Let Us JAVA

7th Edition

Yashavant Kanetkar
Anuj Kanetkar

bpb
www.bpbonline.com

Reprint 2026

Seventh Revised and Updated Edition 2024

First Edition 2011

ISBN: 978-93-5551-755-5

Distributors:

BPB PUBLICATIONS
20, Ansari Road, Darya Ganj
New Delhi-110002
Ph: 23254990/23254991

DECCAN AGENCIES
4-3-329, Bank Street,
Hyderabad-500195
Ph: 24756967/24756400

MICRO MEDIA
Shop No. 5, Mahendra Chambers,
150 DN Rd. Next to Capital Cinema,
V.T. (C.S.T.) Station, MUMBAI-400 001
Ph: 22078296/22078297

To View Complete BPB Publications Catalogue Scan the QR Code:

Published by Manish Jain for BPB Publications, 20 Ansari Road, Darya Ganj, New Delhi-110002 and Printed by him at Akash Press, New Delhi 110020

www.bpbonline.com

Dedicated to

Nalinee and Prabhakar Kanetkar

- Yashavant Kanetkar

Dedicated to

Aai

- Anuj Kanetkar

About The Authors

Yashavant Kanetkar

Through his books and online courses on C, Java, C++, Data Structures, VC++, .NET, Embedded Systems, etc. Yashavant Kanetkar has created, molded, and groomed lacs of IT careers in the last three decades. Yashavant's books have been translated into Hindi, Gujarati, Japanese, Korean and Chinese languages. Many of his books are published in India, USA, Japan, Singapore, Korea, Russia and China.

Yashavant is a much sought-after speaker in the IT field and has conducted seminars/workshops at TedEx, IITs, RECs and global software companies.

Yashavant holds a BE from VJTI Mumbai and M.Tech. from IIT Kanpur. Yashavant's current affiliations include being the Director of KICIT Pvt. Ltd. He can be reached at kanetkar@kicit.com or through www.ykanetkar.com.

Anuj Kanetkar

Anuj Kanetkar is working as a Software Engineer at ServiceNow Inc., Santa Clara. His current passion is anything remotely connected to Java, Security, Distributed Systems, Cloud Computing and Databases. He worked formerly at Veritas Technologies in Pune, India. Anuj holds a Bachelor's degree in Computer Engineering from PICT, Pune and a Master's degree in Computer Science from University of Southern California, Los Angeles.

// Acknowledgments

Let Us Java is not an outcome of our work alone. A book on such a dynamic language required inputs, help and suggestions from several people. Topmost amongst them were our students at Nagpur training center and the participants in various seminars and workshops. Their inputs have gone a long way in getting this book in the shape and form in which you are holding it.

Over the years, we have used Java to build many applications. All these practical experiences and usage scenarios are factored into Let Us Java.

We are indebted to Manish Jain of BPB Publications who had a faith in this book idea, believed in our writing ability, whispered the words of encouragement, and made helpful suggestions from time to time. I hope every author gets a publisher who is as cooperative, knowledgeable, and supportive as Manish.

We thank our family for enduring the late nights, the clicking keyboard and mostly for putting up with yet another marathon book effort.

Contents

1. An Overview of Java **1**
The Evolution 3
The Birth of Java 4
What is Java? 5
Traditional Programming Model 6
How is Java Different? 7
How Java Addresses Security? 8
Java or C++? 9
The Java Environment 10
Tools of the Trade 10
Exercises 12
KanNotes 14

2. Getting Started **17**
Java Data Types 19
Rules for Constructing Constants 21
Rules for Constructing Variable Names 22
Java Keywords 23
The First Java Program 24
Compilation and Execution 28
One More Program 28
Exercises 29
KanNotes 31

3. Java Data Types and Instructions **33**
Data Types Revisited 35
Integer Types 35
Real Types 36
char Data Type 37
boolean Data Type 37
Receiving Input 38
Receiving Input – One More Way 40
Command-line Arguments 41
Java Instructions 42
Type Declaration Instruction 43
Arithmetic Instruction 44
Type Conversion in Arithmetic Instruction 46
Explicit Conversion 48
Hierarchy of Operations 49
Associativity of Operators 50

Constant Variables 51
Console Output in Java 51
*println( )*and *format( )* Functions 51
Control Instructions in Java 53
Exercises 54
KanNotes 57

4. Decision Control Instruction 59
Decisions! Decisions! 61
The *if-else* Statement 61
More Complex Decision Making 64
The *else if* Clause 65
The & and | Operators 68
The ! Operator 69
Hierarchy of Operators Revisited 70
A Word of Caution 70
The Conditional Operators 71
Exercises 73
KanNotes 77

5. Loop Control Instruction 79
Loops 81
The *while* Loop 81
Tips about *while* 83
The *for* Loop 85
Partial *for* Loops 86
Nesting of Loops 87
Multiple Initializations in the *for* Loop 88
The *do-while* Loop 88
The *break* Statement 89
The *continue* Statement 91
Common Usage 92
Exercises 93
KanNotes 97

6. Case Control Instruction 99
Decisions using *switch* 101
The Tips and Traps 102
switch Versus *if-else* Ladder 105
Exercises 105
KanNotes 107

7. Functions 109

What is a Function? 111
Why use Functions? 116
Passing Values between Functions 116
Exercises 119
KanNotes 125

8. Advanced Features of Functions 127
Function Overloading 129
Functions with Variable Number of Arguments 130
Recursion 132
Exercises 134
KanNotes 137

9. Introduction to OOP 139
The Beginning... 141
Structured Programming 142
Object-Oriented Programming 144
Characteristics of OOP 146
Objects 146
Classes 147
Inheritance 147
Polymorphism 149
Containership 149
Reusability 149
Exercises 150
KanNotes 153

10. Classes and Objects 155
Classes and Constructors 160
Object Destruction 163
Terminology 165
A Complex Class 165
this Reference 169
Static Data and Functions 170
Static Block 172
Passing Objects to a Function 173
Inner Classes 174
Exercises 176
KanNotes 180

11. Arrays 183
What are Arrays? 185
A Simple Program using an Array 185

More on Arrays 187
Array Initialization 187
Array Access 188
Bounds Checking 188
Passing Array Elements to a Function 189
Passing Array Reference to a Function 189
Returning an Array 190
Common Array Operations 191
Array of Objects 193
Multi-Dimensional Arrays 194
Passing and Returning 2-D Array 196
Jagged Array 197
Resizing of Arrays 199
Exercises 201
KanNotes 204

12. Strings and Enums 207
What are Strings? 209
More about Strings 210
Splitting Strings 214
StringBuilder Class 215
Array of Strings 215
Sorting Strings 217
Enumerations 218
Use of Enumerated Data Type 219
Enum as A Class 222
Exercises 224
KanNotes 227

13. Inheritance 229
Uses of Inheritance 234
Constructors in Inheritance 237
The *final* Keyword 240
Incremental Development 241
Other Code Reuse Mechanisms 242
Exercises 242
KanNotes 244

14. Polymorphism 247
What is Polymorphism? 249
Abstract Classes and Functions 252
Abstract Functions – Practical Example 256
Interfaces 258

Practical Uses of Interfaces 260
Interfaces–Focused View 261
Interfaces–Different Implementation 264
Interfaces–Unrelated Inheritance 266
default and *static* Methods 268
default Method Ambiguities 268
Exercises 271
KanNotes 274

15. Exception Handling 277
Exception Handling in Java 280
Catching Multiple Exceptions 287
finally Block 289
User-defined Exceptions 290
A More Practical Example 293
Define the Exception Class 295
Throw an Exception 295
try Block 296
The Exception Handler (*catch* Block) 296
How the Whole Thing Works? 296
A Few Tips... 296
Exercises 297
KanNotes 299

16. Effective Input/Output 303
Expectations From an I/O System 305
File, Directory and Drive Operations 305
The Java Streams Solution 310
Stream Classes 312
Byte and Character Operations 313
Reading Strings from a File 315
Record I/O 317
User-defined Streams 319
File Encryption/Decryption 322
Serialization / Deserialization 325
Exercises 328
KanNotes 331

17. Multithreading in Java 335
Multitasking and Multithreading 337
Multithreading in Java 338
Launching Threads 340
Launching Multiple Threads 343

Another Way to Launch Threads 346
A Practical Multithreading Example 348
Synchronization 351
The Synchronized Block 353
Inter-thread Communication 354
Thread Priorities 354
Exercises 355
KanNotes 358

18. Generics 361
Generic Functions 363
Multiple Argument Types 368
Generic Classes 369
Bounded Generics 374
Exercises 375
KanNotes 377

19. Java Collections 379
What is Collections Framework? 381
Array of Names and Numbers 382
Maintaining a Stack 385
Maintaining a Queue 386
Maintaining a Linked List 387
Maintaining a Set 389
Maintaining a Tree 390
Maintaining a HashMap 393
Using the Algorithms 394
Exercises 396
KanNotes 398

20. Lambdas and Functional Programming 401
Functional Interface 403
Lambda Expression 404
Creating and Using Lambda 404
Assigning Lambda to Variable 406
Generic Functional Interface 407
Using Lambda in Multithreading 408
Using Lambda with Collections 410
Functional Programming 411
Stream API 414
Map, Filter, Reduce 416
Mutable and Immutable Lists 418
Standard Functional Interfaces 419

default and *static* Methods of Standard Functional Interfaces 422
Lazy and Eager Operations 425
More Programs 426
The Method Reference Operator 429
Exercises 431
KanNotes 434

21. User Interfaces (in downloadable form) 435
A Simple Swing Application 436
Event Handling 436
One More GUI Application 436
Adapter Classes 436
What Next? 436
Exercises 436
KanNotes 436

22. JDBC 437
Data Organization 439
Common Database Operations 439
Database Operations through Java 441
JDBC Architecture 441
JDBC Driver Types 442
MySQL Database Installation 443
Common JDBC API Components 443
Putting it to Work 444
Exercises 449
KanNotes 451

23. Network and Internet Programming 453
Networking Concepts 454
Networking Model 454
Protocols 454
Packets 454
IP Addresses 454
Sockets 454
Port Numbers 454
Getting Started... 454
What's The Time Now 454
Communicating with Whois Server 454
Give Me the Home Page 454
Two-Way Communication 454
Multiuser Chat Application 454

File Transfer Using UDP 454
Exercises 454
KanNotes 454

24. Miscellany **455**
CLASSPATH Variable 457
strictfp Modifier 457
Bitwise Operators 458
Annotations 459
Packages 461
Creating and Using a Package 461
Split Packages 463
Different Packages, Same Type 465
Nested Packages 467
Package FAQs 468
Packages and Access Mechanism 469
Exercises 470
KanNotes 472

25. The Next Level **475**
Place of Declaration of Local Variables 477
Proper for Loop 477
BigDecimal instead of *float, double* 478
Unnecessary Use of Boxed Primitives 478
Enums over Strings 479
Short Method Parameter List 480
Fail-fast Approach 482
Data Validation 483
Refer Objects by their Interfaces 485
Optional Type 488
Established Object Creation Patterns 492
Static Factory 492
Singleton 495
Builder 496
Dependency injection 503

Periodic Tests I, II, II, IV, V 507
Index 519

OTHER TITLES OF INTEREST

Python Programming
for **Students**
ISBN: 9789355516084

Let Us **Python** -
6th Edition
ISBN: 9789355515414

Let Us **Python**
Solutions - 6th Ed.
ISBN: 9789355515476

Python for **Cybersecurity**
Cookbook
ISBN: 9789355513809

Modern Data Mining
with **Python**
ISBN: 9789355519146

Python GUI with **PyQt**
ISBN: 9789355515575

Building Modern GUIs
with **tkinter** & **Python**
ISBN: 9789355518569

IoT Data Analytics
using **Python**
ISBN: 9789355515759

Python Networking
Solutions Guide
ISBN: 9789355513571

Basic **Core Python**
Programming
ISBN: 9789390684953

Advance
Core Python Programming
ISBN: 9789390684069

Learn Python
Generative AI
ISBN: 9789355518972

Python for **Chemistry**
ISBN: 9789355517975

Python Apps on
Visual Studio Code
ISBN: 9789355519504

Learn Autonomous
Programming with **Python**
ISBN: 9789355517630

Data Visualization
with **Python**
ISBN: 9789355515384

An Overview of Java

Let Us JAVA 7th Edition

CHAPTER 01

You remain well-grounded when you know your roots. The same is true about Java. So, a look at how it came into existence and where it stands amongst other programming languages...

Contents

- The Evolution
- The Birth of Java
- What is Java?
- Traditional Programming Model
- How is Java Different?
- How Java addresses Security?
- Java or C++?
- The Java Environment
- Tools of the Trade
- Exercises
- KanNotes

Before we can begin to write programs in Java, it would be interesting to find out what really is Java, how it came into existence and how does it compare with other computer languages. Also, it is important to know what tools we are going to use for executing programs in this book, from where to get them and how to install them. In this chapter, we will briefly outline these issues.

The Evolution

Approaches to programing keep evolving all the time. These approaches are driven by the computing needs of those times. When these needs cannot be addressed by languages of that era, a need is felt for a new language. These needs have become more and more complex over the years.

In the early days of computing when the need was that a machine should somehow be able to execute instructions, programming was done by manually keying in the binary machine instructions. So long as the programming task was small, programmers were ready to take the pains of keying in instructions in binary.

As the tasks became more complex and the program lengths increased, need was felt for a new language that could make it easier to write programs. That is when Assembly language was invented. In Assembly, instead of binary, small abbreviations were used to write instructions. These abbreviations were nothing but representations of binary instructions. This made life much easier for the programmer. The assembly language programs were very efficient.

As the demands of computing increased, it was felt that learning and using Assembly language are not very easy. To address this need, many languages were invented. These included FORTRAN, BASIC and COBOL. But these turned out to be suitable for specific domains. For example, FORTRAN found widespread acceptance in scientific and engineering applications, whereas COBOL was typically used for building business applications like payrolls, inventory management, etc.

These languages suffered from three important limitations. They are as follows:

(a) They could not be used apart from the domains that they were supposed to serve. So, a change in domain necessitated a programmer to learn a new language.

(b) They could not be used to write system-level code that could interact with hardware easily.

(c) All these languages were not designed around structured programming principles. Hence, in programs of sizeable length it became difficult to follow the flow of control.

As a result, a feeling started growing, could there not be a universal programming language that could address all these three concerns? The answer came in the form of C language. It was invented by Dennis Ritchie at AT&T's Bell Laboratories. Since it was designed by a programmer, and not driven by a committee, it addressed the needs of programmers very well. These included speed, efficiency, and brevity. Programmers loved it and it soon became a dominant programming language. This dominance continued for almost two decades.

As new hardware evolved, and computers gained widespread acceptance, demands from the program grew multi-fold. The complexity of programs hit the roof, and this is where C language started showing signs of strain. It simply did not contain those elements that could handle the complexity of the problem being solved. There was a need for a fresh approach to handle the complexity. This gave birth to a new way of organizing the program, called Object Oriented Programming (OOP). C++ was based on these principles and was invented by Bjarne Stroustrup at AT&T's Bell Labs. 1990 was the decade of C++. Since C++ was built on foundation of C, it became easier for programmers to migrate to this new language quite quickly. It was largely accepted that C++ is a prefect language and there would possibly be no need for a new language. But this belief got dented as you would see in the next section.

The Birth of Java

C and C++ were used for building most applications till late 1990s. The computing world was divided into three camps—Intel, Macintosh, and Solaris. Compliers were available that targeted these microprocessors and created machine language instructions that could get executed on these microprocessors. This was all right for the PC world. However, microprocessor diversity was too much in consumer electronics world. The microprocessors used in washing machines, microwave ovens and other such devices were so many that creating a full-fledged compiler for each microprocessor was impractical. So, a thought started taking shape to create new language that could be used to create software that could run on different microprocessors embedded in various consumer electronic devices. This was the initial motivation that led to the birth of Java.

Thus, creation of an architecturally neutral and portable language for consumer electronics devices was the primary factor for Java to come into existence. However, it gained impetus for a very different reason. World

Wide Web and the Internet were growing like wildfire, and its programming needs were similar to those that Java was trying to address. There were all types of machines that were getting connected to the Internet. A language was needed that could be used to create programs that could run on machines connected to the Internet and had different microprocessors and operating systems. Java fitted this bill perfectly, because it was designed from ground up with this motive in mind, namely, platform-independence (portability).

So, it may not be an exaggeration to state that had the Internet and World Wide Web did not catch the fancy of the world at the same time in which Java was growing, Java would have possibly remained a language to be used only in the consumer electronics world.

With that historic perspective under our belt, we are now well poised to begin learning Java.

What is Java?

Java is a programming language developed at Sun Microsystems in 1995. It was designed by James Gosling. The language derives much of its syntax from C++ (and its predecessor, C), but is simpler to use than C++. The reputation of Java has spread wide and far and has captured the imagination of most software professionals. Literally thousands of applications are being built today in Java for different platforms including desktop, web and mobile.

Possibly why Java seems so popular is because it is reliable, portable, and easy to use. It has modern constructs that are required to represent today's problems programmatically. Java, like C++ makes use of a principle called Object-Oriented Programming (OOP) to organize the program. This organizing principle has lots of advantages to offer. We will be discussing this in detail in Chapter 9.

Let us now try to understand how Java achieves portability and reliability.

Traditional Programming Model

When we execute a program on any computing device like PC, Laptop, Tablet or Smartphone, the instructions in it are executed by the microprocessor present in that device. However, the microprocessor cannot understand the instructions written in languages like C, C++, or Java. Hence, these instructions must first be converted into instructions that can be understood by the microprocessor. These converted instructions are in machine language. This conversion process is known as compilation.

The machine language instructions understood by a microprocessor are often called its Instruction Set. The problem is that instruction sets of different microprocessors are different. Thus, instructions of an Intel microprocessor are different than those of an ARM microprocessor. Therefore, any program being executed on a specific microprocessor needs to be converted into machine language instructions which that microprocessor understands. Thus, for the same program, corresponding machine language instructions would be different for different microprocessors. Hence, if a program is compiled for one microprocessor it may not work on another microprocessor. To make it work on another microprocessor it would have to be compiled for that microprocessor again. This is shown in Figure 1.1.

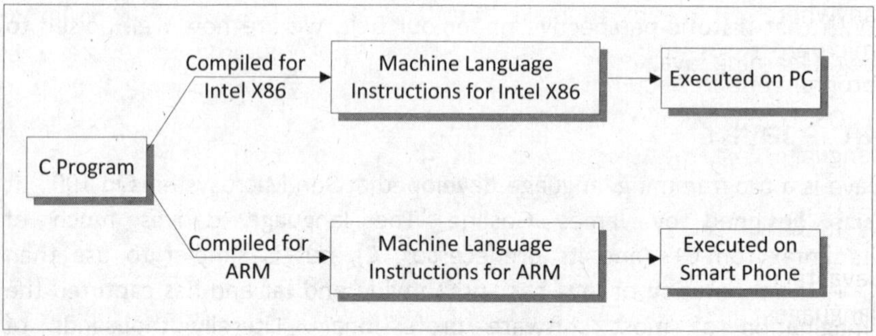

Figure 1.1

Any running program needs to make use of the services of an Operating System (OS) during its execution. These include services like performing input/output, allocating memory, etc. You must be aware that on the same microprocessor, different OS can be used. For example, suppose there are two laptops that have same Intel Pentium microprocessor. On one laptop one can run Windows whereas on the other, one can run Linux. But since the way these OSs' offer different services is different, during conversion to machine language these changes must be accommodated. So, for the same program, machine language instructions for Intel + Windows combination would be different than those for Intel + Linux combination. This is shown in Figure 1.2.

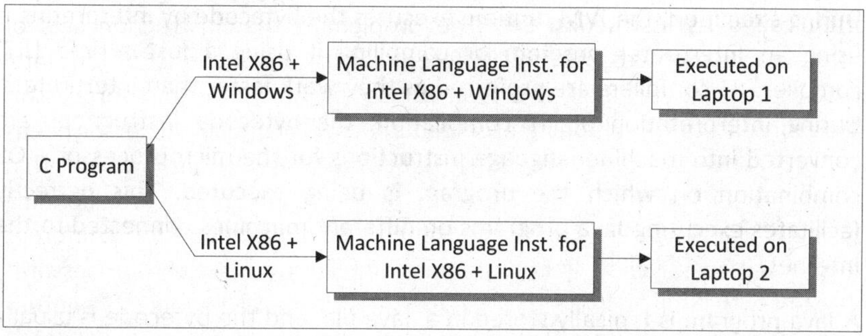

Figure 1.2

Figure 1.1 and Figure 1.2 depict a scenario called "write once, compile anywhere". It means to make the same program work on a different microprocessor + OS combination we are not required to rewrite the program but are required to recompile the program for that microprocessor + OS combination. This is the approach taken by popular traditional languages like C and C++.

How is Java Different?

Java takes a different approach than the traditional approach taken by languages like C and C++. It lets application developers follow a "compile once, run anywhere" scenario. This means that once a Java program is compiled, it can get executed on different microprocessors + OS combinations without the need to recompile the program. This makes Java programs immensely portable across different microprocessors + OS combinations. The microprocessor + OS combination is often called "Platform". Hence Java is often called a platform-independent language or architecturally neutral language. Java programs are considered portable since they can be used on a different microprocessor + OS combination without making any changes in them.

Java achieves this "compile once, run anywhere" and platform independence magic through a program called Java Virtual Machine (JVM). When we compile Java programs, they are not converted into machine language instructions for a specific microprocessor + OS combination. Instead, our Java program is converted into bytecode instructions. These bytecode instructions are similar to machine code, but are intended to be interpreted by JVM. A JVM provides an environment in which Java bytecode can be executed. Different JVMs are written specifically for different host hardware and operating systems. For example, different JVMs are written for Intel + Windows combination, ARM + Linux combination, etc.

During execution, the JVM runtime executes the bytecode by interpreting it using an Interpreter program or compiling it using a just-in-time (JIT) compiler. JIT compilers are preferred as they work faster than interpreters. During interpretation or JIT compilation, the bytecode instructions are converted into machine language instructions for the microprocessor + OS combination on which the program is being executed. This perfectly facilitates executing Java programs on different machines connected to the Internet.

A Java program is typically stored in a .java file, and the bytecode is usually stored in a .class file. A complex program may consist of many .class files. For easier distribution, these multiple class files may be packaged together in a .jar file (short for Java archive). The working of a Java program discussed above is shown in Figure 1.3.

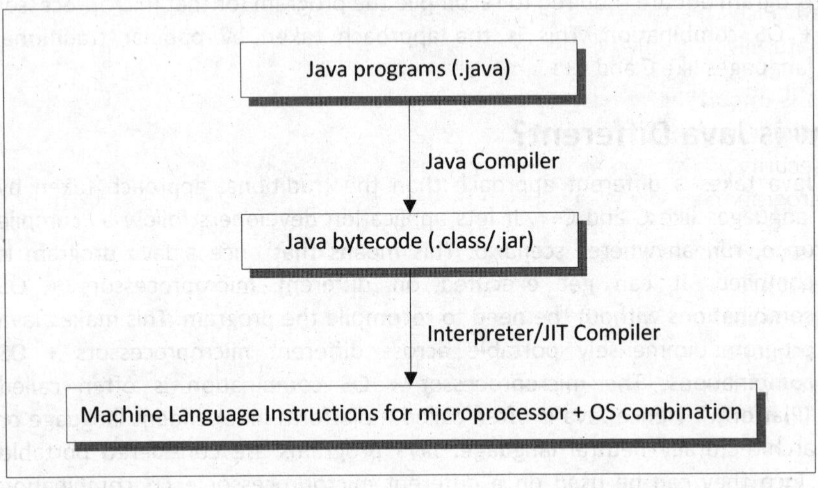

Figure 1.3

How Java addresses Security?

Let us first understand what typically happens when we use some web application on the Internet. Through browser on our PC/Laptop/Tablet/Smartphone we use a URL to reach the application present on some web server on the Internet. The web application sends HTML that gets rendered in our browser. However, except for the simplest of web applications, along with the HTML some executable Java program is also sent to our browser. This program is often small and is called Applet. The purpose of the applet is to make the web application more responsive. For example, if we enter a password, it should be possible to check whether it follows rules for password creation or not right within the browser using the downloaded applet, rather than sending the password to server and get it verified. This certainly improves user experience. This is because the check is being performed on the machine itself rather than on the server machine. This saves a roundtrip to the server.

But when we download an applet, there is always a possibility that the applet may contain malicious code like a Virus or Trojan horse that would cause harm to our machine. JVM prevents this from happening by restricting the applet code from accessing other resources of your machine, other than what it is supposed to. This makes applets secure. Thus, JVM solves two dicey issues in one shot—portability as well as security.

Java or C++?

After learning C, it is often a question whether one should migrate to Java or C++. The answer is both; and that too in any sequence that you want. Though both are Object Oriented programming languages, neither is an advanced version of the other. Learning one before the other would naturally help to learn the second.

It is important to note that both address different sets of problems. C++ primarily addresses complexity, whereas Java addresses portability and security. In my opinion, both languages would continue to rule the hearts of programmers for years to come.

As you start learning Java, you will find that there are many features in it that are like C and C++. This is not by accident, but by intent. Java designers knew that they had to provide a smooth transition path to learners of Java language. That is why Java uses a syntax which is similar in many ways to that of C and it follows many of the object-oriented features of C++, though in a refined fashion.

The Java Environment

We know that JVM contains an Interpreter / JIT that converts bytecode into microprocessor + OS specific machine language instructions. Since instruction sets vary from microprocessor to microprocessor, there exist different JVMs for different platforms. Thus, though any JVM can run any Java program, JVMs themselves are not portable.

JVM is distributed along with a set of standard class libraries that implement the Java Application Programming Interface (API). The Java APIs and JVM together form the Java Runtime Environment (JRE). If your need is only to execute Java programs on your machine, all that you need is JRE. For example, if you wish to play a Java-based game on your machine, you need to install only JRE on your machine for the game to run.

However, if you wish to also develop programs on your machine, you need Java Developer Kit (JDK). JDK contains tools needed to develop Java programs, as well as JRE to run the programs. The tools include compiler (javac.exe), Java application launcher (java.exe), Appletviewer, etc. Compiler converts Java code into bytecode. Java application launcher opens a JRE, loads the class, and calls its **main( )** method. Figure 1.4 shows all these pieces of Java environment.

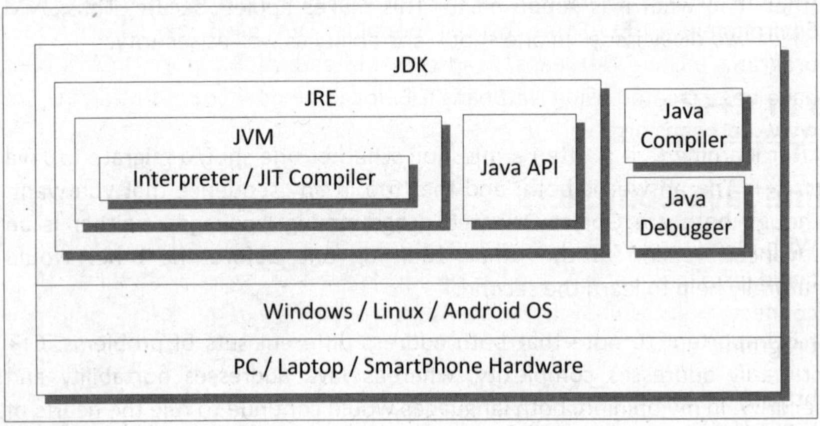

Figure 1.4

Tools of the Trade

To create and run Java programs you need to install two software on your PC. These are:

(a) Java Development Kit (JDK)
(b) Integrated Development Environment like NetBeans or Eclipse

JDK is often also called Standard Edition Development Kit or Java SE 19 JDK or simply Java 19, where 19 is the version number. As years roll by, the version number will go on increasing. JDK contains JVM, JRE, Java compiler and debugger. A compiler is needed to convert the Java program into its equivalent bytecode. A debugger is needed to detect, analyze, and eliminate bugs in the program. Java 19 can be downloaded using the link:

https://www.oracle.com/java/technologies/download

On this download page, select the appropriate version number, OS (Windows/Mac/Linux) and the Microprocessor (x86 or X64) and download the JDK. Next step is to install the downloaded JDK. This is a simple job, and you would be able to do this easily. You simply must double click the downloaded installer file **jdk-19_windows-x64_bin.exe** (assuming Windows and 64-bit machine configuration), and the installer would guide you through the installation process.

When you are developing a Java program you need an editor to type the program. Small Java programs can be typed in one file. But more sophisticated programs may be split across multiple files. To let you type the program, manage multiple files of your program, compile it and debug it, you need a tool that can let you carry out these tasks in a visual and user-friendly manner. This tool is often called an Integrated Development Environment (IDE). Some of the popular IDEs used for building Java programs include NetBeans, Eclipse and IntelliJ. All programs in this book have been created using NetBeans IDE. It can be downloaded using the link www.netbeans.org.

Online Java Compilers

With ubiquitous availability of the Internet, if you wish, you can completely avoid installation of JDK and IDE on your machine. Using a browser, you can connect to any of the following links to type, compile and execute your Java programs:

https://www.onlinegdb.com/
https://www.tutorialspoint.com/compile_java_online.php

The limitation of using online compilers is that you need a steady Internet connection while you are using them.

While using online compilers like the one at onlinegdb.com you must remember to choose the language (Java in our case) from the dropdown. Next, we must type our program and click the Run/Execute button. When we do so, our typed program is sent to the web server where it is compiled and executed. The output created on execution is then sent back and displayed in the browser. If any errors are found in the program during compilation they are also relayed back and displayed in the browser.

Onlinegdb.com also has provisions to create multi-file Java programs, supply command-line arguments, debug a program using the debugger, create folders and store multiple files in it. From the point of view of security, online compiler is not a preferred choice for serious software development in Java. Nevertheless, a good option with zero installation and configuration headaches when you are learning Java.

We are now on surer grounds. We now have the historical perspective of what led to the creation of Java, what problems it primarily attempts to solve, and what tools we need to install to begin Java program development. It would be a good idea to attempt the exercise on the next page to help you fix these ideas, before we begin learning Java language from next chapter onwards.

Exercises

[A] Match the following:

(a) Creator of Java	(1) Provides security and portability
(b) JRE	(2) Platform dependent
(c) Java Program	(3) Bjarne Stroustrup
(d) JVM	(4) Contains compiler and debugger
(e) NetBeans	(5) Needed for executing Java programs
(f) Creator of C++	(6) IDE
(g) JDK	(7) Platform independent
(h) Structured Lang.	(8) Converts Bytecode into m/c language
(i) OOP Language	(9) Java
(j) JVM	(10) James Gosling
(k) Java Compiler	(11) C
(l) Java Interpreter	(12) Converts Java program into Bytecode
(m) Java API	(13) Library of classes

[B] State which of the following statements are True or False:

(a) Different microprocessors use different Instruction sets.

(b) The same JVM is used for all microprocessor + OS combination.

(c) We can get by just installing JRE on a machine on which we intend to only execute Java programs.

(d) NetBeans is just an IDE and does not have a Java compiler built in it.

(e) The Java compiler converts instructions in Java into machine language instructions.

(f) JRE and JDK both are part of JVM.

(g) The way I/O and memory management is done is the same across different OSs.

(h) Traditional programming languages like C and C++ follow "write once, compile anywhere" dictum.

(i) Java follows "compile once, run anywhere" dictum.

(j) Java programs cannot run without JVM.

(k) To run a Java program, you need to install JDK.

(l) Java was conceived to create portable programs for consumer electronic devices.

(m) Multiple .class files can be packaged together to create a .jar file.

(n) During execution Java Interpreter converts Bytecode instructions into machine language instructions.

(o) The instruction set for Intel x86, and Arm microprocessor are different.

[C] Which of the following is highlighting feature of C, C++, and Java?

(a) Structured
(b) Object Oriented
(c) Portable
(d) Secure
(e) Suitable for Internet programming
(f) Simple syntax
(g) Architecturally neutral
(h) Management of complexity

[D] Pick up the correct alternative for each of the following questions:

(a) Which of the following is CORRECT about Java programs?
  (1) Compile often, run once
  (2) Write once, compile anywhere
  (3) Write often, compile anywhere
  (4) Compile once, run anywhere

(b) In traditional programming languages, if a program has been compiled for Intel x86 + Windows combination, what should be done to make the program work on Intel x86 + Linux combination?
  (1) The program should be rewritten
  (2) The program should be recompiled
  (3) The program should be reassembled
  (4) No need to do anything, the same program would work on the new combination

(c) At what stage does byte code get converted into machine language instructions?
  (1) during compilation
  (2) during assembly
  (3) during preprocessing
  (4) during execution

(d) Java is
 (1) microprocessor-independent language
 (2) platform-independent language
 (3) OS-independent language
 (4) library-independent language

(e) For the same Java program to run on different devices we need
 (1) appropriate JVM for those devices
 (2) appropriate compiler for those devices
 (3) appropriate interpreter for those devices
 (4) appropriate preprocessor for those devices

(f) If we are to merely execute a Java program on a machine, then which of the following must be installed on that machine?
 (1) JVM
 (2) JRE
 (3) JDK
 (4) Java API

(g) Which of the following statements is CORRECT?
 (1) Different microprocessors use the same instruction sets
 (2) Different platforms use the same JVM
 (3) To execute a Java program, we need to install JDK
 (4) To execute a Java program, we need to install JRE

[E] Answer the following:

(a) Why do programs written for Linux on a x86 machine do not work on a Windows x86 machine?

(b) If on a machine we wish to develop as well as execute Java programs, should we install JDK or JRE?

(c) Why are programs written in Java considered to be more portable than those written in C and C++?

(d) Why is Java language considered to be architecturally neutral?

(e) What were the pain points that led to creation of Java language?

(f) What are the different components of Java environment?

(g) What do you mean by a computing platform?

KanNotes

- 2 categories of software :
  - System software - OS, Compilers, Device Drivers
  - Application software - software for desktop/laptop, Web, Mobile
- Technologies used in Java world for different platforms :
  - Desktop - J2SE, Mobile - J2ME, Web - J2EE
- Reasons of popularity of Java :
  - Same language for varied applications
  - Rapid Application Development (RAD) possible
  - Easy development cycle
  - Easy to manage large projects
- Acronyms:
  - API = Application Programming Interface
  - JVM = Java Virtual Machine
  - JRE = Java Runtime Environment
  - JDK = Java Development Kit
- API = Library of classes in form of packages
- JVM = Memory Manager + Interpreter / Just In Time (JIT) compiler
- JRE = JVM + API
- JDK = JRE + Development tools like javac, java, debugger
- NetBeans, Eclipse are popular development environments
- Nebeans and Eclipse internally use javac, java, debugger
- Different JREs and JDKs must be downloaded for different Hardware + OS combination
- For execution of Java programs only JRE is needed
- To create and execute Java programs JDK + NetBeans are needed

- In C / C++ our program on building is converted into machine language instructions.
- In Java on compiling our program is converted into ByteCode instructions.
- During execution of Java programs, the ByteCode instructions are converted into machine language instructions and these instructions are executed.
- Byte code instructions of a .java file are stored in corresponding .class file.
- For multiple .java files a .jar (Java Archive) file is created.
- To achieve portability C/C++ use Write once, Compile anywhere principle
- To further improve portability Java uses Compile once, Run anywhere principle

Chapter 02

Getting Started

It is good to wet your feet before you take a dip. See how to create a small program in Java...

Contents

- Java Data Types
  - Rules for Constructing Constants
  - Rules for Constructing Variable Names
- Java Keywords
- The First Java Program
- Compilation and Execution
- One More Program
- Exercises
- KanNotes

Four important aspects of any language are the way it stores data, the way it operates upon this data, how it accomplishes input and output, and how it lets you control the sequence of execution of instructions in a program. We will discuss the first three of these building blocks in this chapter.

Java Data Types

Before we write our first Java program, it is important to understand how data is represented in Java. This is done using a data type. A data type specifies two things:

(a) What value can the data type take?
(b) What operations can be performed on the data type?

For example, an **integer** data type can take values in the range -2147483648 to +2147483647, and operations like addition, subtraction, multiplication, division, etc., can be performed on it. Similarly, a **boolean** data type can take a value true or false and permits comparison operations on it.

Based on where a data type can be created in memory, it is called a **primitive type** (often also known as a **value type**) or a **reference type**.

Java forces primitive data types to get created only in stack and reference types only on heap. For example, an integer (like 2341) always gets created in stack, whereas a string (like "Quest") always gets created in heap. The guiding principle based on which Java makes this decision-making is—all data types that are small in size are created in stack, and all those that occupy larger memory chunks are created in heap.

A primitive type as well as a reference type can be further categorized into pre-defined and user-defined categories. Here pre-defined means the data types that Java provides ready-made, whereas user-defined means those data types which a common user like us can create. For example, integer is a pre-defined primitive data type, whereas Enumeration is a user-defined value type. Figure 2.1 shows the different categories of data types available in Java. Note that the pre-defined value types are often also called Primitives.

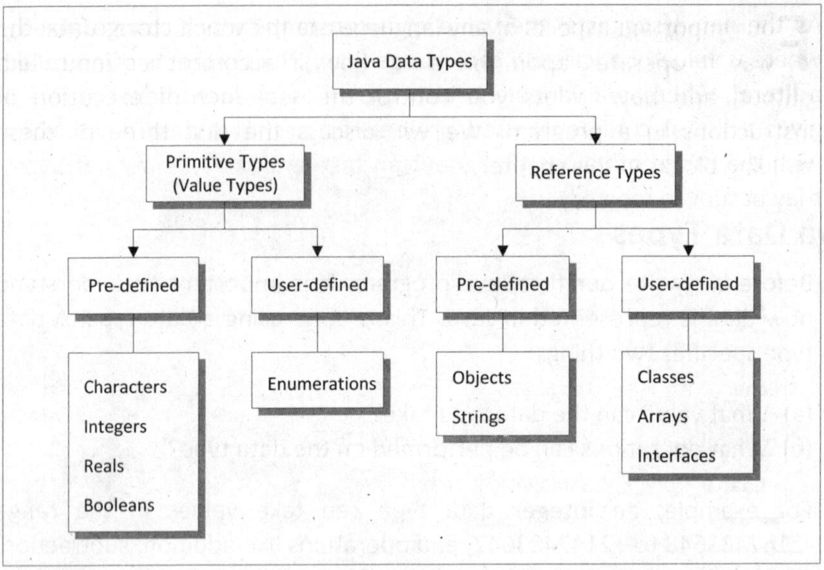

Figure 2.1

Amongst all the data types shown in Figure 2.1, to begin with, we would concentrate on the pre-defined value data types. To use the data types in a Java program, we must create constants and variables. A constant is nothing but a specific value from the range of values offered by a data type, whereas a variable is a container which can hold a constant value. The container is typically a memory location, and the variable is the name given to the memory location. For example, if we use an expression **x = 5**, then the constant value 5 would be stored in a memory location and a name **x** would be given to that location. Whenever we wish to retrieve and use **5**, we must use the variable name **x**. This is shown in Figure 2.2.

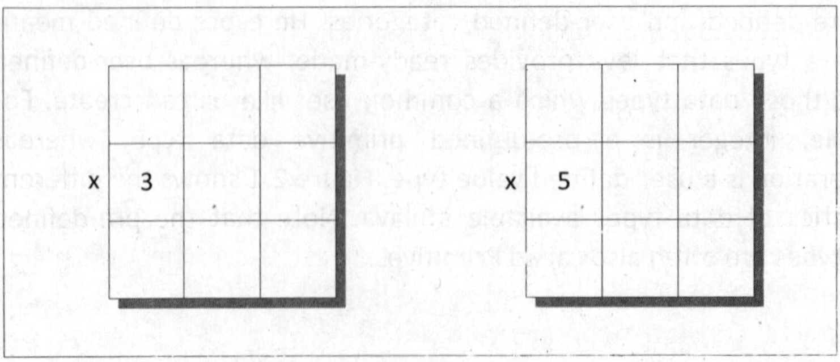

Figure 2.2

As the name suggests, the value of a constant cannot change (fixed), whereas value of a variable can change (vary). A constant is often called a **literal**, whereas a variable is also known as an **identifier**. Figure 2.3 gives a list of commonly used pre-defined primitive data types along with the range of values that they can take and the numbers of bytes they occupy in memory.

Data Type	**Range**	**Size in bytes**
char	0 to 65535	2
int	-2147483648 to +2147483647	4
float	-3.4e38 to +3.4e38	4

Figure 2.3

There are certain rules that one needs to observe while creating constants and variables. These are discussed below.

Rules for Constructing Constants

(a) If no sign precedes a numeric constant, it is assumed to be positive.

(b) No commas or blanks are allowed within a constant.

(c) The bytes occupied by each constant are fixed and do not change from one compiler to another.

(d) Only a float constant can contain a decimal point.

(e) A float constant must be followed by a suffix **f**.

(f) A float constant can be expressed in fractional form (example 314.56f) or exponential form (example 3.1456e2).

(g) A character constant is a single alphabet, a single digit or a single special symbol enclosed within single inverted commas. Both the inverted commas should point to the left. For example, 'A' is a valid character constant, whereas 'A' is not.

Given below are examples of some valid constants.

426	+78.23	-8000	-7605
true	'A'	'+'	'3'

Rules for Constructing Variable Names

(a) A variable name is any combination of alphabets, digits, underscores (_) and dollars ($).

(b) The first character in the variable name must be an alphabet, underscore, or dollar.

(c) No commas or blanks are allowed within a variable name.

(d) Variable names are case-sensitive. So, abc, ABC, Abc, aBc, AbC are treated as different variables.

While creating variable names, conventions given below are commonly followed.

(a) A variable name usually begins with an alphabet. Ex. speed, average

(b) A variable representing money usually begins with $. Ex. $interest, $salary.

(c) If a variable name containing multiple words, the words are either connected using underscore or follow a camel-case notation. Ex. current_speed, currentSpeed, avg_salary, avgSalary.

While following these rules and conventions, one must avoid the temptation of creating long variable names as it unnecessarily adds to the typing effort.

The rules remain same for constructing variables of any type. Naturally the question follows—how is Java able to differentiate between these variables? This is a rather simple matter. Java compiler makes it compulsory for us to declare the type of any variable name that we wish to use in a program. Here are a few examples showing how this is done.

```
Ex.: int  si, m_hra ;
     float  bassal ;
     char  code ;
```

Since there is no limit on maximum allowable length of a variable name, an enormous number of variable names can be constructed using the above-mentioned rules. It is good practice to exploit this enormous choice in naming variables by using meaningful variable names.

Thus, if we want to calculate simple interest, it is always advisable to construct meaningful variable names like **prin**, **roi**, **noy** to represent Principal, Rate of interest and Number of years rather than using the variables **a**, **b**, **c**.

Java Keywords

Keywords are the words whose meaning has already been explained to the Java compiler. When we make the declaration like the one shown below,

```
int  age ;
```

age is a variable, whereas **int** is a keyword. When this declaration is made, we are telling the compiler that the variable **age** be treated as a variable of type integer. But we do not have to be so elaborate, just **int age** conveys the same meaning. This is because the meaning of the keyword **int** has already been explained to the Java compiler.

The keywords cannot be used as variable names because if we do so, we are trying to assign a new meaning to the keyword which is not allowed. There are only 48 keywords available in Java. Figure 2.4 gives a list of these keywords for your ready reference. A detailed discussion of each of these keywords would be taken up in later chapters wherever their use is relevant.

abstract	class	final	int	return	throw
assert	continue	finally	interface	new	switch
boolean	default	float	long	synchronized	throws
break	do	for	native	short	transient
byte	double	if	package	static	try
case	else	implements	private	strictfp	void
catch	enum	import	protected	super	volatile
char	extends	instanceof	public	this	while

Figure 2.4

The First Java Program

Armed with the knowledge of variables, constants and keywords, the next logical step is to combine them to create instructions. However, instead of this, we would like to write our first Java program now. Once we have done that, we will see in detail the instructions that it made use of.

Before we begin with our first Java program, do remember the following rules that are applicable to all Java programs:

(a) Each instruction in a Java program is written as a separate statement. Therefore, a complete Java program would comprise a series of statements.

(b) Blank spaces may be inserted between two words to improve the readability of the statement. However, no blank spaces are allowed within a variable, constant or keyword.

(c) All statements are in small case letters.

(d) Every Java statement must end with a semicolon (**;**).

Let us now write our first Java program. It would simply calculate simple interest for a set of values representing principal, number of years and rate of interest.

```
// Calculation of simple interest
package calofsi ;
public class CalOfSi
{
    public static void main ( String[ ] args )
    {
        float p, r, si ;
        int n ;
        p = 1000.50f ;
        n = 3 ;
        r = 15.5f ;
        si = p * n * r / 100 ;
        System.out.println ( si ) ;
    }
}
```

Now a few useful tips about the program...

- Comment about the program should either be enclosed within /* */ or be preceded by //. For example, the first statement in our program is a comment.
- Though comments are not necessary, it is good practice to begin a program with a comment indicating the purpose of the program, its author and the date on which the program was written.
- Sometimes it is not obvious as to what a particular statement in a program accomplishes. At such times, it is worthwhile mentioning the purpose of the statement (or a set of statements) using a comment. For example

  ```
  /* formula for simple interest */
  si = p * n * r / 100 ;
  ```

- A comment can be split over more than one line, as in,

  ```
  /* This is
     a multi-line
     comment */
  ```

  Such a comment is often called a multi-line comment.

- A Java program is a collection of one or more packages. Each package can contain multiple classes. Each class may contain multiple functions. Each function can contain multiple instructions. This typical organization of a Java program is shown in Figure 2.5.
- Every instruction used in a Java program should belong to a function. Every function must belong to a class and every class must belong to a package. In our program, there is a package called **calofsi,** a class called **CalOfSi** and a function called **main( ). package** and **class** are both keywords.

  Right now, we do not want to go into the details of package and a class. We would learn about packages and classes in later chapters. But it would be a good time to get introduced to the concept of a function.

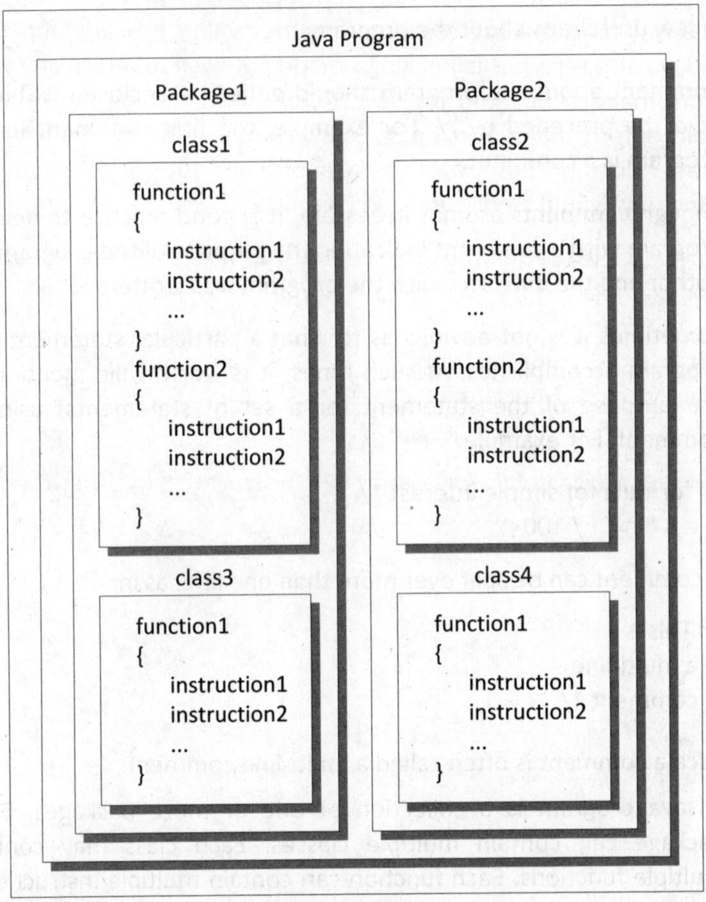

Figure 2.5

- **main( )** is a function. A function contains a set of statements. Though a Java program can contain multiple functions, to begin with, we would concentrate on only those programs which have only one function. All statements that belong to **main( )** are enclosed within a pair of braces { } as shown below.

```
public static void main ( String[ ] args )
{
    statement 1 ;
    statement 2 ;
    statement 3 ;
}
```

- The way functions in a calculator return a value, similarly, functions in Java also return a value. Since we do not wish to return any value from **main( )** function, we have to specify this using the keyword **void** before **main( )**. **main( )** is always preceded by the keyword **static**. The purpose of this keyword and detailed working of functions would be discussed in Chapters 10 and 7 respectively.

- Any variable used in the program must be declared before using it. For example,

```
int p, n ;     /* declaration */
float r, si ;  /* declaration */
si = p * n * r / 100 ;  /* usage */
```

- Any Java statement always ends with a semicolon (;). For example,

```
float r, si ;
r = 15.5f ;
```

- In the statement,

```
si = p * n * r / 100 ;
```

  ***** and **/** are the arithmetic operators. The arithmetic operators available in Java are **+**, **-**, ***** and **/**. Java is very rich in operators. There are a total of 41 operators available in Java.

- Once the value of **si** is calculated, it needs to be displayed on the screen. Unlike other languages, Java does not contain any instructions to display output on the screen. All output to screen is achieved using ready-made library functions. One such function is **println( )**. We have used it to display the value contained in **si** on the screen.

- Actually, **println( )** is a function of **PrintStream** class, and **out** is a **static** object defined in a **System** class. We would learn classes, objects, and static members in Chapter 10. As of now, let us just use the syntax **System.out.println( )** whenever we wish to display output on the screen.

- If we wish we can print multiple values using **println( )** function. This is shown below.

```
System.out.println ( si + " " + p + " " + n + " " + r ) ;
System.out.println ( "Simple interest = Rs. " + si ) ;
System.out.println ( "Principal = " + p + " Rate = " + r ) ;
```

The output of these statements would look like this...

465.2325 1000.5 3 15.5
Simple interest = Rs. 465.2325
Principal = 1000.5 Rate = 15.5

Compilation and Execution

We need to carry out the following steps to create, compile and execute our first Java program. It is assumed that you have installed JDK and NetBeans as per the instructions in Chapter 1.

(a) Start NetBeans from Start | All Programs.

(b) Select File | New Project from the File menu. Select 'Java' from 'Categories' list box and 'Java Application' from 'Projects' box. Click on 'Next' button.

(c) Give a proper name for the project in 'Project Name' text box (say **CalOfSi**). Choose a suitable location for the project folder, then click on Finish.

(d) NetBeans would provide a skeleton program that would contain a **package** statement, a public class **CalOfSi** and a function **main( )**, all defined in a file called **CalOfSi.java**. Note that the name of the file and the name of the public class are the same in all Java programs.

(e) Type the statements of our simple interest program in **main( )**.

(f) Save the program using **Ctrl+S**.

(g) Compile and execute the program using **F6**.

One More Program

We now know how to write an elementary Java program, type it, compile it and execute it. These are the steps that you will have to carry out for every program. So, to help you fix your ideas, here is one more program. It calculates and prints average of 3 numbers.

```
// Calculation of average
package calofavg ;
public class CalOfAvg
```

```
{
    public static void main ( String[ ] args )
    {
        int  x, y, z, avg ;
        x = 73 ;
        y = 70 ;
        z = 65 ;
        avg = ( x + y + z ) / 3 ;
        System.out.println ( avg ) ;
    }
}
```

Exercises

[A] Which of the following is invalid variable name and why?

BASICSALARY   _basic   basic-hra
#MEAN   group.   422
population in 2006   over time   mindovermatter
SINGLE   hELLO   queue.
team'svictory   Plot # 3   2015_DDay

[B] Point out the errors, if any, in the following Java statements:

(a) int = 314.562f * 150 ;

(b) name = 'Ajay' ;

(c) varchar = '3' ;

(d) 3.14f * r * r * h = vol_of_cyl ;

(e) k = (a * b) (c + (2.5fa + b) (d + e) ;

(f) m_inst = rate of interest * amount in rs ;

(g) si = principal * rateofinterest * numberofyears / 100 ;

(h) area = 3.14f * r ** 2 ;

(i) volume = 3.14f * r ^ 2 * h ;

(j) k = ((a * b) + c) (2.5f * a + b) ;

(k) a = b = 3 = 4 ;

(l) count = count + 1 ;

(m) date = '2 Mar 11' ;

[C] Pick up the correct alternative for each of the following questions:

(a) Which of the following is the correct way to write a comment?

(1) // This is a comment
(2) / This is a comment
(3) /* This is a comment
(4) /* This is a /* comment */ */

(b) The maximum value that an integer constant can have is:

(1) -2147483647
(2) 2147483647
(3) 3.4×10^{38}
(4) -3.4×10^{38}

(c) A Java variable cannot start with:

(1) An alphabet
(2) A number
(3) A special symbol other than underscore
(4) Both (2) and (3) above

(d) Which of the following is odd one out?

(1) +
(2) -
(3) /
(4) **

[D] Answer the following:

(a) Assume a suitable value for Ramesh's basic salary. His dearness allowance is 40% of basic salary, and house rent allowance is 20% of basic salary. Write a Java program to calculate his gross salary.

(b) Assume a suitable value for distance between two cities (in km.). Write a Java program to convert and print this distance in meters, feet, inches, and centimeters.

(c) Assume suitable values for marks obtained by a student in five different subjects are input through the keyboard. Write a Java program to find out the aggregate marks and percentage marks obtained by the student. Assume that the maximum marks that can be obtained by a student in each subject is 100.

(d) Assume a suitable value for temperature of a city in Fahrenheit degrees. Write a Java program to convert this temperature into Centigrade degrees and print both temperatures.

(e) Assume suitable values for length and breadth of a rectangle, and radius of a circle. Write a Java program to calculate the area and perimeter of the rectangle, and the area and circumference of the circle.

KanNotes

- Constants = Literals -> Cannot change
  Variables = Identifiers -> May change
- Data Types : 1) Primitives (value types) 2) Reference types
- Primtive types :
  - Char - 2 bytes
  - Integers - byte, short, int, long (sizes - 1, 2, 4, 8 bytes)
  - Real - float, double (sizes - 4, 8 bytes respectively)
  - Boolean - true / false (1 bit)
- Derived types (classes) :
  - Library : String, System, Exception, etc.
  - User-defined : CalOfSi, CalOfAvg, etc.
- Variable names are case-sensitive and should begin with an alphabet
- Total keywords = 48. Example : int, char, float
- A Java program is a collection of one or more packages
- Each package can contain multiple classes

- Each class may contain multiple functions
- A variable must belong to either a function or a class
- No global functions or variables in Java
- public class is accessible from outside the package
- public function is accessible from outside the class
- 3 types of comments :
    - Single line - //
    - Multiline - /* ... */
    - Documentation - /** .... */

Java Data Types and Instructions

Let Us JAVA 7th Edition

CHAPTER 03

Well begun is half done! Learn the basic building blocks of Java language...

Contents

- Data Types Revisited
  - Integer Types
  - Real Types
  - *char* Data Type
  - *boolean* Data Type
- Receiving Input
- Receiving Input - One More Way
- Command-line Arguments
- Java Instructions
- Type Declaration Instruction
- Arithmetic Instruction
  - Type Conversion in Arithmetic Instruction
  - Explicit Conversion
  - Hierarchy of Operations
  - Associativity of Operators
  - Constant Variables
- Console Output in Java
  - *println( )* and *format( )* Functions
- Control Instructions in Java
- Exercises
- KanNotes

In the last chapter we wrote programs with bare minimum knowledge of data types and instructions. As a result, the programs worked only for specific data. If they are to work with other data it would necessitate changes in the program, which is not a good idea. In this chapter we propose to rectify this situation. For that, we must have more in-depth knowledge of data types and instructions. There is a lot of ground to cover here. Let us begin with the data types.

Data Types Revisited

So far, we have used only an **int** to deal with integer values and **float** to deal with real values. However, Java provides many flavors of integers and reals. Let us begin with integers.

Integer Types

Java provides 4 types of integers—**byte**, **short**, **int** and **long** of sizes 1 byte, 2 bytes, 4 bytes and 8 bytes respectively. Figure 3.1 shows different types of integers available in Java along with their sizes and ranges.

Data Type	Range	Bytes	Default Value
byte	-128 to +127	1	0
short	-32768 to +32767	2	0
int	-2147483648 to +2147483647	4	0
long	-9223372036854775808 to +9223372036854775807	8	0

Figure 3.1

Let us now discuss some finer points associated with integer types.

(a) By default, a number without a decimal point is treated as an **int**. During assignment, if the value being assigned exceeds the range of the variable, an error occurs. This is shown below.

```
byte a = 300 ; // error
short b = 40000 ; // error
int c = 2200000000 ; // error
```

(b) If we wish to treat an integer as a long integer, we must add a suffix L or l at its end, as in

```
long int a = 365l * 1000 ;
```

(c) We can use underscores between digits in a number to improve the readability of our code, as shown below.

```
long creditCardNo = 1211_5178_9212_4231L ;
```

Note that we cannot use underscore at the beginning or at the end of a number, or prior to suffix L.

Real Types

Real numbers can be represented as **float** and **double**. The difference between them is the number of bytes occupied by each, their ranges, and their precision. This is shown in Figure 3.2.

Data Type	Range	Default Value	Bytes
float	±1.5 x 10^{-45} to ±3.4 x 10^{38}	0.0f	4
double	±5.0 x 10^{-324} to ±1.7 x 10^{308}	0.0	8

Figure 3.2

There are some finer points associated with these real types. These are discussed below.

(a) By default, a number with a decimal point is treated as a **double.** If we wish to treat it as a **float**, we need to add a suffix **f** or **F** at the end of it to make it a **float**, as shown below.

```
float x = 3.5 ; // error
float y = 3.5f ; // correct
double d = 3.5f ; // correct
double e = 3.5 ; // correct
```

(b) If we want an integer number to be treated as double, use the suffix d or D, for example,

```
double a = 3d ;
```

(c) Any number of underscores can be used between digits in a number to improve the readability of your code, as shown below.

```
float pi = 3.14_28_57F;
```

Note that we cannot use underscore at the beginning or end of a number, prior to suffix F, or adjacent to decimal point.

(d) If the value of a **float** / **double** is too small or too large, then instead of using the normal notation it is easier to specify the number in exponential notation. This is shown below.

```
float a = 0.0000341295f ; // normal notation
double b = 3214.23221 ; // normal notation
float c = 3.41295e-5f ; // exponential notation
double d = 3.21e3 ; // exponential notation
```

(e) A real number is stored in a **float** / **double** it is stored in binary form. During conversion of decimal number into binary, some precision may be lost. So, two real numbers that otherwise appear equal, when represented in binary numbers of different precisions, might turn out to be unequal. For example, 5.375 and 5.375f are not equal. When 5.375 is treated as double, it is represented as a 64-bit binary number, whereas when it is treated as a float, it is represented as a 32-bit binary number, resulting in some loss of precision.

char Data Type

A **char** data type represents a character expressed in Unicode format. The Unicode format has slowly replaced its predecessor, ASCII format. Characters in most of the known written languages used in the world can be represented using Unicode format.

In addition to the normal form, a character constant can also be specified using Unicode representation. This is shown below.

```
char ch = 'X' ;    // character literal
char dh = '\u0058' ;  // Unicode
```

Unicode representation can take a minimum value of '\u0000' (or decimal 0) and a maximum value of '\uffff' (or decimal 65535).

boolean Data Type

boolean data type can take Boolean values, true and false. A variable of the type **boolean** can either be assigned a Boolean value or an expression which evaluates to a Boolean value. This is shown below.

```
boolean a = false ;
System.out.println ( "a = " + a ) ;
```

```
boolean b = 4 > 2 ;
System.out.println ( "b = " + b ) ;
```

The output of this code snippet would be...

```
a = false
b = true
```

We should not use true / false as variable names. Lastly, unlike languages like C and C++, in Java true is not 1 and false is not 0. This is indicated in the following statements:

```
int a ; boolean b ;
a = 3 < 4 ; // error
b = 3 < 4 ; // works
```

Receiving Input

In the simple interest program of Chapter 2, we assumed the values of **p**, **n** and **r** to be 1000.5, 3 and 15.5. Every time we run this program; we would get the same value for simple interest. To calculate simple interest for some other set of values, we would be required to replace the existing set with the new set of values, and again compile and execute the program. Thus, the program is not general enough to calculate simple interest for any set of values without being required to make a change in the program.

To make the program general, the program should ask the user to supply the values of **p**, **n** and **r** through the keyboard during execution. When the user supplies these values, they can be read by the program using the functions of **Scanner** class as illustrated in the program given below.

```
// Calculation of simple interest
package sibyreceivinginput ;
import java.util.* ;
public class SiByReceivingInput
{
    public static void main ( String[ ] args )
    {
        float p, r, si ;
        int n ;
        System.out.println ( "Enter values of p, n and r" ) ;
        Scanner sc = new Scanner ( System.in ) ;
```

```
        p = sc.nextFloat( ) ;
        n = sc.nextInt( ) ;
        r = sc.nextFloat( ) ;
        si = ( p * n * r ) / 100 ;
        System.out.println ( "Simple interest = Rs. " + si ) ;
    }
}
```

Let us now see what happens when we execute this program. To begin with, the first **println( )** outputs the message 'Enter values of p, n, r' in the output window of NetBeans. In this window we are supposed to supply three numbers either in the same line or in three distinct lines.

Our program should read each of these numbers. To do this, we must first create an object of type **Scanner** through the statement

```
Scanner sc = new Scanner ( System.in ) ;
```

Here **System.in** represents the keyboard.

In Chapter 10 we would learn what objects are and how to create them. For now, let us do it mechanically. To be able to use the class **Scanner** we must add the following statement at the beginning of our program, below the **package** statement:

```
import java.util.* ;
```

As mentioned earlier, the classes in Java library are organized in different packages. Through the above statement we are importing all (*) the classes present in the package **java.util**. This makes the class **Scanner** available for use.

Once **Scanner** object is created we have called the functions **nextInt( )** and **nextFloat( )** to receive **int** and **float** from keyboard. Lastly, simple interest is calculated and printed out using the values received as input.

In this program we have received integer and float using the **Scanner** object. Given below are statements through which we can receive other data type values.

```
Scanner sc = new Scanner ( System.in ) ;
byte age = sc.nextByte( ) ;
short villagePopulation = sc.nextShort( ) ;
long mobile = sc.nextLong( ) ;
```

```
double salary = sc.nextDouble( ) ;
Boolean status = sc.nextBoolean( ) ;
char sex = sc.next( ).charAt ( 0 ) ;
String name = sc.nextLine( ) ;
```

Note that to receive a character we have to receive a string by calling **next( )** and then obtain the character at 0th position from this string by calling **charAt( )** function.

Receiving Input - One More Way

There is one more way to receive input from keyboard. It makes use of **InputStreamReader** and **BufferedReader** objects instead of **Scanner** object. The following program shows how to use these objects.

```
package sibyreceivinginput ;
import java.io.* ;
public class SiByReceivingInput
{
    public static void main ( String[ ] args ) throws Exception
    {
        float p, r, si ;
        int n ;
        InputStreamReader isr ;
        BufferedReader br ;
        isr = new InputStreamReader ( System.in ) ;
        br = new BufferedReader ( isr ) ;
        System.out.println ( "Enter values of p, n and r" ) ;
        p = Float.parseFloat ( br.readLine( ) ) ;
        n = Integer.parseInt ( br.readLine( ) ) ;
        r = Float.parseFloat ( br.readLine( ) ) ;
        si = ( p * n * r ) / 100 ;
        System.out.println ( "Simple interest = Rs. " + si ) ;
    }
}
```

Here we have first created two objects of type **BufferedReader** and **InputStreamReader**. Then we have called the **readLine( )** function thrice. To be able to use the classes **BufferedReader** and **InputStreamReader**, we must import them from java.io package.

The numeric values that we supply to the three **readLine( )** functions is treated as string of characters, rather than as numbers. So, we need to convert the strings into numbers. This conversion is done by the **parseFloat( )** and **parseInt( )** functions. These functions belong to a library class called **Float** and **Integer,** respectively. The converted values are then assigned to respective variables. Lastly, simple interest is calculated and printed out.

If we supply wrong input to **readLine( )**, then conversion of this input into an **int / float** through **parseInt( ) / parseFloat( )** would result into an error during execution. There are different ways to take care of this possible error. Of these, we have chosen the easiest one—by writing **throws Exception** besides **main( )**. We would not get into the details of this and the other mechanisms to handle errors that occur during execution. These mechanisms are discussed in detail in Chapter 15.

Command-line Arguments

In our simple interest program, instead of reading values using the **Scanner** object during execution, we can provide the values at command-line itself. This would be another way of supplying input to the program. The modified program would look like this...

```
// Calculation of simple interest
package siusingcmdlineargs ;
import java.lang.* ;
public class SiUsingCmdLineArgs
{
    public static void main ( String[ ] args )
    {
        float p, r, si ;
        int n ;
        p = Float.parseFloat ( args[ 0 ] ) ;
        n = Integer.parseInt ( args[ 1 ] ) ;
        r = Float.parseFloat ( args[ 2 ] ) ;
        si = p * n * r / 100 ;
        System.out.println ( "Simple interest = Rs. " + si ) ;
    }
}
```

To supply the values of **p**, **n** and **r** as command-line arguments, Right click on the project name **siusingcmdlineargs** in the projects window of NetBeans and select 'Properties' from the menu that pops up. On doing so, the Project Properties window is displayed. In this window choose

'Run' from 'Categories' and type the values 1000.50f 3 15.5f in the 'Arguments' text box.

Now you can compile and execute the program as usual using F6. When we execute the program, the command-line arguments are available in **main( )** as an array (collection) of strings in **args**. From this collection we can access the individual strings using **args[0]**, **args[1]** and **args[2]**. These strings contain the values that we gave as command-line arguments. However, we cannot perform arithmetic on these strings. So, it is necessary to first convert them into numbers. This conversion into **float** and **int** is done using the statements:

```
p = Float.parseFloat ( args[ 0 ] ) ;
n = Integer.parseInt ( args[ 1 ] ) ;
r = Float.parseFloat ( args[ 2 ] ) ;
```

Note that **int** and **float** are primitives whereas **Float** and **Integer** are classes. These classes have functions like **parseFloat( )** and **parseInt( )**. The converted numbers are assigned to **p**, **n** and **r**. Finally, simple interest is calculated and printed out. To be able to use **Integer** and **Float** classes we must import them from **java.lang** package.

Java Instructions

Now that we have written a few programs, let us look at the instructions that we have used in these programs. There are basically five types of instructions in Java. The purpose of each of these instructions is given in Figure 3.3.

Instruction	Purpose
Type declaration	To declare the type of variables used in a Java program
Arithmetic	To perform arithmetic operations between constants and variables
Control	To control the sequence of execution of various statements in a Java program
Exception Handling	To handle situations when errors occur during execution of a Java program
Advanced	Instructions for thread synchronization, for handling arithmetic overflow, etc.

Figure 3.3

Since the elementary Java programs would usually contain only the type declaration and the arithmetic instructions; we would discuss only these two instructions at this stage. The other types of instructions would be discussed in detail in the subsequent chapters.

Type Declaration Instruction

This instruction is used to declare the type of variable being used in the program. Any variable used in the program must be declared before using it in any statement.

```
Ex.: int  bas ;
     float rs, grosssal ;
     char  name, code ;
```

There are several subtle variations of the type declaration instruction. These are discussed below.

(a) While declaring the type of variable we can also initialize it as shown below.

```
int i = 10, j = 25 ;
float a = 1.5f, b = 1.99f + 2.4f * 1.44f ;
```

(b) The order in which we define the variables is sometimes important, sometimes not. For example,

```
int  i = 10, j = 25 ;
```

is same as

```
int  j = 25, i = 10 ;
```

However,

```
float  a = 1.5f, b = a + 3.1f ;
```

is alright, but

```
float  b = a + 3.1f, a = 1.5f ;
```

is not. This is because here we are trying to use **a** even before defining it.

(c) The following statements would work:

```
int a, b, c, d ;
a = b = c = 10 ;
```

However, the following statement would not work:

```
int a = b = c = d = 10 ;
```

This is because we are trying to use **b** (to assign to **a**) before defining it.

Arithmetic Instruction

A Java arithmetic instruction consists of a variable name on the left-hand side of =, and variable names and constants on the right-hand side of =. The variables and constants appearing on the right-hand side of = are connected using arithmetic operators like **+**, **-**, *****, and **/**.

Ex.:
```
int budget ;
float alpha, beta ;
budget = 3200 ;
beta = 0.5f ;
alpha = beta + 3.2f * 2 / 5 - 3 ;
```

Here,

***, /, -, +** are the arithmetic operators
= is an assignment operator
2, 3, 5 and 3200 are integer constants
0.5f and 3.2f are float constants
budget is an integer variable
alpha, beta are float variables.

The variables and constants together are called operands. While executing an arithmetic statement the operands on right hand side are operated upon by the arithmetic operators and the result is then assigned, using the assignment operator, to the variable on left hand side.

A Java arithmetic statement could be of three types. These are as follows:

(a) Integer mode arithmetic statement - This is an arithmetic statement in which all operands are either integer variables or integer constants.

```
Ex.: int  i = 10, king, issac = 23, noteit = 45 ;
     i = i + 1 ;
     king = issac * 234 + noteit - 7689 ;
```

(b) Real mode arithmetic statement - This is an arithmetic statement in which all operands are either real constants or real variables.

```
Ex.: float  qbee, si, prin = 100.55f, noy = 1.5f, roi = 5.5f ;
     qbee = 23.123f / 4.5f * 0.3442f ;
     si = prin * noy * roi / 100.0f ;
```

(c) Mixed mode arithmetic statement - This is an arithmetic statement in which some operands are integers and some are real.

```
Ex.: float  si, prin = 100.55f, noy = 1.5f, roi = 5.5f, avg ;
     int  a = 10, b = 20, c =30, num = 40 ;
     si = prin * noy * roi / 100.0f ;
     avg = ( a + b + c + num + 10.5f ) / 5 ;
```

Though Arithmetic instructions look simple to use, one often commits mistakes in writing them. Let us take a closer look at these statements. Note the following points carefully:

(a) Java allows only one variable on left hand side of =. This means, **z = k * l** is legal, whereas **k * l = z** is illegal.

(b) In addition to the division operator Java also provides a modular division operator (%). This operator returns the remainder on dividing one operand with another. Thus, the expression 10 / 2 yields 5, whereas 10 % 2 yields 0. Note that on using %, the sign of the remainder is always same as the sign of the numerator. Thus -5 % 2 yields -1, whereas 5 % -2 yields 1.

(c) Modular division can also be done on floats. If **a** and **b** are floats then **a % b** is computed as **a - n * b**, where **n** is the largest possible integer that is less than or equal to **a / b**. Thus **16.5f % 1.25f** yields **0.25**.

(d) An arithmetic instruction is at times used for storing character constants in character variables.

```
char  a, b ;
a = 'F' ;
b = '+' ;
```

When we do this, the Unicode values of the characters are stored in the variables.

(e) Arithmetic operations can be performed on **int**s, **float**s and **char**s. Thus, the statements,

```
char  x = 'a', y = 'b' ;

int  z ;
z = x + y ;
```

are perfectly valid since the addition is performed on the Unicode values of the characters and not on characters themselves. The Unicode values of 'a' and 'b' are 97 and 98, and hence they can be added.

(f) No operator is assumed to be present. It must be written explicitly. In the following example, the multiplication operator after **b** must be explicitly written:

```
a = c.d.b(xy)               usual arithmetic statement
b = c * d * b * ( x * y )   Java statement
```

(g) If we want to perform an exponentiation operation, we can get it done this way:

```
double  a ;
a = Math.pow ( 3.0, 2.0 ) ;
```

Here **pow( )** function is a function in **Math** class. It is being used to raise 3.0 to the power of 2.0. Note that we should always use **double** values with **pow( )**.

There are many other mathematical functions in **Math** class, like **sqrt( )**, **abs( )**, **sin( )**, **cos( )**, **tan( )**, **log( )**, **log10( )**, etc.

Type Conversion in Arithmetic Instructions

To effectively develop Java programs, it is necessary to understand the rules that are used for the implicit conversion of real and integer values. These are mentioned below. Note them carefully.

(a) An arithmetic operation between an integer and integer always yields an integer result.

(b) An operation between a real and real always yields a real result.

(c) An operation between an integer and real always yields a real result. In this operation, the integer is first promoted to a real and then the operation is performed. Hence the result is real.

A few practical examples shown in Figure 3.4 would put the issue beyond doubt.

Operation	Result	Operation	Result
5 / 2	2	2 / 5	0
5.0 / 2	2.500000	2.0 / 5	0.400000
5 / 2.0	2.500000	2 / 5.0	0.400000
5.0 / 2.0	2.500000	2.0 / 5.0	0.400000

Figure 3.4

Here are a few more implicit conversion rules.

(a) An operation between any **byte**, **short**, **int** or **char** results in an **int**. Hence, the result of these operations should always be assigned to an **int** variable. Otherwise, an error would be reported. The following code segment illustrates this:

```
byte  a = 100, b = 50 ;
byte  c = a + b ;  // error, as resulting int cannot be assigned to a byte
int  d = a + b ;  // works

short  l = 45, m = 20 ;
short  n = l + m ;  // error, as resulting int can't be assigned to a short
int  p = l + m ;  // works

char  ch = 'A', dh = 'B' ;
char  eh = ch + dh  // error, resulting int can't be assigned to a char
int  fh = ch + dh ; // works
```

(b) During assignment, the type on left-hand side may not be the same as the type on right-hand side. In such a case, if the value of the right-hand side is within the range of type on left-hand side, then no error results. The following code snippet illustrates this point:

```
byte s ;
s = 20 ;  // though 20 is an int, it is within range of byte
short a ;
```

```
a = 100 ; // though 100 is an int, it is within range of short
```

If the value of right-hand side is not within the range of type on left hand side then an error is reported. For example,

```
byte s ;
s = 200 ; // error as 200 is not within range of byte
short a ;
a = 40000 ; // error as 40000 is not within range of short
```

(c) A **char** can be implicitly converted to **short**, **int**, **long**, **float**, or **double**. However, there are no implicit conversions from other types to the **char** type. The following code snippet illustrates this:

```
float a = 'A' ; // works
char ch = a ; // error
```

Explicit Conversion

At times we are required to explicitly convert one type into another. This is done using a type casting operation. Let us consider an example.

```
float a, b ;
int x = 6, y = 4 ;
a = x / y ;
b = ( float ) x / y ;
System.out.println ( "Value of a = " + a ) ;
System.out.println ( "Value of b = " + b ) ;
```

And here is the output...

```
Value of a = 1.0
Value of b = 1.5
```

Here **x** and **y** are both integers, hence **x / y** yields an integer, 1. If we do not want the quotient to be truncated, then we can use type casting as we have done in the next statement. Type casting involves putting a pair of ( ) around the data type. In our program the expression (**float**) causes the variable **x** to be converted from type **int** to type **float** before being used in the division operation.

Here is another example of type casting:

```
float a = 6.35f ;
System.out.println ( "Value of a on type casting = " + ( int ) a ) ;
```

```
System.out.println ( "Value of a = " + a ) ;
```

And here is the output...

```
Value of a on type casting = 6
Value of a = 6.35
```

Note that the value of **a** does not change permanently because of typecasting. Rather, it is the value of the expression that undergoes type conversion when we do typecasting.

Hierarchy of Operations

While executing an arithmetic statement, which has two or more operators, we may have some problems as to how exactly does it get executed. For example, does the expression 2 * x - 3 * y correspond to (2x) - (3y) or to 2(x - 3y)? Similarly, does A / B * C correspond to A / (B * C) or to (A / B) * C? To answer these questions satisfactorily, one must understand the 'hierarchy' of operations. Hierarchy decides the order in which the operations in an expression are performed. The hierarchy of commonly used operators is shown in Figure 3.5.

Priority	Operators	Description
1st	* / %	Multiplication, Division, Modular division
2nd	+ -	Addition, Subtraction
3rd	=	Assignment

Figure 3.5

Within parentheses the same hierarchy as mentioned in Figure 3.5 is operative. Also, if there are more than one set of parentheses, the operations within the innermost parentheses would be performed first, followed by the operations within the second innermost pair and so on.

An example would clarify the issue further.

Example 3.1: Determine the hierarchy of operations and evaluate the following expression, assuming that **i** is an integer variable:

i = 2 * 3 / 4 + 4 / 4 + 8 - 2 + 5 / 8

Stepwise evaluation of this expression is shown below.

i = 2 * 3 / 4 + 4 / 4 + 8 - 2 + 5 / 8	
i = 6 / 4 + 4 / 4 + 8 - 2 + 5 / 8	operation: *
i = 1 + 4 / 4 + 8 - 2 + 5 / 8	operation: /
i = 1 + 1 + 8 - 2 + 5 / 8	operation: /
i = 1 + 1 + 8 - 2 + 0	operation: /
i = 2 + 8 - 2 + 0	operation: +
i = 10 - 2 + 0	operation: +
i = 8 + 0	operation: -
i = 8	operation: +

Note that 6 / 4 gives 1 and not 1.5. This is because operations between two integers always evaluate to an integer. Similarly, 5 / 8 evaluates to zero, since 5 and 8 are integers.

Associativity of Operators

When an expression contains two operators of equal priority, the tie between them is settled using the associativity of the operators. All operators in Java have either Left to Right associativity or Right to Left associativity. Let us understand this with the help of a few examples.

Consider the expression a = 3 / 2 * 5 ;

Here there is a tie between operators of same priority, that is between / and *. This tie is settled using the associativity of / and *. Both enjoy Left to Right associativity. Therefore firstly / operation is done followed by *.

Consider one more expression.

a = b = 3 ;

Here both assignment operators have the same priority. So, order of operations is decided using associativity of = operator. = associates from Right to Left. Therefore, the second = is performed earlier than the first =.

Consider yet another expression.

z = a * b + c / d ;

Here * and **/** enjoy same priority and same associativity (Left to Right). Compiler is free to perform * or **/** operation as per its convenience, since no matter which is performed earlier, the result would be same.

Note that the precedence and associativity of all operators is predetermined, and we cannot change it.

Constant Variables

Many times, we have to use constant values in a program. For example, values of pi, Plank's constant or Avogadro's number. Suppose we need the value of pi at several places in a Java program. It would be a bad idea if we directly use the value 3.14 at all these places, as we might commit a typing error at one of the places and this error would go unnoticed by the compiler. To avoid this, we can store the value 3.14 in a **float** variable **pi**, and then use this variable wherever we need the value of pi. This solution suffers from the limitation that being a variable, **pi** is liable to change. So, if by mistake we assign a new value to this variable, the compiler would not be able to report this as an error.

A solution for this is to declare the variable as a constant variable using the keyword **final**. This is illustrated in the code snippet given below.

```
final float pi = 3.14f ;
float radius = 1.5f ;
float area = pi * radius * radius ;
```

Console Output in Java

The screen and keyboard together are called a console. We have already seen how to use the object of **Scanner** class to receive input from keyboard. To send output to screen two functions are popularly used **println( )** and **format( )**. Let us understand these functions now.

println( ) and *format( )* Functions

So far we have used **println( )** function to send output to the screen. Given below is an example of its usage.

```
int avg = 346 ;
float per = 69.5f ;
System.out.println ( "Output:" ) ;
System.out.println ( "Average = " + avg + "\n" + "Percentage = " + per ) ;
```

This code snippet would produce the following output:

```
Output:
Average = 346
Percentage = 69.5
```

In the first **println( )** we have merely printed the string **Output:**, whereas in the next we have converted the integer **avg** and float **per** into strings and then appended them at the end of **Average =** and **Percentage =**, respectively. We have also put a **\n** in between to display the strings in two different lines. Also note that the output of each **println( )** function appears on a new line because it prints the output and sends the cursor to the next line.

If we wish to control the format in which the output is displayed on the screen, we should use the **format( )** or **printf( )** function instead of **println( )** function. They can be used to control details like where the output appears on the screen, how many spaces are present between the two values, the number of places after the decimal points, etc. Its general form looks like this...

```
System.out.format ( "format string", list of variables ) ;
```

The different format specifiers that can be used in the format string of the **format( )** function are shown in Figure 3.7.

Format Specifier	Used for printing
%d	Integers in Decimal form
%e	Real numbers in Exponential form
%f	Real numbers in Fractional form
%o	Integers in Octal form
%X or %x	Integers in Hexadecimal form

Figure 3.7

We can also provide four optional specifiers with the above format specifications—width, zero, comma and sign. Their usage is shown in the following code snippet:

```
int num = 762432 ;
System.out.format ( "%10d\n", num ) ;
System.out.format ( "%010d\n", num ) ;
System.out.format ( "%+10d\n", num ) ;
System.out.format ( "%,10d\n", num ) ;
System.out.format ( "%+,10d\n", num ) ;
```

```
System.out.format ( "%10.2f\n", 5.05 ) ;
System.out.format ( "%10.2f\n", 413.25 ) ;
```

Here is the output of this code snippet.

```
0000762432
   +762432
   762,432
  +762,432
      5.05
    413.25
```

Width indicates the number of columns to be reserved for printing the number. For example, **%10d** indicates that the decimal integer be printed in 10 columns. If the number to be printed is smaller than the columns reserved for printing it, the number is right aligned. If we want to left-align the number we have to use **%-10d**. If width turns out to be smaller than what is required for printing the number, the width gets ignored.

The specifier **%010d** prints the number right aligned in 10 columns with suitable number of zeros padded on the left. **%+10d** adds a **+** sign at beginning of the number. Had the number's value been negative a - sign would have been displayed. **%,10d** introduces comma in the number to make it more readable. Finally, **%+,10d** combines the effect of , and +.

The specifier **%10.2f** right aligns the double in 10 columns with 2 places beyond decimal point.

Control Instructions in Java

As the name suggests, Control Instructions enable us to specify the order in which the various instructions in a program are to be executed by the computer. In other words, the control instructions determine the 'flow of control' in a program. There are four types of control instructions in Java. They are:

(a) Sequence Control Instruction
(b) Selection or Decision Control Instruction
(c) Repetition or Loop Control Instruction
(d) Case Control Instruction

The Sequence control instruction ensures that the instructions are executed in the same order in which they appear in the program.

Decision and Case control instructions allow the computer to take a decision as to which instruction is to be executed next. The Loop control instruction helps computers to execute a group of statements repeatedly. In the following chapters, we are going to learn these instructions in detail.

Exercises

[A] Evaluate the following expressions and show their hierarchy.

(a) g = big / 2 + big * 4 / big - big + abc / 3 ;
(abc = 2.5f, big = 2, assume **g** to be a single)

(b) on = ink * act / 2 + 3 / 2 * act + 2 + tig ;
(ink = 4, act = 1, tig = 3.2f, assume **on** to be an int)

(c) s = qui * add / 4 - 6 / 2 + 2 / 3 * 6 / god ;
(qui = 4, add = 2, god = 2, assume **s** to be an int)

(d) s = 1 / 3 * a / 4 - 6 / 2 + 2 / 3 * 6 / g ;
(a = 4, g = 3, assume **s** to be an int)

(e) t = c + a * y * y / b ;
(a = 2.2, b = 0.0, c = 4.1, y = 3.0, assume **t** to be an float)

(f) R = x * x + 2 * x + 1 / 2 * x * x + x + 1 ;
(x = 3.5, assume **R** to be an float)

[B] Evaluate the result of the following statements.

(a) g = 10 / 5 /2 / 1 ;
(b) b = 3 / 2 + 5 * 4 / 3 ;
(c) a = b = c = 3 + 4 ;
(d) x = 2 – 3 + 5 * 2 / 8 % 3 ;
(e) z = 5 % 3 / 8 * 3 + 4

[C] Convert the following equations into corresponding Java statements:

(a) $$Z = \frac{8.8(a+b)2/c - 0.5 + 2a/(q+r)}{(a+b)*(1/m)}$$

(b) X = -b + (b * b) + 2 4ac

(c) $R = \dfrac{2v + 6.22\ (c + d)}{g + v}$

(d) $A = \dfrac{7.7b\ (xy + a)\ /\ c - 0.8 + 2b}{(x + a)\ (1 / y)}$

[D] Match the following:

(a) Range of char	(1) true4 bytes
(b) Range of int	(2) 2 bytes
(c) Range of float	(3) -2147483648 to 2147483647
(d) Size of int	(4) -3.4e38 to +3.4e38
(e) Size of float	(5) 4 bytes
(f) Size of char	(6) 0 to 65535
(g) Value of bool	(7) 4 bytes
(h) Size of book	(8) 1 bit

[E] Fill in the blanks:

(a) Each character in Java is represented as a ________ character and not as a ASCII character.

(b) All trignometric functions like **sin( )**, **cos( )**, **tan( )**, etc. are present in ______ class.

(c) The result of an arithmetic operation between two **byte** values results into ______.

(d) Addition of a **byte** and a **short** results into a ______.

(e) A ______ can be implicitly converted to **short**, **int**, **long**, while performing arithmetic operation on it.

(f) In Java explicit conversion from one type into another can be done using a _________ operation.

(g) If priority of two operators is same then the order of evaluation is decided by ________ of operators.

[F] State which of the following statements are True or False:

(a) The output of the **println( )** function is always displayed on a fresh line.

(b) In **System.out.println( ), println( )** is a function of **PrintStream** class, and **out** is a **static** object defined in a **System** class.

(c) We can print values of four variables using the following statement:

```
System.out.println ( si, p, n, r ) ;
```

(d) All command-line arguments are received by **main( )** as strings.

(e) An integer value can be assigned to a **short** provided the value is within the range of **short**.

(f) It is not possible to implicitly convert a **float** to a **double**.

(g) The following two statements are same:

```
double a = ( double ) ( 2.5f + 3.5f ) ;
double a = ( double ) 2.5f + 3.5f ;
```

(h) Associativity of operators comes into play only when the precedence of two operators is same.

(i) The following is the correct way to define a constant variable:

```
final float epsilon = 0.1241f ;
```

[G] Answer the following:

(a) Two numbers are input through the keyboard into two locations C and D. Write a Java program to interchange the contents of C and D.

(b) If a five-digit number is input through the keyboard, write a Java program to calculate the sum of its digits.

(c) If a five-digit number is input through the keyboard, write a Java program to reverse the number.

(d) In a town, the percentage of men is 52. The percentage of total literacy is 48. If total percentage of literate men is 35 of the total population, write a Java program to find the total number of illiterate men and women if the population of the town is 80,000.

(e) A cashier has currency notes of denominations 10, 50 and 100. If the amount to be withdrawn is input through the keyboard, write a Java program find the minimum number of currency notes of each denomination the cashier will have to give to the withdrawer.

KanNotes

- 2 ways to make the program general :
  - Receive input from keyboard
  - Receive input from command-line on starting program execution
- Procedure to receive input from command-line in Windows

  ```
  C:\> javac myprogram.java
  C:\> java myprogram.class cat dog parrot
  ```
- Procedure to receive input from command-line in Linux

  ```
  # javac myprogram.java
  # java myprogram.class cat dog parrot
  ```
- Procedure to receive input from command-line in NetBeans under Windows
  - Right click Project | Properties
  - From the dialog that pops up select "Run"
  - Enter "Arguments" as cat dog parrot
- A program can receive input from keyboard using Scanner class function as shown below :

  ```
  Scanner scn = new Scanner ( System.in ) ;
  int n = scn.nextInt() ;
  ```
- A program can receive input through command-line arguments. These arguments are received as strings. If the strings contain numbers then these numeric strings should be converted to integer / float as shown below :

  ```
  int n = Integer.parseInt ( args[ 1 ] ) ; // method 1
  int n = Integer.valueOf ( args[ 1 ] ) ).intValue() ; // method 2
  float p = Float.parseFloat ( args[ 0 ] ) ; // method 1
  float p = ( Float.valueOf ( args[ 0 ] ) ).floatValue() ; // method 2
  ```
- Integer type :
  - 4 types – byte, short, int, long. Most common – int

- Number without a decimal point is byte, short, int, long depending on range in which it fits
  Ex.: 35 – byte   400 – short   45000 – int
- Value being assigned should not exceed the range of the variable

- Real type :
  - 2 types – float, double. Most common – float
  - double is used to deal with very big real values
  - By default number with a decimal point is double
  - Value being assigned should not exceed the range of the variable
- Boolean type :
  - Boolean can take a value true or false
  - Result of a Boolean expression is true / false
  - Do not use true / false as variable names
  - true is not 1 and false is not 0
- Arithmetic Instruction :
  - On LHS of = only variable can occur
  - + - * / % are Arithmetic Operators
  - No operator is assumed to be present
  - Do exponentiation using pow() function
    Ex. : double a = Math.pow (2.0, 5.0) ;
  - Other funs. - sqrt(), abs(), sin(), cos(), tan(), log(), ...
  - Widening conversions take place automatically
    Ex. : long l = 40000 * 2 ;
  - Narrowing conversions report errors. Ex. : short s = 40000 ;
  - Possible loss of precision is reported as error

Decision Control Instruction

Let Us JAVA 7th Edition

CHAPTER 04

All but the simplest of logic would involve decision making on the go. Learn how to make decisions in a Java program...

Contents

- Decisions! Decisions!
- The *if-else* statement
- More Complex Decision Making
  - The *else if* Clause
  - The & and | Operators
  - The ! Operator
  - Hierarchy of Operators Revisited
- A Word of Caution
- The Conditional Operators
- Exercises
- KanNotes

We all need to alter our actions in the face of changing circumstances. If the weather is fine, then I will go for a stroll. If the highway is busy, I will take a diversion. If the pitch takes spin, we will win the match. If she says no, I will look elsewhere. If you like this book, we will write the next edition. You can notice that all these decisions depend on some conditions being met. Java language too must be able to perform different sets of actions depending on the circumstances. In this chapter, we will explore ways in which a Java program can react to changing circumstances.

Decisions! Decisions!

In the programs written in Chapters 2 and 3, the instructions in them got executed sequentially. However, in many programming situations, we want one set of instructions to get executed in one situation, and an entirely different set in another situation. Such situations are dealt with in Java programs using decision control instruction. A decision control instruction can be implemented in Java using:

(a) The **if-else** statement
(b) The conditional operators

Now let us learn each of these and their variations in turn.

The *if-else* Statement

Like most languages, Java uses **if-else** to implement the decision control instruction. The general form of **if** statement looks like this:

```
if ( this condition is true )
{
    execute statement1 ;
    execute statement2 ;
}
else
{
    execute statement4 ;
    execute statement5 ;
}
```

The keyword **if** tells the compiler that what follows is a decision control instruction. The condition following the keyword **if** is always enclosed in a pair of parentheses. If the condition is true, then the statements 1, 2 are executed. If the condition is false, then statements 4 and 5 are executed.

But how do we express the condition itself in Java? And how do we evaluate its truth or falsity? We express a condition using Java's 'relational' operators. They allow us to compare two values to see whether they are equal, unequal, or whether one is greater than the other. Here is how they look and how they are evaluated in Java.

this expression	is true if
x == y	x is equal to y
x != y	x is not equal to y
x < y	x is less than y
x > y	x is greater than y
x <= y	x is less than or equal to y
x >= y	x is greater than or equal to y

Figure 4.1

The relational operators should be familiar to you except for the equality operator == and the inequality operator **!=**. Note that = is used for assignment, whereas == is used for comparison of two quantities. Let us understand the usage of relational operators using a simple program based on Example 4.1.

Example 4.1: In a company an employee is paid as under:

If his basic salary is less than Rs. 1500, then HRA = 10% of basic salary and DA = 90% of basic salary. If his salary is either equal to or above Rs. 1500, then HRA = Rs. 1500 and DA = 98% of basic salary. If the employee's salary is input through the keyboard write a program to find his gross salary.

Now let us look at the program that implements this logic.

```
// Calculation of gross salary
package calofgrosssalary ;
import java.util.* ;
public class CalOfGrossSalary
{
    public static void main ( String[ ] args )
```

```
    {
        float  bs, gs, da, hra ;
        Scanner scn ;
        scn = new Scanner ( System.in ) ;
        bs = scn.nextFloat( ) ;
        if ( bs < 1500 )
        {
            hra = bs * 10 / 100 ;
            da = bs * 90 / 100 ;
        }
        else
        {
            hra = 1200 ;
            da = bs * 98 / 100 ;
        }
        gs = bs + hra + da ;
        System.out.println ( "Gross salary = Rs. " + gs ) ;
    }
}
```

Here is some sample interaction with the program.

```
Enter basic salary
1200
Gross salary = Rs. 2400.0

Enter basic salary
2000
Gross salary = Rs. 4660.0
```

A few points worth noting...

(a) The group of statements in { } after the if is called an 'if block'. Similarly, the statements in { } after the else form the 'else block'.

(b) Notice that the **else** is written exactly below the **if**. The statements in the **if** block and those in the **else** block have been indented to the right. This formatting convention is followed throughout the book to enable you to understand the working of the program better.

(c) Had there been only one statement to be executed in the **if** block and only one statement in the **else** block we could have dropped the pair of braces.

(d) In the first run of the program, the condition evaluates to true, as 1200 (value of **bs**) is less than 1500. In this case the statements in the if block get executed. In the second run, the condition evaluates to false, as 2000 (value of **bs**) is greater than 1500. Now the statements in the else block get executed.

(e) It is perfectly all right if we write an entire **if-else** construct within an **if** block or else block. This is called 'nesting' of **if-else** statements.

(f) At times we may not wish to do anything if the condition in **if** fails. In such a case we should drop the **else** and the associated else block.

More Complex Decision Making

Sometimes decision making becomes complex. We may wish to execute a set of statements if multiple conditions are true, or if one out of multiple conditions is true. To deal with such situations Java provides logical operators, &&, || and !. These are to be read as 'AND' 'OR' and 'NOT', respectively.

The first two operators, **&&** and **||**, allow two or more conditions to be combined in an **if** statement. Let us see how they are used in a program. Consider the following example:

Example 4.2: The marks obtained by a student in 3 different subjects are input through the keyboard. The student gets a division as per the following rules:

Percentage above or equal to 60 - First division
Percentage between 50 and 59 - Second division
Percentage between 40 and 49 - Third division
Percentage less than 40 - Fail

Write a program to determine the division obtained by the student.

Here is the program that implements this logic.

```
// Determining student's division
package studentdiv ;
import java.util.* ;
public class StudentDiv
{
    public static void main ( String[ ] args )
    {
```

```
        int  m1, m2, m3, per ;
        Scanner scn ;

        scn = new Scanner ( System.in ) ;
        System.out.println ( "Enter marks in three subjects" ) ;
        m1 = scn.nextInt( ) ;
        m2 = scn.nextInt( ) ;
        m3 = scn.nextInt( ) ;
        per = ( m1 + m2 + m3 ) * 100 / 300 ;

        if ( per >= 60 )
            System.out.println ( "First division" ) ;

        if ( ( per >= 50 ) && ( per < 60 ) )
            System.out.println ( "Second division" ) ;

        if ( ( per >= 40 ) && ( per < 50 ) )
            System.out.println ( "Third division" ) ;

        if ( per < 40 )
            System.out.println ( "Fail" ) ;
    }
}
```

As can be seen from the second **if** statement, the **&&** operator is used to combine two conditions. 'Second division' gets printed if both the conditions evaluate to true. If one condition evaluates to false, then the whole expression is treated as false.

We could have implemented the same logic without using logical operators, by using nested **if - else** statements. You may try doing this. If you do so you would observe that the program unnecessarily becomes lengthy.

The *else if* Clause

There is one more way in which we can write program for Example 4.1. This involves usage of **else if** blocks as shown below.

```
// else if ladder demo
package elseifladderdemo ;
import java.util.* ;
```

```
public class ElseIfLadderDemo
{
    public static void main ( String[ ] args )
    {
        int  m1, m2, m3, per ;
        Scanner scn ;

        scn = new Scanner ( System.in ) ;
        System.out.println ( "Enter marks in three subjects" ) ;
        m1 = scn.nextInt( ) ;
        m2 = scn.nextInt( ) ;
        m3 = scn.nextInt( ) ;
        per = ( m1 + m2 + m3 ) * 100 / 300 ;

        if ( per >= 60 )
            System.out.println ( "First division" ) ;
        else if ( per >= 50 )
            System.out.println ( "Second division" ) ;
        else if ( per >= 40 )
            System.out.println ( "Third division" ) ;
        else
            System.out.println ( "Fail" ) ;
    }
}
```

You can note that this program reduces the indentation of the statements. In this case, every **else** is associated with its previous **if**. The last **else** goes to work only if all the conditions fail. Also, if the first condition is satisfied, other conditions are not checked. Even in **else if** ladder, the last **else** is optional.

Another place where logical operators are useful is when we want to write programs for complicated logic that ultimately boil down to only two answers. This is shown in Example 4.2 given below.

Example 4.2: A company insures its drivers in the following cases:

- If the driver is married.
- If the driver is unmarried, male and above 30 years of age.
- If the driver is unmarried, female and above 25 years of age.

In all other cases, the driver is not insured. If the marital status, sex, and age of the driver are the inputs, write a program to determine whether the driver is to be insured or not.

Here after checking a complicated set of instructions the final output of the program would be one of the two—either the driver should be insured or the driver should not be insured. Since these are the only two outcomes this problem can be solved using logical operators.

If we list down all those cases in which the driver is insured, then they would be:

(a) Driver is married.
(b) Driver is an unmarried male above 30 years of age.
(c) Driver is an unmarried female above 25 years of age.

Since all these cases lead to the driver being insured, they can be combined using **&&** and **||** as shown in the program below.

```
// Insurance of driver - using logical operators
package driverinsurance ;
import java.util.* ;
public class DriverInsurance
{
    public static void main ( String[ ] args )
    {
        char  sex, ms ;
        int  age ;
        String str ;
        Scanner scn ;

        scn = new Scanner ( System.in ) ;
        System.out.println ( "Enter age, sex, marital status" ) ;
        age = scn.nextInt( ) ;
        sex = scn.next( ).charAt ( 0 ) ;
        ms = scn.next( ).charAt ( 0 ) ;

        if ( ( ms == 'M' ) || ( ms == 'U' && sex == 'M' && age > 30 )
                || ( ms == 'U' && sex == 'F' && age > 25 ) )
            System.out.println ( "Driver is insured" ) ;
        else
            System.out.println ( "Driver is not insured" ) ;
    }
```

```
}
```

In this program, it is important to note that:

- The driver will be insured only if one of the conditions enclosed in parentheses evaluates to true.
- For the second pair of parentheses to evaluate to true, each condition in the parentheses separated by **&&** must evaluate to true.
- Even if one of the conditions in the second parentheses evaluates to false, then the whole of the second parentheses evaluates to false.
- The last two of the above arguments apply to third pair of parentheses as well.

The & and | Operators

Consider the following code snippet:

```
int a = 1, b = 1, c = 5, d ;
if ( a > 3 && ( b = c + 4 ) > 1 )
    d = 35 ;
System.out.println ( b ) ;
```

On execution we would expect the output to be **9**. However, the output turns out to be 1. This so happens because the expression **(b = c + 4) > 1** doesn't get evaluated once **a > 3** fails. This is known as short-circuiting. This can be prevented by rewriting the **if** as follows:

```
if ( a > 3 & ( b = c + 4 ) > 1 )
    d = 35 ;
```

Note that we have used the operator & instead of &&. Using & ensures that both conditions are evaluated even if the first condition turns out to be false. Figure 4.2 summarizes the effects of using &&, ||, & and | operators.

Expression	Condition2 is evaluated
condition1 && condition2	Only if condition1 is true
condition1 & condition2	Always
condition1 || condition2	Only if condition1 is false
condition1 | condition2	Always

Figure 4.2

The ! Operator

So far, we have used only the logical operators **&&** and **||**. The third logical operator is the NOT operator, written as **!**. This operator reverses the result of the expression it operates on. For example, if the expression evaluates to true, then on applying **!** operator to it results into a false. Vice versa, if the expression evaluates to false, then on applying **!** operator to it makes it true. Here is an example of the NOT operator applied to a relational expression.

```
! ( y < 10 )
```

This means "not **y** less than 10". In other words, if **y** is less than 10, the expression will be false, since **(y < 10)** is true. We can express the same condition as **(y >= 10)**.

The NOT operator is often used to reverse the logical value of a single **boolean** variable, as in the expression

```
if ( ! flag )
```

This is another way of saying

```
if ( flag == 0 )
```

Does the NOT operator sound confusing? Avoid it if you want, as the same thing can be achieved without using the NOT operator.

Figure 4.3 summarizes the working of all three logical operators.

Operands		Results					
x	y	!x	!y	x && y	x & y	x || y	x | y
false	false	true	true	false	false	false	false
false	true	true	false	false	false	true	true
true	false	false	true	false	false	true	true
true	true	false	false	true	true	true	true

Figure 4.3

Hierarchy of Operators Revisited

Since we have now added logical operators to the list of operators we know, it is time to review these operators and their priorities. Figure 4.4 summarizes the operators we have seen so far. The higher the position of an operator is in the table, the higher is its priority.

Operators	Type
!	Logical NOT
* / %	Arithmetic and modulus
+ -	Arithmetic
< > <= >=	Relational
== !=	Relational
&& &	Logical AND
|| |	Logical OR
=	Assignment

Figure 4.4

A Word of Caution

A common mistake while using the **if** statement is to write a semicolon (;) after the condition, as shown below.

```
if ( i == 5 ) ;
    System.out.println ( "Reached here" ) ;
```

The ; makes the compiler interpret the statement as if you have written it in following manner:

```
if ( i == 5 )
    ;
System.out.println ( "Reached here" ) ;
```

Here, if the condition evaluates to true, the ; (null statement, which does nothing on execution) gets executed, following which the **println( )** gets executed. If the condition fails, then straightaway the **println( )** gets executed. Thus, irrespective of the result of the condition, the **println( )** gets executed. Compiler would not point out this as an error, since as far as the syntax is concerned, nothing has gone wrong, but the logic has certainly gone awry. Moral is, beware of such a pitfall.

The Conditional Operators

The conditional operators **?** and **:** are sometimes called ternary operators since they take three arguments. In fact, they form a kind of foreshortened if-then-else. Their general form is,

expression 1 ? expression 2 : expression 3

What this expression says is: "if **expression 1** is true, then the value returned will be result of **expression 2**, otherwise the value returned will be result of **expression 3**". Let us understand this with the help of a few examples.

(a)
```
int x, y ;
y = x > 5 ? 3 + 4 : 4 + 7 ;
```

This statement will store 7 in **y** if **x** is greater than 5, otherwise it will store 11 in **y**.

(b)
```
int  y ;
y = a >= 65 && a <= 90 ? 1 : 0 ;
System.out.println ( y ) ;
```

Here 1 would be assigned to **y** if **a >=65 && a <=90** evaluates to true, otherwise 0 would be assigned.

The following points may be noted about the conditional operators:

(c) If we use a function in ? part or in : part the function has to return a value, which can then be assigned to a variable. If we use a function that returns nothing (void) it would result in an error. This is illustrated in the following examples:

```
Ex.:    double j ;
        j = ang > 45 ? Math.sin ( 0.5 ) : Math.cos ( 0.5 ) ;
```

This would work as the sine or cosine value returned would get assigned to **j**.

```
Ex.:    int x ;
        x = act == 1 ? System.out.println ( "Amitabh" ) :
                       System.out.println ( "All and sundry" ) ;
```

This would not work as **println( )** function doesn't return anything, so assignment to **x** cannot happen.

```
Ex.:    double j ;
        System.out.println ( j = 3 > 4 ? 4.4 : 3.3 ) ;
        System.out.println ( 3 > 4 ? 4.4 : 3.3 ) ;
```

These statements would work indicating that conditional operators can be used even inside **println( )** function.

(d) The conditional operators can be nested as shown below.

```
int  big, a, b, c ;
big = a > b ? ( a > c ? 3: 4 ) : ( b > c ? 6: 8 ) ;
```

(e) Check out the following conditional expression:

```
a > b ? g = a : g = b ;
```

This would result in an error, because the result of the expression **g = a** or **g = b** on being returned is not being assigned to any variable. The error can be overcome by rewriting the statement as

```
g = a > b ? a : b ;
```

The limitation of the conditional operators is that after the **?** or after the **:** , only one statement can occur.

Exercises

[A] What will be the output of the following programs:

(a)
```
package sampleproject ;
public class SampleProject
{
    public static void main ( String[ ] args )
    {
        int a = 300, b = 0, c ;
        if ( a >= 400 )
            b = 300 ;
            c = 200 ;
        System.out.println ( b + " " + c ) ;
    }
}
```

(b)
```
package sampleproject ;
public class SampleProject
{
    public static void main ( String[ ] args )
    {
        int x = 10, y = 20 ;
        if ( x == y ) ;
            System.out.println ( x + " " + y ) ;
    }
}
```

(c)
```
package sampleproject ;
public class SampleProject
{
    public static void main ( String[ ] args )
    {
        int i = -4, j, num = -4 ;
        j = i < 0 ? 0 : num * num ;
        System.out.println ( j ) ;
    }
}
```

(d)
```
package sampleproject ;
public class SampleProject
{
```

```
    public static void main ( String[ ] args )
    {
        int k, num = 30 ;
        k = ( num > 5 ? ( num <= 10 ? 100 : 200 ) : 500 ) ;
        System.out.println ( k ) ;
    }
}
```

[B] Point out the errors, if any, in the following programs:

(a)
```
package sampleproject ;
public class SampleProject
{
    public static void main ( String[ ] args )
    {
        int  x = 10 ;
        if ( x >= 2 ) then
            System.out.println ( x ) ;
    }
}
```

(b)
```
package sampleproject ;
public class SampleProject
{
    public static void main ( String[ ] args )
    {
        int x = 10, y = 15 ;
        if ( x % 2 = y % 3 )
            System.out.println ( "Carpathians" ) ;
    }
}
```

(c)
```
package sampleproject ;
public class SampleProject
{
    public static void main ( String[ ] args )
    {
        char  spy = 'a', password = 'z' ;
        if ( spy == 'a' or password == 'z' )
            System.out.println ( "All the birds safe in the nest" ) ;
    }
}
```

(d)
```
package sampleproject ;
```

```
public class SampleProject
{
    public static void main ( String[ ] args )
    {
        int a = 5, b = 6 ;
        a == b ? System.out.println ( a ) ;
    }
}
```

(e)
```
package sampleproject ;
public class SampleProject
{
    public static void main ( String[ ] args )
    {
        int x = 10, y = 20 ;
        boolean ret ;
        ret = ( x == 20 && y != 10 ) ? true : false ;
        System.out.println ( ret ) ;
    }
}
```

[C] Attempt the following:

(a) If the cost and selling price of an item is input through the keyboard, write a program to determine whether the seller has made profit or incurred loss. Also determine how much profit he made or loss he incurred.

(b) Any integer is input through the keyboard. Write a program to find out whether it is an odd number or even number.

(c) Write a program to find the absolute value of a number that is entered through the keyboard.

(d) If the ages of Ram, Shyam and Ajay are input through the keyboard, write a program to determine the youngest of the three.

(e) Write a program to check whether a triangle is valid or not, when the three angles of the triangle are entered through the keyboard. A triangle is valid if the sum of all the three angles is equal to 180 degrees.

(f) If the three sides of a triangle are entered through the keyboard, write a program to check whether the triangle is valid or not. The triangle is valid if the sum of two sides is greater than the largest of the three sides.

(g) If the three sides of a triangle are entered through the keyboard, write a program to check whether the triangle is isosceles, equilateral, scalene or right-angled triangle.

(h) Given the length and breadth of a rectangle, write a program to find whether the area of the rectangle is greater than its perimeter.

(i) Given the coordinates **(x, y)** of the center of a circle and its radius, write a program which will determine whether a point lies inside the circle, on the circle or outside the circle. (Hint: Use **Math.sqrt( )** and **Math.pow( )** functions)

(j) Given a point **(x, y)**, write a program to find out if it lies on the X-axis, Y-axis or on the origin, viz. (0, 0).

(k) Any year is entered through the keyboard, write a program (using logical operators) to determine whether the year is leap or not.

(l) What will be the result of the following expressions:

```
int a = 10 ;
int b = 20 ;
a > 5 && b != 5
a != 0 & b < 34
a > 45 || b > 45
a == 10 | b == 20
a > 5 && b != 3 || a + b >= 10
a > 5 || b != 3 && a + b >= 10
```

(m) Using conditional operators determine

(1) Whether the character entered through the keyboard is a lower case alphabet or not.

(2) Whether a character entered through the keyboard is a special symbol or not.

(3) Whether a character entered through the keyboard is a digit or not.

(4) Whether a character entered through the keyboard is alphanumeric or not.

KanNotes

- Control instructions control the sequence of execution of instructions in a program
- 4 types of control instructions :

  1) Sequence 2) Decision 3) Repetition 4) Case

- Three forms of decision control instruction :

```
if ( condition )
    statement1 ;
else
    statement2 ;
```

{ } are optional here

```
if ( condition )
{
    statement1 ;
    statement2 ;
}
else
{
    statement3 ;
    statement4 ;
}
```

{ } are necessary

```
if ( condition1 )
    statement1 ;
else if ( condition2 )
    statement2 ;
else if ( condition3 )
    statement3 ;
else
    statement4 ;
```

else goes to work if the 3 ifs fail

- Condition is built using relational operators < > <= >= == !=
- a = b is assignment. a == b is comparison
- More complex decision making can be done using logical operators
- Logical operators are &&, ||, &, | and !
- Usage of Logical Operators :

  &&, ||, &, | - To combine two conditions (not numbers)

  ! - To negate the result of a condition (not number)

- Working of logical operators :

condition1 && condition2 - True only if both conditions are true

- condition2 goes to work only if condition1 is true

condition1 & condition2 - True only if both conditions are true

- Both conditions are always evaluated

condition1 || condition2 - True if any one condition is true

- condition2 goes to work only if condition1 is false

condition1 | condition2 - True if any one condition is true

- Both conditions are always evaluated

! condition - If condition is true ! condition is false

- If condition is false ! condition is true

- Hierarchy :

  ! * / % + - < > <= >= && & || | =

- Unary operator - needs only 1 operand. Ex. !
- Binary operator - needs 2 operands. Ex. + - * / % < > <= >= == != && || & |
- ! (a <= b) is same as (a > b). ! (a >= b) is same as (a < b)
- Conditional operators ? : are ternary operators
- General form : result = condition ? value1 : value2
- value1 and value2 must be of same type
- ? : can have only 1 statement each
- ? : can be nested
- ? : always go together. : is not optional
- Always parenthesize assignment operation if used with ? :

Loop Control Instruction

Let Us JAVA 7th Edition

CHAPTER 05

If anything is worth doing, it is worth doing often. Learn how to repeat instructions in a Java program...

Contents

- Loops
- The *while* Loop
  - Tips about *while*
- The *for* Loop
  - Partial *for* Loops
  - Nesting of Loops
  - Multiple Initializations in the *for* Loop
- The *do-while* Loop
- The *break* Statement
- The *continue* Statement
- Common usage
- Exercises
- KanNotes

The programs that we have developed so far used either a sequential or a decision control instruction. These programs always performed the same series of actions, in the same way, exactly once. In programming we frequently need to perform an action over and over, often with variations in the details each time. The mechanism, which meets this need, is the loop control instruction, and loops are the subject of this chapter.

Loops

The versatility of the computer lies in its ability to perform a set of instructions repeatedly. This involves repeating some portion of the program either a specified number of times or until a particular condition is being satisfied. There are three methods by way of which we can repeat a part of a program. They are:

(a) Using a **for** statement
(b) Using a **while** statement
(c) Using a **do-while** statement

Let us now understand each of these methods of looping.

The *while* Loop

It is often the case in programming that you want to do something a fixed number of times. Perhaps you want to calculate gross salaries of ten different persons, or you want to convert temperatures from Centigrade to Fahrenheit for 15 different cities. The **while** loop is ideally suited for such situations. Let us look at a simple program that uses a **while** loop.

```
// Calculation of simple interest for 3 sets of p, n and r
package siusingwhileloop ;
import java.util.* ;
public class SiUsingWhileLoop
{
    public static void main ( String[ ] args )
    {
        float p, r, si ;
        int n, count ;
        Scanner scn ;
        count = 1 ;
        scn = new Scanner ( System.in ) ;
```

```
        while ( count <= 3 )
        {
            System.out.println ( "Enter values of p, n and r" ) ;
            p = scn.nextFloat( ) ;
            n = scn.nextInt( ) ;
            r = scn.nextFloat( ) ;
            si = p * n * r / 100 ;
            System.out.println ( "Simple interest = Rs. " + si ) ;
            count = count + 1 ;
        }
    }
}
```

And here are a few sample runs of this program...

```
Enter values of p, n and r
1000
5
13.5
Simple interest = Rs. 675.0
Enter values of p, n and r
2000
5
13.5
Simple interest = Rs. 1350.0
Enter values of p, n and r
3500
5
3.5
Simple interest = Rs. 612.5
```

The program executes all statements after the **while** 3 times. The logic for calculating the simple interest is written within a pair of braces immediately after the **while** keyword. These statements form the 'body' of the **while** loop. The parentheses after **while** contain a condition. So long as this condition remains true, all statements within the body of the **while** loop get executed repeatedly. To begin with, the variable **count** is initialized to 1 and every time the simple interest logic is executed, the value of **count** is incremented by one. The variable **count** is often called a 'loop counter' or 'index variable'. When the value of **count** reaches 4, the condition in **while** fails and the loop is terminated.

Tips about *while*

Note the following points about **while...**

- The statements within the **while** loop would keep on getting executed till the condition being tested remains true. When the condition becomes false, the control passes to the first statement that follows the body of the **while** loop.
- The condition being tested may use relational or logical operators as shown in the following examples:

```
while ( i <= 10 )
while ( i >= 10 && j <= 15 )
while ( j > 10 && ( b < 15 || c < 20 ) )
```

- The statements within the loop may be a single line or a block of statements. In the first case, the braces are optional as shown below.

```
while ( i <= 10 )
    i = i + 1 ;
```

- Almost always, the while must test a condition that will eventually become false, otherwise the loop will be executed forever, indefinitely as shown below.

```
int  i = 1 ;
while ( i <= 10 )
    System.out.println ( i ) ;
```

- Instead of incrementing a loop counter, we can even decrement it and still manage to get the body of the loop executed repeatedly. This is shown below.

```
int  i = 5 ;
while ( i >= 1 )
{
    System.out.println ( "Make the computer literate!" ) ;
    i = i - 1 ;
}
```

- It is not necessary that a loop counter must only be an **int**. It can even be a **float**.

```
float  a = 10.0f ;
```

```
while ( a <= 10.5f )
{
    System.out.println ( "Raindrops on roses..." ) ;
    System.out.println ( "...and whiskers on kittens" ) ;
    a = a + 0.1f ;
}
```

- A careless use of ; after while will make the loop run infinite number of times as shown in the following code snippet

```
int  i = 1 ;
while ( i <= 10 ) ;
{
    System.out.println ( i ) ;
    i = i + 1 ;
}
```

- Instead of incrementing a loop counter using the statement i = i + 1, we can use the expression **i++** to get the same result.

  Similarly, to reduce the value of a variable by 1, a decrement operator – can be used. Do not use **n+++** to increment the value of **n** by 2. Java does not have an operator **+++**.

- **+=** is a compound assignment operator. It can increment the value of a variable by any suitable value. For example, **i** += 1 increments value of **i** by 1, whereas **j += 10** increments value of **j** by 10. Other compound assignment operators are **-=, *=, /** = and **%=**.

- The ++ and -- operators can be combined with some other operation like assignment, printing or testing of a condition. In such cases the position of ++ decides the order of operations.

  If ++ is used before the variable it is called pre-incrementation and if it is present after the ++ then it is called post-incrementation. The following examples will clarify their usage:

```
int  i = 1 ;
while ( i++ < 10 )  // first test the condition, then increment i
while ( ++i < 10 )  // first increment i, then test the condition
j = ++i ;   // first increment i, then assign to j
j = i++ ;  // first assign i to j, then increment i
System.out.println ( ++i ) ; // first increment i, then print it
System.out.println ( i++ ) ;  // first print i, then increment it
```

The *for* Loop

for is probably the most popular looping instruction. Unlike a **while** loop, the **for** loop allows us to initialize, test and increment the loop counter in a single line as shown below.

```
for ( initialize  counter ; test  counter ; increment  counter )
{
    do this ;
    and this ;
    and this ;
}
```

Let us write down the simple interest program using **for**. Compare this program with the one, which we wrote using **while**.

```
// Calculation of simple interest for 3 sets of p, n and r
package siusingforloop ;
import java.util.* ;
public class SiUsingForLoop
{
    public static void main ( String[ ] args )
    {
        float  p, r, si ;
        int  n, count ;
        Scanner scn ;
        scn = new Scanner ( System.in ) ;
        for ( count = 1 ; count <= 3 ; count = count + 1 )
        {
            System.out.println ( "Enter values of p, n and r" ) ;
            p = scn.nextFloat( ) ;
            n = scn.nextInt( ) ;
            r = scn.nextFloat( ) ;
            si = p * n * r / 100 ;
            System.out.println ( "Simple Interest = Rs. " + si ) ;
        }
    }
}
```

Let us now examine how the **for** statement gets executed:

- When the **for** statement is executed for the first time, the value of **count** is set to an initial value 1.

- Now the condition **count <= 3** is tested. Since **count** is 1, the condition is satisfied, and the body of the loop is executed for the first time.
- Upon reaching the closing brace of **for**, control is sent back to the **for** statement, where the value of **count** gets incremented by 1.
- Again, the test is performed to check whether the new value of **count** exceeds 3.
- If the value of **count** is less than or equal to 3, the statements within the braces of **for** are executed again.
- The body of the **for** loop continues to get executed till **count** does not exceed the final value 3.
- When **count** reaches the value 4, the control exits from the loop and is transferred to the statement (if any) immediately after the body of **for**.

It is important to note that the initialization and incrementation part of a **for** loop can be replaced by any valid expression. Thus, the following **for** loops are perfectly okay.

```
for ( i = 1 ; i <=10 ; System.out.println ( i++ ) )
    ;

Scanner scn = new Scanner ( System.in ) ;
for ( i = scn.nextInt( ) ; i <= 10 ; i++ )
    System.out.println ( i ) ;
```

Partial *for* Loops

We can drop the initialization, test (condition) or incrementation part of a **for** loop. Thus, all the following loops would be correct and would print numbers from 1 to 10.

```
// Method 1 - Normal for loop
int i ;
for ( i = 1 ; i <= 10 ; i = i + 1 )
    System.out.println ( i ) ;

// Method 2 - Drop initialization
int i = 1 ;
for ( ; i <= 10 ; i++ )
```

```
    System.out.println ( i ) ;

// Method 3 - Drop initialization and incrementation
int i = 1 ;
for ( ; i <= 10 ; )
{
    System.out.println ( i ) ;
    i++ ;
}

// Method 4 - Drop initialization, incrementation and test
int i = 1 ;
for ( ; ; )
{
    System.out.println ( i ) ;
    i++ ;
    if ( i > 10 )
        break ;
}
```

Note that despite dropping initialization / incrementation / test, the two semicolons in the for loop are always necessary.

The **for** loop in Method 4 behaves like an infinite loop. Hence, we have checked the value of **i** against 10. If it goes beyond 10, we terminate the **for** loop using the **break** statement.

Nesting of Loops

The way **if** statements can be nested, similarly **while**s and **for**s can also be nested. To understand how nested loops work, look at the program given below.

```
// Demonstration of nested loops
package nestedforloopsdemo ;
public class NestedForLoopsDemo
{
    public static void main ( String[ ] args )
    {
        int  r, c, sum ;
        for ( r = 1 ; r <= 3 ; r++ )  // outer loop
        {
            for ( c = 1 ; c <= 2 ; c++ )  // inner loop
```

```
            {
                sum = r + c ;
                System.out.println ( "r = " + r + " c = " + c +
                                                " sum = " + sum ) ;
            }
        }
    }
}
```

When you run this program, you will get the following output:

```
r = 1 c = 1 sum = 2
r = 1 c = 2 sum = 3
r = 2 c = 1 sum = 3
r = 2 c = 2 sum = 4
r = 3 c = 1 sum = 4
r = 3 c = 2 sum = 5
```

Here, for each value of **r**, the inner loop is cycled through twice, with the variable **c** taking values from 1 to 2. The inner loop terminates when the value of **c** exceeds 2, and the outer loop terminates when the value of **r** exceeds 3.

Multiple Initializations in the *for* Loop

The initialization expression of the **for** loop can contain more than one statement separated by a comma (,). For example,

```
for ( i = 1, j = 2 ; j <= 10 ; j++ )
```

Multiple statements can also be used in the incrementation expression of **for** loop, i.e., you can increment (or decrement) two or more variables at the same time. However, only one statement is allowed in the test expression. This expression may contain several conditions linked together using logical operators.

Use of multiple statements in the initialization expression also demonstrates why semicolons are used to separate the three expressions in the **for** loop. Had commas been used, they could not also have been used to separate multiple statements in the initialization expression, without confusing the compiler.

The *do-while* Loop

The **do-while** loop looks like this:

```
do
{
    this ;
    and this ;
    and this ;
} while ( this condition is true ) ;
```

There is a minor difference between the working of **while** and **do-while** loops. This difference is the place where the condition is tested. The **while** tests the condition before executing any of the statements within the **while** loop. As against this, the **do-while** tests the condition after having executed the statements within the loop.

This means that **do-while** would execute its statements at least once, even if the condition fails for the first time. The **while**, on the other hand, will not execute its statements if the condition fails for the first time.

The *break* Statement

We often come across situations where we want to jump out of a loop instantly, without waiting to get back to the conditional test. The keyword **break** allows us to do this. When **break** is encountered inside any loop, control automatically passes to the first statement after the loop. A **break** is usually associated with an **if**. Let us consider an example where **break** statement would make sense.

Example 5.1: Write a program to determine whether a number is prime or not. A prime number is one, which is divisible only by 1 or itself.

All we must do to test whether a number is prime or not is to divide it successively by all numbers from 2 to one less than itself. If the remainder of any of these divisions is zero, the number is not a prime. If no division yields a zero, then the number is a prime number. The following program implements this logic:

```
// Prime number or not
package primenumberproject ;
import java.util.* ;
public class PrimeNumberProject
{
    public static void main ( String[ ] args )
    {
```

```
        int  num, i ;
        Scanner scn ;
        scn = new Scanner ( System.in ) ;
        System.out.println ( "Enter a number " ) ;
        num = scn.nextInt( ) ;
        i = 2 ;
        while ( i <= num - 1 )
        {
            if ( num % i == 0 )
            {
                System.out.println ( "Not a prime number" ) ;
                break ;
            }
            i++ ;
        }

        if ( i == num )
            System.out.println ( "Prime number" ) ;
    }
}
```

In this program, the moment **num % i** turns out to be zero, (i.e., **num** is exactly divisible by **i**), the message "Not a prime number" is printed and the control breaks out of the **while** loop.

Why does the program require the **if** statement after the **while** loop at all? Well, there are two ways the control could have reached outside the **while** loop:

(a) It jumped out because the number proved to be not a prime.
(b) The loop came to an end because the value of **i** became equal to **num**.

When the loop terminates in the second case, it means that there was no number between 2 to **num - 1** that could exactly divide **num**. That is, **num** is indeed a prime. If this is true, the program should print out the message "Prime number".

The keyword **break** breaks the control only from the **while** in which it is placed. So, in case of nested loops if we use **break** in the inner loop, the inner loop would be terminated. What if we wish to break out of the outer loop? Well, we just must name the outer loop and use **break** to take the control out of the named loop. The following program illustrates how this can be done:

```
first : while ( i++ <= 100 )
{
    while ( j++ <= 200 )
    {
        if ( j == 150 )
            break first ;
        else
            System.out.println ( i + " " + j ) ;
    }
}
```

Note that we have now given a name to the out **while** loop—first. When the condition **j == 150** is satisfied, the statement **break first** gets executed. As a result, control goes outside the loop named **first**, i.e., the outer **while** loop.

The *continue* Statement

In some programming situations, we want to take control to the beginning of the loop, bypassing the statements inside the loop, which have not yet been executed. The keyword **continue** allows us to do this. When **continue** is encountered inside any loop, control automatically passes to the beginning of the loop.

A **continue** is usually associated with an **if**. As an example, let us consider the following program.

```
// Demo of usage of continue keyword
package continuedemoproject ;
public class ContinueDemoProject
{
    public static void main ( String[ ] args )
    {
        int  i, j ;
        for ( i = 1 ; i <= 2 ; i++ )
        {
            for ( j = 1 ; j <= 2 ; j++ )
            {
                if ( i == j )
                    continue ;
```

```
                System.out.println ( i + " " + j ).;
            }
        }
    }
}
```

The output of the above program would be...

1 2
2 1

Note that when the value of **i** equals that of **j**, the **continue** statement takes the control to the **for** loop (inner) bypassing the rest of the statements pending execution in the **for** loop (inner).

The way while working in nested loops we can break the control out of the desired loop by naming a loop, likewise, we can use **continue** with named loops. This is shown below.

```
first : while ( i++ <= 100 )
{
    while ( j++ <= 200 )
    {
        if ( j == 150 )
            continue first ;
        else
            System.out.println ( i + "" + j ) ;
    }
}
```

When **continue first** goes to work, the control is transferred to **while (i++ <= 100)**.

break and **continue** can also be used with **do-while** just as they would be in a **while** or a **for** loop. A **break** takes you out of the **do-while** bypassing the conditional test. A **continue** sends you straight to the test at the end of the loop.

Common Usage

In principle, what can be achieved using one loop can always be achieved using the other two loops. However, in practice people use the three loops for the following purposes:

(a) Repeat logic unknown number of times - **while** loop
(b) Repeat logic finite number of times - **for** loop
(c) Repeat logic at least once - **do - while** loop

If you also follow the same practice, then while reading a program you can recognize the purpose of the loop just by looking at the type of the loop used.

Exercises

[A] What will be the output of the following programs:

(a)
```
package sampleproject ;
public class SampleProject
{
    public static void main ( String[ ] args )
    {
        int i = 1 ;
        while ( i <= 10 ) ;
        {
            System.out.println ( i ) ;
            i++ ;
        }
    }
}
```

(b)
```
package sampleproject ;
public class SampleProject
{
    public static void main ( String[ ] args )
    {
        int x = 4, y, z ;
        y = --x ;
        z = x-- ;
        System.out.println ( x + " " + y + " " + z ) ;
    }
}
```

(c)
```
package sampleproject ;
public class SampleProject
{
    public static void main ( String[ ] args )
```

```
        {
            int x = 4, y = 3, z ;
            z = x-- - y ;
            System.out.println ( x + " " + y + " " + z ) ;
        }
    }
```

(d)
```
package sampleproject ;
public class SampleProject
{
    public static void main ( String[ ] args )
    {
        int x = 4, y = 0, z ;
        while ( x >= 0 )
        {
            if ( x == y )
                break ;
            else
                System.out.println ( x + " " + y ) ;
            x-- ;
            y++ ;
        }
    }
}
```

(e)
```
package sampleproject ;
public class SampleProject
{
    public static void main ( String[ ] args )
    {
        int i ;
        for ( i = 1 ; i <= 5 ; System.out.println ( i ) ) ;
            i++ ;
    }
}
```

[B] Answer the following questions:

(a) An expression contains relational operators, assignment operators, and arithmetic operators. In the absence of parentheses, they will be evaluated in which of the following order:

1. assignment, relational, arithmetic

2. arithmetic, relational, assignment
3. relational, arithmetic, assignment
4. assignment, arithmetic, relational

(b) The **break** statement is used to exit from

1. an **if** statement
2. a **for** loop
3. a program
4. the **main( )** function

(c) In what sequence the initialization, testing and execution of body is done in a **do-while** loop:

1. Initialization, execution of body, testing
2. Execution of body, initialization, testing
3. Initialization, testing, execution of body
4. None of the above

(d) Which of the following statements is used to skip the rest of the instructions in a loop and go for the next iteration of the loop?

1. exit
2. break
3. continue
4. goto

(e) Which of the following statements is true about a **for** loop used in a Java program?

(1) **for** loop works faster than a **while** loop.
(2) All things that can be done using a **for** loop can also be done using a **while** loop.
(3) **for (; ;)** implements an infinite loop.
(4) **for** loop can be used if we want statements in a loop to get executed at least once.

[C] Attempt the following questions:

(a) Write a program to find the factorial value of any number entered through the keyboard.

(b) Two numbers are entered through the keyboard. Write a program to find the value of one number raised to the power of another.

(c) Write a program to print out all Armstrong numbers between 1 and 500. If the sum of cubes of each digit of the number is equal to the number itself, then the number is called an Armstrong number. For example, 153 = (1 * 1 * 1) + (5 * 5 * 5) + (3 * 3 * 3)

(d) Write a program to print all prime numbers from 1 to 300. (Hint: Use nested loops, **break** and **continue**).

(e) Write a program to generate all combinations of 1, 2 and 3 using **for** loops.

(f) According to a study, the approximate level of intelligence of a person can be calculated using the following formula:

i = 2 + (y + 0.5 x)

Write a program that will produce a table of values of **i**, **y** and **x**, where **y** varies from 1 to 6, and, for each value of **y**, **x** varies from 5.5 to 12.5 in steps of 0.5.

(g) Write a program to print the multiplication table of the number entered by the user. The table should be displayed in the following form:

29 * 1 = 29
29 * 2 = 58
...

(h) When interest compounds **q** times per year at an annual rate of **r** % for **n** years, the principal **p** compounds to an amount **a** as per the following formula:

$a = p (1 + r / q)^{nq}$

Write a program to read 10 sets of **p, r, n** & **q** and calculate the corresponding **a**s.

(i) Write a program to add first seven terms of the following series using a **for** loop:

$$\frac{1}{1!} + \frac{2}{2!} + \frac{3}{3!} + \ldots\ldots$$

(j) The natural logarithm can be approximated by the following series.

$$\frac{x-1}{x} + \frac{1}{2}\left(\frac{x-1}{x}\right)^2 + \frac{1}{2}\left(\frac{x-1}{x}\right)^3 + \frac{1}{2}\left(\frac{x-1}{x}\right)^4 + \ldots.$$

If **x** is input through the keyboard, write a program to calculate the sum of the first seven terms of this series.

KanNotes

- Repetition control instruction is used to repeat a set of statements in a program
- It is also called a loop control instruction
- It is implemented using 1) while loop 2) for loop 3) do-while loop
- What can be done using one loop can always be done using the other two
- Usual usage :

  while - to repeat something an unknown number of times
  for - to repeat something a fixed number of times
  do - while - to repeat something at least once

- Equivalent forms of 3 loops :

```
i = 1 ;
while ( i <= 10 )
{
    statement1 ;
    statement2 ;
    i++ ;
}
```

```
for( i = 1 ; i <= 10 ; i++)
{
    statement1 ;
    statement2 ;
}
```

```
i = 1 ;
do
{
    statement1 ;
    statement2 ;
    i++ ;
} while ( i <= 10 ) ;
```

- To create infinite loops use :

```
while ( i <= 10 )
{
    Statement
}
```

```
while ( true )
{
    statement
}
```

```
do
{
    statement
} while ( true ) ;
```

- Multiple initializations, conditions and incrementations in a for loop are acceptable. Ex. :

```
for ( i = 1 , j = 2 ; i <= 10 && j <= 24 ; i++, j += 3 )
{
    statement1 ;    statement2 ;
}
```

- break - terminates the execution of the loop

  continue - abandons rest of the instructions in the loop and goes for the next iteration of the loop

- Usually break and continue are used in this form :

```
while ( condition1 )          while ( condition1 )
{                             {
    if ( condition2 )             if ( condition2 )
        break ;                       continue ;
    statement1 ;                  statement1 ;
    statement2 ;                  statement2 ;
}                             }
```

- i++ increments vale by 1

  i-- decrements value of i by 1

  There are no ** // and %% operators

- The expressions i = i + 1, i++ and ++i are all same

- j = ++i ; first increments i, then assigns the incremented value to j

- j = i++ ; first assigns current value of i to j, then increments i

- while (++i < 10) first increments i, then checks condition

- while (i++ < 10) first checks condition, then increments i

- i = i + 5 is same as i += 5

- Compound assignment operators : += -= *= /= %=

Case Control Instruction

Let Us JAVA 7th Edition

CHAPTER 06

Often one is faced with multiple choices. Learn how to deal with such situations using a switch...

Contents

- Decisions using *switch*
  The Tips and Traps
- *switch* Versus *if-else* Ladder
- Exercises
- KanNotes

In real life, we are often faced with situations where we are required to make a choice between a number of alternatives rather than only one or two. For example, which school to attend, or which hotel to visit, or which movie to see, etc. Serious Java programming is the same; the choice we are asked to make is more complicated than merely selecting between two alternatives. Java provides a case control instruction that allows us to handle such cases effectively, rather than using a series of **if** statements. Case control instruction is, in fact, the topic of this chapter.

Decisions using *switch*

The control instruction that allows us to decide from the number of choices is called a **switch**, or more correctly a **switch-case-default**, since these three keywords go together to make up this control instruction. They most often appear as follows:

```
switch ( expression )
{
    case constant 1 :
        do this ;
        break ;
    case constant 2 :
        do this ;
        break ;
    case constant 3 :
        do this ;
        break ;
    default :
        do this ;
        break ;
}
```

The expression following the keyword **switch** is any Java expression that will yield an integer or a character value. The keyword **case** is followed by an integer or a character constant. Each constant in each **case** must be different from all the others. The "do this ;" lines in the above form of **switch** represent any valid Java statement.

What happens when we run a program containing a **switch**? First, the expression following the keyword **switch** is evaluated. The value it gives is then matched, one-by-one, against the constant values that follow the **case** statements. When a match is found, the program executes the statements following that **case** until a **break** is encountered. On encountering **break** the control goes outside the **switch**. If no match is found with any of the **case** statements, then the statements following the **default** are executed. Let us now look at a program that uses this control instruction.

```
// Demo of usage of switch
package switchdemoproject ;
public class SwitchDemoProject
{
    public static void main ( String[ ] args )
    {
        int i = 2 ;
        switch ( i )
        {
            case 1 :
                System.out.println ( "I am in case 1" ) ;
                break ;
            case 2 :
                System.out.println ( "I am in case 2" ) ;
                break ;
            case 3 :
                System.out.println ( "I am in case 3" ) ;
                break ;
            default :
                System.out.println ( "I am in default" ) ;
                break ;
        }
    }
}
```

The output of this program would be:

I am in case 2

The output is as expected. Note that usage of **break** is mandatory in each case including the **default** case.

The Tips and Traps

Let us now note down a few useful tips about the usage of **switch** and a few pitfalls that should be avoided.

(a) Cases in a **switch** can be written in any order.

(b) Even if there are multiple statements to be executed in each **case**, there is no need to enclose them within a pair of braces.

(c) Every statement in a **switch** must belong to some **case** or the other. If a statement does not belong to any **case**, the compiler would report an error.

(d) If we have no **default** case and no other case is satisfied, then the program simply falls through the entire **switch** and continues with the next instruction (if any,) that follows the closing brace of **switch**.

(e) **switch** cannot have a case looks like:

case i <= 20 :

All that we can have after the case is a **byte**, **short**, **int, char** or **string** constant or an expression that evaluates to one of these constants. Even a **float, double, long** or **boolean** is not allowed.

(f) From JDK 7 onwards strings can also be checked using **switch**.

(g) The advantage of **switch** over **if** is that it leads to a more structured program and the level of indentation is manageable, more so, if there are multiple statements within each **case** of a **switch**.

(h) We can check the value of any expression in a **switch**. Thus, the following **switch** statements are legal:

```
switch ( i + j * k )
switch ( 23 + 45 % 4 * k )
```

(i) Expressions can also be used in cases provided they are constant expressions. Thus **case 3 + 7** is correct, however, **case a + b** is incorrect.

(j) The **break** statement when used in a **switch** takes control outside the **switch**. However, the use of **continue** will not take the control to the beginning of **switch** as one is likely to believe. This is because **switch** is not a looping statement, unlike **while**, **for** or **do-while**.

(k) In principle, a **switch** may occur within another, but in practice, it is rarely done. Such statements would be called nested **switch** statements.

(l) The **switch** statement is very useful while writing menu driven programs. This aspect of **switch** is discussed in the exercise of this chapter.

(m) At times we may want to execute a common set of statements for multiple **cases**. How this can be done is shown in the following example:

```
package switchformsproject ;
import java.io.IOException ;
public class SwitchFormsProject
{
    public static void main ( String[ ] args ) throws Exception
    {
        char ch ;
        System.out.println( "Enter an alphabet a, or b " ) ;
        ch = ( char ) System.in.read( ) ;
        switch ( ch )
        {
            case 'a' :
            case 'A' :
                System.out.println ( "a as in ashar" ) ;
                break ;
            case 'b' :
            case 'B' :
                System.out.println ( "b as in brain" ) ;
                break ;
            default :
                System.out.println ( "wish you knew alphabets" ) ;
                break ;
        }
    }
}
```

Here, we are making use of the fact that once an empty **case** is satisfied, the control simply falls through to the next **case** till it does not encounter a **break** statement. That is why if an alphabet **a** is entered, the **case 'a'** is satisfied and since there are no statements to be executed in this **case**, the control automatically reaches the next **case**, i.e., **case 'A'** and executes all the statements in this **case**.

Also note that any non-empty case must have a **break** statement at the end of it.

Also observe the way we have read the character from the keyboard. Instead of using the usual **Scanner** object, we are using the **System.in.read( )** and converting its return value into a **char**.

switch Versus *if-else* Ladder

There are some things that you simply cannot do with a **switch**. These are:

(a) A **float**, **double**, **boolean**, or **long** expression cannot be tested using a **switch**.

(b) Cases can never have variable expressions (for example it is wrong to say **case a + 3 :**).

(c) Multiple cases cannot use same expressions. Thus a **switch** containing **case 3** : and **case 1 + 2** : is illegal:

(a), (b) and (c) above may lead you to believe that these are obvious disadvantages with a **switch**, especially since there were no such limitations with **if-else**. Then why use a **switch** at all? For speed—**switch** works faster than an equivalent **if-else** ladder. How? Well, this is because the compiler generates a jump table for a **switch** during compilation. As a result, during execution it simply refers to the jump table to decide which case should be executed, rather than checking which case is satisfied.

Note that a lookup in the jump table is faster than evaluation of a condition, especially if the condition is complex.

Exercises

[A] Which of the following case statements are correct:

(a) case 4 / 3 :
(b) case ch :
(c) case a + b :
(d) case 1.5f :
(e) case true :
(f) case 8 % 5 + c / d :
(g) case (temp <= 20) :
(h) case a || b :

[B] State whether the following statements are True or False:

(a) Floats or doubles cannot be checked in a switch.

(b) If there are multiple statements in a case then they should be enclosed within { }.

(c) A case cannot be followed by a variable expression.

(d) Nested switch statements are not allowed.

(e) If break in a switch gets executed the program execution gets terminated.

(f) A switch statement works slower than an equivalent if-else statement.

[C] Point out the rror, if any, in the following program. If there is no error, what will be its output?

```
public class Main
{
    public static void main ( String[ ] args )
    {
        String s = "1.5" ;
        switch ( s )
        {
            case "0.5" :
                System.out.println ( "Good" ) ;
                break ;
            case "1.5" :
                System.out.println ( "Morning" ) ;
                break ;
            case "2.5" :
                System.out.println ( "!!!" ) ;
                break;
        }
    }
}
```

[D] Write a menu driven program which has the following options:

1. Factorial of a number
2. Prime or not
3. Odd or even
4. Exit

Once a menu item is selected the appropriate action should be taken and once this action is finished, the menu should reappear. Unless the user selects the 'Exit' option the program should continue to work.
(Hint: Make use of an infinite **while** and a **switch** statement).

kn KanNotes

- One more form of decision making can be done using switch - case - default
- This should be used when we are to find out whether a variable or an expression has one of the several possible values
- switch should not be used for checking ranges or for solving a yes / no problem
- General form :

```
switch ( expression )  // expression can be constant / variable
{
        case constant expression :
              ...
              break ;
        case constant expression :
              ...
              break ;
        default :
              ...
}
```

- If a case fails, control jumps to the next case
- If a case is satisfied, then all statements below it up to } of switch are executed
- Even though there are multiple statements in a case there is no need to enclose them within { }

- Usually, a break is used at the end of statements in each case
- break takes control out of the switch
- continue DOES NOT take control to the beginning of the switch
- Order in which cases are written does not matter
- Default case is optional
- cases in a switch must always be unique
- switch can be used with byte, short, int, char or string

  switch cannot be used with float, double, long, boolean
- switch works faster than a series of ifs
- switch is popularly used in menu driven programs to check which choice from the menu has been made by the user

Functions

Let Us JAVA 7th Edition

CHAPTER 07

Learn how to improve the functionality of a Java program using Functions...

Contents

- What is a Function?
    - Why use Functions?
- Passing Values between Functions
- Exercises
- KanNotes

A computer program (except for the simplest one) cannot handle all the tasks by itself. Instead, it requests other program-like entities, called 'functions', to get its tasks done. So far our programs had only one function **main( )**. In this chapter we will study how to create multiple functions, how to use them and how to carry out communication between them.

What is a Function?

A function is a self-contained block of statements that perform a coherent task of some kind. Every Java program has one or more functions in it. Let us now look at a simple program containing two functions.

```
// Function call and function definition
package functiondemoproject ;
public class FunctionDemoProject
{
    public static void main ( String[ ] args )
    {
        message( ) ;  /* function call */
        System.out.println ( "Cry, and you stop the monotony!" ) ;
    }
    static void message( )  /* function definition */
    {
        System.out.println ( "Smile, and the world smiles with you..." ) ;
    }
}
```

On execution, the program produces the output given below.

```
Smile, and the world smiles with you...
Cry, and you stop the monotony!
```

Here, we have defined two functions—**main( )** and **message( )**. In fact, we have used the word **message** at two places in the program. Let us understand the meaning of each.

The first usage of **message** is...

```
static void message( )
{
    System.out.println ( "Smile, and the world smiles with you..." ) ;
```

```
}
```

This is the function definition. In this definition right now, we are merely printing a string.

The second usage is...

message( ) ;

Here the function **message( )** is being called from **main( )**. What do we mean when we say that **main( )** 'calls' the function **message( )**? We mean that the control passes to the function **message( )**. The activity of **main( )** is temporarily suspended; it falls asleep while the **message( )** function wakes up and goes to work. When the **message( )** function runs out of statements to execute, the control returns to **main( )**, which comes to life again and begins executing its code at the exact point where it left off. Thus, **main( )** becomes the 'calling' function, whereas **message( )** becomes the 'called' function.

If you have grasped the concept of 'calling' a function you are prepared for a call to more than one function. Consider the following program:

```
// Calling and defining multiple functions
package multiplefunctionproject ;
public class MultipleFunctionProject
{
    public static void main ( String[ ] args )
    {
        System.out.println ( "I am in main" ) ;
        italy( ) ;
        brazil( ) ;
        argentina( ) ;
    }
    static void italy( )
    {
        System.out.println ( "I am in italy" ) ;
    }
    static void brazil( )
    {
        System.out.println ( "I am in brazil" ) ;
    }
    static void argentina( )
    {
        System.out.println ( "I am in argentina" ) ;
```

```
    }
}
```

The output of the above program when executed is as under:

```
I am in main
I am in italy
I am in brazil
I am in argentina
```

Several conclusions can be drawn from this program:

- A Java program can contain one or more classes. Each class can contain one or more functions.
- One of the classes in a Java program must be marked as the 'Main class'. When we create Java project in NetBeans in the 'New Java Application' window there is a check box titled 'Create Main Class'. This check box is by default checked. So, the skeleton code for **Main** class is created for us by NetBeans. This class has the same name as the name of the project. This class is also marked as the class from which execution of the program would begin.

  If we uncheck the check box during project creation, we can later mark any class in our program as **Main** class. To do this, we must right click on the project name and select 'Properties' from the menu that pops up. On doing this the 'Project Properties' window appears. Select 'Run' from this window and in the 'Main Project' text box mention the class name in the syntax **packagename.classname**. For example, for the current project this name would be **multiplefunctionproject.MultipleFunctionProject**.
- Execution always begins with **main( )** function present in the class that has been marked as **Main** class.
- If the class marked as **Main** class contains only one function, it must be **main( )**.
- If the class marked as **Main** class contains more than one function, then one (and only one) of these functions must be **main( )**. This is because program execution always begins with **main( )**.
- There is no limit on the number of functions that might be present in a Java class.

- Each function in a program is called in the sequence specified by the function calls in **main( )**.
- After each function has done its thing, control returns to **main( )**. When **main( )** runs out of statements and function calls, the program ends.

As we have noted earlier, the program execution always begins with **main( )** present in the class marked as **Main** class. Except for this fact, all Java functions enjoy a state of perfect equality. No precedence, no priorities, nobody is nobody's boss. One function can call another function it has already called but has in the meantime left temporarily in order to call a third function which will sometime later call the function that has called it, if you understand what I mean. No? Well, let me illustrate with an example.

```
// Multiple function calls
package functioncallsproject ;
public class FunctionCallsProject
{
    public static void main ( String[ ] args )
    {
        System.out.println ( "I am in main" ) ;
        italy( ) ;
        System.out.println ( "I am finally back in main" ) ;
    }
    static void italy( )
    {
        System.out.println ( "I am in italy" ) ;
        brazil( ) ;
        System.out.println ( "I am back in italy" ) ;
    }
    static void brazil( )
    {
        System.out.println ( "I am in brazil" ) ;
        argentina( ) ;
    }
    static void argentina( )
    {
        System.out.println ( "I am in argentina" ) ;
    }
}
```

And the output would look like...

```
I am in main
I am in italy
I am in brazil
I am in argentina
I am back in italy
I am finally back in main
```

Here, **main( )** calls other functions, which in turn call still other functions. Carefully trace the way control passes from one function to another. Since execution always begins with **main( )**, every function in a program must be called directly or indirectly by **main( )**. In other words, the **main( )** function drives other functions.

Let us now summarize what we have learnt so far.

(a) A function gets called when the function name is followed by a semicolon (;).

(b) A function is defined when a function name is followed by a pair of braces in which one or more statements may be present.

(c) Any function can be called from any other function. Even **main( )** can be called from other functions.

(d) A function can be called any number of times.

(e) The order in which the functions are defined in a program and the order in which they get called need not necessarily be same.

(f) A function can call itself. Such a process is called 'recursion'. We would discuss this aspect of Java functions later in this chapter.

(g) A function can be called from another function, but a function cannot be defined in another function.

(h) There are basically two types of functions:

    Library functions Ex. **readLine( )**, **println( )**, etc.
    User-defined functions Ex. **argentina( )**, **brazil( )**, etc.

    Library functions are commonly required functions grouped together in different classes and stored in a Java API Library. The procedure of calling both types of functions is exactly same.

Why use Functions?

Why write separate functions at all? Why not squeeze the entire logic into one function, **main( )**? It is a very bad style of programming. Instead, break a program into small units and write functions for each of these isolated subdivisions. Do not hesitate to write functions that are called only once. What is important is that these functions perform some logically isolated task.

Passing Values between Functions

The functions that we have used so far have not been very flexible. We called them and they did what they were designed to do. It would be nice to have communication between the 'calling' and the 'called' functions.

Consider the following program. In this program, in **main( )** we receive the values of **a**, **b** and **c** through the keyboard and then output the sum of **a**, **b** and **c**. However, the calculation of sum is done in a different function called **calSum( )**. Since sum is to be calculated in **calSum( )** and values of **a**, **b** and **c** are received in **main( )**, we must pass on these values to **calSum( )**, and once **calSum( )** calculates the sum, we must return it from **calSum( )** back to **main( )**.

```
// Communication between functions
package functioncommunicationproject ;
import java.util.* ;
public class FunctionCommunicationProject
{
    public static void main ( String[ ] args )
    {
        int a, b, c, sum ;
        Scanner scn ;
        scn = new Scanner ( System.in ) ;
        System.out.println ( "Enter any three numbers" ) ;
        a = scn.nextInt( ) ;
        b = scn.nextInt( ) ;
        c = scn.nextInt( ) ;
        sum = calSum ( a, b, c ) ;
        System.out.println ( "Sum = " + sum ) ;
    }
    static int calSum ( int x, int y, int z )
    {
```

```
        int d ;
        d = x + y + z ;
        return ( d ) ;
    }
}
```

And here is the output...

```
Enter any three numbers
10
20
30
Sum = 60
```

There are several things to note about this program:

(a) To pass the values of **a**, **b** and **c** to the function **calSum( )**, while making a call to the function **calSum( )** we have mentioned **a**, **b** and **c** in parentheses:

```
sum = calSum ( a, b, c ) ;
```

In the **calSum( )** function these values get collected in three variables **x**, **y** and **z**:

```
int calSum ( int x, int y, int z )
```

(b) The variables **a**, **b** and **c** are called 'actual arguments', whereas the variables **x**, **y** and **z** are called 'formal arguments'. Actual arguments are often called just arguments, whereas formal arguments are often called parameters. The type, order and number of the actual and formal arguments must always be the same.

Instead of using different variable names **x**, **y** and **z**, we could have used the same variable names **a**, **b** and **c**. But the compiler would still treat them as different variables since they are in different functions.

(c) Since the function **calSum( )** is going to return an **int** we have replaced the usual **void** with **int** while defining **calSum( )**.

(d) In the earlier programs, the moment closing brace (**}**) of the called function was encountered, the control returned to the calling function. No separate **return** statement was necessary to send back the control.

This approach is fine if the called function is not going to return any meaningful value to the calling function. In the above program, however, we want to return the sum of **x**, **y** and **z**. Therefore, it is necessary to use the **return** statement.

(e) The return statement serves two purposes:

(1) On executing the **return** statement, it immediately transfers the control back to the calling function.

(2) It returns the value present in the parentheses after **return**, to the calling function. In the above program, the value of sum of three numbers is being returned.

(f) There is no restriction on the number of **return** statements that may be present in a function. Also, the **return** statement need not always be present at the end of the called function.

(g) Whenever the control returns from a function, the sum being returned is collected in the calling function by equating the called function to some variable. For example,

```
sum = calSum ( a, b, c ) ;
```

(h) All the following are valid **return** statements:

```
return ( a ) ;
return ( 23 ) ;
return ( a + b + c ) ;
return ;
```

The last statement can be used when we wish to return the control to the calling function without returning a value. Note that, in this case, the parentheses after **return** are dropped. In the other **return** statements too, the parentheses can be dropped.

(i) A function can return only one value at a time. Thus, the following statements are invalid:

```
return ( a, b ) ;
return ( x, 12 ) ;
```

(j) If the value of a formal argument is changed in the called function, the corresponding change does not take place in the calling function. For example,

```
// Effect of changing formal arguments
```

```
package formalargchangeproject ;
public class FormalArgChangeProject
{
    public static void main ( String[ ] args )
    {
        int  a = 30 ;
        fun ( a ) ;
        System.out.println ( a ) ;
    }
    static void fun ( int b )
    {
        b = 60 ;
        System.out.println ( b ) ;
    }
}
```

The output of the above program would be:

```
60
30
```

Thus, even though the value of **b** is changed in **fun( ),** the value of **a** in **main( )** remains unchanged. This means that when values are passed to a called function, the values present in actual arguments are not physically moved to the formal arguments; just a photocopy of values in actual argument is made into formal arguments.

(k) Actual arguments can be constants / variables / expressions, whereas formal arguments must always be variables. Thus, the following calls would work without any problem:

```
sum = calSum  ( a, 25, c ) ;
sum = calSum  ( 10 + 2, 25 % 3, a ) ;
```

(l) Nested calls are legal, so also are calls within an expression. Thus, the following calls would work fine:

```
sum = calSum  ( a, calSum ( 25, 10, 4 ), b ) ;
sum = calSum  ( a, 25, c ) * calSum  ( a, 25, c ) + 23 ;
```

Exercises

[A] What will be the output of the following programs:

(a)
```
package sampleproject ;
public class SampleProject
{
    public static void main ( String[ ] args  )
    {
        int a = 10, b = 20 ;
        modify( ) ;
        System.out.println ( a + "  " + b ) ;
    }
    static void modify ( int a, int b )
    {
        a++ ;  b++ ;
    }
}
```

(b)
```
package sampleproject ;
public class SampleProject
{
    public static void main ( String[ ] args  )
    {
        int i = 45, c ;
        c = check ( i ) ;
            System.out.println ( c ) ;
    }
    static int check ( int ch )
    {
        if ( ch >= 45 )
                return ( 100 ) ;
        else
                return ( 10 ) ;
    }
}
```

(c)
```
package sampleproject ;
public class SampleProject
{
    public static void main ( String[ ] args  )
    {
        float area ;
        int radius = 1 ;
        area = areaOfCircle ( radius ) ;
```

```
        System.out.println ( area ) ;
    }
    static float areaOfCircle ( int r )
    {
        float a ;
        a = 3.14f * r * r ;
        return ( a ) ;
    }
}
```

[B] Point out the errors, if any, in the following programs:

(a)
```
package sampleproject ;
public class SampleProject
{
    public static void main ( String[ ] args  )
    {
        int i = 3, j = 4, k, l ;
        k = addMult ( i, j ) ;
        l = addMult ( i, j ) ;
        System.out.println ( k + " " + l ) ;
    }
    static int addMult ( int  ii, int  jj )
    {
        int  kk, ll ;
        kk = ii + jj ;
        ll = ii * jj ;
        return ( kk, ll ) ;
    }
}
```

(b)
```
package sampleproject ;
public class SampleProject
{
    public static void main ( String[ ] args  )
    {
        message( ) ;
        message( ) ;
    }
    public void message( ) ;
    {
        System.out.println ( "Praise worthy effort!" ) ;
```

```
    }
}
```

(c)
```
package sampleproject ;
public class SampleProject
{
    public static void main ( String[ ] args )
    {
        LetUsJava( )
        {
            System.out.println ( "Java is a Cimple  !" ) ;
            System.out.println ( "Others are no match !" ) ;
        }
    }
}
```

(d)
```
package sampleproject ;
public class Main
{
    public static void main ( String[ ] args )
    {
        float area ;
        int radius = 1 ;
        area = AreaOfCircle ( radius ) ;
        System.out.println ( area ) ;
    }
    public float AreaOfCircle ( int r )
    {
        float a ;
        a = 3.14f * r * r ;
        return ( a ) ;
    }
}
```

[C] State whether the following statements are True or False:

(a) The variables commonly used in Java functions are available to all the functions in a program.

(b) To return the control back to the calling function we must use the keyword return.

(c) The same variable names can be used in different functions without any conflict.

(d) Every called function must contain a return statement.

(e) A function may contain more than one return statement.

(f) Each return statement in a function may return a different value.

(g) A function can still be useful even if you do not pass any arguments to it and the function does not return any value back.

(h) A function may be called more than once from any other function.

(i) It is necessary for a function to return some value.

(j) Function definitions cannot be nested; however, function calls can be nested.

[D] Pick up the correct alternative for each of the following questions:

(a) Which of the following return statements is INVALID?
(1) return (x) ;
(2) return (20) ;
(3) return (x + y + z) ;
(4) return (x, y, z) ;

(b) Which of the following statements is CORRECT?
(1) Every called function may not contain a return statement
(2) A function may contain more than one return statement
(3) Each return statement in a function may return a different value
(4) (1), (2) and (3)

(c) Which of the following statements is CORRECT about a function?
(1) A function may be called more than once from another function
(2) It is necessary for a function to return some value
(3) Function calls can be nested
(4) (1), (2) and (3)

(d) Which of the following statements are CORRECT about the code snippet given below:

```
void fun ( int a, int b, int c )
{
}
...
```

```
...
fun ( 10, 20, 30, 40, 50 ) ;
```

(1) Values 40 and 50 will be ignored
(2) Error: Mismatch in number of actual and formal arguments
(3) Error: fun cannot be used as a function name
(4) The program will compile successfully

(e) Which of the following is the CORRECT form of **main( )**?

(1)
```
public static void main ( String[ ] args )
{
}
```

(2)
```
public static void main ( String args )
{
}
```

(3)
```
public static void main ( int argc, char *argv[ ] )
{
}
```

(4)
```
public static void main ( int argc, String argv[ ] )
{
}
```

[E] Answer the following:

(a) Write a function to calculate the factorial value of any integer entered through the keyboard.

(b) Write a function **power (a, b)**, to calculate the value of **a** raised to **b**.

(c) Any year is entered through the keyboard. Write a function to determine whether the year is a leap year or not.

(d) Write a function which receives a **float** and an **int** from **main( )**, finds the product of these two and returns the product which is printed through **main( )**.

(e) If the lengths of the sides of a triangle are denoted by **a**, **b**, and **c**, then the area of triangle is given by

$$area = \sqrt{S(S-a)(S-b)(S-c)}$$

where, S = (a + b + c) / 2

(f) If a function **fun( )** is to receive an **int**, a **float** & a **double** and it is to return a **decimal** then how will you define this function?

KanNotes

- Functions are a group of instructions achieving some intended goal
- Why create functions :

  1) Better complexity management - Easy to Design, Easy to Debug
  2) Provide reuse mechanism - Avoids rewriting same code repeatedly

- Types of functions :

  1) Library – println(), printf(), pow(), parseInt()
  2) User-defined – main()

- Rules for building both are same
- Two things should be done while creating a function :

  1) Function definition
  2) Function call

- General form of a function definition :

```
return-type function-name ( type arg1, type arg2, type arg3 )
{
    statement1 ;  statement2 ;
    return ( variable/constant/expression ) ; // can return only 1 value
}
```

- A function can be called any number of times
- Functions can be defined in any order
- Execution of any Java program always begins with main() present in primary class
- More the function calls, slower the execution

- Communication between functions is done using arguments and return values
- While calling function any number of arguments can be passed, whereas only 0/1 value can be returned. If no value is returned the return type of the function must be void
- Actual & Formal arguments must match in Number, Order and Type
- Actual arguments can be constants / variables / expressions
- Formal arguments can only be variables
- Nested calls are legal

  Ex. : a = Math.sin (Math.cos (b)) ;
- Call within an expression is legal

  Ex. : a = Math.sin (b) + Math.cos (c) ;
- return (s) ; - Return control & value
- return ; - Returns only control. Return type of function must be void
- If values are passed to a function, the function must collect them while defining it
- If value is returned from a function, we can choose to ignore it

Advanced Features of Functions

Let Us JAVA 7th Edition

CHAPTER 08

Functions are more mature in Java. You can appreciate this maturity in this chapter...

Contents

- Function Overloading
- Functions with Variable Number of Arguments
- Recursion
- Exercises
- KanNotes

Functions in Java offers some advanced features which come in quite handy while doing programming. These include functions overloading, defining functions that receive variable number of arguments and recursive functions. This chapter is devoted to discussing these advanced features. Let us begin with function overloading.

Function Overloading

With the facility of function overloading, we can have multiple functions in a class with the same name. For example, if we wish to write functions that return the absolute value of a numeric argument, we can consider writing a separate function for each numeric data type—one that returns absolute value of an **int**, another which returns absolute value of a **long** and yet another which returns absolute value of a **double**.

Since all these functions basically do the same thing, it seems unnecessary to have three different function names. Java overcomes this situation by allowing the programmer to create three different functions with the same name. These functions are called overloaded functions. The following program illustrates how to implement them:

```
// Overloading functions to do different but similar jobs
package functionoverloadingproject ;
public class FunctionOverloadingProject
{
    public static void main ( String[ ] args )
    {
        int i = -25, j ;
        long l = -100000, m ;
        double d = -12.34, e ;

        j = abs ( i ) ;
        m = abs ( l ) ;
        e = abs ( d ) ;
        System.out.println ( "j = " + j + " m = " + m + " e = "+ e ) ;
    }
    static int abs ( int ii )
    {
        return ( ii > 0 ? ii : ii * -1 ) ;
    }
    static long abs ( long ll )
    {
```

```
        return ( ll > 0 ? ll : ll * -1 ) ;
    }
    static double abs ( double dd )
    {
        return ( dd > 0 ? dd : dd * -1 ) ;
    }
}
```

The output of the program would be:

```
j = 25  m = 100000 e = 12.34
```

How does the Java compiler know which of the **abs( )**s should be called when a call is made? It decides that from the type of the argument being passed during the function call. For example, if an **int** is being passed the integer version of **abs( )** gets called, if a **double** is being passed then the double version of **abs( )** gets called and so on. That is quite logical, you would agree.

Overloaded functions must at least differ in the type, number, or order of parameters they accept. Just having different return types is not enough to differentiate them.

It is a bad idea to create overloaded functions that perform different types of actions; functions with the same name should have the same general purpose. For example, if we write an **abs( )** function that returns the square root of a number, it would be both silly and confusing. We must use overloaded functions judiciously. Their purpose is to provide a common name for several similar but slightly divergent functions. Overusing overloaded functions can make a program unreadable.

Functions with Variable Number of Arguments

The functions that we have used so far used to receive a fixed number of arguments. These include the following functions:

```
System.out.println ( "a = " + a ) ;
y = Math.pow ( 2.0, 5.0 ) ;
s = calSum ( a, b, c ) ;
```

Java also permits functions to receive variable number of arguments. For example,

```
System.out.printf ( "%d %d", a, b ) ;
System.out.printf ( "%d %d %f %f", a, b, c, d ) ;
```

Here, in the first call to **printf( )** we are passing 3 arguments, whereas, in the second call we are passing 5 arguments.

Even we can define functions that can receive variable number of arguments. The following program illustrates this:

```
// Receiving varying number of arguments in a function
package varargsproject ;
public class VarArgsProject
{
    public static void main ( String args[ ] )
    {
        double d1 = 10.0 ;  double d2 = 20.0 ;
        double d3 = 30.0 ;  double d4 = 40.0 ;

        System.out.printf ( "Avg = %f\n", average ( d1, d2 ) ) ;
        System.out.printf ( "Avg = %f\n", average ( d1, d2, d3 ) ) ;
        System.out.printf ( "Avg = %f\n", average ( d1, d2, d3, d4 ) ) ;
    }
    static double average ( double... numbers )
    {
        double total = 0.0 ;
        for ( double d : numbers )
            total = total + d ;

        double avg ;
        avg =  total / numbers.length ;
        return avg ;
    }
}
```

Here we are passing different number of arguments to **average( )** function in each call. To make **average( )** capable of receiving such variable number of arguments, a special syntax is used while defining its parameters.

```
static double average ( double... numbers )
{
    ..
}
```

Here **double** is followed by ellipsis (...), meaning that, this function is going to receive different number of doubles in each call. **numbers** is treated as an array. So, while finding the average value, we need to iterate through the array elements. To do this, a special **for** loop syntax has been evolved.

Each time through this **for** loop, **d** takes the next value from the **numbers** array. The number of values present in the array can be obtained using the **length** property of the array. This aspect of the array would be discussed in detail in Chapter 11.

Sometimes we might be required to define a function that receives fixed arguments as well as variable arguments. While defining such function we must ensure that the fixed arguments precede the variable arguments while making the call to such functions.

Recursion

In Java, it is possible for the functions to call themselves. A function is called 'recursive' if a statement within the body of a function calls the same function. Sometimes called 'circular definition', recursion is thus the process of defining something in terms of itself.

Let us now see a simple example of recursion. Suppose we want to calculate the factorial value of an integer. As we know, the factorial of a number is the product of all the integers between 1 and that number. For example, 4 factorial is 4 * 3 * 2 * 1. This can also be expressed as 4! = 4 * 3!, where '!' stands for factorial. Thus, factorial of a number can be expressed in the form of itself. Hence, this logic can be programmed using recursion as shown below.

```
// Calculating factorial using recursive function
package recursivefactorialproject ;
import java.util.* ;
public class Main
{
    public static void main ( String[ ] args )
    {
        int a, fact ;
        Scanner scn ;
        scn = new Scanner ( System.in ) ;

        System.out.println ( "Enter any number " ) ;
```

```
        a = scn.nextInt( ) ;

        fact = rec ( a ) ;
        System.out.println ( "Factorial value = " + fact ) ;
    }
    static int rec ( int x )
    {
        int f ;

        if ( x == 1 )
            return ( 1 ) ;
        else
            f = x * rec ( x - 1 ) ;

        return ( f ) ;
    }
}
```

And here is the output for sample run of the program...

```
Enter any number 3
Factorial value = 6
```

Let us understand this recursive factorial function thoroughly. When value of **a** is 3, **main( )** would call **rec( )** with 3 as its actual argument, and **rec( )** will send back the computed value. But before sending the computed value, **rec( )** calls **rec( )** and waits for a value to be returned. It is possible for the **rec( )** that has just been called to call yet another **rec( )**, the argument **x** being decreased in value by 1 for each of these recursive calls. These recursive invocations end finally when the last invocation gets an argument value of 1, which the preceding invocation of **rec( )** now uses to calculate its own **f** value and so on up the ladder. So, we might say what happens is,

```
rec ( 3 ) returns ( 3 times rec ( 2 ),
    which returns ( 2 times rec ( 1 ),
        which returns ( 1 ) )
```

Foxed? Well, that is recursion for you in its simplest garbs. I hope you agree that it is difficult to visualize how the control flows from one function call to another. Possibly Figure 8.1 would make things a bit clearer.

Assume that the number entered through **readLine( )** is 3. Using Figure 8.1 let us visualize what exactly happens when the recursive function **rec( )** gets called. The first time when **rec( )** is called from **main( )**, **x** collects 3. From here, since **x** is not equal to 1, the **if** block is skipped and **rec( )** is called again with the argument **(x – 1)**, i.e. 2. This is a recursive call. Since **x** is still not equal to 1, **rec( )** is called yet another time, with argument (2 - 1). This time as **x** is 1, control goes back to previous **rec( )** with the value 1, and **f** is evaluated as 2.

Similarly, each **rec( )** evaluates its **f** from the returned value, and finally 6 is returned to **main( )**. The sequence would be grasped better by following the arrows shown in Figure 8.1. Let it be clear that while executing the program, there do not exist so many copies of the function **rec( )**. These have been shown in Figure 8.1 just to help you keep track of how the control flows during successive recursive calls.

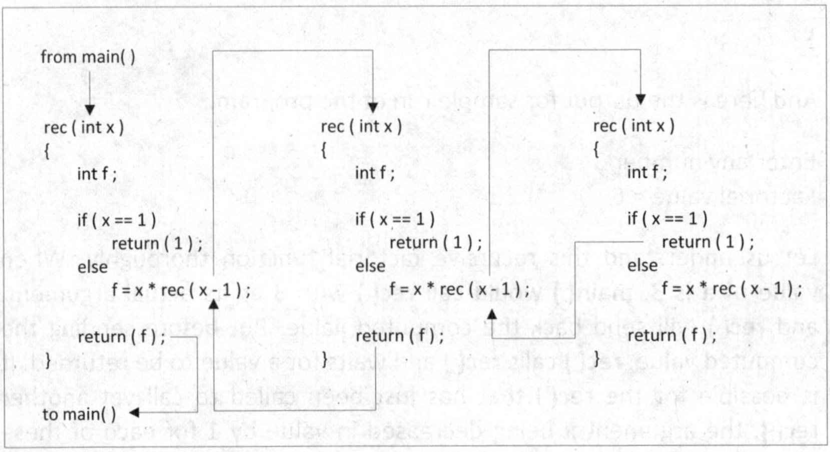

Figure 8.1

Recursion may seem strange and complicated at first glance, but it is often the most direct way to code an algorithm, and once you are familiar with recursion, the clearest way of doing so.

Exercises

[A] Pick up the correct alternative for each of the following questions:

(a) Which of the following return statements is CORRECT?

(1) A Java function always receives a fixed number of arguments.

(2) A Java function always receives a variable number of arguments.

(3) A Java function can receive fixed as well as variable no. of args.
(4) A Java function can never receive variable number of arguments.

(b) Which of the following is CORRECT about the statement given below?

```
System.out.printf ( "%d %d %f %f", a, b, c, d ) ;
```

(1) 4 arguments are being passed to **printf**( )
(2) 1 fixed and 4 variable arguments are being passed to **printf**( )
(3) **printf**( ) is a C library function and cannot be used in Java
(4) 5 fixed arguments are being passed to **printf**( )

(c) If function **fun**( ) given below is called recursively 5 times:

```
int fun ( int a, float b )
{
}
```

(1) 5 sets of **a** and **b** are created
(2) 1 set of **a** and **b** are created
(3) 4 sets of **a** and **b** are created
(4) Infinite sets of **a** and **b** are created

(d) How many **return** statements can be used in a recursive function?

(1) 0
(2) 1
(3) 0 if the function is static, 1 otherwise
(4) Any number depending upon the logic at hand

(e) If variable number of integers are received by a user-defined function called **average**( ), then which of the following is CORRECT way to define **average**( )?

(1)
```
static double average ( double ... numbers )
{
}
```

(2)
```
static double average ( double numbers )
{
}
```

(3)
```
static double average ( double [ ] numbers )
{
```

```
    }
```

(4) static double average (double numbers[ ])

```
    {
    }
```

[B] Answer the following:

(a) Define an overloaded **max( )** function which returns maximum out of two integers / floats / doubles.

(b) Define a function **min( )** that can find out and return minimum out of variable number of integers passed to it.

(c) A 5-digit positive integer is entered through the keyboard, write a recursive function to calculate sum of digits of the 5-digit number.

(d) A positive integer is entered through the keyboard, write a program to obtain the prime factors of the number using a recursive function.

(e) Write a recursive function to obtain the first 25 numbers of a Fibonacci sequence. In a Fibonacci sequence the sum of two successive terms gives the third term. The following are the first few terms of the Fibonacci sequence:

1 1 2 3 5 8 13 21 34 55 89...

(f) A positive integer is entered through the keyboard, write a function to find the binary equivalent of this number using recursion.

(g) Write a recursive function to obtain the running sum of the first 25 natural numbers.

(h) Write the function **fun( )** which finds the minimum number from the variable arguments list passed to it.

```
package sampleproject ;
public class Main
{
    public static void main ( String[ ] args )
    {
        int a = 5, b = 4, res ;
        res = fun ( a, b ) ;
        System.out.println ( res ) ;
        res = fun ( 1, 5, a, b, 7, 99, 100 ) ;
        System.out.println ( res ) ;
```

```
        }
        // Add code here
    }
```

KanNotes

- Function names in a class can be same. Such functions are known as Overloaded Functions
- If function names are same then their arguments must differ in Number, Order or Type
- Usually, overloaded functions carry out similar jobs. Ex. Getting absolute value of different data types
- Functions can receive variable number of arguments.
- If a function receives fixed as well as variable number of arguments, then fixed arguments must be at the beginning and variable number of arguments at the end of argument-list
- Variable number of arguments are received in an array. This array can be processed using a special for loop :

```
static void fun ( int, a, float b, double... numbers )
{
    for ( double d : numbers )
            System.out.println ( d ) ;
}
```

- A function that calls itself is called a recursive function
- Any function, including main() can become a recursive function
- Recursive call always leads to an infinite loop. So, a provision must be made to get outside this infinite loop
- The provision is done by making the recursive call either in the if block or in the else block

- If recursive call is made in the if block, else block should contain the end condition logic
- If recursive call is made in the else block, if block should contain the end condition logic
- Fresh set of variables are born during each function call - normal call and recursive call
- Variables die when control returns from a function
- Recursive function may or may not have a return statement
- Recursion is an alternative for loop in logics which are expressible in the form of themselves
- Recursive calls are slower than an equivalent while / for / do-while loop
- If stuck in an infinite loop while using recursion stack overflow would occur and the program execution would come to an end

Introduction to OOP

Let Us JAVA 7th Edition

CHAPTER 09

Paradigm shift! This chapter would change your thinking about how to organize a program...

Contents

- The Beginning...
- Structured Programming
- Object-Oriented Programming
- Characteristics of OOP
  - Objects
  - Classes
  - Inheritance
  - Polymorphism
  - Containership
  - Reusability
- Exercises
- KanNotes

Data types, control instructions and functions are the basic building blocks of any Java program. With all these topics under our belt it is time to move on to something more complex, namely, Object Oriented Programming.

Java is an Object–Oriented Programming (OOP) language. Many programmers tend to use object-oriented features of Java mechanically. Though this might make the program work, the real advantages of object-oriented programming do not accrue unless you understand the concept of object-oriented programming and what features it offers. Hence, in this chapter we would not write a single program. Instead, we would concentrate on understanding what is OOP and why do we need it.

This chapter addresses these issues and provides an overview of the features to be discussed in the rest of the book. What we say here will necessarily be general and brief. Do not worry if you do not catch everything in this chapter on the first pass; OOP is a bit complex and understanding it takes time. We will be going over these features again in subsequent chapters. There's a lot of ground to cover here, so let us get started.

The purpose of a programming language is to express the solution to a problem with the help of an algorithm (step-by-step procedure). The success of the solution depends on how the solution models (represents) the problem. Different approaches have evolved over the years to model solutions to problems. The primary amongst them are Structured programming model (also called Procedural programming model) and Object-oriented programming model. These models are often called programming paradigms, i.e., principle of program organization. To understand these models, we need to begin by taking a peek at the history of programming models.

The Beginning...

The earliest computers were programmed in binary. Mechanical switches were used to load programs. With the advent of mass storage devices and larger and cheaper computer memories, the first high-level computer programming languages came into existence. With their arrival, instead of thinking in terms of bits and bytes, programmers could write a series of English-like instructions that a compiler could translate into the binary language of computers.

These languages were simple in design and easy to use because programs at that time were primarily concerned with relatively simple tasks like calculations. As a result, the programs were pretty short, limited to about a few hundred lines of instructions.

As the computers' capacity and capability increased, so also did the ability to develop more complex computer programs. However, the earlier programming languages were found wanting in performing the complex programming tasks. These languages suffered from the following limitations:

(a) There were no facilities to reuse the existing program code. Wherever the same piece code was required, it was simply duplicated.

(b) The control of execution within a program was transferred via the dangerous **goto** statement. As a result, there was too much jumping around in the program, often without any clear indication of how, where, and why the control is flowing.

(c) All variables in the program were global. Tracking down spurious changes in global data in long convoluted programs was a very tedious job.

(d) Writing, understanding, and maintaining long programs became a programmer's nightmare.

In short, we can call this methodology of developing programs **Unstructured** programming.

Structured Programming

To overcome the limitations mentioned above, a quest began to develop new languages with new features that would help to create more sophisticated applications. The breakthrough occurred in the late 1960's and early 1970's with the introduction of structured programming. The long programs that the programmer found difficult to comprehend could now be broken down into smaller units of few hundred statements. Functions/subroutines/procedures were introduced in these languages to make the programs more comprehensible to their human creators. The program was now divided into functions, with each function having a clearly defined purpose.

How structured programming overcame the limitations experienced in unstructured programming is given below.

(a) Reuse of existing program code – Wherever the same piece code is required at multiple places in a program, the function containing that code was used. As a result, there was no need to repeat the same code at multiple places.

(b) Excessive use of **goto** statement – This was minimized by introducing powerful control instructions that could transfer the control within the program in an easy-to-understand manner.

(c) Unexpected changes in global variables – With introduction of functions, need for global variables were minimized.

(d) Complexity of programs – Complexity became more manageable as structured programming permitted better organization of the program.

A structured program is built by breaking down a solution into smaller pieces that then become functions within that program. Each function can have its local variables and logic. The execution begins with one function and then all other functions are called directly or indirectly from this function. This is shown in Figure 9.1.

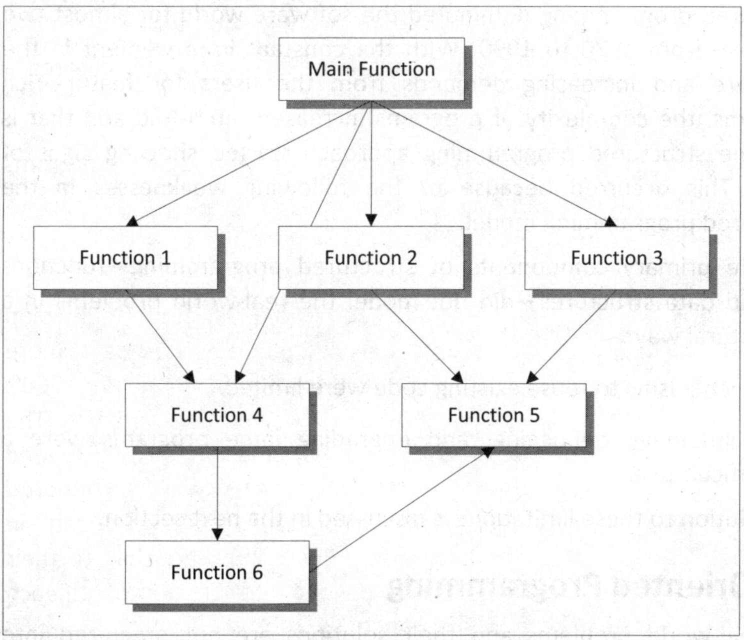

Figure 9.1

In structured programming, there is less need of global variables, which are now replaced by local variables that have a smaller and more controllable scope. Information is passed between functions using parameters and functions can have local variables that cannot be accessed outside the function's scope.

By isolating processes within functions, a structured program minimizes the chance that one function will affect another. This also makes it easier to locate problems, if any. Structured programming helps in writing cleaner code and in maintaining control over each function. All this makes the development and maintenance of code easier as well as efficient.

A new concept came into existence with structured programming—**Abstraction**. Abstraction permits the programmer to look at something without being concerned with its internal details. In a structured program, it is enough to know which task is performed by function. It does not matter to the programmer how that task is performed so long as the function does it reliably. This is called functional abstraction and is the cornerstone of structured programming.

Structured programming dominated the software world for almost two decades—from 1970 to 1990. With the constant improvement in the hardware and increasing demands from the users for feature-rich programs, the complexity of programs increased multi-fold and that is the time structured programming approach started showing signs of strain. This occurred because of the following weaknesses in the structured programming model:

(a) The primary components of structured programming—functions and data structures—did not model the real-world problems in a natural way.

(b) Mechanisms to reuse existing code were limited.

(c) Maintaining, debugging, and upgrading large programs were a difficult task.

The solution to these limitations is discussed in the next section.

Object-Oriented Programming

The real-world problems and their solutions are not organized into values and procedures separate from one another. Instead, they are perceived as objects containing values and procedures that either access or manipulate these values. The world is full of objects and the OOP methodology helps us expresses computer programs in ways that model how people perceive the world.

The fundamental change in OOP is that a program is designed around the data being operated upon, rather than around the operations themselves. This is to be expected once we appreciate that the prime purpose of the program is to access or manipulate data. The basic idea behind object-oriented language is to combine into a single unit, both the data and the functions that operate on the data. Such a unit is called an object.

An object's functions, called member functions or methods, typically provide the only way to access its data. If you want to access a data item in an object, you call a member function in the object. It will read the item and return the value to you. You cannot access the data directly.

If you want to modify the data in an object, you call the member functions in the object. No other functions can access the data. This simplifies writing, debugging, and maintaining the program.

A Java program typically consists of several objects which communicate with each other by calling one another's member functions. The organization of a Java program is shown in Figure 9.2.

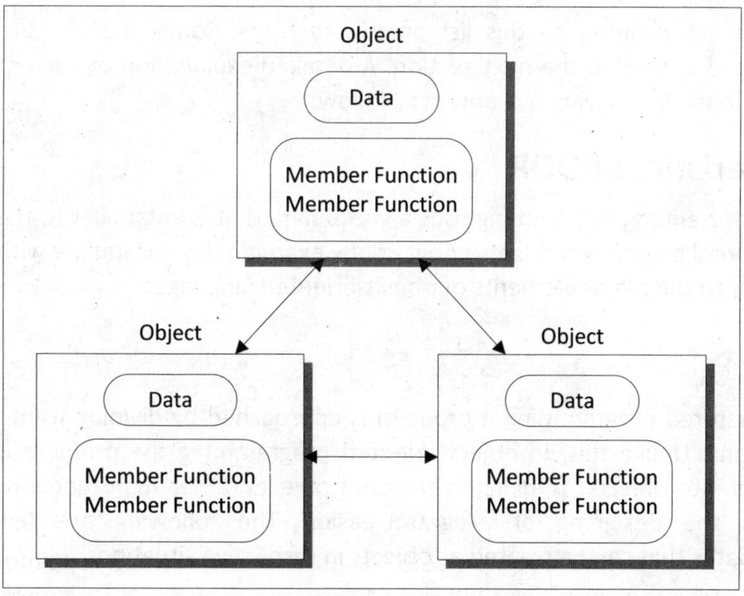

Figure 9.2

When you approach a programming problem in an object-oriented manner, you no longer ask how the problem will be divided into functions, but rather how it will be divided into objects. Thinking in terms of objects, rather than functions, has a surprisingly helpful effect on how easily programs can be designed. This results from the close match between objects in the programming world and objects in the real world.

The match between programming objects and real-world objects is the happy result of combining data and functions. The resulting objects offer a revolution in program design. No such close match between programming constructs and the concepts being modeled exists in a procedural language.

There is more to OOP than just binding the data and functions together. Given below are some of the new concepts introduced in OOP.

(a) Data hiding
(b) Encapsulation
(c) Inheritance
(d) Containership
(e) Polymorphism
(f) Generics
(g) Exception handling

Do not get daunted by this list of new features. Some of these are explained in brief in the next section. A detailed explanation of each of these concepts is given in chapters to follow.

Characteristics of OOP

Object-oriented programming uses a vocabulary that is unfamiliar to the procedural programmer. Let us now briefly examine this vocabulary with regards to the major elements of object-oriented languages.

Objects

In structured programming a problem is approached by dividing it into functions. Unlike this, in object-oriented programming the problem is divided into objects. Thinking in terms of objects rather than functions makes the designing of program easier. The following are few candidates that can be treated as objects in respective situations:

- Employees in a Payroll processing system
- GUI elements like windows, menus, icons, etc.

- Elements in computer games like cannons, guns, animals, etc.
- Customers, salespersons in a sales tracking system

Classes

Most languages offer primitive data types like **int**, **long** and **float**. Their data representation and response to arithmetic, assignment and relational operators are defined as part of the language. However, not all the information about real world objects can be represented using these limited built-in data types. The programmer often needs to create his own data types by defining a **class** for it.

For example, there can be a user-defined data type to represent dates. Programmers must define the behavior of dates by designing a **Date** class. This class expresses the format of a date and the operations that can be performed on it. The way we can declare many variables of the primitive type **int**, we can define many objects of the **Date** class. A class serves as a blueprint or a plan or a template. It specifies what data and what functions will be included in objects of that type. Defining a class does not create any objects, just as the mere existence of a type **int** does not create any variables.

Inheritance

OOP permits you to create your own data types (classes) just like the types built into the language. However, unlike the built-in data types, the user-defined classes can use other classes as building blocks. Using a concept called **inheritance**, new classes can be built on top of the old ones. The new class referred to as a **derived** class, can inherit the data and functions of the original, or the **base** class. The new class can add its own data elements and functions in addition to those it inherits from its base class.

For example, we can build a set of classes that describe a library of publications. There are two primary types of publications— periodicals and books. We can create a general **Publication** class by defining data items for the publisher's name, the number of pages and the accession number. Publications can be retrieved, stored, and read. These would be the functions of **Publication** class.

Next, we can define two classes named **Periodical** and **Book**. Both these classes can be derived from the base class **Publication**. This is natural because a periodical as well as a book would have properties like publisher name, number of pages and the accession number.

In addition to this, a periodical also has a volume and issue number and contains articles written by different authors. Data items for these should be included in the definition of the **periodical** class. The **Periodical** class will also need a function, subscribe.

Data items for the **Book** class will include the names of its author, a cover type (hard or soft) and its ISBN (International Standard Book Number). This class would also have a function called **subscribe**. As you can see, the **Book** class and the **Periodical** class share the characteristics of **Publication** class while having their own unique attributes. This entire scenario is depicted in Figure 9.3.

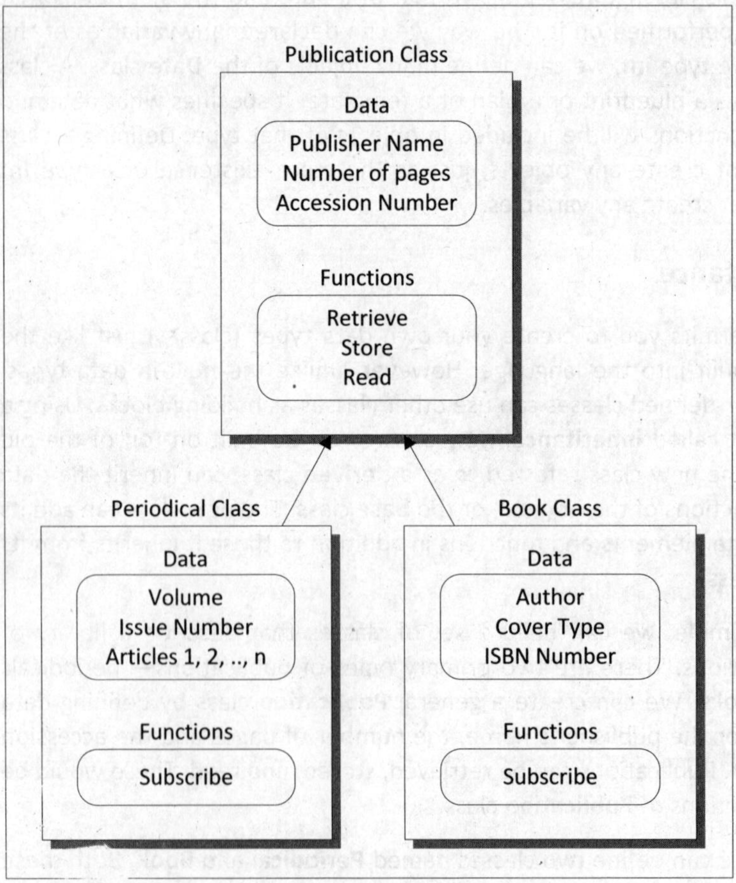

Figure 9.3

Polymorphism

Extending the same example of the Publication, Periodical and Book, let us now understand another important concept. Our base class, Publication, defines methods for storing and retrieving data. A periodical may be stored in a binder, while a book is usually placed on a shelf. Furthermore, the way to find a specific periodical is different from finding a book. Periodicals are located through a guide to periodical literature, while books are found using a card catalog system. Based on this we can design a 'find through periodical literature' function for a periodical and a 'find through card catalog' function for a book.

OOP provides an elegant facility called **polymorphism** to handle such situations. In our example, the retrieval method for a periodical is different from the retrieval method for a book, even though the result is same. Polymorphism permits us to define a function for retrieving a publication that can work for both periodicals and books. When a periodical is retrieved, the retrieve function that is specific to a periodical is used, but when a book is retrieved, the retrieve function associated with a book is used. The result is that a single function name can be used for the same operation performed on related derived classes even if the implementation of that function varies from class to class. This concept of polymorphism (one thing with several distinct forms) can be extended even to operators, as we would see in later chapters.

Containership

In a typical supermarket, each item on sale can be represented using a class. These items in turn belong to different categories like cosmetics, food, cold drink, clothes, books, electronics, etc. Such relationships can be represented using containership. For example, objects like cold-cream, facewash, shampoo are contained inside a category object called cosmetics. You will be able to observe this containership relationship in many real-world problems.

Reusability

Object-oriented programs are built from reusable software components. Once a class is completed and tested, it can be distributed to other programmers for use in their own programs. This is called reusability. If those programmers want to add new features or change the existing ones, new classes can be derived from existing ones. The tried and tested capabilities of base classes do not need to be redeveloped. Programmers can devote time to writing new code instead of wasting time in rewriting existing code. This way software becomes easier to test, since programming errors can be isolated within the new code of derived classes.

For example, you might have written (or purchased from someone else) a class that creates a menu system. You are happy with the working of this class and you do not want to change it, but you want to add the capability of displaying *help* for each menu item. To do this, you simply create a new class that inherits all the capabilities of the existing one but adds *help* feature. This ease with which existing software can be reused is a major benefit of OOP.

Exercises

[A] State whether the following statements are True or False:

(a) Object-oriented programming permits reusability of the existing code.

(b) Languages earlier than procedural programming languages made use of only global variables.

(c) It is easier to write, understand and maintain programs if they use Object-Oriented programming model as compared to Structured programming model.

(d) As compared to procedures, data is not given enough importance in Procedural programming.

(e) Structured programming model does not represent the real-world problem as well as the Object-oriented programming model.

(f) A class permits us to build user-defined data types.

(g) Objects are to classes as variables are to built-in data types.

(h) Deriving a new class from an existing class promotes reusability of code.

(i) Encapsulation facilitates a single function name to be used for the same operation performed on related derived classes.

(j) In polymorphism even though the function names are same, their implementation may vary from class to class.

(k) Multiple objects can be created from the same class.

(l) Object-oriented Programming paradigm stresses dividing the logic into smaller parts and writing procedures for each part.

(m) Classes and objects are cornerstones of structured programming paradigm.

(n) Object-oriented programming paradigm gives equal importance to data and the procedures that work on the data.

(o) Java is a structured programming language.

[B] Fill in the blanks:

(e) The two major components of an object are ____ and _____.

(f) The ability of a function to act in different ways on different data types is called _________.

(g) The process of building new classes from existing ones is called ________.

(h) If a class A inherits its properties from class B, then A and B are known as _____ class and _____ class, respectively.

(i) Pascal and C are ______ languages, whereas Java is _____ language.

(j) The phenomenon of nesting one object within another is known as __________.

(k) ________ are nothing but user-defined types.

[C] Pick up the correct alternative for each of the following questions:

(a) Calling multiple functions from **main**( ) is a feature of
(1) Structured programming
(2) Object-oriented programming
(3) Functional programming
(4) Dynamic programming

(b) Dividing a given job into multiple smaller jobs is a feature used by

(1) Structured programming
(2) Object-oriented programming
(3) Functional programming
(4) Event-driven programming

(c) Which relationship should be established between a **Vehicle** class and a **Car** class?
(1) Encapsulation
(2) Polymorphism
(3) Containership
(4) Inheritance

(d) Which relationship should exist between Car, maruti and bmw?
(1) All should be classes
(2) All should be objects
(3) Car should be a class and maruti and bmw should be objects
(4) Car should be an object and maruti and bmw should be classes

(e) From OOP perspective, Customers and SalesPersons in a Sales Tracking System should be represented as
(1) classes
(2) objects
(3) interfaces
(4) methods

(f) From OOP perspective, Employees in a Payroll Processing Systems should be represented as
(1) classes
(2) objects
(3) interfaces
(4) methods

(g) Classes in an OOP system are
(1) Primitives
(2) User-defined types
(3) Interfaces
(4) Methods

(h) An object contains
(1) only data
(2) only member functions
(3) data and member functions

(4) only abstract functions

[D] Answer the following questions:

(a) What is the basic difference between structured programming model and object-oriented programming model?

(b) Give at least 5 examples of classes and objects.

(c) What do you mean by encapsulation?

(d) What do you mean by inheritance?

(e) What do you mean by polymorphism?

(f) In structured programming data is given a step-motherly treatment and the whole emphasis is on doing things. What does this mean in the programmer's language?

(g) What do you mean by abstraction?

(h) Is it necessary to create good abstractions?

(i) Why did people change over from structured programming to object-oriented programming?

(j) What is the difference between classes and objects in layman's terms?

(k) What is the difference between classes and objects in programmer's terms?

KanNotes

- Programming paradigm means a way of organizing a program.
- Two major programming paradigms are :
  1) Structure programming paradigm - adopted by C, Pascal
  2) Object Oriented Programming (OOP) paradigm - adopted by C++, Java, C#, VB.NET
- Structured programming :
  1) Emphasis on breaking the given task into smaller sub-tasks
  2) For each sub-task functions are written
  3) These functions are called directly or indirectly from main()

4) No importance given to data, it is just passed from one function to another as required

- Disadvantage of Structured programming - It is difficult to write programs involving complex tasks

- Object Oriented Programming (OOP) :

  1) Emphasis is on identifying objects in a given problem and then writing programs to facilitate interaction between objects
  2) Objects contain data and functions that can access/manipulate the data
  3) Equal importance to data as data and functions go together

- Example of classes and objects :

  Class – Human being   Objects – Amitabh, Sachin, Rahul
  Class – Birds   Objects – Sparrow, Crow, Parrot

- Class has Properties (data) and Methods (functions) :

  Ex. Vehicle has properties like wheels, engine, fuel

- Objects have specific values for properties :

  Car – 4 wheels, 4-stroke engine, Diesel
  Motorbike – 2 wheels, 2-stroke engine, Petrol

- Objects are always nameless and are created using new operator on heap

CHAPTER 10

Classes and Objects

Classes and objects are to OOP, what functions were to Structured programming. A good foundation about classes and objects would make you a sound Java programmer...

Contents

- Classes and Constructors
- Object Destruction
- Terminology
- A Complex Class
- ***this*** Reference
- Static Data and Functions
- Static Block
- Passing Objects to a Function
- Inner Classes
- Exercises
- KanNotes

Having familiarized ourselves with the basic principles of object-oriented programming, it is time we start implementing these principles through Java programs. Let us begin with classes and objects.

In all programs that we have created so far, we have just defined functions inside a class. Java permits us to combine data and functions together in a class. The functions defined within a class have a special relationship with the data elements present within the class. Placing data and functions (that work upon the data) together into a single entity is the central idea in object-oriented programming.

To begin with, let us look at a program that demonstrates the syntax and general features of classes in Java. In all the programs that we did so far we had only one class. This class used to be created by the NetBeans wizard with the name same as the Project name. For the first time we are now going to see a program that uses two classes. While creating this project in NetBeans we would give the project name as **ClassesAndObjectsProject**. As a result, the wizard would create a package called **classesandobjectsproject** containing a class called **ClassesAndObjectsProject**. Additionally, we would create the **Rectangle** class in the same package. Here's the listing of the program.

```
// Demonstration of classes and objects
package classesandobjectsproject ;
import java.util.* ;
class Rectangle
{
    private int len, brd ;
    public void getData( )
    {
        Scanner scn ;
        scn = new Scanner ( System.in ) ;
        System.out.println ( "Enter length and breadth " ) ;
        len = scn.nextInt( ) ;
        brd = scn.nextInt( ) ;
    }
    public void setData ( int l, int b )
    {
        len = l ;
        brd = b ;
    }
```

```
    public void displayData( )
    {
        System.out.println ( "length = "+ len ) ;
        System.out.println ( "breadth = "+ brd ) ;
    }
    public void areaPeri( )
    {
        int a, p ;
        a = len * brd ;
        p = 2 * ( len + brd ) ;
        System.out.println ( "area = "+ a ) ;
        System.out.println ( "perimeter = "+ p ) ;
    }
}
public class ClassesAndObjectsProject
{
    public static void main ( String[ ] args )
    {
        Rectangle r1, r2, r3 ; // define three references

        r1 = new Rectangle( ) ;
        r2 = new Rectangle( ) ;
        r3 = new Rectangle( ) ;

        r1.setData ( 10, 20 ) ; // set data in elements of the object
        r1.displayData( ) ;      // display the data set by setData( )
        r1.areaPeri( ) ;         // calculate and print area and perimeter

        r2.setData ( 5, 8 ) ;
        r2.displayData( ) ;
        r2.areaPeri( ) ;

        r3.getData( ) ; // receive data from keyboard
        r3.displayData( ) ;
        r3.areaPeri( ) ;
    }
}
```

Look at the definition of **Rectangle** class in our program. The keyword **class** is followed by the name of the class, i.e., **Rectangle**. The body of a class is delimited by braces. The **Rectangle** class contains two data items **len** and **brd** and four functions **setData( ), getData( ), displayData( )** and

areaPeri( ). As their names suggest, the first function sets the data items (**len** and **brd**) to values passed to it, the second function receives the values of data items, the third displays these values, whereas the fourth calculates and prints the area and perimeter.

The data items defined in a class are often called data members, whereas the functions defined in it are called member functions or methods. The member functions provide controlled access to the data members of class. This controlled access is managed through two keywords—**private** and **public**.

Note that we have defined the data members as **private**. As a result, they cannot be accessed directly from outside the **Rectangle** class. Thus, the data remains safe from accidental manipulation.

Only the member functions of **Rectangle** class can access the **private** data members. To permit access to these member functions from outside the **Rectangle** class, they have been defined as **public**. Thus, when we wish to access or manipulate the data members from outside the class we call the **public** member functions, which in turn access the **private** data members. This is what we mean by controlled access.

Usually, the data members in a class are **private** and the member functions are **public**. This ensures that data remains safe from inadvertent manipulation. However, there is no rule that data must be **private** and functions **public**. In fact, in some situations you may be required to use **private** functions and **public** data.

Do not confuse data hiding with the security techniques used to protect computer data. Security techniques prevent illegal users from accessing data. Data hiding, on the other hand, is used to protect well-intentioned users from honest mistakes.

Let us now understand the meaning of the term **object** and how they are created. An object is an **instance** of a class, and the process of creating an object is called **instantiation**. In our program we have created three objects through the statements:

```
r1 = new Rectangle( ) ;
r2 = new Rectangle( ) ;
r3 = new Rectangle( ) ;
```

All the three objects are created in memory and each one of them would have data members **len** and **br** in them. None of these objects have names. The addresses at which these objects are created in memory are stored in variables **r1**, **r2** and **r3**. These variables are known as references to objects. Figure 10.1 illustrates this.

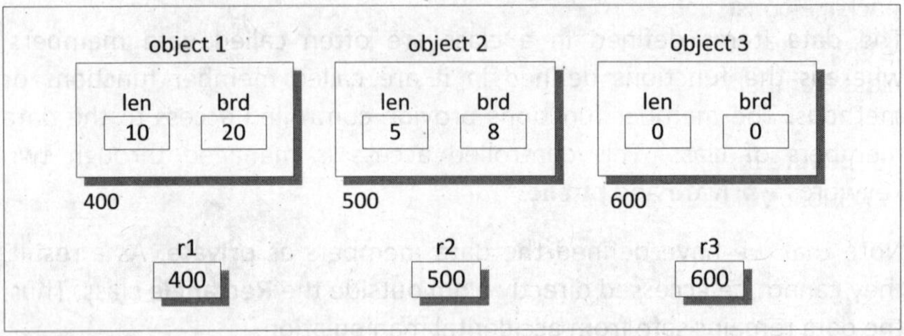

Figure 10.1

Once the objects are created, we can use them to call member functions of the class. For example, we can call the member function **setData( )** from **main( )** using the object whose address is stored in the reference **r1**, through the statement:

```
r1.setData ( 10, 20 ) ;
```

The 10 and 20 that are being passed to **setData( )** would be collected in **l** and **b** and would then be assigned to **len** and **br** of object whose address is present is reference **r1**.

Similarly, when we make the call to

```
r2.setData ( 5, 8 ) ;
```

5 and 8 get set up in **len** and **br** of object whose address is present in **r2**.

The dot operator (.) used to call **setData( )** through **r1** and **r2** is called 'class member access operator'. Calls to other functions like **displayData( )** and **areaPeri( )** are similar.

Note that objects are created at a place in memory called heap, whereas, references to objects are created at a place in memory called stack.

Classes and Constructors

In the last section we had our first tryst with classes in Java. Just to reiterate, a class contains data and functions that operate upon this data. Both data and functions can be **private** or **public**, which essentially decides the access to the data and functions within the class. Let us now move one step further. Observe the following program carefully.

```
// Different types of constructors
package constructorsproject ;
import java.util.* ;
class Number
{
    private int i ;
    public void setData ( int j )
    {
        i = j ;
    }
    public void getData( )
    {
        Scanner scn ;
        scn = new Scanner ( System.in ) ;
        System.out.println ( "Enter any integer" ) ;
        i = scn.nextInt( ) ;
    }
    public Number( ) // zero argument constructor
    {
    }
    public Number ( int j ) // one argument constructor
    {
        i = j ;
    }
    public void displayData( )
    {
        System.out.println ( "value of i = "+ i ) ;
    }
}
public class ConstructorsProject
{
    public static void main ( String[ ] args )
    {
        Number  n1, n2, n3 ;

        n1 = new Number( ) ;
        n1.displayData( ) ;
        n1.setData ( 200 ) ; // first method to set data in object
        n1.displayData( ) ;
```

```
        n2 = new Number( ) ;
        n2.displayData( ) ;
        n2.getData( ) ;  // second method to set data in object
        n2.displayData( ) ;

        n3 = new Number ( 100 ) ;  // third method to set data in object
        n3.displayData( ) ;
    }
}
```

This program shows three ways in which we can give values to data items in an object. One is through the member function **setData( )** to whom we pass the value to be set up. Another way is by receiving values through keyboard as shown in function **getData( )**. That brings us to the third method, which uses an entity called 'constructor' (or in short, Ctor). The constructor is a special member function that allows us to set up values while creating an object, without the need to make a separate call to a member function like **setData( )**. Thus, constructor is a member function that is called automatically whenever an object is created.

There are some unusual aspects to constructor functions. First, it is no accident that they have the same name as the class of which they are members. In fact, it is a rule that the class and the constructor function within it must have same names. This is how the compiler knows that the member function is a constructor.

Secondly, no return type is used for constructors. Why not? Since the constructor is called automatically when an object is created, returning a value would not make sense.

In our program the statements

```
n1 = new Number( ) ; // calls zero-argument constructor
n2 = new Number( ) ; // calls zero-argument constructor
n3 = new Number ( 100 ) ; // calls one-argument constructor
```

create three objects of the type **Number** and call the appropriate constructor function. Note the use of the **new** operator while creating objects. This operator allocates memory for the object and then calls that object's constructor function.

If you notice carefully, you would find that there are two constructors with the same name **Number( )**. Hence, we call these constructors

overloaded constructors. Which of the two constructors gets called when an object is created, depends on how many arguments are used in the creation of the object.

Since we have not done anything in the zero-argument constructor, the value of **i** is set to 0 for objects referred by **n1** and **n2**. This can be verified from the output of the program. The value of **i** for **n1** and **n2** can later be reset, as done here through calls to **setData( )** and **getData( )**.

If data can be set in an object through the constructor function as well as through the **setData( )** function, why should we define both in a class? This is because the constructor function can be called only during creation of an object, whereas the **setData( )** function can be called multiple times once an object is created. So initial data can be set in an object through the constructor and it can be changed later (if required) through the **setData( )** function.

What would happen if we declare an object of a particular class type and the class does not have a constructor? Nothing. Because when no constructor is present in a class, the compiler inserts a zero-argument constructor in it. Note that if we declare a one-argument constructor, it is necessary on our part to define the zero-argument constructor as well.

Object Destruction

When the object is created using the operator **new**, memory is allocated for it. Should we not free this memory when we are done with using this object? This is not necessary, as this is done for us by JVM. It has a program called **Garbage Collector**, which it runs periodically. When it runs, it checks for objects that are no longer being used by an application. It then reclaims (frees) the memory used to store all such objects. So, as far as memory management for objects is concerned, we do not have to worry much about it, and can safely rely on garbage collector to do it for us. This is unlike traditional OO languages like C++ where programmers must manage the memory explicitly.

However, in many Java programs, memory is not the only resource that is used. Other resources like files, network connections, and database connections, are also used. When we no longer need the objects that use these resources the objects should release these resources in a disciplined manner. If this is not done resource leaks will happen. This is a waste of resources. At times, if the pool of resources gets exhausted then the program may even stop running. Java provides a mechanism called **finalize( )** function to give up the resources when the object is no longer needed. This function is defined inside the class and is called by the garbage collector just before reclaiming the object.

Thus the **finalize( )** function is opposite of a constructor. The constructor is called when an object is created. Similarly, when an object is destroyed by the garbage collector the **finalize( )** function is called. Note that we have no control over when the **finalize( )** function is called by the Garbage Collector.

The following program shows **finalize( )** at work:

```
/* Object destruction using finalize( ) */
package objectdestructionproject ;
class Example
{
    private int data ;
    public Example( ) // contstuctor (same name as class)
    {
        System.out.println ( "Inside the constructor" ) ;
    }

    protected void finalize( ) throws Throwable
    {
        super.finalize( ) ;
    }
}
public class ObjectDestructionProject
{
    public static void main ( String[ ] args )
    {
        Example e = new Example( ) ;
    }
}
```

When the object referred to by **e** gets created, the constructor gets called. When control goes outside **main( )** this object is no longer used. When the garbage collector finds this, it calls the **finalize( )** function. **finalize( )** function does not receive any parameter, nor does it return any value. The **finalize( )** method cannot be called explicitly. Also, we should not declare it as **public**.

In the **finalize( )** method we have simply called the base class **finalize( )** method. Note that all classes in Java including the **Example** class are derived from a base class called **Object**. We would learn more about this derivation process in Chapter 13.

In this program we have done precious little inside the **finalize( )** function. In a program in which the object uses files, network and database connections the **finalize( )** method should perform operations like closing open files, terminating network connections, terminating database connections and other cleanup work.

Terminology

Consider the following code snippet:

```
Sample s1, s2 ;
s1 = new Sample ( 1.0f, 2.0f ) ;
s2 = new Sample( ) ;
s2.Function ( s1 ) ;
```

From the code it is obvious that we are creating two objects of the **Sample** class and calling its zero-argument and two-argument constructors. Can you guess what are we passing to **Function( )**? Simple, object **s1**. Well, actually speaking, no. This is because **s1** is not an object, but a reference to an object. The object does not have a name and we always access it using its address stored in reference **s1**. But it is quite common to call reference **s1** as object **s1**. Though this is slightly incorrect, it gives a lot of convenience and hence we too would be using this terminology in the rest of the chapter and in the chapters to follow.

A Complex Class

As we know, a complex number consists of a real part and an imaginary part. The following program puts the concept of constructor to a practical stint by developing a class to implement complex numbers:

```
// Implementation of complex numbers
package complexnumbersproject ;
import java.util.* ;
class Complex
{
    private float real, imag ;
    public Complex( )
    {
```

```
    }
    public Complex ( float r, float i )
    {
        real = r ;
        imag = i ;
    }
    public void getData( )
    {
        float r, i ;
        Scanner scn ;
        scn = new Scanner ( System.in ) ;
        System.out.println ( "Enter real and imaginary part" ) ;
        r = scn.nextFloat( ) ;
        i = scn.nextFloat( ) ;
        real = r ;
        imag = i ;
    }
    public void setData ( float r, float i )
    {
        real = r ;
        imag = i ;
    }
    public void displayData( )
    {
        System.out.println ( "real = "+ real ) ;
        System.out.println ( "imaginary = "+ imag ) ;
    }
    public Complex addComplex ( Complex y )
    {
        Complex t ;
        t = new Complex( ) ;
        t.real = real + y.real ;
        t.imag = imag + y.imag ;
        return t ;
    }
    public Complex mulComplex ( Complex y )
    {
        Complex t ;
        t = new Complex( ) ;
        t.real = real * y.real - imag * y.imag ;
        t.imag = real * y.imag + y.real * imag ;
```

```
        return t ;
    }
}
public class ComplexNumbersProject
{
    public static void main ( String[ ] args )
    {
        Complex c1, c2, c3 ;
        c1 = new Complex( ) ;
        c1.setData ( 2.0f, 2.0f ) ;
        c2 = new Complex( ) ;
        c3 = new Complex( ) ;
        c3 = c1.addComplex ( c2 ) ;
        System.out.println( "Complex c3:" ) ;
        c3.displayData( ) ;

        Complex c4, c5, c6 ;
        c4 = new Complex( ) ;
        c4.getData( ) ;
        c5 = new Complex ( 2.5f, 3.0f ) ;
        c6 = new Complex( ) ;
        c6 = c4.mulComplex ( c5 ) ;
        System.out.println ( "Complex c6:" ) ;
        c6.displayData( ) ;

        Complex c7 ;
        c7 = new Complex( ) ;
        c7 = c1.addComplex ( c2.mulComplex ( c3 ) ) ;
        System.out.println ( "Complex c7:" ) ;
        c7.displayData( ) ;
    }
}
```

In this program we have once again used overloaded constructors and functions **getData( )** and **setData( )** to set up values of data items in different objects. To add two complex numbers we have called the member function **addComplex( )** through the statement,

c3 = c1.addComplex (c2) ;

Here, the complex numbers **c1** and **c2** are being added and the result is being stored in **c3**. Out of **c1** and **c2**, **c2** is being passed explicitly, whereas **c1** becomes accessible to **addComplex( )** through a mechanism of **this** reference. This mechanism would be discussed in the next section. The syntax for arguments that are objects is the same as that for arguments that are simple data types like **ints** or **floats**. The complex object's reference returned by **addComplex( )** is collected in **c3**.

The call to **mulComplex( )** function works similarly:

```
c6 = c4.mulComplex ( c5 ) ;
```

There is another interesting call in this program:

```
c7 = c1.addComplex ( c2.mulComplex ( c3 ) ) ;
```

Here, result of multiplication of **c2** and **c3** gets added to **c1** and the result of addition gets stored in **c7**. What you must be wondering is, where does the result of multiplication of **c2** and **c3** gets stored when it is returned by **mulComplex( )**? Well, this result gets collected in a temporary object, and then this temporary object is passed to **addComplex( )**.

We could as well have implemented the addition and multiplication functions in the manner shown below.

```
void addComplex ( Complex x, Complex y )
{
    Complex t ;
    real = x.real + y.real ;
    imag = x.imag + y.imag ;
}
void mulComplex ( Complex x, Complex y )
{
    real = x.real * y.real - x.imag * y.imag ;
    imag = x.real * y.imag + y.real * x.imag ;
}
```

If we implement the functions in this fashion, the way they are called would also change. The calls would now look like this:

```
c3.addComplex ( c1, c2 ) ;
c6.mulComplex ( c4, c5 ) ;
```

Here, in the first call **c1** and **c2** are being passed explicitly, whereas, **c3** would be available to **addComplex( )** through the **this** reference mechanism. Similarly, in the second call, **c4** and **c5** are being passed explicitly, whereas **c6** would be available through the **this** reference mechanism. Can we use both the forms of **addComplex( )** and **mulComplex( )** in the same class? Of course, you can. They would then be treated as overloaded functions. In such a case, you would have the flexibility of calling them in any of the two ways discussed above.

this Reference

Whenever we call a member function of a class using an object, in addition to the parameters that are explicitly being passed to the function, address of the object is also passed to it implicitly. This address is implicitly collected by the member function in a reference with a special name—**this**. Thus, through **this** reference every member function has access to address of the object through which it is called. **this** reference ceases to exist when the control returns from the member function. **this** reference can be treated like any other reference to an object. It can be used to access the data in the object it points to. The following program shows the working of **this** reference:

```
// Working of this reference
package thisreferenceproject ;
class Example
{
    private int i ;
    public void setData ( int ii )
    {
        i = ii ; // one way to set data
        this.i = ii ; // another way to set data
    }
    public void showData( )
    {
        System.out.println ( i ) ; // one way to display data
        System.out.println ( this.i ) ; // another way to display data
    }
}
public class ThisReferenceProject
{
    public static void main ( String[ ] args )
    {
        Example e1 ;
        e1 = new Example( ) ;
```

```
        e1.setData ( 10 ) ;
        e1.showData( ) ;
    }
}
```

Here is the output of the program...

```
10
10
```

Since **this** reference contains the address of the object, using it we can reach the data member of the **Example** object through statements like:

```
this.i = ii ; // another way to set data
System.out.println ( this.i ) ; // another way to display data
```

But if we can set the value in **i** and display it without using **this** reference, then why bother about it? There is one situation where we cannot get by without using **this** reference. Suppose that we had defined the **setData( )** function as shown below.

```
public void setData ( int i )
{
    this.i = i ;
}
```

Note that here we have collected the value passed to **setData( )** in the variable **i** and not in **ii**. This local **i** would now conflict with the **private int i** of the **Example** class. So, we cannot expect the **private int i** to get set if we use the statement,

```
i = i ;
```

In this case the only way to refer to the **private int i** of the **Example** object is to use the **this** reference through a statement,

```
this.i = i ;
```

Static Data and Functions

A class can contain instance data members and static data members. Multiple objects have their own instance data members, whereas all of them would share the static data members. Static data members are useful when we wish to share some data between all objects. For example, if we wish to keep track of the number of objects that have been created so far from a class, we can track it using a static data member, as shown below.

```
// Working of static data member and static member function
package sample ;
public class Sample
{
    public static void main ( String[ ] args )
    {
        Ex e1 = new Ex ( 10 ) ;
        Ex.showCount( ) ;
        Ex e2 = new Ex ( 20 ) ;
        Ex.showCount( ) ;
        Ex e3 = new Ex ( 30 ) ;
        Ex.showCount( ) ;
    }
}
class Ex
{
    private int i ;
    private static int count = 0 ;
    public Ex ( int val )
    {
        i = val ;
        count += 1 ;
    }
    public static void showCount( )
    {
        System.out.println ( count ) ;
    }
}
```

In class **Ex** we have an instance data member **i** and a static data member **count**. Each of the three **Ex** objects would have their own **i**, which would be set up with values 10, 20, 30 respectively. All the three objects would share a common **count** variable which would be incremented each time a new object is created. So, the latest value of **count** can tell us how many **Ex** objects have been created so far. This value is printed through a static function **showCount( )**. Note the syntax of calling a **static** function—**classname.staticfunctionname( )**. Also note that a static function can access only static data.

Static Block

A **static** block is like **static** data members in the sense that it belongs to a class and not to a particular object. The **static** block is executed when the class is first loaded. It is typically used to initialize all the static data of the class at one place. In this block we can also use control instructions to validate the static data before initializing it. We cannot access non-static variables or methods in this block. Look at the following program:

```
// Usage of static block
package staticblockproject ;
import java.util.Calendar ;
public class StaticBlockProject
{
    public static void main ( String[ ] args )
    {
        Sample.showDate( ) ;
    }
}
class Sample
{
    private static int y ;
    private static int m ;
    private static int d ;

    // static block
    static
    {
        Calendar cal = Calendar.getInstance( ) ;
        y = cal.get ( Calendar.YEAR ) ;
        m = cal.get ( Calendar.MONTH ) ;
        d = cal.get ( Calendar.DAY_OF_MONTH ) ;
    }
    public static void showDate( )
    {
        System.out.println ( "Year: " + y ) ;
        System.out.println ( "Month: " + m ) ;
        System.out.println ( "Day: " + d ) ;
```

```
    }
}
```

In the static block we have called the **static** method **getInstance( )** of the **Calendar** class. This method creates a **Calendar** object and fills it up with current day, month, and year data. We then extracted this data by calling the **get( )** method of **Calendar** class.

Passing Objects to a Function

The way we can pass primitives to a function, we can also pass objects to a function. Since objects are nameless, while passing an object, we pass only its reference. The called function can collect this passed reference in another reference. Since only the address of the object has been passed, this reference in the function also points to the same object. So, using it, if we change the values in the object, then we are changing the original object. The following program illustrates this fact.

```
// Passing objects to a function
package passingobjectsproject
public class PassingObjectsProject
{
    public static void main ( String[ ] args )
    {
        Ex e = new Ex( ) ;
        e.setData ( 1, 2.5f ) ;
        e.displayData( ) ;
        fun ( e ) ;
        e.displayData( ) ;
    }
    static void fun ( Ex  p )
    {
        p.setData ( 3, 8.5f ) ;
    }
}
class  Ex
{
    private int  i ;
    private float  f ;
    public void setData ( int  x, float  y )
    {
        i = x ;
```

```
        f = y ;
    }
    public void displayData( )
    {
        System.out.println ( i + " " + f ) ;
    }
}
```

The second call to **displayData( )** prints the values 3 and 8.5, proving that through **fun( )** when we manipulate the object, the original object gets modified.

Inner Classes

Inner classes are classes defined within another class. They offer a way to organize and group related classes together, improving code modularity and reusability. The inner classes can be **static** or non-static. If non-static, they can access all members of the enclosing class. If static, they can access only static members of enclosing class. The working of both these inner classes is shown in the following program:

```
// Working of inner classes
package innerclassdemoproject ;
public class InnerClassDemoProject
{
    private int outerField = 10 ;
    private static int outerStaticField = 20 ;
    public void message( )
    {
        System.out.println ( "Hi from instance method" ) ;
    }
    public static void staticMessage( )
    {
        System.out.println ( "Hello from static method" ) ;
    }
    public class InnerClass
    {
        public void accessOuterFields( )
        {
            System.out.println ( "outer field: " + outerField ) ;
            System.out.println ( "outer static field: " + outerStaticField ) ;
        }
```

```
        public void accessOuterMethods( )
        {
            message( ) ;
            staticMessage( ) ;
        }
    }
    public static class StaticInnerClass
    {
        public void accessOuterFields( )
        {
            //System.out.println ( "outer field: " + outerField ) ;
            System.out.println ( "outer static field: " + outerStaticField ) ;
        }
        public void accessOuterMethods( )
        {
            //message( ) ;
            staticMessage( ) ;
        }
    }
    public static void main ( String[ ] args )
    {
        // creating and using non-static inner class
        // outer class instance needed
        InnerClassDemoProject m = new InnerClassDemoProject( ) ;
        InnerClassDemoProject.InnerClass inner ;
        inner = m.new InnerClass( ) ;
        inner.accessOuterFields( ) ;
        inner.accessOuterMethods( ) ;

        // creating and using static inner class
        // no outer class instance needed
        InnerClassDemoProject.StaticInnerClass innerStatic ;
        innerStatic = new InnerClassDemoProject.StaticInnerClass( ) ;
        innerStatic.accessOuterFields( ) ;
        innerStatic.accessOuterMethods( ) ;
    }
}
```

Here we have defined a class **InnerClassDemoProject** containing two inner classes—**InnerClass** and **StaticInnerClass**. The **InnerClass** can access both static and instance data and methods of the outer class. It requires an instance of the outer class to be created first. The

StaticInnerClass can only access the static field and static method of the outer class, and it doesn't need an outer class instance for creation. The main method shows how to use both inner classes to interact with the outer class's members. Inner class's utility can be appreciated while learning the Builder pattern in Chapter 25.

Exercises

[A] What will be the output of the following programs?

(a)
```
package sampleproject ;
class MyDate
{
    private int dd, mm, yy ;
    public MyDate( )
    {
        System.out.println ( "Reached here" ) ;
        System.out.println ( this ) ;
    }
}
public class SampleProject
{
    public static void main ( String[ ] args )
    {
        MyDate today = new MyDate( ) ;
        MyDate tomorrow = new MyDate( ) ;
    }
}
```

(b)
```
package sampleproject ;
class StudentRecord
{
    private int m1, m2, m3 ;
    private float percentage ;
    public StudentRecord( )
    {
        m1 = m2 = m3 = 0 ;
        percentage = 0.0f ;
    }
    public void calculatePercentage ( int x, int y, int z )
    {
        m1 = x ; m2 = y ; m3 = z ;
```

```
        percentage = ( m1 + m2 + m3 ) / 3.0f ;
    }
    public void displayPercentage( )
    {
        System.out.println ( "Percentage = " + percentage ) ;
    }
}
public class SampleProject
{
    public static void main ( String[ ] args  )
    {
        StudentRecord s1 ;
        s1 = new StudentRecord( ) ;
        s1.displayPercentage( ) ;
        s1.calculatePercentage ( 35, 35, 35 ) ;
        s1.displayPercentage( ) ;
    }
}
```

(c)

```
package SampleProject ;
class Sample
{
    public static int d,m,y ;

    static
    {
        d = m = y = 10 ;
    }
    public Sample( )
    {
        y++ ;  m++ ;  d++ ;
    }
    public static void Show( )
    {
        System.out.println ( "y : " + y ) ;
        System.out.println ( "m: " + m ) ;
        System.out.println ( "d: " + d ) ;
    }
}
class SampleProject
{
```

```
    static void main ( string[ ] args )
    {
        Sample s = new Sample( ) ;
        s.Show( ) ;
    }
}
```

[B] Answer the following questions:

(a) What are the two major components of an object?

(b) Where do objects get created in memory?

(c) Once objects are created in memory, are they accessed using their names or their references?

(d) Do member functions occupy space in objects?

(e) Can we create an object **s** of class **Sample** through a statement,

sample s ;

(f) How does a member function come to know on which object it has to work upon?

(g) What is the type of **this** reference?

(h) When does **this** reference get created?

(i) Is it true that all objects in Java are created dynamically? If true, why?

(j) Is it true that in class data members are always private, whereas member functions are always public?

(k) Is it true that a class declaration creates space in memory for the members defined in it?

(l) Is it necessary that a constructor in a class should always be **public**?

(m) Is the size of an object equal to sum of sizes of data members and member functions within the class?

(n) Define a class **Cartesian** which stores the Cartesian co-ordinates of a point. Define another class **Polar** which stores Polar co-ordinates of a point. Make a provision to convert co-ordinates from Cartesian to Polar and vice-versa.

// Polar to Cartesian conversion

```
x = radius * cos ( angle )
y = radius * sin ( angle )

// Cartesian to Polar conversion
angle = a tan ( x / y )
radius = sqrt ( x * x + y * y )
```

(o) Can we access non-static or instance member functions from the **static** block?

(p) If a method is called using two different objects, then would **this** reference contain the same addresses during each call?

[C] Attempt the following questions:

(a) When the following code snippet is executed would contents of **s1** and **s2** be same or different?

```
// Sample is a user-defined class
Sample s1, s2 ;
s1 = new Sample( ) ;
s2 = new Sample( ) ;
```

(b) When the following code snippet is executed where would the object and the reference be created in memory?

```
Sample c ;
c = new Sample( ) ;
```

(c) Is it true that objects are always nameless and depending upon their size they either get created in the stack or on the heap?

(d) What is Garbage Collector? How is it important when working with classes and objects in Java?

(e) How many times can a constructor be called during the lifetime of the object?

(f) Is it possible for you to prevent an object from being created by using zero-argument constructor? If yes, how?

(g) Constructor cannot return any value. If the constructor fails, how do you let the caller know?

(h) Is it possible to call constructor for a class explicitly?

(i) What is a static constructor? When is it called?

(j) Is it possible to invoke Garbage Collector explicitly? If yes, how can it be done?

(k) Is it recommended that you provide **finalize( )** a method in all your classes?

(l) Can **static** procedures access instance data? If not, why not?

KanNotes

- Classes are user-defined data types
- Classes indicate how the objects created from them would look like
- Objects have specific data. Each object is a specific instance of a class
- Data values in objects are often called instance data or state of the object
- In a class data members are usually private, whereas member functions are usually public
- public members of a class are accessible from outside the class
- private members of a class are NOT accessible from outside class
- Within a class any member can access any other member
- By default, class members are public
- Usually, data in a class is kept private and the data is accessed / manipulated through public member functions of the class
- In principle every object has instance data and member functions
- In practice each object has instance data, whereas member functions are shared amongst objects
- Sharing is justified as from one object to another member functions are going to remain same

- Objects are nameless
- Objects are referred using references created on stack
- Objects are created on heap using new operator, which returns address (reference) of the object on its creation
- Usage of "this" reference is optional
- this is a constant reference - final
- this reference cannot be modified during execution of the method
- this reference dies once control returns from the method
- Two ways to initialize an object :

  Method 1 :

  Using member function like getData( ) / setData( )
  Benefit 1 - Data is protected from manipulation
  Benefit 2 - Better validation as it is done at one place
  Benefit 3 - Validation done by class designer

  Method 2 :

  Using special member function – Constructor
  Benefit 1 - Program is better organized
  Benefit 2 - Guaranteed initialization through constructor (Ctor)
- When an object is created, space is allocated in memory and Ctor is called
- Name of Ctor must be same as name of class
- Ctor is a function
- Ctor doesn't return any value
- Ctor gets called automatically when an object is created
- Ctor is called only once during entire lifetime of an object
- Ctor can be overloaded
- If we don't define a Ctor, compiler inserts a 0-arg Ctor

- A class may have Ctor as well as setData()

  Ctor – To initialize object
  setData() – To modify object

- finalize() method is called when an object is about to be destroyed

- finalize( ) method is called by Java Runtime just before garbage collection

- finalize() method is Not called when an object goes out of scope

- finalize() method is used to free non-Java resource like file handle of font

- A class can contain instance data and static data

- A class can contain instance functions and static functions

- Instance functions can access instance data and static data

- Static functions can access only static data

- Access from outside the class :

  Instance function : Object.function()
  Static function : Class.function()
  Object.function() - works, but is misleading

- An instance function can be called only after creating an object

- A static function can be called anytime

- this reference is never passed to a static function

- Static block gets executed exactly once when the class is loaded

- A static block can contain control instructions for validating data

- A static block is used to initialize all static data at one place

- Functions are called only by value. There is no call by reference. So, when we pass an object to a function, we are actually passing its reference, by value

Arrays

Let Us JAVA 7th Edition

CHAPTER 11

Data abounds in nature and its problems. So, when you have a lot of it to deal with, Array is a good answer...

Contents

- What are Arrays?
  - A Simple Program using an Array
- More on Arrays
  - Array Initialization
  - Array Access
  - Bounds Checking
  - Passing Array Elements to a Function
  - Passing Array Reference to a Function
  - Returning an Array
- Common Array Operations
- Array of Objects
- Multi-Dimensional Arrays
  - Passing and Returning 2-D Array
- Jagged Array
- Resizing Arrays
- Exercises
- KanNotes

Java language provides a capability that enables the user to design a set of similar data types, called array. This chapter describes how arrays can be created and manipulated in Java. We would also discuss how and why arrays are implemented as objects.

What are Arrays?

Suppose we wish to arrange the percentage marks obtained by 50 students in ascending order. To do this we must first be able to hold 50 students marks in memory. In such a case, we have two options to store these marks in memory:

(a) Construct 50 variables, each containing one student's marks.
(b) Construct one variable capable of storing all 50 values.

Obviously, the second alternative is better, as it would be much easier to handle one variable than handling 50 variables. Such a variable capable of storing multiple values is called an array.

An array is a collection of similar elements—all **int**s, or all **float**s, or all **char**s, etc. Usually, the array of characters is called a 'string', whereas an array of **int**s or **float**s is called simply an array. Remember that we cannot have an array of 10 numbers, of which 5 are **int**s and 5 are **float**s.

A Simple Program using an Array

Let us try to write a program to find average marks obtained by a class of 30 students in a test. Here is the program...

```
// First array program
package firstarrayprogramproject ;
import java.util.* ;
public class FirstArrayProgramProject
{
    public static void main ( String[ ] args )
    {
        int i, avg, sum = 0 ;
        int[ ] marks ;
        Scanner scn ;
        marks = new int[ 30 ] ;

        scn = new Scanner ( System.in ) ;

        // store data in the array
        for ( i = 0 ; i <= 29 ; i++ )
```

```
        {
            System.out.println ( "Enter marks " ) ;
            marks[ i ] = scn.nextInt( ) ;
        }

        // read data from the array
        for ( i = 0 ; i <= 29 ; i++ )
            sum = sum + marks[ i ] ;

        avg = sum / 30 ;
        System.out.println ( "Average marks = "+ avg ) ;
    }
}
```

There is a lot of new material in this program, so let us understand it part-by-part.

Array Declaration

Like other variables, an array needs to be declared. In our program, we have done this with the statement:

```
int[ ] marks ;
```

This statement tells the compiler that **marks** is a reference to an array of integers.

Once the reference to the array is declared, we need to allocate space for the array in memory. This is done using the statement,

```
marks = new int[ 30 ] ;
```

This statement allocates space for 30 integers in memory and returns the base address (starting address) of this memory chunk. This returned address is stored in the reference **marks**. The array that gets created in heap does not have any name. It is always referred to using **marks,** the reference to the array, which is stored in the stack.

Accessing Elements of an Array

Once an array is created, its individual elements can be accessed using the element's position in the array. All the array elements are counted, starting with 0. Thus, **marks[2]** is not the second element of the array, but the third. In our program, we are using the variable **i** to refer to various elements of the array. This variable can take different values and hence can refer to different elements in the array in turn. This ability to use variables to represent position of array elements makes arrays very useful.

Entering Data into an Array

Here is the section of code that places data into an array:

```
for ( i = 0 ; i <= 29 ; i++ )
{
    System.out.println ( "Enter marks " ) ;
    marks[ i ] = scn.nextInt( ) ;
}
```

First time through the loop, **i** has a value 0, so the first value read through **nextInt( )** function will be stored in **marks[0]**. This process will be repeated 30 times till the last values gets stored at **marks[29]**.

Reading Data from an Array

The balance program reads the data back out of the array and uses it to calculate the average. The **for** loop is much the same, but now the body of the loop causes each student's marks to be added to a running total stored in a variable **sum**. When all the marks have been added up, the result is divided by 30, the number of students, to get the average.

More on Arrays

Array is a very popular data type with Java programmers. This is because of the convenience with which arrays lend themselves to programming. The features which make arrays so convenient to program would be discussed below, along with the possible pitfalls in using them.

Array Initialization

In the program in the previous section, we used an array that did not have any values in it to begin with. We managed to store values in it during program execution. Let us now see how to initialize an array while declaring it. The following are a few examples that demonstrate this:

```
int[ ] ages = new int[ ] { 32, 24, 31, 25, 26 } ;
float[ ] press = { 12.3f, 34.2f, -23.4f, -11.3f } ;
int[ ] num = { 2, 4, 1, 5, 6, 3 } ;
```

If the array is initialized where it is declared, there is no need to use the **new** operator for creating an array as shown in the second and the third examples above. Also, when we initialize the arrays in this manner, we are not allowed to mention the size of the array in **[ ]**.

Note that both the following definitions are acceptable.

```
int[ ] num = { 2, 4, 1, 5, 6, 3 } ;
int num[ ] = { 2, 4, 1, 5, 6, 3 } ;
```

Array Access

In Java we can access array elements using any of the following three methods:

```
int[ ] marks = { 55, 65, 75, 56, 78, 78, 90 } ;
int i ;

// method 1
for ( i = 0 ; i <= 6 ; i++ )
    System.out.print ( marks[ i ] + "  " ) ;

// method 2
for ( i = 0 ; i <= marks.length - 1 ; i++ )
    System.out.print ( marks[ i ] + " " ) ;

// method 3
for ( int j : marks )
    System.out.print ( j + " " ) ;
```

The first method is as usual. In the second method we have obtained the number of elements in the array using its **length** property. In the third method, we don't have to worry about the number of elements in the array, as **j** takes different values present in **marks[ ]** array during each iteration through the loop.

Bounds Checking

In Java while accessing array elements if we exceed the bounds of the array an error would be reported during execution of the program. For example, if the following code snippet is executed an error would be reported as **num[6]** does not exist.

```
int [ ] num = { 2, 4, 12, 5, 45, 5 } ;
num[ 6 ] = 72 ;
```

Passing Array Elements to a Function

Like normal variables, we can also pass array elements to a function by calling the function. This is illustrated below.

```
// Demonstration of passing array elements
package passingarrayelementsproject ;
public class PassingArrayElementsProject
{
    public static void main ( String[ ] args )
    {
        int [ ] marks = { 55, 65, 75, 56, 78, 78, 90 } ;
        int i ;

        for ( i = 0 ; i <= 6 ; i++ )
            modify ( marks[ i ] ) ;

        for ( i = 0 ; i <= 6 ; i++ )
            System.out.println ( marks[ i ] ) ;
    }
    static void modify ( int  m )
    {
        m = m * 2 ;
    }
}
```

And here's the output...

```
55 65 75 56 78 78 90
```

Here, we are passing an individual array element at a time to the function **modify( )**. Since at a time only one element is being passed, this element is collected in an integer variable **m**. Even though we are doubling each element received in **m** in the **modify( )**, on returning when we print all array elements we find that they have not been doubled at all. This is because we passed each array element by value.

Passing Array Reference to a Function

If we want the modifications that we make in the **modify( )** function to be reflected back in **main( )**, then we need to pass the reference to the array, instead of passing each individual element. This is shown in the following program:

```
// Passing array reference
package passarrayreferenceproject ;
public class PassArrayReferenceProject
{
    public static void main ( String[ ] args )
    {
        int[ ] marks = { 55, 65, 75, 56, 78, 78, 90 } ;
        int i ;

        modify ( marks ) ;

        for ( i = 0 ; i <= marks.length - 1 ; i++ )
            System.out.print ( marks[ i ] + " " ) ;
    }
    static void modify ( int[ ] m )
    {
        int i ;
        for ( i = 0 ; i <= m.length - 1 ; i++ )
            m[ i ] = m[ i ] * 2 ;
    }
}
```

The output of the program would be as under:

```
110 130 150 112 156 156 180
```

The array reference passed to **modify( )** is collected in another array reference **m**. **m** is a reference to the same array, as it contains the same address that is present in **marks**. Using this reference when we modify the array elements we are changing the array that we defined in **main( )**. So once control returns to **main( )**, using **marks** when we print this array we find that the array elements stand doubled.

Returning an Array

The way we can pass an array to a function, can we return an array from a function? Certainly. Even here what we would be returning would only be a reference to the array. The following program shows how this can be done:

```
// Returnin an array from a function
package returningarrayproject ;
public class ReturningArrayProject
```

```
{
    public static void main ( String[ ] args )
    {
        int[ ] p ;
        p = func( ) ;
        for ( int i = 0 ; i <= p.length - 1 ; i++ )
            System.out.println ( p[ i ] + " " ) ;
    }
    static int[ ] func( )
    {
        int [ ] arr = { 10, 20, 30, 40, 50 } ;
        return arr ;
    }
}
```

Here the reference to the array **arr** is returned from **func( )** and collected in reference **p** in **main( )**. Using this reference when we iterate through the array in the **for** loop, we can access all the elements of **arr**.

Common Array Operations

There are certain operations that are very commonly carried out on arrays. For example, rearranging array elements in ascending or descending order, or searching for an element in an array, etc. To carry out these operations the Java Library provides a class called **Arrays**. The following program shows how to perform these operations using the **Arrays** class:

```
// Performing different array operations
package morearrayoperationsproject ;
import java.util.* ;
public class MoreArrayOperationsProject
{
    public static void main ( String[ ] args )
    {
        int [ ] arr = { 23, 45, 11, 54, 89, 32 } ;
        int i ;

        System.out.println ( "Original array" ) ;
        for ( i = 0 ; i < arr.length ; i++ )
            System.out.print ( arr[ i ] + " " ) ;
```

```
        Arrays.sort ( arr ) ;
        System.out.println ( "\nSorted array" ) ;
        for ( i = 0 ; i < arr.length ; i++ )
            System.out.print ( arr[ i ] + " " ) ;

        int index = Arrays.binarySearch ( arr, 54 ) ;
        System.out.println ( "\nElement 54 found at "+ index ) ;

        int[ ] newarr = new int[ 6 ] ;
        newarr = Arrays.copyOf ( arr, arr.length ) ;
        System.out.println ( "New array contents" ) ;
        for ( i = 0 ; i < newarr.length ; i++ )
            System.out.print ( newarr[ i ] + " " ) ;

        Arrays.fill ( arr, 0 ) ;
        System.out.println ( "\nCleared array" ) ;
        for ( i = 0; i < arr.length; i++ )
            System.out.print ( arr[ i ] + " " ) ;
        System.out.println( );
    }
}
```

Given below is the output of the program...

```
Original array
23 45 11 54 89 32
Sorted array
11 23 32 45 54 89
Element 54 found at 4
New array contents
11 23 32 45 54 89
Cleared array
0 0 0 0 0 0
```

The **sort( )** function arranges the elements of the array in ascending order, whereas, the **binarySearch( )** function searches for an element in the sorted array and reports its position in the array. The **copyOf( )** function copies the contents of one array into another, whereas **fill( )** function sets each array elements value to 0. You can watch these effects in the output of the program. All these functions are **static** functions, hence the syntax used to call them is

classname.functioname( ). You can try your hand at other functions present in the **Arrays** class to get a hang of them.

You can also rely on context-sensitive help to get to know methods of the **Arrays** class. That is, as you type the word array and a '.' NetBeans pops up a list of methods available in this class. This list acts as a quick reference.

Array of Objects

So far, we have constructed an array of pre-defined types like integers or floats. It is also possible to create an array of user-defined types as well. For example, we can create an array of 3 **Sample** objects as shown below.

```
// Creating and handling an array of objects
package arrayofobjectsproject ;
class Sample
{
	private int i ;
	private float a ;
	public Sample ( int ii, float aa )
	{
		i = ii ;
		a = aa ;
	}
	public void display( )
	{
		System.out.println ( "i = " + i + " a = "+ a ) ;
	}
}
public class ArrayOfObjectsProject
{
	public static void main ( String[ ] args )
	{
		Sample[ ] arr = new Sample[ 3 ] ;
		arr[ 0 ] = new Sample ( 10, 3.14f ) ;
		arr[ 1 ] = new Sample ( 20, 6.28f ) ;
		arr[ 2 ] = new Sample ( 30, 3.55f ) ;
		for ( Sample s : arr )
			s.display( ) ;
	}
}
```

The output of the program would be as follows:

```
i = 10 a = 3.14
i = 20 a = 6.28
i = 30 a = 3.55
```

As objects get created in a heap, strictly speaking the array is not an array of objects, but an array of references to objects. This is shown in Figure 11.1.

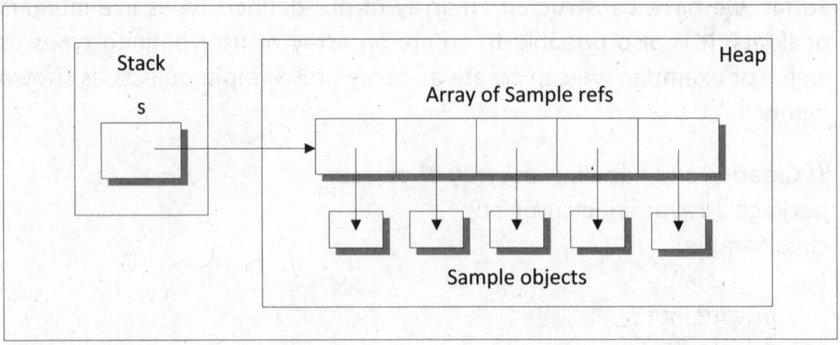

Figure 11.1

Once the array is created we can iterate through it using the **for** loop, calling **display( )** function for each object in turn. This is justified by the output of the program.

There is a more compact way in which we could have initialized the array of objects. This is shown below.

```
Sample[ ] arr = {
                        new Sample ( 10, 3.14f ),
                        new Sample ( 20, 6.28f ),
                        new Sample ( 30, 3.55f )
                    } ;
```

Multi-Dimensional Arrays

So far, we have explored arrays with only one dimension. It is also possible for arrays to have two or more dimensions. The two-dimensional array is also called a matrix. Here is a simple program that stores numbers in a matrix and then reports the biggest number and its position in the matrix.

```
// Working with 2D arrays
```

```
package twodarrayproject ;
public class Main
{
    public static void main ( String[ ] args )
    {
        int[ ][ ] a = { { 7, 2, 6, 1 }, { 3, 5, 4, 8 }, { 6, 2, 9, 50 } } ;
        int i, j, big ;
        int r, c ;

        big = a[ 0 ][ 0 ] ;
        r = 0 ;
        c = 0 ;
        for ( i = 0 ; i < a.length ; i++ )
        {
            for ( j = 0 ; j < a[ i ].length ; j++ )
            {
                if ( a[ i ][ j ] > big )
                {
                    big = a[ i ][ j ] ;
                    r = i ;
                    c = j ;
                }
            }
        }
        System.out.println ( "Biggest number = "+ big ) ;
        System.out.println ( "Row = " + r + " Col = "+ c ) ;
    }
}
```

There are two parts to the program—in the first part, we define and initialize a 2-D array of 3 rows and 4 columns of integers, whereas, in the second part through a set of **for** loops, we find out the value of the biggest number in the 2-D array.

In **a[i][j]** the first subscript of the variable **a**, is row number. The second subscript tells which of the four columns we are talking about. Remember the counting of rows and columns begin with zero. Thus, 7 is stored in **a[0][0]**, 8 is stored in **a[1][3]** and so on.

Instead of initializing the 2-D array in-place we can also receive its values from the keyboard as shown below.

```
int [ ][ ] a = new int[ 3 ][ 4 ] ;
```

```
Scanner scr = new Scanner ( System.in ) ;
for ( int i = 0; i < a.length ; i++ )
{
    for ( int j = 0 ; j < a[ i ].length ; j++ )
        a[ i ][ j ] = scn.nextInt( ) ;
}
```

On similar lines we can construct a 3-D array as a collection of several 2-D arrays.

Passing and Returning 2-D Array

We can pass a 2-D array to a function by passing its reference. Similarly, we can return a 2-D array from a function by returning its reference. This is illustrated in the following program:

```
// Passing and returning 2D array
package passingandreturning2darraysproject ;
public class PassingAndReturning2dArraysProject
{
    public static void main ( String[ ] args )
    {
        int[ ][ ] a = { { 1, 2, 3 }, { 4, 5, 6 } } ;
        int sum ;

        sum = getSum ( a ) ;
        System.out.println ( "Sum = "+ sum ) ;
        int[ ][ ] d ;
        d = getArray( ) ;
        int i, j, prod = 0 ;
        for ( i = 0 ; i < d.length ; i++ )
        {
            for ( j = 0 ; j < d[ i ].length ; j++ )
                prod = prod + d[ i ][ j ] ;
        }
        System.out.println ( "Product = "+ prod ) ;
    }
    public static int getSum ( int[ ][ ] b )
    {
        int i, j ;
        int s = 0 ;
        for ( i = 0 ; i < b.length ; i++ )
        {
```

```
            for ( j = 0 ; j < b[ i ].length; j++ )
                s = s + b[ i ][ j ] ;
        }
        return ( s ) ;
    }
    public static int[ ][ ] getArray( )
    {
        int[ ][ ] c = { { 1, 2, 3 }, { 4, 5, 6 }, { 7, 8, 9 } } ;
        return c ;
    }
}
```

And here is the output...

```
Sum = 21
Product = 45
```

Here in **main( )** we have defined a 2-D array and then passed it to the function **getSum( )**. The **getSum( )** function collects the reference to the 2-D array passed to it in **b**. Using this reference, it then accesses all the array elements and adds them up. This sum is then returned to **main( )** which promptly prints it.

Next, **main( )** calls the function **getArray( )**. This function defines another 2-D array **c**, and returns its reference to **main( )**. When control returns from **getArray( )** even though the reference **c** dies, since the reference **d** points to the 2-D array, the array doesn't get collected by the Garbage Collector. Once in **main( )** it iterates through the 2-D array, this time calculating the product of all its elements. This product is then printed out.

From this program it is evident that whenever we must pass or return an array, all that we have to do is pass or return a reference to the array.

Jagged Arrays

It is not necessary that each row of a 2-D array always have the same number of columns. For example, the arrangement of seats in an auditorium is like a 2-D array, but the number of seats in each row may not be equal. If we are to represent these seats in a 2-D array in Java we have to use jagged arrays. A jagged array permits an unequal number of elements in each row of a 2-D array.

Let us now construct a 2-D jagged array containing 3 rows. The number of elements in these three rows is 4, 3 and 2, respectively. So, the arrangement of this jagged array would be as shown in Figure 11.2.

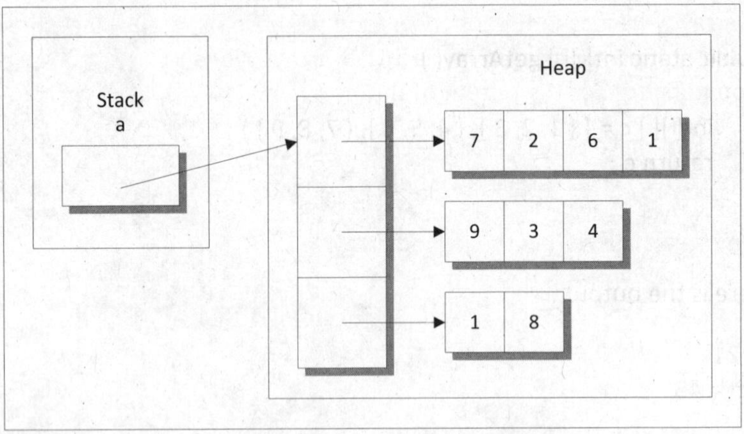

Figure 11.2

Here is a program that implements this jagged array.

```
// Implementation of a 2-D Jagged array
package twodjaggedarrayproject ;
public class Main
{
    public static void main ( String[ ] args )
    {
        int[ ][ ] a = new int[ 3 ][ ] ;
        a[ 0 ] = new int[ 4 ] ;
        a[ 1 ] = new int[ 3 ] ;
        a[ 2 ] = new int[ 2 ] ;
        a[ 0 ][ 0 ] = 7 ; a[ 0 ][ 1 ] = 2 ; a[ 0 ][ 2 ] = 6 ; a[ 0 ][ 3 ] = 1 ;
        a[ 1 ][ 0 ] = 9 ; a[ 1 ][ 1 ] = 3 ; a[ 1 ][ 2 ] = 4 ;
        a[ 2 ][ 0 ] = 1 ; a[ 2 ][ 1 ] = 8 ;
        for ( int i = 0 ; i < a.length ; i++ )
        {
            for ( int j = 0 ; j < a[ i ].length ; j++ )
                System.out.print ( a[ i ][ j ] + ", " ) ;

            System.out.println( ) ;
        }
    }
}
```

In this program **a** is a reference that refers to an array of references. Each reference in this array refers to a 1-D array of integers. Note how we have iterated through the jagged array. In the outer **for** loop we have used **a.length** to obtain number of 1-D integer arrays present in the jagged array, whereas in the inner for loop we have used **a[i].length** to obtain the number of integers in each 1-D array. We would like to leave it for you to figure out the output of this program.

There are two more ways in which we could have defined and initialized the jagged array. These are shown below.

```
// one more way to define the jagged array
int[ ][ ] a = { new int[ 4 ], new int[ 3 ], new int[ 2 ] } ;
a[ 0 ][ 0 ] = 7 ; a[ 0 ][ 1 ] = 2 ; a[ 0 ][ 2 ] = 6 ; a[ 0 ][ 3 ] = 1 ;
a[ 1 ][ 0 ] = 9 ; a[ 1 ][ 1 ] = 3 ; a[ 1 ][ 2 ] = 4 ;
a[ 2 ][ 0 ] = 1 ; a[ 2 ][ 1 ] = 8 ;
```

```
// yet another way to define the jagged array
int[ ] a1 = new int[ ] { 7, 2, 6, 1 } ;
int[ ] a2 = new int[ ] { 9, 3, 4 } ;
int[ ] a3 = new int[ ] { 1, 8 } ;
int[ ][ ] a = { a1, a2, a3 } ;
```

The way we can pass a normal 2-D array to a function, we can also pass or return a jagged 2-D array to/from a function.

Resizing Arrays

As we know, arrays are created on the heap dynamically during execution of the program. As a result, we can do two things with an array:

(a) We can decide the number of elements in the array at run-time and do not have to make any commitment about it while writing the program.

(b) Once the array is created, we can increase or decrease its size during execution.

Let us now see how this can be done programmatically.

```
// Flexible arrays and resizing of arrays
package resizingarrayproject ;
import java.util.* ;
```

```
public class ResizingArrayProject
{
    public static void main ( String[ ] args )
    {
        int[ ] arr, newarr ;
        int i, num, newnum ;
        Scanner scn ;

        scn = new Scanner ( System.in ) ;
        System.out.println ( "Enter number of students" ) ;
        num = scn.nextInt( ) ;
        arr = new int[ num ] ;

        System.out.println ( "Enter marks for "+ num + " students" ) ;
        for ( i = 0 ; i < arr.length ; i++ )
            arr[ i ] = scn.nextInt( ) ;

        System.out.println ( "Enter additional number of students" ) ;
        newnum = scn.nextInt( ) ;
        newarr = new int[ num + newnum ] ;

        // copy existing students marks to the new array
        for ( i = 0 ; i < arr.length ; i++ )
            newarr[ i ] = arr[ i ] ;

        System.out.println ( "Enter marks for "+ newnum +
                             " new students" ) ;
        for ( i = arr.length ; i < newarr.length ; i++ )
            newarr[ i ] = scn.nextInt( ) ;

        System.out.println ( "The new array now contains" ) ;
        for ( i = 0 ; i < newarr.length ; i++ )
            System.out.print ( newarr[ i ] + " " ) ;
    }
}
```

Shown below is some sample interaction with the program.

```
Enter number of students
5
Enter marks for 5 students
55
```

43
65
78
66
Enter additional number of students
3
Enter marks for 3 new students
70
80
90
The new array now contains
55 43 65 78 66 70 80 90

Look at the way **arr** and **newarr** are defined in one statement:

```
int[ ] arr, newarr ;
```

The **int[ ]** applies to **arr** as well as **newarr**. Both are treated as references to an integer array.

Both these arrays are flexible in the sense that their size is decided by the user of this program during execution. The arrays are created based on the values of **num** and **newnum** supplied by the user during execution.

To increase the size of the array we have created a new array (**newarr**), copied elements of existing array (**arr**) into it and then filled additional values into it after the copied elements.

Once this is done, if we so desire, we can delete the old array by settings its reference to null. If we do so, the Garbage Collector would reclaim the array.

The way this program lets you increase the size of an existing array during execution; if the need arises, we can also shrink the size of an existing array during execution.

Exercises

[A] Answer the following questions:

(a) Which of the following array declarations is correct?

int a (25) ;

```
int size = 10, b[ size ] ;
int[ ] c = { 0, 1, 2 } ;
```

(b) What will happen if you assign a value to an element of an array whose subscript exceeds the size of the array?

(c) When you pass an array as an argument to a function, what gets passed?

(d) How will you initialize a three-dimensional array **thread[3][2][3]**? How will you refer to the first and last element in this array?

(e) What will be the output of the following code snippet?

```
int[ ][ ] a = new int[ 2 ][ ] ;
a[ 0 ] = new int[ ] { 6, 1, 4, 3 } ;
a[ 1 ] = new int[ ] { 9, 2, 7 } ;
System.out.println ( a[ 1 ].Length ) ;
```

(f) What will be the output of the following code snippet?

```
int[ ][ ][ ] a = new int[ 3 ][ 2 ][ 3 ] ;
System.out.println ( a.length ) ;
```

(g) What does a refer to in the following statement?

```
int[ ][ ][ ] a = new int[ 2 ][ ][ ] ;
```

(h) How will you obtain the number of elements present in the array given below?

```
int[ ] a = { 25, 30, 45, 15, 60 } ;
```

(i) How will you define and initialize an array of 5 integers? How will you increase its size to 10 elements?

(j) Which of the following statements are correct about the Java code snippet given below?

```
int[ ][ ] a = new int[ 2 ][ ] ;
a[ 0 ] = new int[ ] { 6, 1, 4, 3 } ;
a[ 1 ] = new int[ ] { 9, 2, 7 } ;
```

1. **a** is a reference to a 2-D jagged array.
2. **a[0]** refers to 0th 1-D array and a[1] refers to the 1st 1-D array.
3. **a** refers to a[0] and a[1].
4. **a** refers to a[1] and a[2].

(k) How many ways are there to iterate through elements in a 1-D array? What are their pros and cons?

(l) What is the advantage of using 2-D jagged array over 2-D rectangular array?

(m) Is it true that rectangular arrays do not have access to the methods of **Arrays** Class?

[B] Attempt the following:

(a) Twenty-five numbers are entered from the keyboard into an array. The number to be searched is entered through the keyboard by the user. Write a program to find if the number to be searched is present in the array and if it is present, display the number of times it appears in the array.

(b) Twenty-five numbers are entered from the keyboard into an array. Write a program to find out how many of them are positive, how many are negative, how many are even and how many are odd.

(c) Write a program that interchanges the odd and even elements of an array.

(d) Write a program to copy the contents of one array into another in the reverse order.

(e) Write a program to obtain transpose of a 4 x 4 matrix. The transpose of a matrix is obtained by exchanging the elements of each row with the elements of the corresponding column.

(f) The **X** and **Y** coordinates of 10 different points are entered through the keyboard. Write a program to find the distance of the last point from the first point (sum of distances between consecutive points).

(g) Create a jagged array of integers. This array should consist of two 2-D arrays. The first 2-D array should contain 3 rows having length of 4, 3 and 2, respectively. Second 2-D array should contain 2 rows with length 3 and 4, respectively. Initialize array with suitable elements and display them without using **for** loops.

KanNotes

- Array is a variable capable of holding > 1 value at a time
- Two basic properties of an array :
  1) Similarity - All array elements are similar to one another
  2) Adjacency - All array elements are stored in adjacent memory locations
- 3 ways to declare an array if array elements are not known beforehand :

```
int per[ ] = new int[ 10 ] ;
int per[ ] ; per = new int[ 10 ] ;
int [ ] per ; per = new int[ 10 ] ;
```

- If all array elements are known before-hand array can be defined as

```
int a[ ] = { 7, 6, 11, -2, 26 } ; // Cannot mention the size in this case
```

- Array elements are always counted from 0 onwards. So arr[9] is 10th element
- Array elements can be calculated as in arr[5] = 3 + 7 % 2 ;
- Arithmetic on array elements is allowed as in arr[6] = arr[1] + arr[3] / 16 ;
- Java performs bounds checking on an array and warns if we exceed the bounds
- Three ways to process an array element by element :

```
int a[ ] = { 7, 9, 16, -2, 8 } ; int i ;
for ( i = 0 ; i <= 4 ; i++ )
    System.out.println ( a[ i ] ) ;

for ( i = 0 ; i < a.length ; i++ )  // length is property of an array
    System.out.println ( a[ i ] ) ;

for ( int item : a )  // special for loop for processing an array
    System.out.println ( item ) ;
```

- Array is implemented as an object; hence it is nameless. It is created on the heap and its reference is set in the stack. The reference contains the base address of the array object.
- It is possible to increase or decrease the array size during execution
- It is possible to free the array during execution for the garbage collector to collect it
- Passing an array to a function and returning an array from a function is similar as in both cases we are passing a reference or returning a reference

```
public static void int [] display ( int [] p ) // p - array reference
{
    int a[] = { 1, 4, 6, 2, 8 } ;
    return a ; // returns an array reference
}
```

- 2D array is a collection of several 1D arrays

  int a[ ][ ] = { { 2, 3, 11, 4 }, { 4, 7, 8, 9 }, { 33, 2, 1, 1 } } ;

  Cannot mention dimensions as array is being initialized in place
  { } for each 1D array are compulsory
  , after each 1D array is compulsory
  a is a reference, it would be created on stack
  a would refer to an array of references (on heap). Each reference in this array would refer to a 1D array of integers
- a.length will give 3 as there are 3 1D arrays in the 2D array
- a[2].length will give 4 as there are 4 elements in the 2nd 1D array
- Passing and returning a 2D array is similar to passing and returning a 1D array

CHAPTER 12

Strings and Enums

Strictly Speaking, we can create Java programs without Strings and Enums. But, once you see the elegance that they add to your work, you would never give them up...

Contents

- What are Strings?
- More about Strings
- Splitting Strings
- *StringBuilder* Class
- Array of Strings
- Sorting Strings
- Enumerations
- Use of Enumerated Data Type
- Enum as A Class
- Exercises
- KanNotes

In the last chapter, you learnt how to define arrays of various sizes and dimensions, how to initialize them, how to pass them to a function, etc. With this knowledge under your belt, you should be ready to handle strings, which are, simply put, a special kind of array. And strings and the ways to manipulate them are going to be the topics of discussion in this chapter.

What are Strings?

The way a group of integers can be stored in an integer array, similarly a group of characters can be stored in a character array. Character arrays can be used to manipulate text, such as words and sentences. The nature of operations that can be carried out on a collection of characters is slightly different than the operations that can be carried out on a collection of numbers. For example, characters in an array can be converted to upper case or lower case. There is no such parallel operation on a numeric array. So common is the usage of character arrays, that to deal with them, Java library provides a special class called **String**. Java makes further relaxation while creating objects of this class—even though it is a reference type, we don't have to use the **new** operator to create it. We can create it like an **int** or a **float**. This is shown below.

```
String s1 = "Lionel" ;
String s2 = "Messi" ;
```

Here **s1** and **s2** are references to two **String** objects. We can display these strings simply by saying:

```
System.out.println ( s1 ) ;
System.out.println ( s2 ) ;
```

The **String** class has an overloaded + operator using which we can append one string at the end of another. This is shown below.

```
String s1 = "Lionel" ;
String s2 = "Messi" ;
s1 = s1 + s2 ;
System.out.println ( s1 ) ;
```

This would produce the output LionelMessi. This code snippet makes it appear as if the string **s2** simply got attached at the end of **s1**, thereby changing **s1**. However, something different happened internally. This is because strings in Java are immutable. So, when we attempted to do the append operation, a new string object containing "LionelMessi" got created and **s1** was made to refer to this new string object instead of the old string object "Lionel".

Look at the following code:

```
String s1 = "Hoopster" ;
String s2 = "Hoopster";
if ( s1 == s2 )
    System.out.println ( "Equal" ) ;
else
    System.out.println ( "Unequal" ) ;
```

Here, when we create the second string, a new string object is not created. Instead **s2** is made to refer to the same string "Hoopster" to which **s1** is referring. Thus, **s1** and **s2** both are referring to the same string. Therefore, the condition in **if** is satisfied. As opposed to this, in the following code **s3** and **s4** are referring to two different string objects, so the condition in **if** fails.

```
String s3 = new String ( "Hoopster" ) ;
String s4 = new String ( "Shuttler" ) ;
if ( s3 == s4 )
    System.out.println ( "Equal" ) ;
else
    System.out.println ( "Unequal" ) ;
```

In this case to check whether the contents of the two **String** objects are same we should use the following code:

```
if ( s3.equals ( s4 ) )
    System.out.println ( "Equal" ) ;
else
    System.out.println ( "Unequal" ) ;
```

More about Strings

Let us now try different operations on strings. For this we will take help of several methods defined in the **String** class. It is not possible to discuss every of these methods. Instead, we would show how to use the more commonly needed methods with the help of a program. Here is the program...

```
// Different string operations
package usingstringsproject ;
public class Main
{
    public static void main ( String[ ] args )
    {
        String s1 = "kicit" ;
        String s2 = "Nagpur" ;
        System.out.println ( "Char at 3rd pos: " + s1.charAt ( 2 ) ) ;

        String s3 ;
        s3 = s1.concat ( s2 ) ;
        System.out.println ( s3 ) ;
        System.out.println ( "Length of s3: " + s3.length( ) ) ;

        s3 = s3.replace ( "p", "P" ) ;
        System.out.println ( s3 ) ;

        s3 = String.copyValueOf ( s2.toCharArray( ) ) ;
        System.out.println ( s3 ) ;

        int c ;
        c = s2.compareTo ( s3 ) ;
        if ( c < 0 )
            System.out.println ( "s2 is less than s3" ) ;
        else if ( c == 0 )
            System.out.println ( "s2 is equal to s3" ) ;
        else
            System.out.println ( "s2 is greater than s3" ) ;

        if ( s1 == s3 )
            System.out.println ( "s1 is equal to s3" ) ;
        else
            System.out.println ( "s1 is not equal to s3" ) ;

        s3 = s1.toUpperCase( ) ;
        System.out.println ( s3 ) ;

        s3 = s2.concat ( "Mumbai" ) ;
        System.out.println ( s3 ) ;
```

```
        s3 = s2.replace ( s2.charAt ( 0 ), ' ' ) ;
        System.out.println ( s3 ) ;

        int fin, lin ;
        fin = s1.indexOf ( "i" ) ;
        System.out.println ( "First index of i in s1: " + fin ) ;
        lin = s1.lastIndexOf ( "i" ) ;
        System.out.println ( "Last index of i in s1: " + lin ) ;

        String s ;
        s = s1.substring ( fin, lin + 1 ) ;
        System.out.println ( "Substring: " + s ) ;

        int i = 10 ;
        float f = 9.8f ;
        s3 = String.format ( "Value of i = %d Value of f = %f" , i, f ) ;
        System.out.println ( s3 ) ;
    }
}
```

The output of the program is shown below:

```
Char at 3rd pos: c
kicitNagpur
Length of s3: 11
kicitNagPur
Nagpur
s2 is equal to s3
s1 is not equal to s3
KICIT
NagpurMumbai
 agpur
First index of i in s1: 1
Last index of i in s1: 3
Substring: ici
Value of i = 10 Value of f : 9.8
```

Let us now understand the operations that we have performed on strings in this program. To begin with, we have created two **String** variables **s1** and **s2** and initialized them to "kicit" and "Nagpur" respectively. To access individual characters of a **String,** we have to use the method **charAt( )**. Thus **s1.charAt (2)** fetches the character 'c' in the string **s1**. Unlike an array, we cannot access the 3rd character using **s1[2]**.

The **concat( )** method concatenates two strings, stores it in a new string object and returns its reference, which is stored in **s3**. Thus, the object referred to by **s3** would contain "kicitNagpur". The **length( )** method of a **String** class returns the number of characters in a string. The length of **s3** in our program is 11. The **replace( )** method replaces all the instances of a character (mentioned as the first parameter) with the character given as the second parameter. Here we have replaced 'p' with a 'P' in string referred to by **s3**. The **copyValueOf( )** method is a **static** method that returns a **String** that represents the character sequence in the character array passed to it.

The **compareTo( )** method compares two strings alphabetically. This means a string with a starting alphabet 'a' will always be lesser than a string with a starting alphabet as 'b'. This method returns a negative integer if the **String** object that has called the **compareTo( )** method contains a string which is lesser than the string contained in the object whose reference is passed as the method's parameter. It returns a positive number if the string objects are interchanged. It returns zero when both strings are equal.

In the same way the == operator compares two strings and returns a **bool**—**true** if the strings are equal and **false** if they are not. To carry out string comparison in a case insensitive manner there is another method called **compareToIgnoreCase( )**.

The **toUpperCase( )** method creates a new object, stores in it the converted upper case string and returns the address of this object. This address is collected in **s3**. Note that **s1** is not affected here. Hence, we can draw a conclusion that the object which we use to call the methods to manipulate the string, does not affect the object.

The **indexOf( )** method returns the index of first occurrence of a given character in the **string**. Similarly, **lastIndexOf( )** method returns the index of last occurrence of a given character in the **string.** In our program the first index of 'i' happens to be 1 whereas the last index is 3.

The **substring( )** method returns a new string which starts at an index passed as the first parameter and ends at an index passed as the second parameter to the method.

The **format( )** method is a **static** method which builds a new string object using strings and numbers. Here we have collected the address of the newly created string object in **s3**.

If we want, we can combine calls to **String** class functions as shown below.

```
String s1 = "Hello" ;
s1 = s1.toUpperCase( ).substring ( 2, 5 ) ;
System.out.println ( s1 ) ;
```

Here firstly, Hello is converted to HELLO using **toUpperCase( )** and from this string LLO is extracted using **substring( )**.

Function **isEmpty( )** is very commonly used when validating user input in many Java applications. This function allows us to check in one shot if the string is empty, i.e., its length is 0. In the absence of this function, we would have been required to write an equivalent **if** as shown below:

```
if ( s == "" )
```

Function **contains( )** returns true if input string is present anywhere in the current string object. It enables us to search for substrings within a large string efficiently.

Splitting Strings

While processing strings in Java applications, it is required to split a string into parts based on certain *separator*, thereby getting an array of strings. The following program illustrates how this splitting of strings can be done:

```
// Split string operations
package splitandjoinproject ;
import java.io.* ;
public class SplitAndJoinProject
{
    public static void main ( String[ ] args ) throws Exception
    {
        File f =new File ( "." ) ;
        String d = f.getCanonicalPath() ;
        String[ ] parts = d.split ( "\\\\" ) ;
        System.out.println ( "Complete path: " + d ) ;
        System.out.println ( "Dir name: " +  parts [ parts.length - 1 ] ) ;
```

```
    }
}
```

And here is the output for this program...

```
Complete path: D:\Books\J_LUJ\Programs\SplitAndJoinProject
Dir name: SplitAndJoinProject
```

In this program, firstly we have obtained the complete path of the current directory (represented by .) by calling the method **getCanonicalPath( )** of the **File** class.

Then we have used the **split( )** method to separate different elements of this path based on separator '\'. The last part of the array of string thus obtained gives us the directory from which program is being executed.

StringBuilder Class

As we noted in the previous section, when a string is manipulated, it is not changed in-place. Instead, a new object containing the manipulated string is created and the reference which was pointing to the earlier string is now made to point to this new manipulated string.

Instead of this, if we want the same string to get manipulated in-place, then Java library provides a **StringBuilder** class for this. When we create a string using this class, we can modify it by appending, removing, replacing, or inserting characters. For carrying out these operations it has methods like **append( )**, **delete( )**, **replace( )** and **insert( )**.

Based on what operations that we wish to perform on the string created using **StringBuilder**, we can set the maximum number of characters that the object can store. This can be done by using the **EnsureCapacity( )** method.

Array of Strings

Very often we are required to deal with a set of strings rather than only one string. In such cases we should create an array of strings. The following program shows how to declare and process such an array. In this program we have stored names of persons in a string array called **masterList**. The program asks you to type your name. When you do so, it checks your name against the names in **masterList** to see if you are worthy of entry to the palace. Here's the program...

```
// Using array of strings
```

```
package arrayofstringsproject ;
import java.util.* ;
public class ArrayOfStringsProject
{
    public static void main ( String[ ] args )
    {
        String[ ] masterList = new String [ ] {
                                                "Akshay", "Parag",
                                                "Raman", "Srinivas",
                                                "Gopal", "Rajesh"
                                              } ;

        int i, a ;
        boolean flag ;
        String yourName ;

        Scanner scn = new Scanner ( System.in ) ;
        System.out.println ( "Enter your name " ) ;
        yourName = scn.nextLine( ) ;

        flag = false ;
        for ( i = 0 ; i <= 5 ; i++ )
        {
            a = masterList[ i ].compareTo ( yourName ) ;
            if ( a == 0 )
            {
                System.out.println ( "You can enter the palace" ) ;
                flag = true ;
                break ;
            }
        }
        if ( flag == false )
            System.out.println ( "Sorry, you are a trespasser" ) ;
    }
}
```

And here is the output for two sample runs of this program...

```
Enter your name Dinesh
Sorry, you are a trespasser
Enter your name Raman
You can enter the palace
```

Notice how the array of strings **masterList** has been created. In fact, it is an array of **String** references. That is, it contains base addresses of respective names. For example, address of **String** object representing "Akshay" is stored in **masterList[0]**, base address of **String** object representing "Parag" is stored in **masterList[1]** and so on. This is depicted in Figure 12.1.

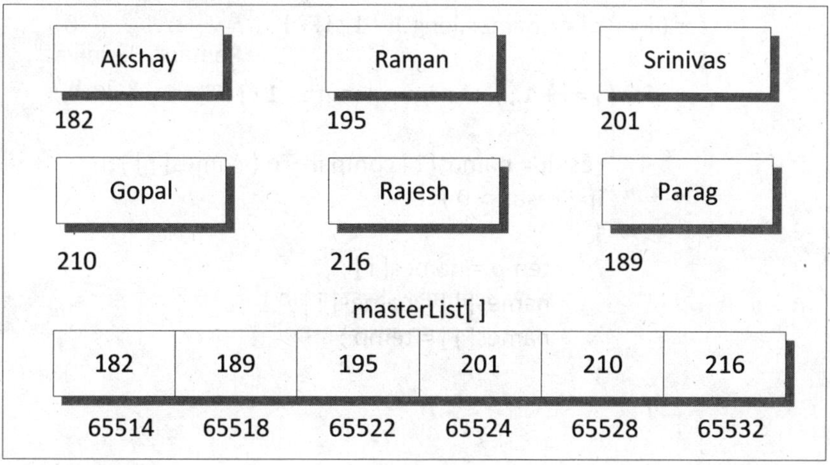

Figure 12.1

While comparing the strings using **compareTo( )**, true is returned if the strings match, otherwise false is returned. The variable **flag** is used to keep a record of whether the control reached inside the **if** or not. To begin with, we set **flag** to false. Later through the loop, if the names match, **flag** is set to true. When the control reaches beyond the **for** loop, if **flag** is still set to false, it means none of the names in the **masterList** matched with the one supplied from the keyboard.

Sorting Strings

Let us now create a program that stores names of persons in an array of strings, sorts these names in alphabetical order using the Bubble Sort logic and finally prints the sorted list of names. Here is the program...

```
// Sorting array of Strings
package sortingstringsproject ;
public class SortingStringsProject
{
    public static void main ( String[ ] args )
    {
```

```
        String[ ] names = new String[ ] {
                                        "Akshay", "Parag",
                                        "Raman", "Srinivas",
                                        "Gopal", "Rajesh"
                                    } ;
        int i, j, result ;
        String temp ;
        for ( i = 0 ; i <= names.length - 1 ; i++ )
        {
            for ( j = i + 1 ; j <= names.length - 1 ; j++ )
            {
                result = names[ i ].compareTo ( names[ j ] ) ;
                if ( result > 0 )
                {
                    temp = names[ i ] ;
                    names[ i ] = names[ j ] ;
                    names[ j ] = temp ;
                }
            }
        }
        for ( String n : names )
            System.out.println ( n ) ;
    }
}
```

To sort the strings, we have used the Selection Sort logic. To compare the alphabetical order of strings, we have used the function **compareTo( )** which returns a value greater than 0 if the two strings being compared are not in alphabetical order. In such a case we swap the positions of the two strings in the array. Once the sorting of all strings is over, we have printed the sorted list using a **for** loop.

Enumerations

The enumerated data type gives you an opportunity to invent your own data type and define what values the variable of this data type can take. This can help in making the program listings more readable, which can be an advantage when a program gets complicated or when more than one programmer would be working on it. Using enumerated data type can also help you reduce programming errors.

As an example, one could invent a data type called **MaritalStatus** which can have four possible values—Single, Married, Divorced or Widowed. Here's how **MaritalStatus** data type can be implemented.

```
enum MaritalStatus
{
    single, married, divorced, widowed
}
MaritalStatus  person1, person2 ;
```

This declaration has two parts:

(a) The first part declares the data type and specifies its possible values. These values are called 'enumerators'.

(b) The second part defines variables of this data type.

Now we can give values to these variables:

```
person1 = MaritalStatus.married ;
person2 = MaritalStatus.divorced ;
```

Internally, the compiler treats the enumerators as integers. Each value on the list of permissible values corresponds to an integer, starting with 0. Thus, in our example, single is stored as 0, married is stored as 1, divorced as 2 and widowed as 3.

Lastly, the enumerators used in an **enum** should not contain white space in its name. Thus "elgible bachelor" would be an unacceptable enumerator for the **MaritalStatus**.

Use of Enumerated Data Type

Enumerated variables are usually used to clarify the operation of a program. For example, if we need to use employee departments in a payroll program, it makes the listing easier to read if we use values like assembly, manufacturing, accounts rather than the integer values 0, 1, 2, etc. The following program illustrates the point we are trying to make:

```
// Using Enumerations
package usingenumproject ;
enum Department
{
    assembly, manufacturing, accounts, stores
}
```

```
class Employee
{
    private String name ;
    private int age ;
    private float salary ;
    private Department dept ;
    public Employee ( String n, int a, float s, Department d )
    {
        name = n ;
        age = a ;
        salary = s ;
        dept = d ;
    }
    public void displayData( )
    {
        System.out.println ( name + " "+ age + " " + salary+ " " + dept );
        if ( dept == Department.accounts )
            System.out.println ( name + " is an accountant\n" ) ;
        else
            System.out.println (name + " is not an accountant\n" ) ;
    }
}
public class UsingEnumProject
{
    public static void main ( String[ ] args )
    {
        Employee e = new Employee ( "Sandeep Shah", 28, 15575.50f,
                                    Department.manufacturing ) ;
        e.displayData( ) ;
    }
}
```

And here is the output of the program...

```
Sandeep Shah 28 15575.5 manufacturing
Sandeep Shah is not an accountant
```

Let us now dissect the program. We first defined the data type **enum Department** and specified the four possible values, namely, assembly, manufacturing, accounts, and stores. Then we declared a class **Employee** to manage employee data. It contains **name**, **age**, **salary** and **dept**. Of these, the last one is special—it is a variable of the type

Department. The constructor of the **Employee** class is invoked from **main( )**. In this call to the constructor, the value of the department in which the employee is working is passed as **Department.manufacturing**. This is much more informative to anyone reading the program than simply passing a value 1 to represent the manufacturing department. In the constructor, the enum value passed to it is assigned to **private** variable of the class through the statement,

```
dept = d ;
```

In the next part of the program, the values assigned to **Employee e** are printed by calling the function **displayData( )**. Note that even though an integer value is assigned to **Dept**, while printing it, it prints **manufacturing** and not 1. Thus, **enum** data type comes in very handy whenever we wish to use named constants in a Java program. Here are a few more **enum** declarations that would make programming quite convenient.

```
enum Days { Mon, Tue, Wed, Thu, Fri, Sat, Sun }
enum Color { Red, Green, Blue }
enum Months { January, February, March, April, May, June, July,
              August, September, October, November, December }
```

You must have noticed that in the previous program when we tried to print the department, it was printed as manufacturing though the underlying value was an integer. At times, we may want to access and print the integer value instead of the string. The following program shows how this can be done. This time however we are going to use an **enum CarTypes** instead of **Department**. Here is the program...

```
// Printing enumerators as String Value pairs
package enumstringvaluepairsproject ;
enum CarTypes
{
    suv, hatchBack, sedan, convertible
}
public class EnumStringValuePairsProject
{
    public static void main ( String[ ] args )
    {
        CarTypes car1 = CarTypes.sedan ;
```

```
        System.out.println ( "Value of car1 is " + car1 ) ;
        System.out.println ( "Value of car1 is " + car1.ordinal( ) ) ;
        System.out.println ( "Car names and their values:" ) ;
        for ( CarTypes c : CarTypes.values( ) )
            System.out.println ( c + " = " + c.ordinal( ) ) ;
    }
}
```

Given below is the output of the program:

```
Value of car1 is Sedan
Value of car1 is 2
Car names and their values:
suv = 0
hatchBack = 1
sedan = 2
convertible = 3
```

Here, to begin with we have declared an **enum** called **CarTypes** containing enumerators to represent different types of cars. Then we have created an enum variable **car1** and assigned the value **CarTypes.sedan** to it. Then we have printed the string "sedan" and the underlying value, i.e., 4 through two **println( )** calls. Note that to get the integer value we have called the **ordinal( )** method. This method returns the position of the enumeration constant in its enum declaration.

Enum as A Class

An enum is implemented as a class with specific characteristics that distinguishes it from a regular class. Given below is a list of reasons that highlights the differences between an enum and a class.

(a) A class can have fields (instance variables) to maintain state, while an enum is limited to representing fixed sets of constants.

(b) Methods in a class can perform complex operations on instance variables. Methods in an enum may perform limited operations.

(c) A class can support inheritance and polymorphism, whereas an enum cannot.

(d) A class can define custom constructors with parameters, allowing for the creation of objects with different initial states. Enums can have only private or package-private constructors, which means they cannot be called from outside the enum type or its package.

(e) Instance variables in a class can be modified after instantiation. Enum, by design, is typically immutable and represent fixed sets of constants that cannot be modified at runtime.

The following program shows how an enum can encapsulate fixed data and behavior.

```
// Encapsulating fixed data and behavior in enum
package enumsdataandbehaviourproject ;
enum Shape
{
    CIRCLE ( 0, 3 ), SQUARE( 4, 2 ), EQUILAT_TRIANGLE ( 3, 4 ) ;
    private final int numSides ;
    private final int lineThickness ;

    Shape ( int num, int thickness )
    {
        numSides = num ;
        lineThickness = thickness ;
    }
    public int getSides( )
    {
        return numSides ;
    }
    public int getThickness( )
    {
        return lineThickness ;
    }
    public double calcPeri ( double sideLength )
    {
        switch ( this )
        {
            case CIRCLE :
                return 2 * Math.PI * sideLength ;
            case SQUARE :
                return numSides * sideLength ;
            case EQUILAT_TRIANGLE :
                return numSides * sideLength ;
            default :
                return -1 ;
        }
    }
```

```
}
public class EnumsDataAndBehaviourProject
{
    public static void main ( String[ ] args )
    {
        double side = 5.0 ; // length of a side for all shapes
        for ( Shape s : Shape.values( ) )
        {
            System.out.println ( "Shape: " + s ) ;
            System.out.println ( "Number of sides: " + s.getSides( ) ) ;
            System.out.println ( "Perimeter: " + s.calcPeri ( side ) ) ;
            System.out.println ( "Line thickness: " + s.getThickness( ) ) ;
            System.out.println( ) ;
        }
    }
}
```

Note that **CIRCLE (0, 3)** invokes the private constructor with 0 as number of sides and 3 as line thickness. This means that each enum constant (CIRCLE, SQUARE, EQUILAT_TRIANGLE) has its own set of fixed values (sides and line thickness).

Exercises

[A] Answer the following questions:

(a) What will be the output of the Java code snippet given below?

```
String s1 = "Kicit" ;
System.out.println ( s1.indexOf ( 'c' ) ) ;
System.out.println ( s1.length( ) ) ;
```

(b) What will be the output of the Java code snippet given below?

```
String s1 = "Nagpur" ;
String s2 ;
s2 = s1.concat ( "Mumbai" ) ;
System.out.println ( s2 ) ;
```

(c) What will be the output of the Java code snippet given below?

```
String s1 = "Five Star" ;
String s2 = "FIVE STAR" ;
int c ;
```

```
c = s1.compareTo ( s2 ) ;
System.out.println ( c ) ;
```

(d) What will be the output of the Java code snippet given below?

```
String s1 = "ALL MEN ARE CREATED EQUAL" ;
String s2 ;
s2 = s1.substring ( 12, 3 ) ;
System.out.println ( s2 ) ;
```

(e) With reference to the following statements, how will you copy the contents of **s1** into **s2**?

```
String s1 = "String" ;
String s2 ;
```

(f) How will you find out the index of the second 's' in the string "She sells sea shells on the sea-shore"?

(g) What will be the output of the following code snippet?

```
class Employee
{
    enum MaritalStatus { MARRIED, UNMARRIED, DIVORCED } ;
    public static void main ( String args[ ] )
    {
        MaritalStatus ms = MARRIED ;
        System.out.println ( ms ) ;
    }
}
```

[B] Pick up the correct alternative for each of the following questions:

(a) Which of the following is the CORRECT way to create a String object?

(1) String s = "Hello" ;
(2) String s[ ] = "Hello" ;
(3) char s[ ] = new char [20] ; s = "Hello" ;
(4) string s = "Hello" ;

(b) Where is **str** created in the following code snippet:

```
String str = "Good Morning" ;
```

(1) Stack
(2) Heap
(3) Virtual Memeory
(4) Disk file

(c) What does str contain in the following code snippet:

String str = "Bye Bye" ;

(1) Address of nameless String object
(2) Bye Bye
(3) B
(4) Addressof B

(d) What is the name of the **String** object in the following code snippet:

String s = "Snakes and Pythons" ; String t = s ;

(1) s
(2) t
(3) Snakes and Pythons
(4) Object is nameless

(e) In the following code snippet, what does **t** contain?

String s = "Horses for courses" ; String t ;
t = s ;

(1) "Horses for courses"
(2) Address of nameless String object
(3) s
(4) H

(f) Which of the following is true about an enum value?
(1) It is always public
(2) It is always static
(3) It is always final
(4) A, B and C

[C] Attempt the following questions:

(a) Write a program that uses an array of strings **str**[ ]. Receive two strings **str1** and **str2** and check if **str1** is embedded in any of the strings in **str[ ]**. If **str1** is found, then replace it with **str2**.

```
String str[ ] = {
                    "We will teach you how to...",
                    "Move a mountain",
                    "Erase the past",
                    "Make a million",
                    "...all through Java!"
```

};

For example, if **str1** contains "mountain" and **str2** contains "car", then the second string in **str** should get changed to "Move a car".

(b) Write a program to reverse the strings stored in the following array:

```
String s[ ] = {
                "To err is human...",
                "But to really mess things up...",
                "One needs to know Java!!"
              };
```

(c) Write a program to delete all vowels from a sentence.

(d) Write a program that will read a line and delete from it all occurrences of the word 'the'.

(e) Write a program that takes a set of names of individuals and abbreviates the first, middle and other names except the last name by their first letter.

(f) Write a program to count the number of occurrences of any two vowels in succession in a line of text. For example, in the sentence

"Please read this application and give me gratuity"

Such occurrences are ea, ea, ui.

(g) Create a class called **Window** containing data members **height**, **width**, **cursortype** and **windowcolor**. Of these, the last two should be enumerations. Create two objects of **Window** type and set and print values of these objects. Make sure that the enum values are printed as strings.

KanNotes

- Strings are used to manage an array of characters
- Strings in Java are immutable
- The String class has an overloaded + to concatenate strings
- Different operations can be performed on string using functions of the String class

- charAt( ) - obtain character at specified position
- concat() - concatenate two strings
- length() - obtain length of a string
- replace() - a substring in a string with another
- compareTo - compare two strings
- toUpperCase() - convert string to uppercase
- indexOf() - obtain first index of a substring in a string
- lastIndexOf() - obtain last index of a substring in a string
- substring() - extract substring from a string

- To manipulate a string in-place use StringBuilder class
- Use methods like append( ), delete( ), replace( ) and insert() to manipulate a string represented using StringBuilder class.
- To maintain several strings, it is possible to create an array of strings
- Enumerations are user-defined types that are used to make programs more readable

CHAPTER 13

Inheritance

Inheritance is all about genes... they better be good! So true in life, quite so in programming...

Contents

- Uses of Inheritance
- Constructors in Inheritance
- The *final* Keyword
- Incremental Development
- Other Code Reuse Mechanisms
- Exercises
- KanNotes

Now that we have familiarized ourselves with classes—the building blocks of object oriented programming—let us deal with another important Java concept called **Inheritance**. Inheritance is probably the most powerful feature of object-oriented programming after classes themselves. Inheritance is the process of creating new classes, called **derived classes**, from existing classes. These existing classes are often called **base classes**. The derived class inherits all the capabilities of the base class but can add new features and refinements of its own. By adding these refinements, the base class remains unchanged.

Most important advantage of Inheritance is that it permits code reusability. Once a base class is written and debugged, it need not be touched again but at the same time it can be adapted to work in different situations. Reusing existing code saves time and effort and increases a program's reliability. Inheritance can also help in the original conceptualization of a programming problem, and in the overall design of the program.

The code reusability is of great help in the case of distributing class libraries. A programmer can use a class created by another person or company, and, without modifying it, derive other classes from it that are suited to particular programming situations. Let us now understand the concept of inheritance using a program.

Suppose we have designed a class called **Index** that serves as a counter. Suppose that the **Index** class can only increment the counter and not decrement it. To achieve this, we can insert a decrement function directly into the source code of the **Index** class. However, there are several reasons why we might not want to do this. Firstly, the **Index** class works well and has been thoroughly tested and debugged. This is an exaggeration in this case, but it would be true in a larger and more complex class. Now, if we start modifying the source code of the **Index** class, the testing process will have to be carried out again.

Sometimes, there might be another reason for not modifying the **Index** class—we might not have access to its source code, especially if it had been distributed as part of a class library.

To avoid these problems, we can use inheritance to create a new class based on **Index**, without modifying **Index** itself. Here's how this can be achieved.

```
// Demonstrating implementation and usage of Inheritance
package inheritanceusageproject ;
```

```
// base class
class Index
{
    protected int count ;

    public Index( )
    {
        count = 0 ;
    }
    public void display( )
    {
        System.out.println ( "count = " + count ) ;
    }
    public void increment( )
    {
        count += 1 ;
    }
}
// derived class
class Index1 extends Index
{
    public void decrement( )
    {
        count -= 1 ;
    }
}
public class InheritanceUsageProject
{
    public static void main ( String[ ] args )
    {
        Index1 i ;
        i = new Index1( ) ;
        i.increment( ) ;
        i.display( ) ;
        i.decrement( ) ;
        i.display( ) ;
    }
}
```

The first line of the **Index1** class,

```
class Index1 extends Index
```

specifies that the class **Index1** has been derived from the base class **Index**. By doing this, **Index1** inherits all the features of the base class **Index**. **Index1** doesn't need a constructor or the **increment( )** function, since they are already present in the base class. Figure 13.1 shows the relationship between the base class and the derived class. Note that the arrow in Figure 13.1 means "derived from". The direction of the arrow says that the derived class can refer to the functions and data in the base class, while the base class has no access to the derived class data or functions.

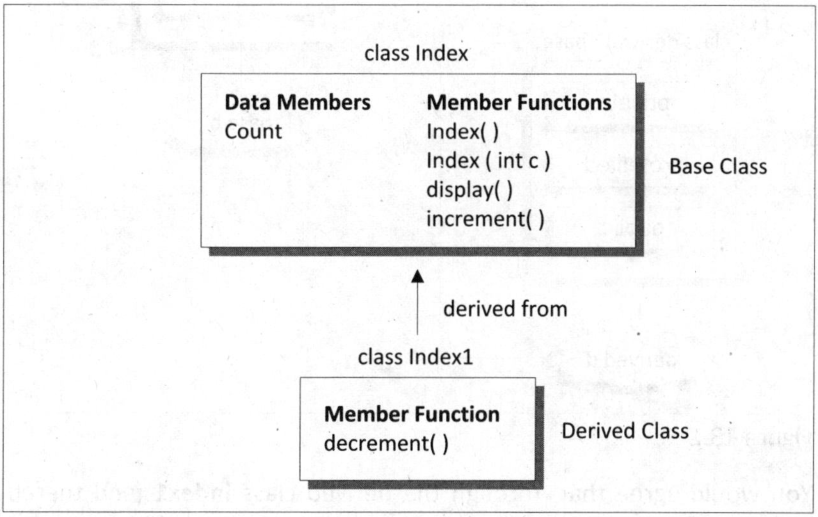

Figure 13.1

Since we have not declared any constructor in **Index1**, the compiler would insert an empty zero-argument constructor in it. When we create an object **i**, the constructor in the base class gets called followed by the empty zero-argument constructor in the derived class. When we call the function **increment( )** it is searched in the derived class. Since the derived class doesn't contain such a function, **increment( )** from base class is used to increment **count**.

Note that **count** has been marked as **protected**. Had it been **private** it would not have been available outside the **Index** class. By marking it as **protected**, it is now available in the **Index** class as well as in the inheritance chain, i.e. in functions of **Index1** class.

We don't want to make **count** as **public**, as that would allow it to be accessed from outside the class, and thereby eliminate the advantages of data hiding. Figure 13.2 clearly indicates who can access what, in a base class–derived class relationship.

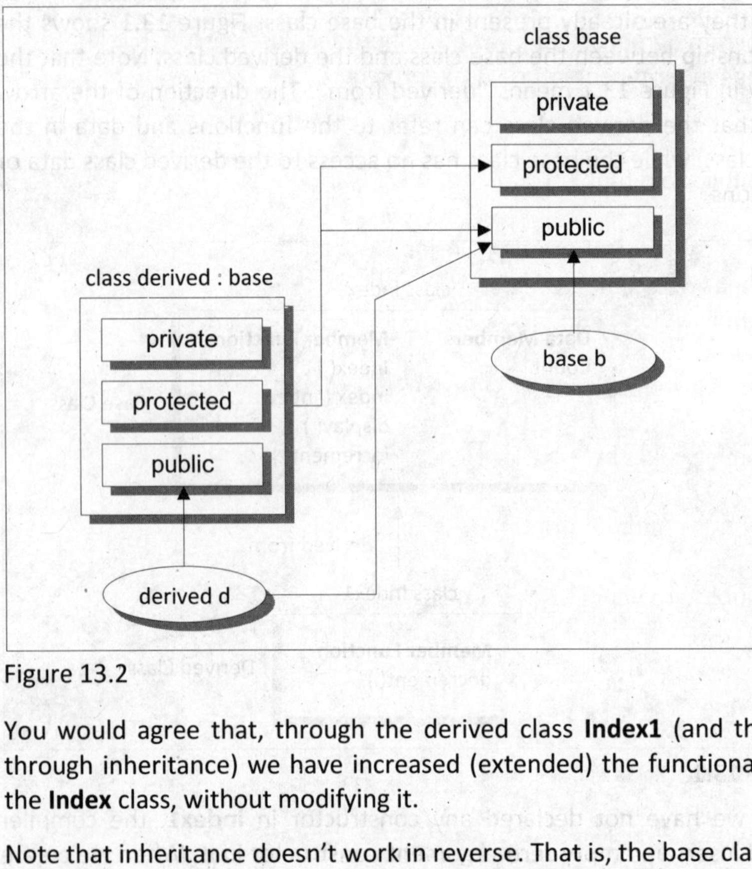

Figure 13.2

You would agree that, through the derived class **Index1** (and thereby through inheritance) we have increased (extended) the functionality of the **Index** class, without modifying it.

Note that inheritance doesn't work in reverse. That is, the base class and its objects have no knowledge about any classes derived from the base class. This means, in our program, had we built an object **j** from the class **Index**, then the **decrement( )** function would have remained inaccessible to this object.

Uses of Inheritance

Now that we have a basic idea about inheritance, let us see in which scenarios inheritance is used in Java. The four common usages of inheritance are as follows:

(a) Use existing functionality
(b) Override existing functionality
(c) Provide new functionality
(d) Combination of existing and new functionality

Let us now look at a few examples of these usage patterns. We would begin with a scenario which demonstrates usage of all the four features mentioned above. Here is the program...

```
// Program demonstrating various Inheritance usage scenarios
package inheritancefeaturesusageproject ;
class Ex
{
	public void fun( )
	{
		System.out.println ( "Inside Ex - fun( )" ) ;
	}
	public void save( )
	{
		System.out.println ( "Inside Ex - save( )" ) ;
	}
	public void enc( )
	{
		System.out.println ( "Inside Ex - enc( )" ) ;
	}
	public void open( )
	{
		System.out.println ( "Inside Ex - open( )" ) ;
	}
}
class NewEx extends Ex
{
	public void save( )
	{
		System.out.println ( "Inside NewEx - save( )" ) ;
	}
	public void enc( )
	{
		System.out.println ( "Inside NewEx - enc( )" ) ;
	}
	public void autoUpdate( )
	{
		System.out.println ( "Inside NewEx - autoUpdate( )" ) ;
	}
	public void open( )
	{
		System.out.println ( "Inside NewEx - open( )" ) ;
```

```
        super.open( ) ;
    }
}
public class InheritanceFeaturesUsageProject
{
    public static void main ( String[ ] args )
    {
        NewEx e = new NewEx( ) ;
        e.fun( ) ;
        e.save( ) ;
        e.enc( ) ;
        e.autoUpdate( ) ;
        e.open( ) ;
    }
}
```

Given below is the output of the program...

```
Inside Ex - fun( )
Inside NewEx - save( )
Inside NewEx - enc( )
Inside NewEx - autoUpdate( )
Inside NewEx - open( )
Inside Ex - open( )
```

Here we have defined two classes—**Ex** as base class and **NewEx** as derived class. The **Ex** class contains member functions **fun( )**, **save( )**, **enc( )** and **open( )**, whereas **NewEx** class contains member functions **save( )**, **enc( )**, **open( )** and **autoUpdate( )**. In **main( )** we have created an object of **NewEx** class and then called different member functions. Now look at the output of the program to appreciate the different inheritance usage scenarios.

When we called the function **fun( )** it was first searched in the **NewEx** class. Since it was not found in **NewEx**, it was then searched in the base class. In the base class it was found. As a result, the base class function got called and the message "Inside Ex – fun( )" got printed. This demonstrates that we have used one of the features of the base class, namely **fun( )**, as it is, through a derived class object.

When we called **save( )**, again the function was searched in derived class **NewEx**. Since the function was found in **NewEx**, this version of **save( )** (and not the one in **Ex** class) got called. This demonstrates that through inheritance we can override existing functionality. Same is the case with the function **enc( )**.

When we called the function **autoUpdate( )** the function was searched and found in **NewEx**. Since there was no **autoUpdate( )** function in base class this is the case where a totally new functionality is provided through inheritance.

Lastly, when we called **open( )** the function was searched and found in **NewEx**. This version of **open( )** got called and this function in turn called the base class version of **open( )** through the statement **super.open( )**. The resulting output was:

Inside NewEx - open( )
Inside Ex - open( )

This indicates the usage of inheritance to combine new functionality with old.

Note the following important points about Inheritance relationships:

(a) We can even derive a class from a class which itself has been derived from another class. Thus, multiple levels of inheritance can exist.

(b) A class cannot have multiple base classes. That is, a derived class cannot be derived from more than one class.

Constructors in Inheritance

As we know, the base class member functions can be called from derived class member function using the syntax:

```
super.functionName( ) ;
```

Here **super** is a keyword and **functionName( )** is the name of the function in the base class. Unless explicitly called, the base class function doesn't get called from the body of the derived class function. Constructors in the inheritance chain are given a different treatment. Regarding constructors in the inheritance chain, we have to keep two things in mind:

(a) When a derived class object is created, the constructor of the base class followed by constructor of derived class gets called.

(b) While constructing a derived class object, if we do not call the base class constructor then, by default, the zero-argument constructor of base class gets called.

Let us illustrate these facts with the help of a program. Here is the program...

```
// Demonstrates calls to constructors in Inheritance chain
package constructorsininheritanceproject ;
class a
{
    public a( )
    {
        System.out.println ( "a's 0-arg Ctor" ) ;
    }
    public a ( int xx )
    {
        System.out.println ( "a's 1-arg Ctor" ) ;
    }
}
class b extends a
{
    public b( )
    {
        System.out.println ( "b's 0-arg Ctor" ) ;
    }
    public b ( int x )
    {
        super ( x ) ;
        System.out.println ( "b's 1-arg Ctor" ) ;
    }
}
public class ConstructorsIninheritanceProject
{
    public static void main ( String[ ] args )
    {
        b y = new b( ) ;
        b z = new b ( 10 ) ;
    }
}
```

Given below is the output of the program...

```
a's 0-arg Ctor
b's 0-arg Ctor
a's 1-arg Ctor
b's 1-arg Ctor
```

From the output we can see that when we construct the objects **y** and **z**, firstly the constructor of base class gets called, followed by constructor of the derived class. While constructing the object **y** the zero-argument constructor of base class got called automatically. However, while constructing **z** the one-argument constructor had to be called explicitly through the syntax:

```
super ( x ) ;
```

Had we not used **super (x)**, then the zero-argument constructor of base class would have been called.

You must be wondering why it is necessary that the construction proceed from base towards derived. This can be best understood with the help of the following program:

```
// Order of construction of object in Inheritance chain
package orderofconstructionproject ;

class base1
{
    protected int i ;

    public base1( )
    {
        i = 4 ;
    }
}
class der extends base1
{
    private int j ;

    public der( )
    {
        j = i * 4 ;
    }
}
public class OrderOfConstructionProject
```

```
{
    public static void main ( String[ ] args )
    {
        der d = new der( ) ;
    }
}
```

Here **i** is marked as a **protected** member, hence it is available to functions in the derived class **der**. For a moment, assume that the order of construction is not from base towards derived. In that case, firstly the constructor of **der** would get called. And since **i** is available in constructor and the base class constructor has not been called so far, it has not been set with a value so far. As a result, **j** would not be set properly. Thus, the value in the object **d** would not be set correctly. Unlike, this if the order of construction is from base towards derived then object **d** would be set initialized properly.

The *final* Keyword

By default, we can inherit a new class from any existing class. At times, we may want that inheritance should not be permitted on a class. This can be achieved by using a **final** keyword as shown in the following program:

```
// Demonstrates prevention of Inheritance
package preventinheritanceproject ;
final class base1
{
}
class derived extends base1
{
    public void fun( )
    {
        System.out.println ( "Too much noise, too little substance" ) ;
    }
}
public class PreventInheritanceProject
{
    public static void main ( String[ ] args )
    {
        derived d = new derived( ) ;
        d.fun( ) ;
```

```
    }
}
```

This program doesn't even cross the compilation hurdle. On compilation it reports an error—cannot derive from final 'preventinheritanceproject.base1'. This so happens, because we have marked the base class as non-inheritable by using the keyword **final**.

Though method overriding is one of the most important features of Java, at times you may want to prevent it from occurring. We can prevent a method from being overridden by declaring it as **final** in the base class. The following code snippet illustrates this:

```
// Demonstrates prevention of overriding
class base1
{
    final public void fun( )
    {
        System.out.println ( "In the final method" ) ;
    }
}
class derived extends base1
{
    public void fun( )
    {
        System.out.println ( "Illegal" ) ;
    }
}
```

Incremental Development

One of the advantages of inheritance is that it supports incremental development. It allows you to introduce new code without causing bugs in existing code. By inheriting from an existing, functional class and adding data members and member functions (and redefining existing member functions) you leave the existing code—that someone else may still be using—untouched and unbugged. If a bug happens, you know it's in your new code, which is much shorter and easier to read, than if you had modified the body of existing code.

It's rather amazing how cleanly the classes are separated. You don't even need the source code for the member functions to reuse the code. Just the byte-code containing the compiled member functions would do.

It's important to realize that program development is an incremental process. Nobody ever conceived the program in its entirety at the start of the project. The program should try to create and manipulate objects of various types to express a model in the terms given to you by the problem definition. Rather than constructing the program all at once it should grow out as an organic, evolutionary creature. Of course, at some point after things stabilize you need to take a fresh look at your class hierarchy with an aim to collapse it into a sensible structure. Inheritance fits this bill to perfection.

Other Code Reuse Mechanisms

Java facilitates code reuse at 2 levels—Source code level and Byte code level. In the source code level reuse mechanism, the code cannot be reused to build new code, unless the source code is available. Source code level reuse is done in Java using Generic functions and Generic classes. Generics let us write generalized functions / classes and the compiler creates specific functions / classes from it. For creating specialized functions / classes source code must be available. Chapter 18 discusses this reuse mechanism in detail.

Byte code level reuse is implemented in Java using Containership and Inheritance. Containership should be used when the two classes have a "has a" relationship between them. For example, a problem may have two classes Address and Employee. An Employee object may contain an Address object, apart from other data like name, age, salary etc.

Inheritance should be used when the two classes have a "like a" relationship. For example, if a problem has two classes—Window and Button, then the Button class can be inherited from Window class since Button is like a Window.

Containership and Inheritance can be implemented even if source code is not available.

Exercises

[A] State whether the following statements are True or False:

(a) We can derive a class from a base class even if the base class's source code is not available.

(b) The way a derived class member function can access base class **protected** and **public** members, the base class member functions can access **protected** and public **member** functions of derived class.

(c) **private** members of base class cannot be accessed by derived class member functions or objects of derived class.

(d) The size of a derived class object is equal to the sum of sizes of data members in base class and the derived class.

(e) Creating a derived class from a base class requires fundamental changes to the base class.

(f) If a base class contains a member function **func( )**, and a derived class does not contain a function with this name, an object of the derived class cannot access **func( )**.

(g) If no constructors are specified for a derived class, objects of the derived class will use the constructors in the base class.

(h) If a base class and a derived class each include a member function with the same name, the member function of the derived class will be called by an object of the derived class.

(i) A class D can be derived from class C, which is derived from class B, which is derived from class A.

(j) It is illegal to make objects of one class members of another class.

[B] Answer the following questions:

(a) Implement a **MyString** class containing the following functions:

- Function to display the length of a string.
- Function **toLower( )** to convert upper case letters to lower case.
- Function **toUpper( )** to convert lower case letters to upper case.

(b) Suppose there is a base class **B** and a derived class **D** derived from **B**. **B** has two **public** member functions **b1( )** and **b2( )**, whereas **D** has two member functions **d1( )** and **d2( )**. Write these classes for the following different situations:

- **b1( )** should be accessible in **main( )**, **b2( )** should not be.
- Neither **b1( )**, nor **b2( )** should be accessible in **main( )**.
- Both **b1( )** and **b2( )** should be accessible in **main( )**.

(c) If a class **D** that is derived from class **B**, then which of the following can an object of class **D** located in **main( )** access?

- **public** members of **D**
- **protected** members of **D**
- **private** members of **D**
- **public** members of **B**
- **protected** members of **B**
- **private** members of **B**

(d) In an inheritance chain which out of **static**, **protected**, **private** and **public** members of base class are accessible to the derived class members?

(e) Which of the following can be facilitated by the Inheritance mechanism?

1. Use the existing functionality of base class.
2. Override the existing functionality of base class.
3. Implement new functionality in the derived class.
4. Implement polymorphic behavior.
5. Implement containership.

(f) How can you prevent inheritance from a class in Java?

(g) If the base class has two versions of the overloaded function, and derived class contains one version of it, then using the derived class object can we call the other version of the base class?

(h) What will be the size of the derived class object if the base class contains two private integers, one static integer and the derived class contains two static integers and one private integer?

KanNotes

- Java facilitates code reuse at 2 levels : a) Source code level b) Byte code level

- Source code level reuse is done using Generic functions and Generic classes
- Generics let us write generalized functions / classes and the compiler creates specific functions / classes from it
- For creating specialized functions / classes source code must be available
- Byte code level reuse is done using Containership and Inheritance
- Containership should be used when the two classes have a "has a" relationship
- Inheritance should be used when the two classes have a "like a" relationship
- Containership and Inheritance can be implemented even if source code is not available
- Inheritance terminology : base - derived, parent - child, subclass, superclass
- Protected members are available in the inheritance chain
- Derived class object contains all base class data
- Derived class object may not be able to access all base class data
- Inheritance facilitates :

  Inheritance of existing feature : To implement this just establish inheritance relationship
  Suppressing an existing feature : Hide base class implementation by defining same function in derived class
  Extending an existing feature : Call base class function from derived class by using super.Baseclassfunction( ) ;
- Construction of an object always proceeds from base towards derived
- Base class constructor can be called using super( )

- If a class is marked as final, then a new class cannot be derived from it
- If a function is marked as final, then the function cannot be overridden in the derived class

Chapter 14

Polymorphism

Let Us JAVA 7th Edition

The more caps one can wear, more versatile one becomes. Polymorphism is same...

Contents

- What is Polymorphism?
- Abstract Classes and Functions
- Abstract Functions – Practical Example
- Interfaces
- Practical Uses of Interfaces
  - Interfaces–Focused View
  - Interfaces–Different Implementation
  - Interfaces–Unrelated Inheritance
- *default* and *static* Methods
- *default* Method Ambiguities
- Exercises
- KanNotes

After classes and inheritance, polymorphism is the third essential feature of an object-oriented programming language. Programmers who switch to Java after having learnt C seem to do so in two steps. In the first step they start using classes, objects, constructors, function overloading, etc. While doing this, they are using Java as a "object-based" programming language. This means that, at this stage, they start appreciating the benefits of grouping data together with the functions that act upon it, the value of constructors and perhaps some simple inheritance.

Many programmers carry the wrong impression that since they have started using classes, objects, function overloading and inheritance they have graduated into the object-oriented world. Though, on the face of it, everything may appear nice, neat, and clean, don't get fooled. If you stop here, you're missing out on the greatest part of the language, which is the jump to true object-oriented programming. You can do this only when you have learnt polymorphism.

What is Polymorphism?

Overloading of functions is one kind of polymorphism—one thing existing in several distinct forms. We have already dealt with this type of polymorphism. The other type of polymorphism simplifies the syntax of performing the same operation with a hierarchy of classes. Thus, you can use polymorphism to keep the interface to the classes clean, because you do not have to define unique function names for similar operations on each derived class.

When polymorphism is used, a program that appears to be calling a function of one class may be calling a function of a different class. But why on earth would we want this? Suppose we have three different classes called **Line, Circle** and **Rectangle**. Each class contains a **draw( )** function to draw the relevant shape on the screen. If we are to draw a picture containing numerous lines, circles, and triangles we can create an array of references which would hold addresses of all the objects in the picture. The array definition may look like,

```
Shape[ ] arr ;
arr = new Shape[ 50 ] ;
```

When it is time to draw the picture, we can simply run the loop,

```
for ( i = 0 ; i < 50 ; i++ )
```

```
arr[ i ].draw( ) ;
```

When **arr[i]** contains the address of the **Line** object it would call the **Line** class's **draw( )** function. Similarly, when it contains the address of the **Circle** object it would call the **Circle** class's **draw( )** function. This is amazing for two reasons:

(a) Functions from different classes are executed through the same function call.

(b) The array **arr[ ]** has been defined to contain **Shape** references and not **Line** or **Circle** references.

This concept is called polymorphism. The functions have the same appearance, the **draw( )** function, but different actual functions are used. Which **draw( )** function would get used depends on the contents of **arr[i]**. However, for this polymorphic approach to work, several conditions must be met. These are:

(a) The classes **Line**, **Circle** and **Rectangle** all must be derived from the same base class, **Shape**.

(b) The **Shape** base class must contain a **draw( )** function.

All this would be too much to digest at one shot. So let us break it into pieces and try to understand it part by part through simple programs. Here is the first one...

```
// Illustrates use of upcasted reference
package polymorphismproject ;
class One
{
    public void display( )
    {
        System.out.println ( "In base class" ) ;
    }
}
class OneOfOne extends One
{
    public void display( )
    {
        System.out.println ( "In OneOfOne class" ) ;
    }
}
```

```
class TwoOfOne extends One
{
    public void display( )
    {
        System.out.println ( "In TwoOfOne class" ) ;
    }
}
public class PolymorphismProject
{
    public static void main ( String[ ] args )
    {
        One ptr ;
        OneOfOne o1 = new OneOfOne( ) ;
        TwoOfOne o2 = new TwoOfOne( ) ;
        ptr = o1 ;
        ptr.display( ) ;
        ptr = o2 ;
        ptr.display( ) ;
    }
}
```

Here **OneOfOne** and **TwoOfOne** are classes derived from the base class **One**. Each of these three classes has a member function **display( )**.

Inside **main( )** having created the objects **o1**, **o2** (from the two derived classes) and a reference **ptr** to base class, we have assigned the address of a derived class object to the base class reference through the statement,

```
ptr = o1 ;
```

Should this not give us an error since we are assigning an address of one type to a reference of another? No, since in this case the compiler relaxes the type checking. The rule is that references to objects of a derived class are type-compatible with references to objects of the base class. Assigning the address of a derived class object to a base class reference is called **upcasting**.

When we execute the statement,

```
ptr.display( ) ;
```

Which function gets called—**display( )** of **OneOfOne** or **display( )** of **One**? Well, the function in the derived class gets called. On execution of the program, we get the following output:

```
In OneOfOne class
In TwoOfOne class
```

As can be seen from the output, instead of the base class, the member functions of the derived classes got executed. Thus, the same function call,

```
ptr.display( ) ;
```

executes different functions, depending on the contents of **ptr**. The rule here is that the compiler selects the function to be called based on the *contents* of the reference **ptr**, and not on the *type* of the reference.

Deciding which function to call in known as binding. As **ptr** may contain address of an object of the **OneOfOne** class or of the **TwoOfOne** class, the compiler is unable to bind the call to a specific version of **display( )**. Hence the decision is deferred until the program is executed. At runtime, when it is known what object is pointed to by **ptr**, the appropriate version of **display( )** gets called. This is called **Late Binding** or **Dynamic Binding**. Late binding requires some overhead but provides increased power and flexibility.

Thus, this program can provide the feature mentioned at the beginning of this discussion—accessing functions of different classes using the same function call.

Abstract Classes and Functions

We can add another refinement to the function declared in the base class of the last program. Since the function **display( )** in the base class never gets executed we can easily do away with the body of this function and mark it using the keyword **abstract**, as shown below.

```
abstract class One
{
    public abstract void display( ) ;
}
```

The **abstract** function never has any statements in it. An abstract function must be contained in an **abstract** class. That is why we have marked **One** as an abstract class as shown above. We can never create an object from an abstract class. So, the following statement would report an error:

```
One o = new One ;
```

But when would a situation arise where we want to prevent the creation of an object? Well, let us go back to our previous example. Suppose there is base class called **Shape** containing a **draw( )** function. From this **Shape** class three classes **Line**, **Circle** and **Rectangle** are derived. In this case we would never want to make an object of the **Shape** class; we would only make objects of the derived classes as they would help us draw specific shapes. In this case we would define **Shape** as an abstract class and **draw( )** as an abstract function in this class. We would then provide an implementation of **draw( )** function in each of the derived classes. These **draw( )** functions would let us draw specific line, circle or rectangle shapes.

Whenever an abstract function is placed in the base class, you must override it in all the derived classes from which you wish to create objects. If you don't implement the function in the derived class, then the derived class is treated as an abstract class.

Let us now reiterate a few facts that we have learnt in this section. A clear understanding of them is utmost necessary.

To help you fix your understanding of abstract classes and functions let us write one more program. Figure 14.1 shows the hierarchy of classes that we propose to implement in this program.

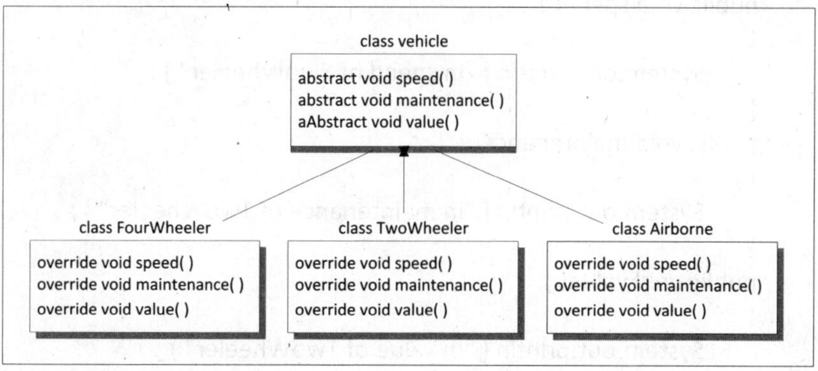

Figure 14.1

Given below is the code for the program that implements this class hierarchy.

```
// Program that illustrates working of abstract class & abstract functions
package abstractclassexampleproject ;
abstract class Vehicle
{
    public abstract void speed( ) ;
    public abstract void maintenance( ) ;
    public abstract void value( ) ;
}
class FourWheeler extends Vehicle
{
    public void speed( )
    {
        System.out.println ( "In speed of FourWheeler" ) ;
    }
    public void maintenance( )
    {
        System.out.println ( "In maintenance of FourWheeler" ) ;
    }
    public void value( )
    {
        System.out.println ( "In value of FourWheeler" ) ;
    }
}
class TwoWheeler extends Vehicle
{
    public void speed( )
    {
        System.out.println ( "In speed of TwoWheeler" ) ;
    }
    public void maintenance( )
    {
        System.out.println ( "In maintenance of TwoWheeler" ) ;
    }
    public void value( )
    {
        System.out.println ( "In value of TwoWheeler" ) ;
    }
}
class Airborne extends Vehicle
```

```
{
    public void speed( )
    {
        System.out.println ( "In speed of Airborne" ) ;
    }
    public void maintenance( )
    {
        System.out.println ( "In maintenance of Airborne" ) ;
    }
    public void value( )
    {
        System.out.println ( "In value of Airborne" ) ;
    }
}
public class AbstractClassExampleProject
{
    public static void main ( String[ ] args )
    {
        Vehicle maruti, bajaj, jumbo ;

        maruti = new FourWheeler( ) ;
        bajaj = new TwoWheeler( ) ;
        jumbo = new Airborne( ) ;

        maruti.speed( ) ;
        maruti.maintenance( ) ;
        maruti.value( ) ;

        bajaj.speed( ) ;
        bajaj.maintenance( ) ;
        bajaj.value( ) ;

        jumbo.speed( ) ;
        jumbo.maintenance( ) ;
        jumbo.value( ) ;
    }
}
```

Here is the output of the program...

```
In speed of FourWheeler
In maintenance of FourWheeler
```

In value of FourWheeler
In speed of TwoWheeler
In maintenance of TwoWheeler
In value of TwoWheeler
In speed of Airborne
In maintenance of Airborne
In value of Airborne

We would leave it to you to analyze the output of this program.

Abstract Functions – Practical Example

We hope that by now you have understood the mechanism of abstract functions. Let us now see where we can use them effectively. Suppose we wish to write an application which must print a document on the printer. The application should be able to print on any printer. All that it must know is the name of the printer. To do the printing, application should merely call the **print( )** function. Note that every printer uses its own way of printing. We can implement this scenario by creating classes as shown in Figure 14.2.

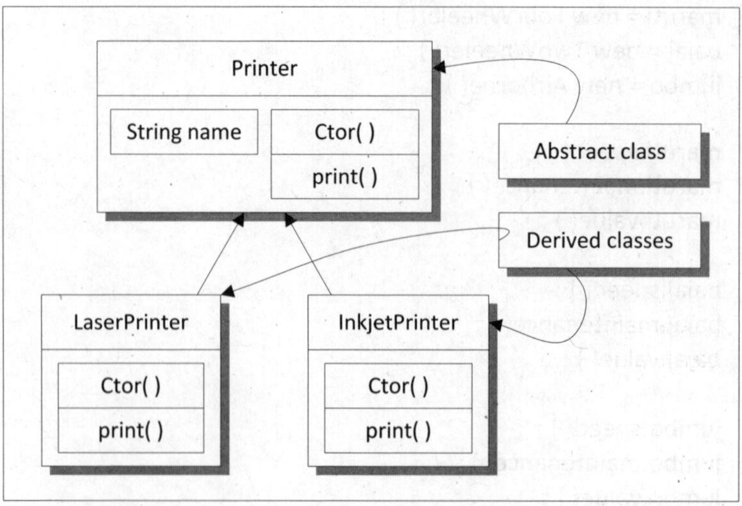

Figure 14.2

Given below is the implementation of the classes shown in Figure 14.2.

```
// Application that does printing using abstract class
package printingappproject ;
abstract class Printer
```

```
{
    protected String name ;

    public Printer ( String n )
    {
        name = n ;
    }
    public abstract void print ( String docName ) ;
}
class LaserPrinter extends Printer
{
    public LaserPrinter ( String n )
    {
        super ( n ) ;
    }
    public void print ( String docName )
    {
        System.out.println ( ">> LaserPrinter.print" ) ;
    }
}
class InkjetPrinter extends Printer
{
    public InkjetPrinter ( String n )
    {
        super ( n ) ;
    }
    public void print ( String docName )
    {
        System.out.println ( ">> InkjetPrinter.print" ) ;
    }
}
public class PrintingAppProject
{
    public static void main ( String[ ] args )
    {
        Printer p = new LaserPrinter ( "LaserJet 1100" ) ;
        p.print ( "hello1.pdf" ) ;
        p = new InkjetPrinter ( "IBM 2140" ) ;
        p.print("hello2.doc" ) ;
    }
}
```

Here is the output of the program...

```
>> LaserPrinter.print
>> InkjetPrinter.print
```

In this program we first defined an abstract class called **Printer**. This class has a string that can store the name of the printer through the constructor. It also has an abstract function called **print( )**. This **print( )** function has been implemented in the two derived classes—**LaserPrinter** and **InkjetPrinter**. Though in these implementations we have just displayed messages, in real-life it would contain the logic to do the printing on laser and inkjet printer, respectively. Based on whose address is present in the reference **p**, the **print( )** of the appropriate derived class would get called through the dynamic binding mechanism that we learnt earlier.

Given below is the summary of all that we learnt about abstract classes and functions.

(a) Object cannot be created from an abstract class.
(b) An abstract class can contain abstract as well as non-abstract functions.
(c) Abstract class may contain instance and static variables. These variables may be inherited.
(d) Abstract methods do not have a body.
(e) Abstract classes can participate in inheritance.
(f) If a class contains abstract methods, the class must be abstract.
(g) Abstract functions cannot be private.

Interfaces

An interface usually contains only the signatures of methods (i.e., function declarations). The implementation of these methods is done in the class that implements the interface. For example, we can declare an interface called **Mouse**, and then implement this interface in a class **GeniusMouse** as shown below.

```
// Illustrates declaration and implementation of interface
package interfaceexampleproject ;
interface Mouse
{
    void lBtnDown ( int x, int y ) ;
    void rBtnDown ( int x, int y ) ;
}
```

```
class GeniusMouse implements Mouse
{
    @Override public void lBtnDown ( int x, int y )
    {
        System.out.println ( "Left Button: " + x + " " + y ) ;
    }
    @Override public void rBtnDown ( int x, int y )
    {
        System.out.println ( "Right Button: " + x + " " + y ) ;
    }
}
public class InterfaceExampleProject
{
    public static void main ( String[ ] args )
    {
        GeniusMouse m = new GeniusMouse( ) ;
        m.lBtnDown ( 10,20 ) ;
        m.rBtnDown ( 30,40 ) ;
    }
}
```

Here is the output of the program...

```
Left Button: 10 20
Right Button: 30 40
```

To declare an interface Java provides a keyword called **interface**. The syntax for defining the class that implements an interface is like the one used for inheritance, except the use of keyword **implements** instead of **extends**.

In **main( )** we have simply created an instance of **GeniusMouse** and called the implementations of interface methods **lBtnDown( )** and **rBtnDown( )**. The output of the program is simple to follow.

Note the use of an annotation **@Override** in the **GeniusMouse** class. Though not compulsory, we should use it every time we implement an interface method or override a base class method. This practice offers two benefits. By using **@Override** we can take advantage of the compiler checking to make sure we actually are overriding a method when we think we are. This way, if we make a common mistake of misspelling a method name or not correctly matching the parameters, we will be warned that your method does not actually override as we think it does. Secondly, it makes our code easier to understand.

It might occur to you that the effect that we obtained in this program could have been achieved using an abstract class, instead of an interface. We could have defined an abstract class like this:

```
abstract class Mouse
{
    public abstract void lBtnDown ( int x, int y ) ;
    public abstract void rBtnDown ( int x, int y ) ;
}
```

These abstract methods could have been implemented in **GeniusMouse**. That leads to an important question—how is an abstract class different than an interface? Well, here are the differences...

(a) Abstract class functions may have a body, whereas interface functions never have a body.

(b) Abstract class may contain static, const or instance variables, whereas an interface cannot contain any variables.

(c) Abstract class can be inherited from only one base class, whereas an interface can be inherited from multiple interfaces.

One similarity that abstract classes and interfaces share is, we cannot create objects from either of them.

Now that we have created our first program that uses an interface, it is time for some small tips about interfaces. These are given below.

(a) Interfaces are not derived from **Object** class.
(b) Interfaces are not derived from any base interface.
(c) A class can implement multiple interfaces.
(d) Interfaces can be inherited.
(e) Multiple interface inheritance is allowed.
(f) Class cannot implement an interface partially.

Practical Uses of Interfaces

In my opinion, more than the syntax and the mechanism, it is more important to know the situations in which we should use interfaces. We would discuss three scenarios where interfaces are commonly used. These are as follows:

(a) Interfaces permit us to have a focused view of a large implementation.
(b) Interfaces permit us to provide different implementations of same tasks.
(c) Interfaces let us inherit in a class desired qualities from unrelated sources.

Let us now understand each of these situations in detail, with the help of suitable programs.

Interfaces–Focused View

Often in professional software you would find a class that contains so many functions that a quick glance would possibly not give us an idea about their purpose. Instead, if we find that the class implements a particular interface then we would quickly get an idea about what the class is intending to do. For example, if we come to know that a class implements three interfaces—**IEncrypt**, **ICompress** and **IAuthenticate**, then we can guess that the class has something to do with encryption, compression, and authentication. The following program defines and implements these interfaces:

```
// Illustrates how interfaces permit us to have a focused view of an
// implementation
package interfacesfocusedviewproject ;
interface IEncrypt
{
    void encrypt( ) ;
    void decrypt( ) ;
}
interface ICompress
{
    void compress( ) ;
    void decompress( ) ;
}
interface IAuthenticate
{
    void login( ) ;
    void logout( ) ;
}
class FocusedView implements IEncrypt, ICompress, IAuthenticate
{
    @Override public void encrypt( )
    {
```

```
        System.out.println ( ">> encrypt" ) ;
    }
    @Override public void decrypt( )
    {
        System.out.println ( ">> decrypt" ) ;
    }
    @Override public void compress( )
    {
        System.out.println ( ">> compress" ) ;
    }
    @Override public void decompress( )
    {
        System.out.println ( ">> decompress" ) ;
    }
    @Override public void login( )
    {
        System.out.println ( ">> login" ) ;
    }
    @Override public void logout( )
    {
        System.out.println ( ">> logout" ) ;
    }
}
public class InterfacesFocusedViewProject
{
    public static void main ( String[ ] args )
    {
        FocusedView o = new FocusedView( ) ;

        IEncrypt ie = o ;
        ie.encrypt( ) ;
        ie.decrypt( ) ;

        ICompress ic = o ;
        ic.compress( ) ;
        ic.decompress( ) ;

        IAuthenticate ia = o ;
        ia.login( ) ;
        ia.logout( ) ;
    }
```

}

Given below is the output of the program...

```
>> encrypt
>> decrypt
>> compress
>> decompress
>> login
>> logout
```

Few things that you can notice about the program are

(a) The class **FocusedView** implements three interfaces— **IEncrypt**, **ICompress** and **IAuthenticate**. The order in which the interfaces are mentioned in the list while defining the class does not matter.

(b) In **main( )** we have created a **FocusedView** object, assigned its address to an interface reference (say **ICompress**) and then called the methods (**Compress( )** and **Decompress( )**) that belong to that interface (**ICompress**).

(c) If we call the method **Compress( )** using authentication interface reference **ia**, it would result in a compilation error. This means using an interface reference only methods belonging to that interface alone can be called.

(d) While typing the program when we type "**ia.**", the help shows only those methods that belong to **IAuthenticate** interface. This makes the development of the **FocusedView** class easy, as we get to concentrate only on that part of the class which we are developing right now.

(e) Though the **FocusedView** class implements only interfaces, we may as well derive **FocusedView** from another class. In that case, while defining the class the base class name should precede the interfaces as shown below.

```
class FocusedView extends BaseClass implements IEncrypt,
                                   ICompress, IAuthenticate
{
    // code
}
```

Interfaces–Different Implementations

There are different ways in which we can maintain data in memory. For example, we can store it in an array or a linked list. Each of these data structures would organize the same data in different manners. Hence the actual implementation of operations like counting the number of elements, adding a new element, removing an existing element, etc. would be different for these two data structures. However, it would be nice if the way to use these operations remains the same. Thus, no matter whether we are using an array or a linked list, we should be able to get the current number of elements in any of them by calling the method **count( )**. Likewise, it should be possible to add a new element to each of them by calling the method **add( )**. This is possible by using an interface as shown in the following program:

```
// Same interface, different implemenations
package differentimplementationsproject ;
interface IListMethods
{
    int count( ) ;
    void add ( Object o ) ;
    void remove ( Object o ) ;
}
class MyArray implements IListMethods
{
    @Override public int count( )
    {
        System.out.println ( ">> MyArray.count" ) ;
        return 0 ;
    }
    @Override public void add ( Object o )
    {
        System.out.println ( ">> MyArray.add" ) ;
    }
    @Override public void remove ( Object o )
    {
        System.out.println ( ">> MyArray.remove" ) ;
    }
}
class MyLL implements IListMethods
{
    @Override public int count( )
    {
```

```
        System.out.println ( ">> MyLL.count" ) ;
        return 0 ;
    }
    @Override public void add ( Object o )
    {
        System.out.println ( ">> MyLL.add" ) ;
    }
    @Override public void remove ( Object o )
    {
        System.out.println ( ">> MyLL.remove" ) ;
    }
}
public class DifferentImplementationsProject
{
    public static void main ( String[ ] args )
    {
        IListMethods i ;

        i = new MyArray( ) ;
        i.add ( 1 ) ;
        i.remove ( 1 ) ;
        i.count( ) ;

        i = new MyLL( ) ;
        i.add ( 1 ) ;
        i.remove ( 1 ) ;
        i.count( ) ;
    }
}
```

The program produces the following output:

```
>> MyArray.add
>> MyArray.remove
>> MyArray.count
>> MyLL.add
>> MyLL.remove
>> MyLL.count
```

Here we have defined an interface **IListMethods** containing methods **count( )**, **add( )** and **remove( )**. All these methods have been implemented in the classes **MyArray** and **MyLL**. In **main( )** we have created objects of **MyArray** and **MyLL**, stored their references in the interface reference **i** and then called the three methods in turn. In each method we have just printed a message. In true implementation the methods would contain the logic for counting, addition, or deletion.

Same interface, but different implementation is a very common theme followed in good object-oriented software development. Java permits us to use this feature through interfaces.

Interfaces–Unrelated Inheritance

We know that we cannot inherit a class from multiple base classes. However, it is possible to create a class which inherits from one base class and implements one or more interfaces. But when would such a need arise? The need arises when we wish to inherit desired qualities from unrelated sources. For example, a person may want to inherit the looks of "John Abraham" and character of "Dr. Abdul Kalam". Looks of a person may include hairstyle, whereas character may include patriotism. These are unrelated qualities. Also, we cannot create a **Person** class and then inherit it from **Actor** class and **Character** class, as multiple inheritance is not permitted in Java. Moreover, you can appreciate that looks can be inherited, whereas character must be implemented. So, to represent this scenario we can create an **Actor** class and an **ICharacter** interface. Then we can create another class **Person** which is derived from **Actor** class and implements **ICharacter** interface. This is shown in the following program:

```
// Demonstrates inheritance from unrelated sources
package unrelatedinheritanceproject ;
interface ICharacter
{
    void patriotism( ) ;
}
class Actor
{
    protected String hairstyle = "Spikes" ;

    public void style( )
    {
        System.out.println ( ">> Actor.Style: " + hairstyle ) ;
    }
}
class Person extends Actor implements ICharacter
{
```

```
    public void doActing( )
    {
        System.out.println ( ">> Person.doActing" ) ;
    }
    public void style( )
    {
        super.style( ) ;
        System.out.println ( ">> Person.style" ) ;
    }
    public void patriotism( )
    {
        System.out.println ( ">> Character.patriotism" ) ;
    }
}
public class UnrelatedInheritanceProject
{
    public static void main ( String[ ] args )
    {
        Actor m ;
        Person p ;

        p = new Person( ) ;
        m = p ;
        m.style( ) ;

        ICharacter i ;
        i = p ;
        i.patriotism( ) ;
    }
}
```

Here, we have created a base class called **Actor** and an Interface called **ICharacter**. The base class has a method called **style( )** and the interface has a method called **patriotism( )**. Then we created a class called **Person**. This class inherits from **Actor** class and implements **ICharacter** interface. In **main( )** we have created an object of **Person** class and stored its address in **Actor** reference **m** as well as **ICharacter** reference **i**. Then using **m** and **i** we have called the **style( )** and **patriotism( )** methods. The output of the program is given below.

```
>> Actor.Style: Spikes
>> Person.style
```

```
>> Character.patriotism
```

default and *static* Methods

Apart from method prototypes, an interface can also contain *default* and *static* methods. These methods can have a body too. Given below is an interface that contains all three.

```
public interface MyInterface
{
    void existingMethod1( ) ;       // method signature
    void existingMethod2( ) ;       // method signature
    default void newMethod( )
    {
        // Default implementation for newMethod
    }
    static void helperMethod( )
    {
        // implementation for helper method
    }
}
```

Let us now understand the purpose of **default** and **static** methods.

Suppose there is an interface which has been implemented in ten different classes by different team members. Now you wish to add one more method to the interface which you are planning to implement in your implementation of the class. But if you do this, other implementations of the interface would break. In such cases you can add the method with a body in the interface and mark it as **default**. When you do so, other implementations would simply inherit the default implementation. Thus, **default** methods allow the addition of new methods to interfaces without breaking existing implementations. This way interface maintainers can add new methods with default implementations over time without affecting existing code. This is particularly useful when evolving APIs.

Static methods act as helper functions that are related to the interface, but do not depend on an instance of the implementing class. A **static** method defined in the interface can be overridden in a class that is implementing the interface.

default Method Ambiguities

There are three types of ambiguities that may arise with default methods. These are discussed below with the help of examples.

(a) If interfaces **I1** and **I2** contain a **default** method **newMethod( )** and **Sample** class implements **I1** and **I2**, an error would be reported as the compiler would be unable to decide which **default** method to inherit in **Sample** class. This problem can be resolved by overriding **newMethod( )** in **Sample** class. From this method default method of both interfaces can be called using **super** keyword.

```
interface I1
{
    default public void newMethod( )
    {
        System.out.println ( "In I1 Interface" ) ;
    }
}
interface I2
{
    default public void newMethod( )
    {
        System.out.println ( "In I2 Interface" ) ;
    }
}
class Sample implements I1, I2
{
    @Override
    public void newMethod( )
    {
        System.out.println ( "In Sample class" ) ;
        I1.super.newMethod( ) ;
        I2.super.newMethod( ) ;
    }
}
public class Main
{
    public static void main ( String[ ] args )
    {
        Sample s = new Sample( ) ;
        s.newMethod( ) ;
    }
}
```

(b) Suppose interface **I** contains a **default** method **newMethod( )**, and interfaces **I1** and **I2** are derived from **I**. So **newMethod( )** would be inherited in **I1** and **I2**. If **Sample** class implements **I1** and **I2**, would compiler report an error? No, because **I1** and **I2** has inherited same **newMethod( )** so it doesn't confuse the compiler.

```
interface I
{
    default public void newMethod( )
    {
        System.out.println ( "In I Interface" ) ;
    }
}

interface I1 extends I
{
}
interface I2 extends I
{
}
class Sample implements I1, I2
{
}
public class Main
{
  public static void main ( String[ ] args )
  {
    Sample s = new Sample( ) ;
    s.newMethod( ) ;
  }
}
```

(c) Suppose interface **I** contains a **default** method **newMethod( )**, and interfaces **I1** and **I2** are derived from **I**. **I1** contains its own implementation of **newMethod( )**, whereas **I2** inherits **newMethod( )** from **I**. If **Sample** class implements **I1** and **I2**, would compiler report an error? No, in such cases complier chooses the most recent implementation of **newMethod( )** in the inheritance chain. Hence it calls **newMethod( )** of interface **I1**.

```
interface I
{
    default public void newMethod( )
    {
        System.out.println ( "In I Interface" ) ;
```

```
    }
}
interface I1 extends I
{
    default public void newMethod( )
    {
        System.out.println ( "In I1 Interface" ) ;
    }
}
interface I2 extends I
{
}
class Sample implements I1, I2
{
}
public class Main
{
    public static void main ( String[ ] args )
    {
        Sample s = new Sample( ) ;
        s.newMethod( ) ;
    }
}
```

Exercises

[A] State whether the following statements are True or False:

(a) Java permits calling of derived class functions using a base class reference.

(b) Abstract functions can never have a body, whereas Abstract constructors can have a body.

(c) We can never build an object from an abstract class.

(d) While building an object it doesn't matter whether the base class constructor is called first or the derived class constructor is called first.

(e) Which of the following statements are correct about Interfaces used in Java?

1. All interfaces are derived from an **Object** class.
2. Interfaces can be inherited.
3. All interfaces are derived from an **Object** interface.
4. Interfaces can contain only method declarations.
5. Interfaces can contain static data and methods.
6. Interfaces can contain one or more default methods.
7. One class can implement only one interface.
8. In a program if one class implements an interface then no other class in the same program can implement this interface.
9. From two base interfaces a new interface cannot be inherited.
10. Interfaces cannot be inherited.
11. If a class implements an interface partially, then it becomes an abstract class.
12. A class cannot implement an interface partially.
13. A class that implements an interface can explicitly implement members of that interface.
14. The functions declared in an interface have a body.
15. Interfaces members are automatically public.
16. To implement an interface member, the corresponding member in the class must be **public** as well as **static**.
17. An explicitly implemented member can be accessed through an instance of the interface.
18. Interfaces can be overloaded.
19. A class can implement multiple interfaces.
20. An interface can implement multiple classes.
21. The static attribute can be used with a method that implements an interface declaration.

[B] Answer the following questions:

(a) How are interfaces different from classes?

(b) Does Java support partial implementation of interfaces?

(c) Which different type of polymorphism does Java support?

[C] Pick up the correct alternative for each of the following questions:

(a) If a function **fun( )** is overloaded multiple times in a class, then calls to this function are bound at
(1) compile time
(2) preprocessing time
(3) execution time
(4) linking time

(b) "Function binding" means
(1) deciding which function to call
(2) deciding which function to define
(3) deciding which function to compile
(4) deciding which function to assemble

(c) A class **Trial** and a class **Example** implement an interface called **IAuthenticate**. Which of the following concepts is being put to work here?
(1) Containership
(2) Polymorphism
(3) Operator overloading
(4) Static binding

(d) If a class contains an abstract function, the class must be
(1) singleton
(2) abstract
(3) static
(4) friend

(e) From which class is any abstract class derived?
(1) Base
(2) Object
(3) Abstract
(4) Appropriate preprocessor for those devices

(f) What will happen on execution of the following code snippet?

```
abstract class One
{
```

```
    public abstract void display( ) ;
}
One o = new One( ) ;
```

(1) An object of class One will get created
(2) Error, since class One doesn't contain a constructor
(3) Error, since an object cannot be created from an abstract class
(4) (2) and (3)

KanNotes

- Upcasted reference - when a base class reference contains address of derived class object
- Binding means deciding which function to call
- If binding is done at the time of compilation, it is called Early Binding
- If binding is done at the time of execution, it is called Late Binding
- Java does Early Binding while calling private, static and final methods
- Java uses Late Binding when method to be called cannot be determined at compile time
- Early Binding is also known as Static Binding or Compile time Binding
- Late Binding is also known as Dynamic Binding or Runtime Binding
- For Late Binding the function being called must be present in base class as well as derived class
- To prevent an object from getting created from a class declare it as an abstract class
- To prevent a base class method getting called through derived class object mark the method as abstract in the base class
- An abstract class can contain :

  Abstract & non-abstract functions
  Abstract methods do not have a body

Instance & static variables
Variables may be inherited

- Abstract classes can participate in inheritance
- If a class contains abstract methods, class has to be abstract
- Interface is an entity through which we interact with a system, person, organization, etc.
  - Examples of Hardware Interfaces - RS232, USB, PCI, I2C, SATA
  - Examples of Software Interfaces - Text, GUI
  - Example of Programming Interface - Functions / Methods
  - An interface is a collection of functions declarations, static methods and default methods
  - Implementation (definition) of functions declared in an interface is done in classes that implement the interface
  - Different classes may implement the same interface
  - A class can implement any number of interfaces
  - Interface indicates what a class must do
  - Definition of interface functions indicate how to do it
  - Difference between Interface and Abstract class :

    Functions :
    - Abstract class functions may have a body
    - Interface functions never have a body

    Instance variables :
    - Abstract class may contain variables. These variables may be inherited
    - Interface may contain variables. These variables are by default static and final
  - Interfaces are useful in 3 situations :

- When a similar operation is to be performed on different collections
- When a focused view is needed in a large implementation
- When a class must inherit desired qualities from unrelated sources

Exception Handling

Let Us JAVA 7th Edition

CHAPTER 15

Exceptions can't be eliminated completely. They are bound to occur in a Java program. You better know how to deal with them in an OO manner...

Contents

- Exception Handling in Java
- Catching Multiple Exceptions
- The *finally* Block
- User-defined Exceptions
- A More Practical Example
    - Define the Exception Class
    - Throw an Exception
    - The *try* Block
    - The Exception Handler (*catch* Block)
    - How the Whole Thing Works?
- A Few Tips...
- Exercises
- KanNotes

Programming is a difficult art. No matter how much confidence you have in your programming ability, several things may go wrong during its development. This includes typing errors, compilation errors, linking errors runtime errors. The first three types of errors are comparatively easy to tackle. But when errors occur during execution, your program must deal with the situation in an elegant fashion. This chapter discusses how to deal with such types of errors.

The errors that occur at runtime—i.e., during execution of the program—are called Exceptions. The reasons why exceptions occur are numerous. Some of the more common ones are as follows:

(a) Falling short of memory
(b) Inability to open a file
(c) Exceeding the bounds of an array
(d) Attempting to initialize an object to an impossible value
(e) Division by zero
(f) Stack overflow
(g) Arithmetic overflow or underflow
(h) Attempt to use an unassigned reference
(i) Unable to connect to Server

When such exceptions occur, the programmer must decide a strategy according to which he would handle the exceptions. The strategies could be displaying error messages on the screen, or displaying a dialog box in case of a GUI environment, or requesting the user to supply better data or simply terminating the program execution. Which of these strategies would be adopted depends on whether the exceptional condition can be anticipated or not. Figure 15.1 shows some examples of these exceptional conditions.

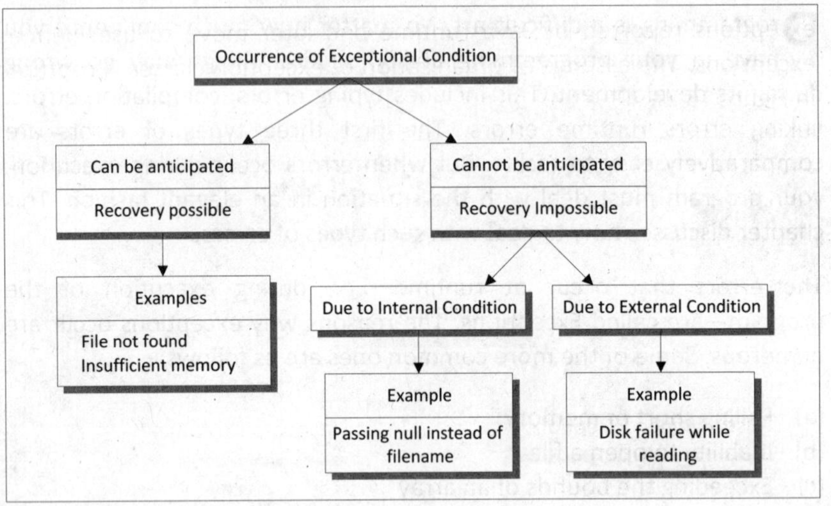

Figure 15.1

Exception Handling in Java

Java provides a systematic, object-oriented approach to handling runtime errors. The exception mechanism of Java uses three keywords—**throw**, **catch**, and **try**. Let us understand their purpose.

Suppose during execution of a member function of a class an error occurs, then Java runtime informs the application that an error has occurred. This process of informing is called **throwing** an exception. This involves two steps:

(a) Creating an object called exception object and storing information about the exceptional condition in it.

(b) Throwing the exception object using the keyword **throw**.

Java runtime creates the exception object from ready-made exception classes provided in the Java Library. Each exception class represents a different exception situation. For example, there is an exception class that represents a divide by zero situation, another which represents an inability to open file, etc. All these classes are derived from a base class called **Exception**, which in turn is derived from an **Object** class.

If we anticipate an exception situation other than the ones represented through these exception classes, then we can define our own exception class, create an object from this class and then throw that object to report the error situation. To begin with, we would concentrate on the exceptions reported by Java runtime and later move to user-defined exceptions. The essence of organization of exception classes is captured in Figure 15.2.

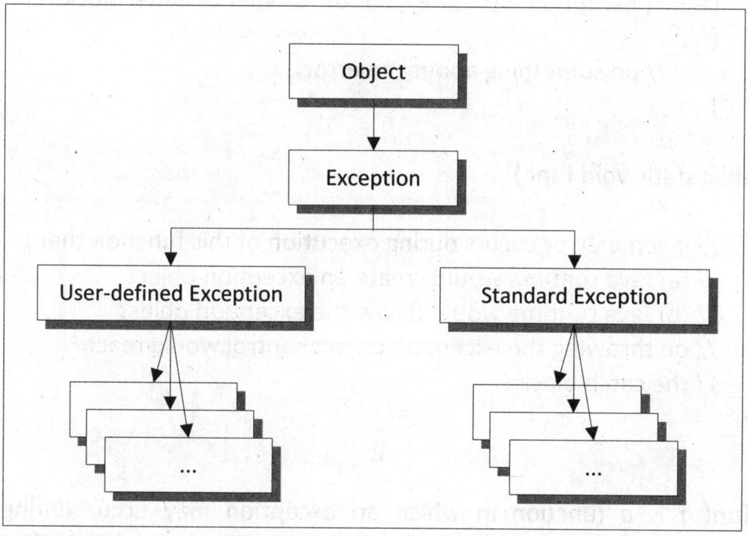

Figure 15.2

The code in the application that anticipates an exception to occur during its execution is enclosed in a **try block**. When the exception occurs, and an exception object is thrown the control is transferred to another section of code in the application called **exception handler** or a **catch block**. Thus, runtime errors generated in the **try** block are caught in the **catch** block. Code that doesn't expect an exception to occur need not be present within the **try** block.

The following code snippet shows the organization of **try** and **catch** blocks. It is not a working program, but it clearly shows how and where the various elements of the exception mechanism are placed.

```
// Elements of exception mechanism
package exceptionexampleproject ;
public class ExceptionExampleProject
{
    public static void main ( String[ ] args )
    {
        // normal code
        // try block – code where an exception condition is anticipated
        try
```

```
        {
            fun( ) ;
        }
        catch ( Exception e )    // exception handler or catch block
        {
            // do something about the error
        }
    }
    public static void fun( )
    {
        // if some error occurs during execution of this function then:
        // (a) Java runtime would create an exception object
        // (b) Java runtime would throw the exception object
        // on throwing the exception object control would reach
        // the catch block
    }
}
```

Here **fun( )** is a function in which an exception may occur during execution. Hence the call to **fun( )** has been placed in the **try** block. If an exception indeed occurs during execution of **fun( )** then the Java runtime creates an exception object and throws it. This thrown exception object is caught in **Exception** reference **e** in the **catch** block that immediately follows the **try** block.

There are three things that our code can do on receiving a thrown object. These are as follows:

(a) Do nothing and let the default exception handler handle the exceptional condition

(b) Rectify the situation that led to the exceptional condition and continue the execution

(c) Perform a graceful exit

These three possibilities are depicted in Figure 15.3.

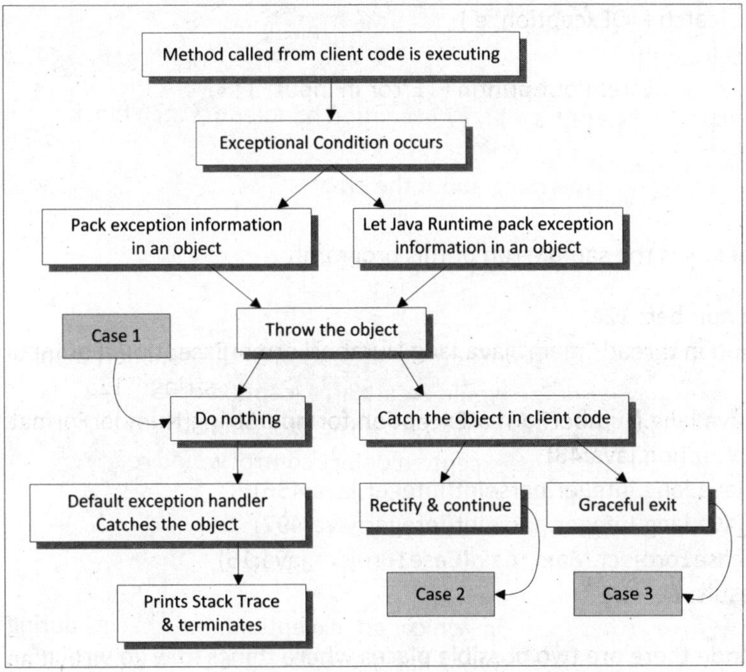

Figure 15.3

Let us now see programs for all these cases to get a real grasp of these situations. Here is the first one...

```
// Case 1 - Do nothing when an exception occurs
package case1project ;
import java.io.* ;
public class Case1Project
{
    public static void main ( String[ ] args ) throws
                                        NumberFormatException
    {
        int num ;
        try
        {
            BufferedReader br = new BufferedReader (
                            new InputStreamReader ( System.in ) ) ;

            System.out.print ( "Enter a number: " ) ;
            num = Integer.parseInt ( br.readLine( ) ) ;
            System.out.println ( num ) ;
        }
```

```
        catch ( IOException  e )
        {
            System.out.println ( "Error in input" ) ;
        }
    }
}
```

Given below is the sample run of this program...

```
Enter a number: 12a
Exception in thread "main" java.lang.NumberFormatException: For input
                                                         string: "12a"
    at java.lang.NumberFormatException.forInputString(NumberFormat
      Exception.java:48)
    at java.lang.Integer.parseInt(Integer.java:456)
    at java.lang.Integer.parseInt(Integer.java:497)
    at case1project.Main.main(Case1Project.java:15)
Java Result: 1
```

In our code there are two possible places where things may go wrong:

(a) While reading using **readLine( )**
(b) While converting string into integer using **parseInt( )**

How do we know this? Well, these functions have advertised these exceptions through their prototypes, which read like this:

```
public String readLine( ) throws IOException
public static int parseInt ( String s ) throws NumberFormatException
```

As you can see, these prototypes indicate that if something goes wrong with **readLine( )**, then it would throw **IOException** and if something goes wrong with **parseInt( )**, then it would throws **NumberFormatException**. This is known as advertising an exception.

For these advertised exceptions, we may adopt any of the following three approaches:

(a) Catch both the exceptions ourselves.
(b) Catch one and throw the other further, so that the default exception handler can deal with it.
(c) Throw both the exceptions further, so that the default exception handler can deal with them.

In our program we have followed approach (b)—we have caught **IOException** and thrown further the **NumberFormatException**.

From the output of the program you can see that when we enter the number as "12a" and attempt to convert it into a string through a call to **Integer.parseInt( )**, an exception occurs. Since we have thrown this exception further, Java runtime prints a stack trace and then terminates the execution of the program. You should read the stack trace from bottom to top. If you do that, you can follow that the error occurred in the file "Case1Project" while executing line number 15. This line is present in **main( )** and contains a call to **Integer.parseInt( )**. And during execution of this function an exception occurred, as the input "12a" could not be converted into a number. Finally, it also reports the name of the exception—**NumberFormatException**.

Let us now look at the second case, where we would attempt to rectify the exception situation by prompting the user to provide correct input and then continue the execution of the program from the point where the exception occurred. Here is the program...

```
// Case 2 – Rectify and continue when an exception occurs
package case2project ;
import java.io.* ;
public class Case2Project
{
    public static void main ( String[ ] args )
    {
        int num ;
        while ( true )
        {
            try
            {
                BufferedReader br = new BufferedReader (
                                new InputStreamReader ( System.in ) ) ;

                System.out.println ( "Enter a number: " ) ;
                num = Integer.parseInt ( br.readLine( ) ) ;
                break ;
            }
            catch ( IOException  e )
            {
                System.out.println ( "Error in input" ) ;
```

```
            }
            catch ( NumberFormatException  e )
            {
                System.out.println ( "Incorrect Input" ) ;
            }
        }
        System.out.println ( "You entered: " + num ) ;
    }
}
```

Shown below is a sample interaction with this program.

```
Enter a number:
12a
Incorrect Input
Enter a number:
12
You entered: 12
```

As you can see, when we provide the input as “12a” an exception occurs. But rather than terminating the execution, this time the program prompts the user to enter another number. When we supply “12”, it gets converted into a number and then displayed Thus, we are now able to rectify the exceptional situation and continue with the execution of the program.

You can note three things about the **catch** block:

(a) **catch** block must immediately follow the **try** block.

(b) When an exception occurs, control goes to **catch** block.

(c) After **catch** block is executed, control goes to the next line after **catch** block unless there is a **return** or **throw** in the **catch** block.

Let us now turn our attention to case 3. It may not always be possible to recover from the exceptional situation. In such cases rather than printing the ugly and intimidating stack trace to the user, our program should report an error and gracefully terminate the execution. The program given below shows how this can be achieved.

```
// Case 3 – Exit gracefully when an exception occurs
package case3project ;
import java.io.*  ;
public class Case3Project
{
```

```
    public static void main ( String[ ] args )
    {
        int num ;
        try
        {
            BufferedReader br = new BufferedReader (
                                        new InputStreamReader ( System.in ) ) ;

            System.out.println ( "Enter a number: " ) ;
            num = Integer.parseInt ( br.readLine( ) ) ;
            System.out.println ( "You entered: " + num ) ;
        }
        catch ( IOException  e )
        {
            System.out.println ( "Error in input" ) ;
        }
        catch ( NumberFormatException e )
        {
            System.out.println ( "Incorrect Input" ) ;
        }
    }
}
```

From the interaction with the program shown below, you can see that when we supply the input as “12a” the program reports that the input is incorrect and then terminates the execution.

```
Enter a number:
12a
Incorrect Input
```

Catching Multiple Exceptions

If one thing can go wrong, then multiple things may also go wrong. So true in real life, this is also true in programming. That is, while executing a piece of code there is a possibility of multiple exceptions. These can be tackled by providing multiple **catch** blocks for one **try** block. A program that illustrates how this can be done is given below.

```
// Multiple exceptions
package multipleexceptionsproject ;
import java.io.*  ;
```

```
public class MultipleExceptionsProject
{
    public static void main ( String[ ] args )
    {
        int i, j ;
        try
        {
            BufferedReader br = new BufferedReader (
                                    new InputStreamReader ( System.in ) ) ;

            System.out.println ( "Enter i: " ) ;
            i = Integer.parseInt ( br.readLine( ) ) ;

            System.out.println ( "Enter j: " ) ;
            j = Integer.parseInt ( br.readLine( ) ) ;

            System.out.println ( "You entered: " + i + " "+j ) ;
            System.out.println ( "Result: "+ i / j ) ;
        }
        catch ( IOException  e )
        {
            System.out.println ( "Error in input" ) ;
        }
        catch ( NumberFormatException ne )
        {
            System.out.println ( "Incorrect Input" ) ;
        }
        catch ( ArithmeticException ae )
        {
            System.out.println ( "Arithmetic Exception, div by 0" ) ;
        }
        catch ( Exception e )
        {
            System.out.println ( "Unknown Error: " + e ) ;
        }
    }
}
```

Here we have accounted for three possibilities while executing the code in the **try** block. These are as follows:

(a) The input is incorrect, i.e., a value like “12a” is entered

(b) The denominator is equal to 0
(c) Some unknown error

To deal with each of these situations we have provided separate **catch** blocks. Based on which exception occurs, Java runtime creates an appropriate exception object and throws it. That is why in each **catch** block the thrown object is collected in a different exception object. For example, if the input is incorrect then the exception object that is thrown is collected in an object of the type **NumberFormatException**. Unlike this, if the denominator is 0 then the exception object that is thrown is collected in an object of the type **ArithmeticException**.

There are two important things that you should note here:

(a) At one time only one **catch** block goes to work.
(b) Order of **catch** blocks is important. Their order should be derived to base as regards the exception object.

Let us elaborate on the second point mentioned above. Since the **NumberFormatException** and **ArithmeticException** classes are derived from the **Exception** class, their **catch** blocks should occur before the one that catches an **Exception** object.

finally Block

At times, we want that no matter whether an exception occurs or not, some statements must be executed. **finally** block is the solution for these situations. The program given below illustrates its usage.

```
// Usage of finally block
package finallyblockproject ;
import java.io.* ;
public class FinallyBlockProject
{
    public static void main ( String[ ] args )
    {
        FileWriter fw = null ;

        try
        {
            fw = new FileWriter ( "a.txt" ) ;
            fw.write ( "Hello World\n" ) ;
        }
```

```
        catch ( IOException ie )
        {
            System.out.println ( "Encountered IO Error" ) ;
        }
        finally
        {
            try
            {
                if ( fw != null )
                    fw.close( ) ;
            }
            catch ( IOException e )
            {
                System.out.println ( "Error in input" ) ;
            }
        }
    }
}
```

Though we intend to deal with File Input/Output in great detail in a later chapter, in this program we can have our first tryst with it. To write data into a disk file, we must first create a **FileWriter** object by passing to its constructor the name of the file into which we propose to write. The actual writing is done by calling the **write( )** function of the **FileWriter** class. If an exception occurs during construction of the **FileWriter** object or during writing, then the **catch** block would appropriately report it.

Now comes the crucial part—no matter whether writing is done successfully or not, before exiting the file that has been opened by the constructor, must be closed. The **finally** block serves this purpose. Statements in the **finally** block always get executed no matter whether an exception occurs or not. This is true even if a **return** statement is encountered beforehand. As you must have guessed, **finally** is a keyword, and is used following the **catch** block(s). In our **finally** block we have first checked whether the **FileWriter** object has been created successfully. If so, we have called the **close( )** method to close the file associated with the **FileWriter** object.

User-defined Exceptions

In all the programs in this chapter we have been using exception objects created from Java exception classes. It is time we explore the possibility of user-defined exception classes. Such classes are required when an exception condition that occurs cannot be represented using the standard exception classes. For example, a banking application may throw an exception when the amount being withdrawn makes the balance in an account go below the minimum prescribed limit. Another example could be when the amount of transaction in a credit card application is more than the credit limit of a credit card. In such cases we need to define our own exception class, and when an exception occurs, we need to create an object of this exception class and throw it. The following program illustrates this in a simple banking application:

```
// Usage of user-defined exception
package userdefinedexceptionproject ;
class Customer
{
    private String name ;
    private int accno ;
    private int balance ;
    public Customer ( String n, int a, int b )
    {
        name = n ;  accno = a ; balance = b ;
    }
    public void withdraw ( int amt ) throws BankException
    {
        if ( balance - amt <= 500 )
        {
            throw new BankException ( accno, balance ) ;
        }

        balance -= amt ;
    }
}
class BankException extends Exception
{
    private int acc ;
    private int bal ;
    public BankException ( int a , int b )
    {
        this.acc = a ;
        this.bal = b ;
    }
    public void inform( )
    {
```

```
        System.out.println ( "Acc. No.: "+ acc ) ;
        System.out.println ( "Balance: "+ bal ) ;
    }
}
public class UserDefinedExceptionProject
{
    public static void main ( String[ ] args )
    {
        try
        {
            Customer c = new Customer ( "Rahul", 2453, 900 ) ;
            c.withdraw ( 450 ) ;
        }
        catch ( BankException  ex )
        {
            System.out.println ( "Transaction failed" ) ;
            ex.inform( ) ;
        }
    }
}
```

Given below is the output of the program...

```
Transaction failed
Acc. No.: 2453
Balance: 900
```

In this program apart from the normal class that contains **main( )**, we have defined two new classes—**Customer** and **BankException**. From **main( )** we have constructed an object of **Customer** class to contain name, account number and balance amount. Then we have called the **withdraw( )** method from the **try** block to withdraw an amount of Rs. 450 from the customer's account. Since the amount being withdrawn makes the balance go below Rs. 500, an exception occurs. To represent this exceptional condition, an object of **BankException** (derived from **Exception** class) class is created. The account number and current balance values are stored in this **BankException** object. This object is then thrown using the keyword **throw**. This takes the control straightway to the **catch** block that matches the **try** block, from where **withdraw( )** method was called. In the **catch** block we have called the method **inform( )** which promptly displays the error message

"Transaction failed" along with account number and the current balance.

A More Practical Example

Admittedly, the examples that we have used so far to understand exception handling were a bit amateurish. Let's now try to use exception handling in a more practical situation. We would try to implement a stack data structure. We would use exception handling to report errors in two situations:

(a) When the program attempts to store more objects in the stack than what it can accommodate.

(b) When the program tries to remove an object from the empty stack.

Here is the program that uses exceptions to handle these two errors.

```
// Use of exceptions to report errors while maintaining a stack
package stackswithexceptionsproject ;
class Stack
{
    private int capacity ;
    private int size ;
    private Object[ ] data ;
    public Stack ( int cap )
    {
        data = new Object[ cap ] ;
        capacity = cap ;
        size = 0 ;
    }
    public void push ( Object o ) throws StackException
    {
        if ( size == capacity )
            throw new StackException ( "Stack full" ) ;

        data[ size ] = o ;
        size++ ;
    }
    public Object pop( ) throws StackException
    {
        if ( size <= 0 )
            throw new StackException ( "Stack empty" ) ;
```

```
        size-- ;
        return data[ size ] ;
    }
    public int getSize( )
    {
        return size ;
    }
}
class StackException extends Exception
{
    private String errormsg ;

    public StackException ( String msg )
    {
        this.errormsg = msg ;
    }
    public void inform( )
    {
        System.out.println ( errormsg ) ;
    }
}
public class StacksWithExceptionsProject
{
    public static void main ( String[ ] args )
    {
        Stack s = new Stack ( 3 ) ;
        try
        {
            s.push ( "Vinod" ) ;
            s.push ( "Sanjay" ) ;
            s.push ( 25 ) ;
            s.push ( 3.14f ) ;
        }
        catch ( StackException ex )
        {
            System.out.println ( "Problem in stack" ) ;
            ex.inform( ) ;
        }

        try
```

```
        {
            while ( s.getSize( ) > 0 )
                System.out.println ( s.pop( ) ) ;
        }
        catch ( StackException ex )
        {
            System.out.println ( "Problem in stack" ) ;
            ex.inform( ) ;
        }
    }
}
```

Given below is the output that the program produces on execution:

```
Problem in stack
Stack full
25
Sanjay
Vinod
```

We have purposefully kept the capacity of the stack small so that it's easier to trigger an exception while adding objects to the stack. We would leave it for you to go through the program and figure out how it produces this output, as an exercise. Also, you can try to implement the Queue data structure on similar lines as stack.

From the above two programs—Banking and Stack—we can now generalize how to deal with user-defined exceptions. There are four parts involved in the exception handling mechanism. These are as under:

Define the Exception Class

We have defined such exception classes in our programs—**BankException** and **StackException**. Both classes were inherited from **Exception** class and had a constructor using which an exception object can be created. Additionally these classes had a method called **inform( )** to report error messages.

Throw an Exception

When an exceptional situation occurs an exception object is created and thrown. In our first program an exception could occur in one situation—when the balance goes below 500, whereas, in the second program there were two exceptional situations—when the stack becomes full and we try to store another object in it, or when we try to remove an object from an empty stack. In the first program, we create and throw a **BankException** object, whereas in the second we create and throw a **StackException** object. On throwing an exception the control is transferred to the exception handler, i.e., the **catch** block.

try Block

The statements that might cause exceptions have been enclosed in a pair of braces and preceded by the **try** keyword. This code is the program's normal code. We would have written it even if we weren't using exceptions. Note that all the code in the program need not be in a **try** block. Just the code that anticipates the occurrence of exceptional condition during execution should be in **try** block.

The Exception Handler (*catch* Block)

The code that handles an exception is enclosed in braces, preceded by the **catch** keyword, with the exception object that it proposes to catch mentioned in parentheses.

How the Whole Thing Works?

Let's summarize the events that take place when an exception occurs:

(a) Code is executing normally outside a **try** block.
(b) Control enters the **try** block.
(c) A statement in the **try** block causes an error in a member function called from it.
(d) The member function creates and throws an exception object.
(e) Control transfers to the exception handler (**catch** block) following the **try** block.

You can appreciate how clean is this code. Just about any statement in the **try** block can cause an exception, but we don't need to worry which one. The **try-throw-catch** arrangement handles it all for us, automatically.

A Few Tips...

To round off all that we have learnt about exception handling, here are a few finer points about it that you must note:

(a) Don't catch and ignore. For example, it is a wrong practice to write a **catch** block like this:

```
catch ( Exception e )
{
}
```

Programmers are tempted to write this when runtime errors occur in their program and they wish to avoid displaying of an ugly and elaborate stack trace of the exception.

(b) Don't use exception handling for cosmetic purposes. It should serve the purpose of rectifying the exceptional situation or perform a graceful exit.

(c) Always try to distinguish between types of exceptions by writing multiple **catch** blocks wherever relevant.

(d) It is not necessary that the statement that causes an exception be located directly in the **try** block. It may as well be present in a function that is being called from the **try** block.

(e) A **try** block can be present inside another **try** block.

(f) If the inner **try** block doesn't have a corresponding **catch block**, then the outer **try** block's **catch** handlers are inspected for a match when an exception occurs.

(g) If we are writing a class library for somebody else to use, we should anticipate what could cause problems to the program using it. At all such places we should throw exceptions.

(h) If we are writing a program that uses a class library, we should provide **try** and **catch** blocks for any exceptions that the library may throw.

(i) Exceptions impose an overhead in terms of program size and (when an exception occurs) in time. So, we should not try to overuse it. Make it optimally elaborate—not too much, not too little.

Exercises

[A] State whether the following statements are True or False:

(a) The exception handling mechanism is supposed to handle compile time errors.

(b) It is necessary to declare the exception class within the class in which an exception is going to be thrown.

(c) Every thrown exception must be caught.

(d) For one **try** block there can be multiple **catch** blocks.

(e) When an exception is thrown an exception class's constructor gets called.

(f) **try** blocks cannot be nested.

(g) Proper destruction of an object is guaranteed by exception handling mechanism.

(h) All exceptions occur at runtime.

(i) Exceptions offer an object-oriented way of handling runtime errors.

(j) If an exception occurs, then the program terminates abruptly without getting any chance to recover from the exception.

(k) No matter whether an exception occurs or not, the statements in the **finally** clause (if present) will get executed.

(l) A program can contain multiple **finally** clauses.

(m) **finally** clause is used to perform cleanup operations like closing the network/database connections.

(n) While throwing a user-defined exception multiple values can be set in the exception object.

(o) In one function, there can be only one **try** block.

(p) An exception must be caught in the same function in which it is thrown.

(q) All values set up in the exception object are available in the **catch** block.

(r) If our program does not catch an exception, then the Java Runtime catches it.

(s) It is possible to create user-defined exceptions.

(t) All types of exceptions can be caught using the **Exception** class.

(u) For every **try** block there must be a corresponding **finally** block.

[B] Answer the following questions:

(a) If we do not catch the exception thrown at runtime then who will catch it?

(b) Explain in short the most compelling reasons for using exception handling over conventional error handling approaches.

(c) Is it necessary that all classes that can be used to represent exceptions be derived from base class **Exception**?

(d) What is the use of a **finally** block in Java exception handling sequence?

(e) How does nested exception handling work in Java?

KanNotes

- While creating and executing a Java program things may go wrong at 3 different stages :
  During Compilation : Reported by – Compiler, Action – Rectify program
  During Linking : Reported by – Linker, Action – Proper import statements
  During Execution (runtime) : Reported by – Java Runtime, Action – Tackle it on the fly
- Examples of Runtime errors :
  Memory Related - Stack / Heap overflow, Exceeding the bounds of an array
  Arithmetic Related - Divide by zero, Arithmetic overflow or underflow
  Others - Attempt to use an unassigned reference, File not found
- 2 Types of Exceptional conditions :

(a) Checked Exceptions - Compiler checks whether they have been handled
Ex. File not found, Insufficient memory
(b) Unchecked exceptions - Up to us whether to handle them or not

- 2 Types of Unchecked Exceptions :

(a) Due to Internal Condition - k/a Runtime Exceptions
Ex. : Passing null instead of filename
(b) Due to External Condition - k/a Errors
Ex. : Disk failure while reading

- How to determine - Checked or Unchecked
    - Follow trail by clicking on exception
    - It is a Checked Exception, if you reach "Exception" class
    - It is an Unchecked Exception, if you reach "RuntimeException" or "Error" class

- When a method called from client code is executing an Exceptional Condition may occur. This condition can be tackled in 2 Ways :

(a) Pack exception information in an object and throw it
(b) Let Java Runtime pack exception information in an object and throw it

- Two things that can be done when the exception object is thrown :

(a) Throw it further
(b) Catch the object in client code

- If we throw the exception object further - Default exception handler Catches the object, Prints Stack Trace & terminates

- If we catch the exception object in client code, we can either perform a graceful exit or rectify the exceptional situation & continue

- 2 ways to create Exceptional Condition objects

From Java API exception classes
From User-defined exception classes

- Advantage of tackling exceptions in OO manner :
    - More info can be packed into Exception objects

- Propagation of exception objects to caller is managed by Java Runtime

- How Java facilitates OO exception handling :
  - By providing keywords - try, catch, finally, throw, throws
  - By providing readymade exception classes - For Checked as well as Unchecked Exceptions
  - Advertise - Let methods advertise possibility of an exception
  - Force - Make users handle advertised exception

- How to use try - catch

  try block - Enclose in it the code that you anticipate would cause an exception
  catch block - Catch the thrown exception in it. It must immediately follow the try block

- When exception is thrown control goes to catch block. Once catch block is executed, control goes to the next line after catch block(s), unless there is a return or throw in the catch block

- When a method advertises that it will throw an exception, you have to either catch or rethrow it.

- try block :
  - Can be nested inside another try block
  - If inner try doesn't have a catch, outer try's catch handlers are inspected for a match

- catch block :
  - Multiple catch blocks for one try block are OK
  - At a time only one catch block goes to work
  - Order of catch blocks is important - Derived to Base

- finally block :
  - finally clause is optional
  - Code in finally always runs, no matter what! Even if a return or break occurs first
  - it is placed after catch blocks (if they exist)
  - try block must have catch block and/or finally block

- Exception handling tips :
    - Don't catch & ignore an exception
    - Don't catch everything using "Exception", distinguish between types of exceptions
    - Make it optimally elaborate - Not too much, not too little

Let Us JAVA 7th Edition

CHAPTER 16

Effective Input / Output

No point in creating a program that tells secrets to itself. Input / Output with the outside world is the way of life for a program...

Contents

- Expectations from an I/O System
- File, Directory and Drive Operations
- The Java Streams Solution
- Stream Classes
- Byte and Character Operations
- Reading Strings from a File
- Record I/O
- User-defined Streams
- File Encryption/Decryption
- Serialization / Deserialization
- Exercises
- KanNotes

Almost all programs have to perform Input/Output (I/O) in some form or the other. There is not much use in writing a program that spends all its time telling a secret to itself. And since all languages have been dealing with input/output since the very first program came into existence, it is quite natural to expect that a modern object-oriented language like Java provides a *mature* input/output system. This chapter proposes to explore the ways provided by Java to effectively carry out I/O needs of a program.

Expectations from an I/O System

Since mankind has been creating software and writing programs for more than five decades now, a programmer has begun to expect some solid support from a language's I/O system to cater to his/her program's I/O needs. These expectations are as follows:

(a) **Communication with different sources and destinations**: A Java program should be able to carry out reading operations from input devices like keyboard, port, disk, etc., and perform writing operations to disk, printer, port, etc.

(b) **Capability to I/O varied entities**: A Java program should be able to I/O byte, char, numbers of all kinds, strings, records, and objects.

(c) **Multiple means of communication**: A Java program should be able to carry out I/O in different modes like sequential and random.

(d) **Communication with file system**: A Java program should be able to interact with file system entities like files and directories and be able to access and manipulate paths, times, dates, access permissions, etc.

Let us now see how Java meets these expectations.

File, Directory and Drive Operations

We are often required to programmatically perform operations on files, directories and drives. For example, we may wish to create, copy, delete, move, or open a file. Similarly, we may wish to create, move, and navigate through directories and subdirectories. To carry out such operations Java library provides a ready-made class called **File**. Based on the requirement, we can appropriately use the methods of this class to carry out the relevant file/directory operations.

Let us now create programs that use **File** class. We would begin with one that receives the name of a file as input and then checks whether such a file exists or not. If it does, then it reports the relevant information about this file. Here is the program...

```
// Obtain information about a file
package fileinfoproject ;
import java.io.* ;
import java.util.Date ;
public class FileInfoProject
{
    public static void main ( String[ ] args ) throws Exception
    {
        String str ;
        try
        {
            BufferedReader br = new BufferedReader ( new
                                 InputStreamReader ( System.in ) ) ;
            System.out.print ( "Enter filename: " ) ;
            str = br.readLine( ) ;

            File f ;
            f = new File ( str ) ;
            if ( f.exists( ) )
            {
                String dname = f.getParent( ) ;
                System.out.println ( "Directory name: " + dname ) ;
                String fname = f.getName( ) ;
                System.out.println ( "File name: " + fname ) ;
                String abspath = f.getAbsolutePath( ) ;
                System.out.println ( "Full Name: " + abspath ) ;

                long size = f.length( ) ;
                System.out.println ( "Size: " + size ) ;
                String ext ;
                int dot = str.lastIndexOf ( "." ) ;
                ext = str.substring ( dot ) ;
                System.out.println ( "Extension = " + ext ) ;
                System.out.println ( "Last Modified = " +
                                      new Date ( f.lastModified( ) ) ) ;
            }
        }
        catch ( IOException e )
        {
```

```
            System.out.println ( "Error in input" ) ;
        }
    }
}
```

And now a sample interaction with this program...

```
Enter filename: c:\a.txt
Directory name: c:\
File name: a.txt
Full Name: c:\a.txt
Size: 2748
Extension = .txt
Last Modified = Tue Feb 09 16:29:24 IST 2010
```

The program is straight-forward. To begin with, it receives the name of the file—"C:\a.txt" (you may give any other file's path as input). Next, it creates a **File** object for this file and then extracts all the details of this file using different methods of the **File** class. To be able to use **File** class and **Date** class it is necessary to add the suitable **import** statements at the beginning of the program.

In addition to the methods used here, there are several other methods in the **File** class. You may explore them on your own.

Let us now create a program that gives a listing of all files in a directory. Here is the program...

```
// Recursive listing of files in directories
package directorylisterproject ;
import java.io.* ;
public class DirectoryListerProject
{
    public static void main ( String[ ] args )
    {
        File d ;
        d = new File ( "." ) ;
        ListFiles ( d, "" ) ;
    }
    static void ListFiles ( File d, String indent )
    {
        String str ;
        System.out.println ( indent + d.getName( ) + "/" ) ;
```

```
        for ( File fi : d.listFiles( ) )
        {
            str = indent + "  " + fi.getName( ) ;
            System.out.println ( str ) ;
        }
        // implement accept function of FileFilter interface
        FileFilter dirFilter = new FileFilter( )
        {
            public boolean accept ( File file )
            {
                return file.isDirectory( ) ;
            }
        }
        for ( File di : d.listFiles ( dirFilter ) )
            ListFiles ( di, indent + "  " ) ;
    }
}
```

On executing the program on my machine, it produced the following output:

```
./
 build
 build.xml
 manifest.mf
 nbproject
 src
 build/
  classes
  classes/
   .netbeans_automatic_build
   .netbeans_update_resources
   directorylisterproject
   directorylisterproject/
    DirectoryListerProject$1.class
    DirectoryListerProject.class
 nbproject/
  build-impl.xml
  genfiles.properties
  private
  project.properties
  project.xml
```

```
  private/
    private.properties
 src/
  directorylisterproject
  directorylisterproject/
    DirectoryListerProject.java
```

In the output every directory has been purposefully marked with a / to help identify an entry as a directory. Each nested directory is indented to the right to show the hierarchy clearly.

At the heart of the program is the function **ListFiles( )**. This function is first called from **main( )** with two arguments—"." and "". The first argument indicates from where to start the listing and second indicates the starting indentation level. "." means current directory. Thus, for our program **DirectoryListerProject** is the starting directory. In the **ListFiles( )** function we have first obtained and printed all files in this directory. In course of this, if we came across any directory then we have called **ListFiles( )** recursively to list files in this directory.

Let us now look at another interesting program. This one obtains and reports information about all the drives present in a machine. To obtain the list of drives, it uses the **listRoots( )** method of the **File** class. Then through a **for** loop it iterates through this list, gathering details of each drive using the methods of the **File** class. Rest of the program is straightforward. Here is the program...

```
// Obtain information about all drives
package driveinfoproject ;
import java.io.* ;
public class DriveInfoProject
{
    public static void main ( String[ ] args )
    {
        for ( File d : File.listRoots( ) )
        {
            System.out.println ( "Drive = " + d ) ;
            System.out.println ( "Total Space = "+ d.getTotalSpace( ) ) ;
            System.out.println ( "Free Space = "+ d.getFreeSpace( ) ) ;
            System.out.println ( " " ) ;
        }
    }
}
```

The machine on which we executed this program had 6 drives. Out of these 3 were hard disk drives whereas the other 3 were DVD reader, DVD read/write drive, and a virtual drive. The output that we got on this machine is given below.

```
Drive = C:\
Total Space = 179583315968
Free Space = 18052345856

Drive = D:\
Total Space = 59624124416
Free Space = 20760801280

Drive = E:\
Total Space = 10737414144
Free Space = 6717689856

Drive = F:\
Total Space = 0
Free Space = 0

Drive = G:\
Total Space = 0
Free Space = 0

Drive = H:\
Total Space = 0
Free Space = 0
```

The Java Streams Solution

To meet the expectations of a mature I/O system Java designers decided that all I/O should be performed using I/O Streams. A stream is a sequence of bytes that travel from source to destination over a communication path. A program can read data from a stream or write data to a stream. The streams are linked to physical devices by Java I/O system. Most of the communication details are hidden from us by the I/O system and we are required to concentrate only on what we wish to read from where, and what we wish to write where. Figure 16.1 should help you understand this concept better.

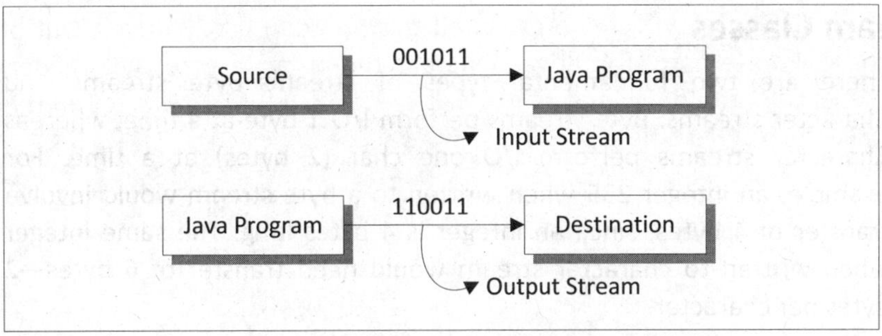

Figure 16.1

Streams are implemented using classes in **java.io** package. This abstraction of I/O operations using streams offers one important benefit—no matter from where we are reading or where we are writing, stream behaves similarly. For example, whether we are reading from a keyboard or a disk we call the same **readLine( )** method. The implementation of the **readLine( )** method is different for different devices. Thus, because of stream-based I/O the programmer doesn't have to worry about the specific details of the operating system and underlying devices while performing I/O as shown in Figure 16.2. The differences in the devices and the OS are hidden away from us into different stream classes in the **java.io** package.

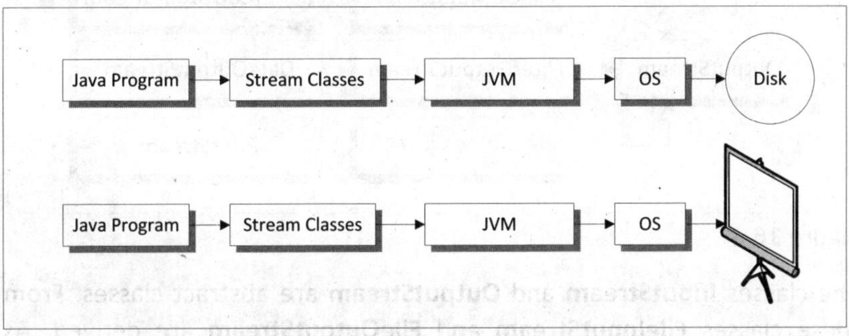

Figure 16.2

The two fundamental operations that can be performed on a stream are Reading and Writing. Reading involves transferring data from a stream into a data structure, such as an array of bytes. Writing consists of transferring data from a data source into a stream.

Every stream may not support reading and writing. Most stream classes contain methods called **canRead( )** and **canWrite( )** using which we can determine which operations that stream supports.

Stream Classes

There are two fundamental types of streams–Byte streams and Character streams. Byte streams perform I/O 1 byte at a time, whereas Character streams perform I/O one char (2 bytes) at a time. For example, an integer 235 when written to a byte stream would involve transfer of 4 bytes, since an integer is 4 bytes long. The same integer when written to character stream would need transfer of 6 bytes—2 bytes per character.

There are several classes available in the Java library to perform stream-based input/output of bytes/characters. Figure 16.3 and Figure 16.4 show the hierarchy of these classes.

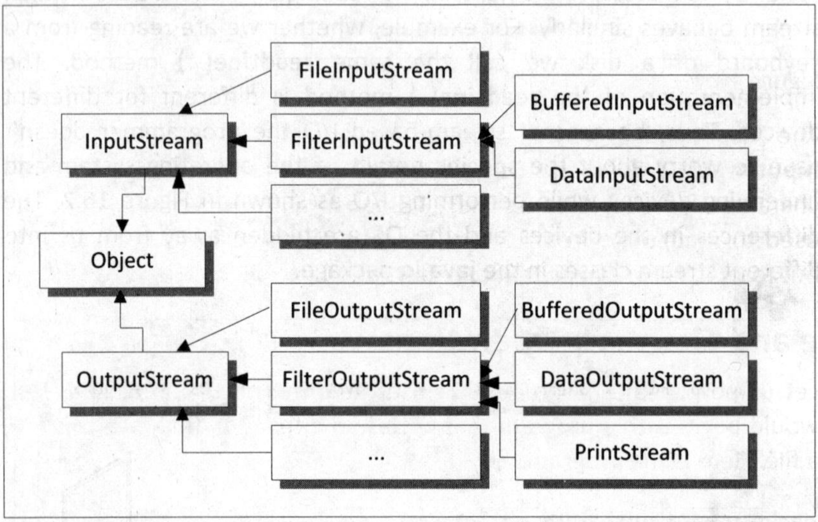

Figure 16.3

The classes **InputStream** and **OutputStream** are abstract classes. From these classes **FileInputStream** and **FileOutputStream** are derived. As their names suggest, these classes read/write streams of bytes from/to file. The **FilterInputStream** class uses some input stream as source of data and filters it based on some criterion. The **BufferedInputStream** class provides the buffering ability. Buffering is used to improve read/write performance of a stream. The **DataInputStream** class provides the ability to read Java primitives.

Figure 16.4 shows the hierarchy of classes used for performing character-based input/output.

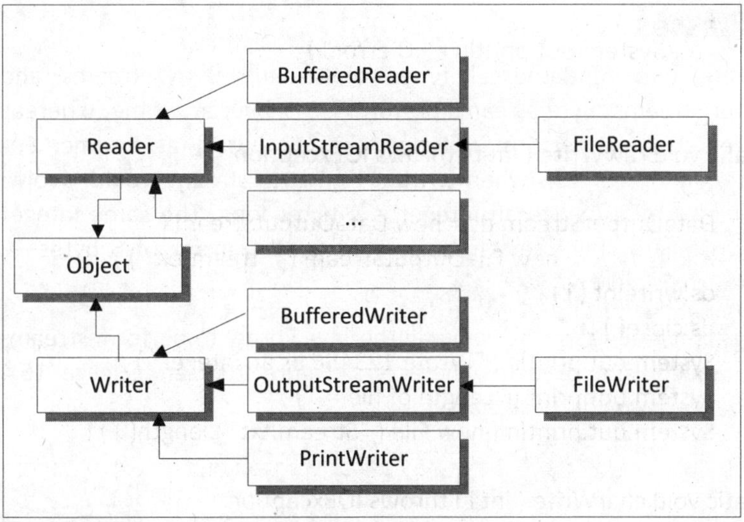

Figure 16.4

The **Reader** and **Writer** classes are abstract classes. The classes **InputStreamReader** and **OutputStreamWriter** are used to read/write character from/to stream. The **FileReader** and **FileWriter** classes are used to read/write from/to file. The **PrintWriter** class is used to carry out formatted writing in text representation.

Byte and Character Operations

Let us now create programs that use the different stream classes. We would begin with a program that writes an integer in multiple ways into a file. Here is the program...

```
package byteandcharacterstreams ;
import java.io.* ;
public class ByteAndCharacterStreams
{
    public static void main ( String[ ] args )
    {
        int i = 123456 ;
        try
        {
            rawWrite ( i ) ;
            charWrite ( i ) ;
            unicodeWrite ( i ) ;
        }
        catch ( IOException e )
```

```
        {
            System.out.println ( "IO error" ) ;
        }
    }
    static void rawWrite ( int i ) throws IOException
    {
        DataOutputStream ds = new DataOutputStream (
                    new FileOutputStream ( "Stream.txt" ) ) ;
        ds.writeInt ( i ) ;
        ds.close( ) ;
        System.out.println ( "Wrote 123456 as an integer" ) ;
        System.out.print ( "Length of file = " ) ;
        System.out.println ( new File ( "Stream.txt" ).length( ) ) ;
    }
    static void charWrite ( int i ) throws IOException
    {
        FileWriter fw = new FileWriter ( new File ( "Char.txt" ) ) ;
        fw.write ( ( ( Integer ) i ).toString( ) ) ;
        fw.close( ) ;
        System.out.println ( "Wrote 123456 as a string" ) ;
        System.out.print ( "Length of file = " ) ;
        System.out.println ( new File ( "Char.txt" ).length( ) ) ;
    }
    static void unicodeWrite ( int i ) throws IOException
    {
        OutputStreamWriter ow = new OutputStreamWriter (
            new FileOutputStream ( "CharU.txt" ), "UTF-16" ) ;
        ow.write ( ( ( Integer ) i ).toString( ) ) ;
        ow.close( ) ;
        System.out.println ( "Wrote 123456 as a Unicode string" ) ;
        System.out.print ( "Length of file = " ) ;
        System.out.println ( new File ( "CharU.txt" ).length( ) ) ;
    }
}
```

On executing this program, it produces the output shown below.

```
Wrote 123456 as an integer
Length of file = 4

Wrote 123456 as a string
Length of file = 6
```

```
Wrote 123456 as a Unicode string
Length of file = 14
```

The program writes the same integer into 3 files in different ways. For example, it is written as an **int** in the first file, as a **string** in the second and as a **Unicode string** in the third. These writing operations are done through three methods defined in the program—**rawWrite( )**, **charWrite( )** and **unicodeWrite( )**.

Note that after writing the same integer value (123456), the sizes of the three files "Raw.txt", "Char.txt" and "CharU.txt" are reported as 4, 6 and 14 bytes, respectively. This indicates that during raw writing, each byte value of the 4-byte integer is written. Unlike this, during character writing, the integer was first converted into a string "123456" and then written to the file character-by-character. In Unicode writing, each character of the string was written as a 2-byte character.

Before writing to a file, the file is opened using either the **FileOutputStream** or **File** object. While writing the integer as an **int**, a **DataOutputStream** object is used, whereas, while writing it as a string or a Unicode string, a **FileWriter** and **OutputStreamWriter**, respectively are used. Objects of these writers are created before using them to call the **writeInt( )** and **write( )** methods. Instead of the statement,

```
DataOutputStream ds = new DataOutputStream (
                        new FileOutputStream ( "Stream.txt" ) ) ;
```

we can split it into two parts

```
fos = new FileOutputStream ( "Stream.txt" ) ;
DataOutputStream ds = new DataOutputStream ( fos ) ;
```

The **close( )** function is called at the end of writing operations to close the current stream and release any resources associated with the current stream.

The rest of the program is simple to understand. You can modify this program to write float values to a file.

Reading Strings from a File

Let us now create a program which can read a file's content and display them on screen. For this we would read the file contents a line at a time, meaning as a string of characters. Here is the program...

```
// Reading strings from a file
package displayfilecontentsproject ;
import java.io.* ;
public class DisplayFileContentsProject
{
    public static void main ( String[ ] args ) throws IOException
    {
        File f ;
        f = new File ( "D:\\DisplayFileContents\\src\\
                    displayfilecontents\\DisplayFileContents.java" ) ;
        if ( f.exists( ) && f.canRead( ) )
        {
            BufferedReader br = null ;
            try
            {
                br = new BufferedReader ( new FileReader ( f ) ) ;
                String line ;
                while ( ( line = br.readLine( ) ) != null )
                    System.out.println ( line ) ;
            }
            catch ( FileNotFoundException ex )
            {
                System.out.println ( "Can't open " + f.getName( ) ) ;
            }
            finally
            {
                if ( br != null )
                    br.close( ) ;
            }
        }
    }
}
```

When we run this program, it displays the contents of the file "DisplayFileContents.java". In the program, to begin with, we created a **File** object, and then using it, we have checked whether the file exists, and whether we have a permission to read the file. If so, we have proceeded to read the file a line at a time using the **BufferedReader** object that has a **FileReader** object reference stored in it. Every line read is displayed on the screen using **println( )**.

Record I/O

Suppose we wish to write records of employees into a file and then read them back from the file and display them on the screen. Each record contains id, name, and salary of an employee. Here is the program...

```
// receives employee records, writes them to file,
// reads them back and displays them on screen
package recordioproject ;
import java.io.* ;
public class RecordIOProject
{
    public static void main ( String[ ] args ) throws IOException
    {
        // prepare for writing records
        FileOutputStream  fos ;
        fos = new FileOutputStream ( "emp.dat" ) ;
        OutputStreamWriter osw ;
        osw = new OutputStreamWriter ( fos ) ;

        // prepare for console input
        InputStreamReader  isr1 ;
        isr1 = new InputStreamReader ( System.in ) ;
        BufferedReader  br1 = new BufferedReader ( isr1 ) ;

        // receive employee data, write it to file
        String  choice = "y", temp1, temp2, temp3 ;
        while ( choice.equals ( "y" ) )
        {
            System.out.println ( "Enter employee id: " ) ;
            temp1 = br1.readLine( ) ;
            System.out.println ( "Enter employee salary: " ) ;
            temp2 = br1.readLine( ) ;
            System.out.println ( "Enter employee name: " ) ;
            temp3 = br1.readLine( ) ;
            osw.write ( temp1 + "@" + temp2 + "@" + temp3 + "\n" ) ;
            System.out.println ( "Want another ( y/n ): " ) ;
            choice = br1.readLine( ) ;
        }
        osw.close( ) ;

        // prepare for reading records
```

```
        FileInputStream  fis ;
        fis = new FileInputStream ( "emp.dat" ) ;
        InputStreamReader isr2 ;
        isr2 = new InputStreamReader ( fis ) ;
        BufferedReader  br2 ;
        br2 = new BufferedReader ( isr2 ) ;

        String  rec, str[ ] ;
        // read employee data, display it on screen
        System.out.println ( "\nEmployees Info: " ) ;
        while ( true )
        {
            try
            {
                rec = br2.readLine( ) ;
                str = rec.split("@", 3) ;
                System.out.println ( "Id: " + str[ 0 ] ) ;
                System.out.println ( "Salary: " + str[ 1 ] ) ;
                System.out.println ( "Name: " + str[ 2 ] ) ;
            }
            catch ( Exception e )
            {
                if ( fis != null )
                    fis.close( ) ;
            }
        }
    }
}
```

To begin with we have created objects of **FileOutputStream**, and **OutputStreamWriter** classes. Of these, the **FileOutputStream** object is used to write employee data to a file. To carry out this writing we have used the function **write( )**. Once a set of records are written, we have closed the stream.

In the next part of the program, we have done the reverse, we have read the data from the same file "emp.dat" and displayed it on the screen. While reading, each record is read as a string. Hence to split it into id, salary and name we have used the **split( )** function. Here is the sample interaction with the program...

```
Enter employee id: 101
```

```
Enter employee salary: 12000
Enter employee name: Dinesh
Want another ( y/n ): y
Enter employee id: 201
Enter employee salary: 13500
Enter employee name: Shailesh
Want another ( y/n ): y
Enter employee id: 301
Enter employee salary: 13300
Enter employee name: Seema
Want another ( y/n ): n

Employees Info:
101
12000.0
Dinesh
201
13500.0
Shailesh
301
13300.0
Seema
```

User-defined Streams

Apart from using the standard streams Java permits us to define our own streams and their behavior. For example, we can define a filter stream called **UppercaseFilterStream** which would convert all characters passed through it into uppercase characters. Such a stream class should be derived from **FilterStream** class. The following program illustrates how this can be done:

```
// Converts all chars read from a file into uppercase using a filter stream
package filterstreamproject ;
import java.io.* ;
class UppercaseFilterReader extends FilterReader
{
    public UppercaseFilterReader ( Reader s )
    {
        super ( s ) ;
    }
    public int read ( char[ ] cbuf, int off, int count ) throws IOException
```

```
    {
        int nb = in.read ( cbuf, off, count ) ;

        for ( int i = off ; i < off + nb ; i++ )
            cbuf[ i ] = transform ( cbuf[ i ] ) ;

        return nb ;
    }
    private char transform ( char ch )
    {
        if ( Character.isLowerCase ( ch ) )
            return Character.toUpperCase ( ( char ) ch ) ;

        return ch ;
    }
}
public class FilterStreamProject
{
    public static void main ( String[ ] args ) throws
                        FileNotFoundException, IOException
    {
        File f = new File ( "C:\\a.txt" ) ;
        if ( f.exists( ) )
        {
            UppercaseFilterReader ufr ;
            BufferedReader br ;
            ufr = new UppercaseFilterReader (
                new FileReader ( "C:\\a.txt" ) ) ;
            br = new BufferedReader ( ufr ) ;
            String line ;
            while ( ( line = br.readLine( ) ) != null )
                System.out.println ( line ) ;
            br.close( ) ;
            ufr.close( ) ;
        }
    }
}
```

On executing this program, it opens the file "a.txt" from C:\ and converts the text in it into uppercase. The uppercase characters are then displayed on the screen. In my case the "a.txt" file contained some interesting text. Once converted to uppercase it looked like this...

I CDNUOLT BLVEIEE TAHT I CLUOD AULACLTY UESDNATNRD WAHT I WAS RDANIEG. THE PHAONMNEAL PWEOR OF THE HMUAN MNID, AOCCDRNIG TO A RSCHEEARCH AT CMABRIGDE UINERVTISY, IT DSENO'T MTAETR IN WAHT OERDR THE LTTERES IN A WROD ARE, THE OLNY IPROAMTNT TIHNG is TAHT THE FRSIT AND LSAT LTTEER BE IN THE RGHIT PCLAE.. THE RSET CAN BE A TAOTL MSES AND YOU CAN SITLL RAED IT WHOTUIT A PBOERLM. TIHS IS BCUSEAE THE HUAMN MNID DEOS NOT RAED ERVEY LTETER BY ISTLEF, BUT THE WROD AS A WLOHE. AZANMIG HUH? YAEH AND I AWLYAS TGHUHOT SLPELING WAS IPMORANTT!

The **UppercaseFilterReader** class is derived from the abstract class **FilterReader.** We have added three methods to the **UppercaseFilterReader** class. These are constructor, **read( )** and **transform( )**. In the constructor, we simply pass the **FileReader** object passed to it, to the base class constructor. The **read( )** function reads the specified number of bytes from a given offset position in the stream and stores them in a buffer. It then calls the **transform( )** function to transform each character in the buffer into corresponding uppercase character.

In **main( )** we have first created a **FileReader** object. This object has then been passed to the constructor of **UppercaseFilterStream**, which passed it to the constructor of its base class—**FilterReader**. This class's constructor stores object reference in a private variable. Next, we have created a **BufferedReader** object and stored in it the **UppercaseFilterStream** object's reference. In both cases containership is being used as shown in Figure 16.5.

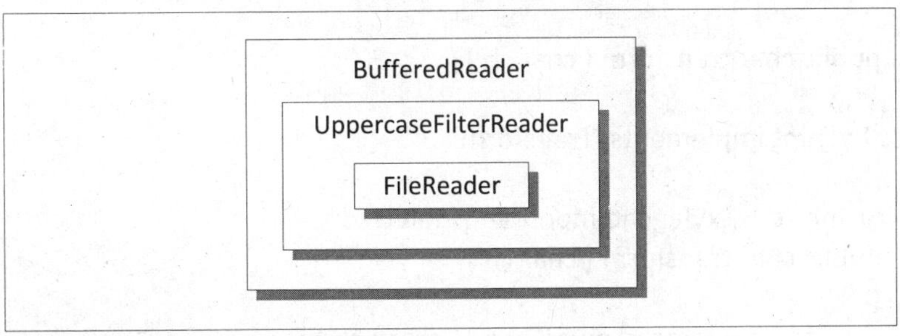

Figure 16.5

Once the construction of objects is over, we have called the **readLine( )** method of **BufferedReader** class. This method in turn calls the **read( )** method of the **UppercaseFilterStream** class. Here firstly the characters are read from the input stream by calling the **read( )** method of **FileReader** class. These characters are collected in the buffer **cbuf**. This buffer's contents are then converted to uppercase by calling the **transform( )** function for each character in the buffer. Thus, we can change the behavior of a stream by implementing the desired behavior through a filter stream class.

File Encryption/Decryption

Security has gained paramount importance in the digital world. Often, we wish to secure our data from others. There are various techniques through which this can be done. One of the most common techniques is to encrypt the data in such a fashion that even if the encrypted data falls into other people's hands they are unable to obtain the original data from it. At the same time, we should be able to get back the original data by decrypting the encrypted data. Many Encryption/Decryption schemes are popularly used today to secure the data from misuse. Our intention here is not to discuss these schemes. Instead, we wish to evolve a very simple encryption/decryption scheme. In this scheme during encryption, we would replace every lowercase alphabet in the source stream with another predetermined lowercase character. During decryption we would do the reverse. This type of encryption/decryption scheme is often called a Substitution Cipher. Given below is the program which implements the Substitution Cipher.

```
// Substitution Cipher implementation
package substitutioncipherproject ;
import java.io.* ;
interface ITransform
{
    public char transform ( char ch ) ;
}
class Encrypt implements ITransform
{
    String str = "xyfagchbimpourvnqsdewtkjzl" ;
    public char transform ( char ch )
    {
        if ( Character.isLowerCase ( ( char ) ch ) )
            ch = str.charAt ( ch - ( char ) 'a' ) ;

        return ch ;
    }
```

```
}
class Decrypt implements ITransform
{
    String str = "xyfagchbimpourvnqsdewtkjzl" ;
    public char transform ( char ch )
    {
        if ( Character.isLowerCase ( ( char ) ch ) )
            ch = ( char ) ( str.indexOf ( ( char ) ch ) + 'a' ) ;

        return ch ;
    }
}
class TransformWriter extends FilterWriter
{
    private ITransform trans ;
    public TransformWriter ( Writer s, ITransform t )
    {
        super ( s ) ;
        this.trans = t ;
    }
    public void write ( char[ ] buf, int off, int len )
    {
        for ( int i = off ; i < off + len ; i++ )
            buf [ i ] = trans.transform ( buf[ i ] ) ;

        try
        {
            out.write ( buf, off, len ) ;
        }
        catch ( IOException ex )
        {
            System.out.println ( "IO error" ) ;
        }
    }
}
public class SubstitutionCipherProject
{
    public static void main ( String[ ] args ) throws IOException
    {
        doEncDec ( "C:\\a.txt", "enc.txt", true ) ;
        doEncDec ( "enc.txt", "dec.txt", false ) ;
```

```
    }
    static void doEncDec ( String source, String target,
                            boolean IsEncrypt ) throws IOException
    {
        ITransform trans ;
        if ( IsEncrypt )
            trans = new Encrypt( ) ;
        else
            trans = new Decrypt( ) ;

        FileReader sstream ;
        BufferedReader sr ;
        sstream = new FileReader ( new File ( source ) ) ;
        sr = new BufferedReader ( sstream ) ;
        FileWriter tstream ;
        TransformWriter tw ;
        BufferedWriter sw ;
        tstream = new FileWriter ( new File ( target ) ) ;
        tw = new TransformWriter ( tstream, trans ) ;
        sw = new BufferedWriter ( tw ) ;
        String line ;
        while ( ( line = sr.readLine( ) ) != null )
            sw.write ( line + "\r\n" ) ;
        sw.close( ) ;
        sr.close( ) ;
    }
}
```

We have three classes in this program—**Encrypt**, **Decrypt** and **TrasformWriter**. Of these, the **Encrypt** and **Decrypt** classes implement an interface called **ITransform**. This interface contains a function **transform( )** which is implemented to do encryption in the **Encrypt** class and decryption in the **Decrypt** class.

Let us see how it does the encryption. It maintains an arbitrary string of lowercase characters. Once it receives a character to be encrypted it obtains an index value by doing the operation **ch – 'a'**, where **ch** is the character to be encrypted. It then uses this index value to pick a character from the arbitrary string. Thus, this character is used as a *substitute* for the character to be encrypted. Decryption works in exactly the reverse way. The character to be decrypted is searched in the same arbitrary string (as the one used for encryption). Once this character is found, 'a' is added to its index value to obtain the original character. That forms the crux of our substitution cipher.

The **TransformWriter** class uses the substitution cipher by calling the **transform( )** function of either the **Encrypt** class or the **Decrypt** class depending on whether encryption or decryption is being carried out.

A helper function **doEncDec( )** is called from **main( )** twice—first time to carry out the encryption and second time to carry out the decryption. The files used in these calls are shown in Figure 16.6.

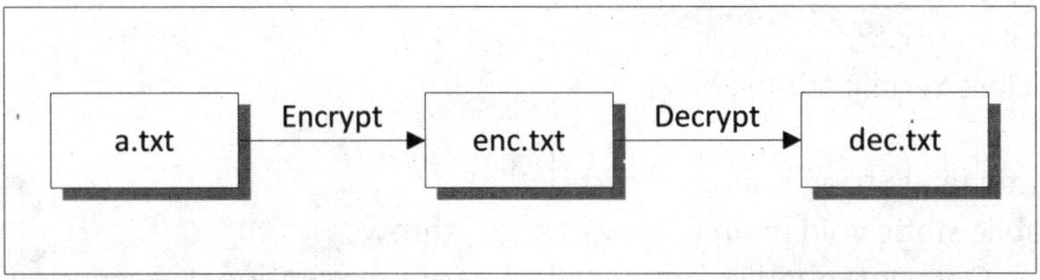

Figure 16.6

Rest of the program is similar to the uppercase filter stream program that we discussed in the last section. So, we would not repeat the explanation here.

From this program and the one that we discussed in the last section we can make the following important observations:

(a) Stream is a very important abstraction for data modelling in a variety of applications. Being able to manipulate stream data effectively is immensely important in Java programming. The streams implementation in Java enables us to do that quite effectively. For example, the data that we are manipulating in our stream may come from a file stored on disk, a network socket or simply a buffer in memory.

(b) We too can create our customized stream classes. When we do so, we need to implement the abstract methods inherited from the base class.

Serialization / Deserialization

So far, we have seen how to write characters, strings, or records to a persistent storage medium like file by using a file stream. What if we wish to write an entire object itself to a file? Well, it is possible to do so using a mechanism called Serialization. During serialization the contents of an object are converted into a byte stream. Deserialization is the reverse process where the byte stream is used to recreate the object in memory. Target of serialization need not be a file; it can even be a network or a database. This means that the object can be written to a file, passed over a network or be stored in a database.

Given below is the program that serializes a **Product** object (containing id, name, and price) to a disk file and then deserializes it back into memory.

```
package serializationproject ;
import java.io.* ;
import java.util.* ;
public class SerializationProject
{
    static final String fname = "cart.dat" ;
    public static void main ( String[ ] args ) throws
        ClassNotFoundException, FileNotFoundException, IOException
    {
        FileOutputStream  fos ;
        ObjectOutputStream  out ;
        Scanner  sc ;
        int id ;  String name ;  float price ;
        String  choice = "y" ;
        Product p ;
        fos = new FileOutputStream ( fname ) ;
        out = new ObjectOutputStream ( fos ) ;
        sc = new Scanner ( System.in ) ;
        while ( choice.equals ( "y" ) )
        {
            System.out.println ( "Enter object values:" ) ;
            id = sc.nextInt( ) ;
            name = sc.next( ) ;
            price = sc.nextFloat( ) ;
            p = new Product ( id, name, price ) ;
            out.writeObject ( p ) ;
            System.out.println ( "Want another ( y/n ): " ) ;
            choice = sc.next( ) ;
        }
        FileInputStream  fis ;
        ObjectInputStream  in ;
        fis = new FileInputStream ( fname ) ;
        in = new ObjectInputStream ( fis ) ;
```

```
        try
        {
            while ( true )
            {
                p = ( Product ) in.readObject( ) ;
                System.out.println ( p ) ;
            }
        }
        catch ( IOException e )
        {
            if ( in != null )
                in.close( ) ;
            System.out.println ( "End of file" ) ;
        }
    }
}
class Product implements Serializable
{
    private int pid ;
    private String pname ;
    private float pprice ;

    public Product ( int id, String name, float price )
    {
        pid = id ;  pname = name ;  pprice = price ;
    }
    public String toString( )
    {
        return "[ " + pid + ", " + pname + ", " + pprice + " ]";
    }
}
```

Here in a **while** loop we have received id, name and price of a product, constructed a Product object from it and then serialized to a file using the **ObjectOutputStream::writeObject( )** method. Once we have serialized a few objects, in another **while** loop we have deserialized them by calling the **ObjectInputStream::readObject( )** method. Note that it is necessary to cast the return value of **readObject( )** function from **Object** into **Product**. While reconstructing the object during deserialization, constructor of **Product** class is not called, as the necessary information to reconstruct the object is read from the file. On reconstructing the **Product** object, when it is displayed, the **toString( )**

function of **Product** class gets called. For objects of **Product** class to be serializable, it must implement the **Serializable** interface.

Now a few tips about serialization:

(a) Only the objects of those classes can be serialized which implement the **java.io.Serializable** interface.

(b) **Serializable** interface has no data member or method in it.

(c) **static** members are associated with the class and not objects of that class; hence they are not serialized.

(d) If we do not want to serialize some instance variable of an object, it should be marked as such using the keyword **transient**.

(e) All classes inherited from a class that implements the **Serializable** interface are themselves serializable.

(f) The byte stream used in serialization is platform independent. Hence, an object serialized on one platform can be deserialized on a different platform.

Exercises

[A] State whether the following statements are True or False:

(a) **System.out** refers to standard output stream (console).

(b) **System.in** refers to standard input stream (keyboard).

(c) **System.err** refers to standard error stream (console).

(d) Standard output/input/error streams are already open and ready to supply/accept input/output data.

(e) The **File** class is used to perform file operations, whereas **Directory** class is used to carry out directory-related operations.

(f) All stream classes of Java library are derived from a base class **Object**.

(g) All stream classes of Java library are defined in the **java.io** package.

(h) **InputStreamReader** and **OutputStreamWriter** classes are used to perform character oriented I/O.

(i) **FileInputStream** and **FileOutputStream** classes are used to perform byte oriented I/O.

(j) If we wish to write characters to a file in Unicode, then we should use the enum **Encoding.Unicode** while creating the **OutputStreamWriter** object.

(k) It is possible to create user-defined filter streams by inheriting our stream class from **FilterReader / FilterWriter** class.

(l) The streams implementation in Java is such that the stream doesn't have to know the source or destination of the data.

[B] Answer the following questions:

(a) What are the common expectations from a mature input/output system?

(b) Can we inherit new classes from **File** class available in the Java library?

(c) How would you check whether a given file exists or not?

(d) Is it possible to check the number of drives, the type of each drive and the drive format type through a Java program? If yes, how?

(e) What is a stream?

(f) What are the two fundamental types of I/O streams?

(g) Consider the following code snippet:

```
File f = new File ( " d:\\Test.java" ) ;
BufferedReader b = new BufferedReader ( new FileReader ( f ) ) ;
String s ;
// add statement here
```

Which statement will you add to read the file line-by-line and print each line?

(h) Suppose a **Student** object contains roll number, name and age. Write a program to serialize 5 Student objects to a disk file 'student.dat'. Once serialized, deserialize these objects and display their data on the screen.

[C] Pick up the correct alternative for each of the following questions:

(a) A number 485000 when written to a file using byte stream will occupy
(1) 4 bytes
(2) 8 bytes
(3) 12 bytes
(4) 2 bytes

(b) A number 485000 when written to a file using character stream will occupy
(1) 4 bytes
(2) 8 bytes
(3) 6 bytes
(4) 2 bytes

(c) Given a File object **fobj**, how will you determine whether it represents a file or a directory?
(1) System.out.println (fobj) ;
(2) if (fobj.isDirectory( ))
(3) if (fobj.isFolder( ))
(4) if (fobj.FileOrDirectory( ))

(d) Which import statement should be used to avail of classes that use character stream?
(1) import java.bytestream.*
(2) import java.io.*
(3) import java.inputoutput.*
(4) import io.*

(e) Which import statement should be used to avail of classes that use character stream?
(1) import java.bytestream.*
(2) import java.io.*
(3) import java.inputoutput.*
(4) import io.*

(f) Which of the following statements is CORRECT?
(1) Serialization is a process of storing an object in a file
(2) Deserialization is a process of reading an object from a file

(3) To carry out serialization and deserialization ObjectInputStream and ObjectOutputStream classes should be used
(4) 1, 2 and 3

(g) Which of the following can be serialized/deserialized?
(1) int, float
(2) Integer, Float
(3) Any reference type
(4) Any reference type that implements serializable interface

(h) Which methods are present in the Serializable interface?
(1) serialize( ), deserialize( )
(2) read( ), write( )
(3) in( ), out( )
(4) It is an empty interface

KanNotes

- Expectations from an IO System :
  - We should be able to communicate with sources & destinations
  - We should be able to I/O varied entities
  - We should be able to communicate in multiple ways
  - We should be able to deal with underlying file system
- Java solution - Perform all IO using Streams
- Stream is a sequence of bytes that travel from source to destination over a communication path
- Streams are implemented by classes in java.io package
- Linking of Streams to physical devices is done by Java IO system
- Java program performs IO by reading / writing from / to a stream
- Benefits of using Streams
  - Streams hide details of communication from programmer
  - Methods are same, implementation changes as per device
- Types of streams : 1) Byte Streams 2) Character streams

- Byte stream perform i/o one byte at a time. They are used to i/o binary data
- Character streams perform i/o one char (2 bytes) at a time. Used to i/o textual data
- To write 485000 to a file as sequence of bytes use byte stream
- To write "485000" as a sequence of Unicode characters to a file use character stream
- Byte Stream classes
    - FileInputStream, FileOutputStream - R/W streams of bytes from file
    - FilterInputStream, FilteroutputStream - Filters data being read or written
    - BufferedInputStream - Provides buffering ability
    - DataInputStream - Provides ability to read Java primitives
- Character stream classes
    - InputStreamReader, OutputStreamWriter - R/W char from/to stream
    - FileReader, FileWriter - R/W characters from/to file
    - PrintWriter - Formatted writing in text representation
- System class contains 3 predefined public static variables - in, out, err which are accessible from any part of the program
    - out refers to standard output stream (screen)
    - in refers to standard input stream (keyboard)
    - err refers to standard error stream (screen)
- These streams are already open and are ready to receive/send input/output data
- In System.out.println ("Hello") ;
    - System - class
    - out - PrintStream object reference
    - out - public static member of System class
    - println(), print() – Members of PrintStream class

- How to decide which classes to use when :
  - What is your data format - text or binary
    Binary – InputStream, OutputStream
    Text – Reader, Writer
  - Do you want random access capability?
    Use RandomAccessFile class
  - Wish to serialize/deseralize object?
    Use ObjectInputStream, ObjectOutputStream
  - What are your sources and sinks for data?
    Sockets, files, strings - All can be used by Byte and Character Streams
  - Do you need to use filtering?
    Derive your class from FilterReader class

Let Us JAVA 7th Edition

Multithreading in Java

CHAPTER 17

The ability to do multiple things simultaneously is a great asset in life. So also in programming...

Contents

- Multitasking and Multithreading
- Multithreading in Java
- Launching Threads
- Launching Multiple Threads
- Another Way to Launch Threads
- A Practical Multithreading Example
- Synchronization
- The Synchronized Block
- Inter-thread Communication
- Thread Priorities
- Exercises
- KanNotes

Multithreading is the ability to perform several jobs simultaneously. Knowingly or unknowingly, we make use of multithreading frequently in everyday life. For example, while driving a car we carry out several activities in parallel. We listen to music, we follow the traffic rules, and we talk to the co-passengers. All this, without losing the focus, i.e., driving. There can be several such examples where we carry out several activities at the same time. Since programmers are people, and programming is the art of solving people's problems, it is only natural that in programming in general, and in Java in particular, too, there is an effort to do several activities simultaneously.

Multitasking and Multithreading

Most modern OSs can execute several tasks in memory at a time. This ability to execute several tasks simultaneously is known as Multitasking. For example, while using Windows we can simultaneously print a document on the printer, receive e-mails, download files, and compile programs. All these operations are carried out through different programs that are being executed in memory at the same time.

This ability of Windows to execute several tasks can be taken a step further, whereby we execute different parts of a program simultaneously. This can be experienced while working with many popular Windows software. Here are a few examples...

(a) While copying files one part of the 'Copy' program displays the copying progress through a green-colored progress bar, whereas another part of the program carries out the actual copying.

(b) While working with MS-Word one part of the program lets us type the document, whereas two other parts perform the spelling check and grammar check.

(c) In anti-viral software one part of the program scans the disk files for viruses, whereas the other part lets us interact with the user interface of the software.

This ability to execute different parts of the same program simultaneously is known as Multithreading.

If a multithreaded program is executing on a machine with a single microprocessor, though it may appear that the processor is performing several tasks simultaneously, it is not so. What happens is that the processor divides the execution time equally amongst all the running threads. Thus, each thread gets the processor attention in a round robin manner. Once the time-slice allocated for a thread expires, the operation that it is currently being performed is put on hold and the processor now directs its attention to the next thread. Thus, at any given moment, if we take a snapshot of memory, the processor is executing only one thread. The switching of attention from one thread to another happens so fast that we get the effect as if the processor is executing several threads simultaneously.

In modern machines with multiple processors, the threads would be executed simultaneously, as each processor can execute a separate thread.

Multithreading has several advantages to offer. These are listed below.

(a) **Responsiveness:** Take MS-Word example again. Had the spell checker and the grammar checker not run as different threads, we would have been required to write documents and submit it to the checkers from time to time. This would have resulted in low responsiveness. Since the checkers run in different threads, our document gets checked as we type, thereby increasing the responsiveness of the application.

(b) **Organization:** Threading simplifies program organization. In the 'File Copy' example if both the operations—displaying the progress bar and the actual copying—run in the same thread, then after copying a few thousand bytes we would be required to advance the progress bar. If we run the copying code and the progress bar code in separate threads, we can avoid cluttering the copying code with progress bar code and vice versa.

(c) **Performance:** Many a time it happens that a program needs to wait for user input or must give some output. The I/O devices are generally slower than the processor. So, the application waits for the I/O operation to finish. Instead, if we use another thread for the I/O operation, the processor time can be allotted to other important tasks that can work independent of the I/O operation, thereby improving the performance.

Multithreading in Java

To help you appreciate the challenges of multithreading you can try a simple experiment. Make two phone calls to your friends and try to carry out conversation with both concurrently. This would involve major challenges—talking to one friend, putting him on hold, remembering where you left off, picking up the other receiver, talking to the other friend, putting him on hold, picking up the first receiver, carrying on the conversation from the point where you left off, and above all making the conversation sensible for everybody involved.

Java offers features that let you run multiple threads in a program. To create multiple threads the programmer must specify which parts of the program he intends to execute concurrently. Although on the face of it this might appear simple, rest assured that often multithreaded programs are tricky and demand a substantial effort on your part to master all the issues involved in multithreading.

Any simple Java program has a single thread of execution. This running thread has a name (called main), a priority and a group to which it belongs. If we wish we can change the name of the thread. This has been demonstrated in the program given below.

```
// Displaying thread properties
package mainthreadproject ;
public class MainThreadProject
{
    public static void main ( String args[ ] )
    {
        Thread  t = Thread.currentThread( ) ;
        System.out.println ( "Current thread: " + t ) ;
        t.setName ( "mythread" ) ;
        System.out.println ( "After name change: " + t ) ;
        String  s = t.getName( ) ;
        System.out.println ( "Thread name: " + s ) ;
    }
}
```

And here is the output of the program...

```
Current thread: main, 5, main
After name change: mythread, 5, main
Thread name: mythread
```

The object representing the running thread is obtained by calling the **static** method **currentThread( )** of the **Thread** class. If we print this object using **println( )** we get the name of the thread, its priority and its thread group. Note from the output that 5 is the default priority. 1 represents the lowest priority and 10 the highest, thus 5 is the average priority.

Once we have obtained the **Thread** object, we can set or get the name of the current thread using the methods **setName( )** and **getName( )** respectively.

It is possible to make multiple threads to belong to one group. If this is done, then it is possible to manipulate all those threads together, rather than individually. For example, we can start or suspend all the threads within a group with a single method call.

Launching Threads

There are two mechanisms to launch new threads in a Java program. These are:

(a) By extending the **Thread** class
(b) By implementing the **Runnable** interface

We wish to learn both ways to launch a thread and assess the utility of each. Let us begin with a program that uses the first way.

```
// Creating and launching threads
package sampleproject ;
public class SampleProject
{
    public static void main ( String args[ ] )
    {
        Ex t = new Ex( ) ;
        t.start( ) ;
        for ( int i = 0 ; i < 5 ; i ++ )
            System.out.println ( "Main thread" ) ;
    }
}
class Ex extends Thread
{
    public void run( )
    {
        for ( int i = 0 ; i < 5 ; i++ )
            System.out.println ( "New thread" ) ;
    }
}
```

Here we have derived the **Ex** class from the **Thread** class and defined a **run( )** method inside it. The method simply prints a message "New Thread" 5 times. In **main( )** we have created an object of **Ex** class, called the **start( )** method and then printed the message "Main Thread" 5 times.

The **start( )** method is defined in **Thread** class and by inheritance is available to **Ex** objects. Once we call the **start( )** method, the thread gets scheduled. This means we are informing the thread scheduler that the new thread is ready to run. When the thread scheduler deems fit, it would start executing this new thread by calling its **run( )** method.

The output of the program is shown below.

```
Main thread
Main thread
Main thread
Main thread
Main thread
New thread
New thread
New thread
New thread
New thread
```

Ideally the messages "Main thread" and "new Thread" should have been inter-mingled. But this did not happen because once the timeslot got allotted to the main thread, in that timeslot it printed all the messages before the timeslot could be snatched away and allotted to the new thread. Had each loop been executed 1000 times, then during each timeslot allocated to the two threads, each would not have been able to print all 1000 messages. This would have resulted in inter-mingling of messages.

Another way to get the inter-mingled messages is to put each thread to sleep for 1000 milliseconds when they get the timeslot. This would ensure that in the first timeslot that they get, they do not finish the entire printing. This change is shown below.

```
// Better thread implementation
package sampleproject ;
public class  SampleProject
{
    public static void main ( String args[ ] )
    {
        Ex  t  = new  Ex( ) ;
```

```
        t.start( ) ;
        try
        {
            for ( int  i = 0 ; i < 5 ; i ++ )
            {
                System.out.println ( "Main thread" ) ;
                Thread.sleep ( 1000 ) ;
            }
            catch ( Exception e )
            {
            }
        }
    }
}
class Ex extends Thread
{
    public void run( )
    {
        try
        {
            for ( int  i = 0 ; i < 5 ; i++ )
            {
                System.out.println ( "New thread" ) ;
                Thread.sleep ( 1000 ) ;
            }
        }
        catch ( Exception e )
        {
        }
    }
}
```

The static **sleep( )** method of the **Thread** class postpones the execution of next instruction by 1000 milliseconds. As a result, now the output is inter-mingled as shown below.

```
Main thread
Main thread
Main thread
New thread
New thread
Main thread
```

Main thread
New thread
New thread
New thread

Notice that the call to **sleep( )** method has to be present in the try block, as it is likely to throw an exception. Though, not the best of the ways, for the sake of simplicity we have used an empty **catch** block to catch the exception that **sleep( )** may throw.

Launching Multiple Threads

Do not be under the impression that we can create only one thread from the class derived from the **Thread** class. It is possible to create multiple threads from the same class. This is illustrated in the following program.

```
// Launching multiple threads
package sampleproject ;
public class  SampleProject
{
    public static void main ( String args[ ] )
    {
        Ex t1 = new Ex( ) ;
        t1.start( ) ;
        t1.setname ( "First" ) ;
        Ex t2 = new Ex( ) ;
        t2.start( ) ;
        t2.setname ("Second" ) ;
        Ex t3 = new Ex( ) ;
        t3.start( ) ;
        t3.setname ( "Third" ) ;
        try
        {
            for ( int i = 0 ; i < 10 ; i ++ )
            {
                System.out.println ( "Main thread" ) ;
                Thread.sleep ( 500 ) ;
            }
        }
        catch ( Exception e )
        {
```

```
        }
    }
}
class Ex extends Thread
{
    public void run( )
    {
        Thread  t ;

        t = Thread.currentThread( ) ;
        String  s = t.getName( ) ;

        for ( int i = 0 ; i < 10 ; i++ )
            System.out.println ( s ) ;
    }
}
```

Given below is the output of the program.

```
First
First
First
First
First
Third
Third
Third
Third
Third
Third
Main thread
Second
Second
Second
Second
Main thread
Main thread
Main thread
:::
```

Here, while launching the three threads we have given a name to each, which is displayed in a loop, when those threads get a timeslot. In which situation we would want to launch multiple threads from the same class? Imagine if the thread is to display an animation from a GIF file. Then by launching different threads we can display different animations in different parts of the screen simultaneously.

When we launch several threads from the main thread there is a possibility that the main thread ends whereas the launched threads continue to execute. If we wish that main thread should be the last thread to finish execution, then we can employ the **join( )** method of the **Thread** class to ensure this, as shown below.

```
// Joining threads
package sampleproject ;
public class  SampleProject
{
    public static void main ( String args[ ] )
    {
        Ex t1 = new Ex( ) ;
        t1.start( ) ;
        t1.setname ( "First" ) ;
        Ex t2 = new Ex( ) ;
        t2.start( ) ;
        t2.setname ( "Second" ) ;
        Ex t3 = new Ex( ) ;
        t3.start( ) ;
        t3.setname ( "Third" ) ;
        try
        {
            for ( int i = 0 ; i < 10 ; i ++ )
            {
                System.out.println ( "Main thread" ) ;
                Thread.sleep ( 500 ) ;
            }
        }
        catch ( Exception e )
        {
        }
        System.out.println ( t1.isAlive( ) ) ;
        System.out.println ( t2.isAlive( ) ) ;
        System.out.println ( t3.isAlive( ) ) ;
        t1.join( ) ;
        t2.join( ) ;
```

```
        t3.join( ) ;
        System.out.println ( t1.isAlive( ) ) ;
        System.out.println ( t2.isAlive( ) ) ;
        System.out.println ( t3.isAlive( ) ) ;
    }
}
```

On execution, out of the calls to **isAlive( )** some threads may return false if those threads have finished execution. By calling **join( )** the main thread would wait for the alive threads to finish their execution, before it terminates. Naturally, the second set of calls to **isAlive( )** would return false for each call.

Another Way to Launch Threads

So far we have been extending the **Thread** class and implementing the **run( )** method in it to launch new threads. This method has one important limitation. Once our class is derived from **Thread** class we cannot inherit it from any other class, as Java doesn't support multiple inheritance. If we wish to keep our class open for derivation from some other class and still be able to launch new threads, we should do so by implementing a **Runnable** interface in it. This method of launching new threads is given below.

```
// Second way to launch threads
package sampleproject ;
public class SampleProject
{
    public static void main ( String args[ ] )
    {
        Runnable x = new Ex( ) ;
        Thread t = new Thread ( x, "One" ) ;
        t.start( ) ;
        for ( int i = 0 ; i < 10 ; i ++ )
            System.out.println ( "Main thread" ) ;
    }
}
class Ex implements Runnable
{
    public void run( )
    {
        int i ;
```

```
        for ( i = 0 ; i < 10 ; i++ )
            System.out.println ( Thread.currentThread( ).getName( ) ) ;
    }
}
```

Note that here we have not derived **Ex** from **Thread** class. Instead, we are implementing the **Runnable** interface in it. The **Runnable** interface has only one method in it—**run( )**.

To begin with, we have created an object of **Ex** class. Then, while creating an object of the **Thread** class, to its constructor we have passed the **Ex** object and a string "One" which would be the name of the thread that is launched. Then, from **main( )** we have called the **start( )** method of the **Thread** class for the instance **t**. By doing this, we are informing JVM to schedule a thread. As a result, the **run( )** method gets called. In the **run( )** method we have simply printed the name of the current thread (i.e. "one").

Here is one more program that uses **Runnable** interface to launch threads. The difference is that this program launches multiple threads for each instance of the **Ex** class.

```
// Launching multiple threads
package sampleproject ;
public class SampleProject
{
    public static void main ( String args[ ] )
    {
        Runnable x1 = new Ex( ) ;
        Thread t1 = new Thread ( x1, "One" ) ;
        t1.start( ) ;
        Runnable x2 = new Ex( ) ;
        Thread t2 = new Thread ( x2, "Two" ) ;
        t2.start( ) ;
        Runnable x3 = new Ex( ) ;
        Thread t3 = new Thread ( x3, "Three" ) ;
        t3.start( ) ;
        for ( int i = 0 ; i < 10 ; i ++ )
            System.out.println ( "Main thread" ) ;
    }
}
class Ex implements Runnable
{
```

```
    public void run( )
    {
        int i ;
        for ( i = 0 ; i < 10 ; i++ )
            System.out.println ( Thread.currentThread( ).getName( ) ) ;
    }
}
```

A Practical Multithreading Example

Suppose we wish to copy the contents of one folder into another. Naturally, if the source folder contains multiple files, each file must be opened, and its contents copied into a file in the target folder. If this operation is done in a loop in a single thread, then unless copying of the first file is over, the copying of second file cannot begin. Instead, a better approach would be to do the copying in multiple threads. Given below are two programs that follow the single thread and the multithread approach. To simplify things, instead of copying files, we simply open each source file, read it to the end and report the number of lines present in each file.

```
// Approach 1 : Read files in a single thread
package singlethreadproject ;
import java.io.* ;
public class SingleThreadProject
{
    static public void main ( String args[ ] ) throws Exception
    {
        System.out.println ( "Starting Time: " +
                                    System.currentTimeMillis( ));
        for ( int i = 0 ; i < args.length ; i++ )
        {
            FileReader fr = new FileReader ( args[ i ] ) ;
            BufferedReader br = new BufferedReader ( fr ) ;
            LineNumberReader l = new LineNumberReader ( br ) ;

            while ( l.readLine( ) != null )
                Thread.sleep ( 10 ) ;

            System.out.println ( "Lines in " + args[ i ] + ":" +
                                    l.getLineNumber( ) ) ;
        }
```

```
        System.out.println ( "Ending Time: " +
                                        System.currentTimeMillis( ) ) ;
    }
}
```

The program reads three files **a.txt**, **b.txt** and **c.txt** that are provided to it as command-line arguments. To add these files to your project in NetBeans, right click on the project folder and select New | Empty File from the menu that pops up. Give the name of the file (say, **a.txt**) and type a few lines in it. Similarly add **b.txt** and **c.txt** to your project. Once this is done, add these filenames as command-line arguments through Right-click project name | Properties | Run | Arguments.

In the program, we print the current time in milliseconds before we start reading the files and after the reading is finished. This is done using the function **System.currentTimeMillis( )**. The actual reading of a file is done by using the **LineNumberReader** class. This class has a method **getLineNumber( )** which reports the number of lines present in the file that it has read.

When we executed this program, we got the following output:

```
Starting Time: 1484131339431
Lines in a.txt:13
Lines in b.txt:25
Lines in c.txt:37
Ending Time: 1484131340184
```

Your output may vary as depending on the contents of the three files their reading times may vary. A quick calculation would show the difference in times to be 753 milliseconds.

Now let us look at the program that follows the multithreaded approach to achieve the same goal. Here it is...

```
// Approach 2 : Read files in multiple threads
package multithreadproject ;
import java.io.* ;
public class MultithreadProject
{
    static public void main ( String args[ ] ) throws Exception
    {
        System.out.println ( "Starting time: " +
```

```
                                    System.currentTimeMillis( ) ) ;
        linecounter  t[ ] = new linecounter [ args.length ] ;
        for ( int  i = 0 ; i < args.length ; i++ )
        {
            t[ i ] = new linecounter ( args[ i ] ) ;
            t[ i ].start( ) ;
        }
        for ( int  i = 0 ; i < args.length ; i++ )
            t[ i ].join( ) ;
        System.out.println ( "Ending Time: " +
            System.currentTimeMillis( ) ) ;
    }
}
class linecounter extends Thread
{
    String  fname ;
    linecounter ( String  str )
    {
        fname = str ;
    }
    public void run( )
    {
        try
        {
            FileReader  fr = new FileReader ( fname ) ;
            BufferedReader  br  = new BufferedReader ( fr ) ;
            LineNumberReader  l = new LineNumberReader ( br ) ;
            while ( l.readLine( ) != null )
                Thread.sleep ( 10 ) ;
            System.out.println ( "Lines :" + fname + " : " +
                                    l.getLineNumber( ) ) ;
        }
        catch ( Exception  e )
        {
        }
    }
}
```

This time on execution the following times are reported:

```
Starting Time: 1484196850259
Lines: a.txt : 13
```

```
Lines: b.txt : 25
Lines: c.txt : 37
Ending Time: 1484196850646
```

This time the time difference is 387 milliseconds. Clearly the multithreaded approach is a better option than the single-threaded approach in such situations.

Synchronization

Software development is a team effort. Unless team members cooperate with one another and synchronize their work with the rest of the team, the team cannot go far. Similarly, if in a program there are several threads running, unless their activities are synchronized with one another the disaster is not far away. For example, if a program instantiates two threads and if both the threads use the same resource and both change it simultaneously the situation would become unreliable and erratic.

Let me illustrate the need for synchronization of threads using a simple example. Consider the following method.

```
void display ( String msg )
{
    System.out.print ( "[" ) ;
    System.out.print ( msg ) ;
    Thread.sleep ( 1000 ) ;
    System.out.println ( "]" ) ;
}
```

Suppose three different threads decide to call this method to display a message. It is expected that this method would display the message passed to it within a pair of [ ]. However, it produces the following output if the strings passed to it from three threads are KICIT, Nagpur and India respectively.

```
[India[Nagpur[KICIT]
]
]
```

To rectify this, we need to synchronize the activities of each thread. How this can be achieved is shown in the following program.

```
// Synchronization of threads
```

```
package sampleproject ;
public class SampleProject
{
    static public void main ( String args[ ] ) throws Exception
    {
        Output c = new  Output( ) ;
        Ex  t1 = new Ex ( c, "KICIT" ) ;
        t1.start( ) ;
        Ex  t2 = new Ex ( c,"Nagpur" ) ;
        t2.start( ) ;
        Ex  t3 = new Ex ( c,"India" ) ;
        t3.start( ) ;
        t1.join( ) ;
        t2.join( ) ;
        t3.join( ) ;
    }
}
class Ex extends Thread
{
    private Output  o ;
    private String  message ;

    public Ex ( Output c, String  msg )
    {
        o = c ;
        message = msg ;
    }
    public void run( )
    {
        o.display ( message ) ;
    }
}
class Output
{
    synchronized void display ( String  msg )
    {
        System.out.print ( "[" + msg ) ;
        try
        {
            Thread.sleep ( 1000 ) ;
        }
```

```
        catch ( InterruptedException  e )
        {
        }
        System.out.println ( "]" ) ;
    }
}
```

On execution, this program produces the desired output shown below.

```
[KICIT]
[NAGPUR]
[INDIA]
```

In this program we have defined two classes—**Ex** and **Output**. In **main( )** we have created one object of **Output** class and three objects of **Ex** class. The **Ex** class is derived from the **Thread** class. When objects of **Ex** class are created, along with object of **Output** class, a message to be printed is passed to its constructor. It stores this message in a private string **message**. This **message** is passed to the **display( )** method of **Output** class, when **display( )** is called from **run( )**.

We want you to note a standard technique here. Since we do not explicitly call the **run( )** method, any objects that **run( )** needs should be passed to the constructor of the class to which **run( )** belongs, so that **run( )** can access them. In our case, we needed the **Output** object to call **display( )** from the **run( )** method. That is why we passed it to the constructor while creating the **Ex** objects.

Note that the **display( )** function in the **Output** class has been marked as **synchronized**. This ensures that once one thread makes a call to **display( )**, unless the execution of **display( )** in this thread is finished, the call by other threads to **display( )** would be put on hold. This results in producing the systematic output that we desire.

The Synchronized Block

At times it may happen that a class has been developed with a view to using it in single thread situations. But later, a need arises to use it in a multithreaded situation. If we do not have access to its source code, we cannot mark the methods in it as **synchronized**. In such situations, the solution is to use a synchronized block.

In the context of our program in the previous section, suppose we do not have access to source code of **Output** class. So we cannot mark

display( ) as synchronized method. In this case we need to simply make the call to **display( )** in a **synchronized** block as shown below, to get the desired output.

```
public void run( )
{
    synchronized ( o )
    {
        o.display ( message ) ;
    }
}
```

Inter-thread Communication

The programs in the Synchronization section unconditionally blocked other threads from asynchronous access to certain methods. To improve the overall performance of the program there should be a mechanism to notify a waiting thread that it can start running. This means that one thread should be able to communicate with the other. To achieve this Java provides three methods—**wait( )**, **notify( )** and **notifyAll( )**. Given below is the purpose of each of these methods.

Method	Purpose
wait( )	Tell calling thread to go to sleep till notified
notify( )	Wakes up thread that called wait( ) on same object
notifyAll( )	Wakes up all threads that called wait( ) on same object

Figure 17.1

One of the places where usage of this method makes sense is in implementing a classical Computer Science algorithm called Producer - Consumer algorithm. This algorithm is described in the Exercise at the end of this chapter.

Thread Priorities

If we wish, we can assign priorities to each running thread. This helps the scheduler to determine the order in which these threads are executed. Threads with higher priority are more important to a program and are allocated processor time before lower-priority threads. A Java thread can have three standard Priorities: MAX_PRIORITY, NORM_PRIORITY. These represent numbers 1, 10 and 5. Java provides the following functions to set a new priority for a thread and to obtain a thread's current priority.

```
final void setPriority ( int level )
final int getPriority( )
```

Exercises

[A] State whether the following statements are True or False:

(a) Multithreading always improves the speed of execution of the program.

(b) A running task may have several threads running in it.

(c) Multitasking is the same as multithreading.

(d) If we create a class that inherits from the **Thread** class, we can still inherit our class from some other class.

(e) Default thread priority is 10.

(f) A higher priority thread can preempt a lower priority thread.

(g) It is possible to change the name of the running thread.

(h) To launch a thread we must explicitly call the **run( )** method defined in a class that implements the **Runnable** interface.

(i) To launch a thread we must explicitly call the **run( )** method defined in a class that extends the **Thread** class.

(j) To synchronize a method defined in a class, we must have access to the source code of the class.

[B] Pick up the correct alternative for each of the following questions:

(a) What will happen if a Java program that launches 5 threads is executed on a machine which has a single processor?
(1) 5 threads will get launched

(2) 1 thread will get launched
(3) 0 thread will get launched
(4) Error will occur since a single processor cannot handle 5 threads

(b) Which of the following are the CORRECT way to create a thread?
(1) Create a class and inherit it from Thread class
(2) Implement the Runnable interface
(3) Create a class and inherit it from CWinThread
(4) A and B

(c) Consider the following code snippet:

```
class Ex extends Thread
{
}
Ex t = new Ex( ) ;
t.start( ) ;
```

Which of the following should be done to create a multithreaded program?
(1) Define a **run**( ) method in the **Ex** class
(2) Define a **run**( ) method in the **Ex** class and call it using **t.run**( )
(3) Implement the **Runnable** interface in class **Ex**
(4) Derive class **Ex** from the **Runnable** class

(d) Which of the following statement is CORRECT about the code snippet given below:

```
class Ex extends Thread
{
    public void run( )
    {
    }
}
```

(1) **run**( ) method gets called when the thread gets a timeslot
(2) We need to call **run**( ) explicitly
(3) **start**( ) will call **run**( )
(4) **run**( ) will be called by a method present in a class that implements the **runnable** interface

(e) If in a Java program one thread lets you type a document, and another thread performs spellcheck on the same document then the two threads
(1) should be synchronized
(2) need not be synchronized

(3) should be executed one after the other
(4) should be launched through 2 separate programs

(f) We wish to synchronize the working of methods present in a legacy Java program whose source code is not available. How will you achieve this?
(1) Hunt for the source code
(2) Use synchronized block
(3) Mark the methods from where legacy methods are called synchronized
(4) Reimplement the legacy code and then mark methods in it as synchronized

(g) Suppose we wish to copy contents of one directory into another and display the progress in copying through a green-colored progress bar. Which of the following will be the CORRECT way to implement this requirement?
(1) Create one program to copy and another program to display progress bar. Run two programs simultaneously.
(2) Create two threads in one program—do copying in one thread and display progress bar in another thread.
(3) Create a single threaded program which performs both the tasks.
(4) Create two programs, call one from the other.

[C] Answer the following questions:

(a) Which are the two methods available for launching threads in a Java program?

(b) What are the pros and cons of using two different methods of launching threads in a Java program?

(c) Which methods should be used to improve the performance of a multithreaded Java program that uses synchronization?

(d) If **Ex** class implements the **Runnable** interface, then can we launch multiple threads for objects of **Ex** class? If yes, how?

(e) Write a multithreaded program that copies contents of one folder into another. The source and target folder paths should be input through keyboard.

(f) Producer - Consumer algorithm is a popularly used algorithm in Computer Science. It is a technique for generating requests (by producer) and processing the generated requests (by consumer). Write a program to implement this algorithm to meet the following specifications:

- The Producer produces numbers in sequence 0, 1, 2, ...
- Consumer consumes the produced numbers by printing them
- Both Producer and Consumer work as independent threads
- Consumer must wait while Producer is producing
- Once Producer has produced it would send a signal to Consumer
- Producer must wait while Consumer is consuming
- Once Consumer has consumed it should send a signal to Producer

KanNotes

- Multitasking - Ability to execute multiple tasks at a time
  Task = Process
- Multithreading - Ability to execute multiple parts of a program at a time
  Part = Thread = separate path of execution
- Examples of Multitasking :
  - Several Windows applications running in memory
  - Multiple instances of Paint or Notepad in memory
- Examples of Multitasking :
  - Scroll Web page as graphic continues to load
  - Printing one Word document while opening another
  - Replying an email while downloading another
- Advantages of Multithreading
  - Improves application's responsiveness
  - Simplifies program organization
  - Do other things while waiting for slow I/O operations
  - Exploitation of Multiple Processors
- Thread is a Java API class. It contains following useful methods :

- currentThread() - returns current thread's object
- setName() - sets up name for a thread
- getName() - returns name of the specified thread
- sleep() - Postpone execution of next instruction by specified milliseconds

- Two methods to launch a thread :
  - By extending the Thread class
  - By implementing Runnable interface

- Extending Thread class
  - Easy to use
  - Thread related functions can be overridden
  - Disadvantage : Cannot use in Multiple Inheritance situations

- Implementing Runnable Interface

  Can be used in Multiple Inheritance situations

  Disadvantage : Cannot override Thread class functions

- If multiple files are to be read then the reading time can be reduced by carrying out the reading in multiple concurrent threads

- When >= 2 threads access same shared resource if we wish to ensure that the resource is used by only 1 thread at a time, then it can be achieved using Synchronized methods

- If a method is declared as Synchronized then when it is called by multiple threads, when the first thread is executing it, others are made to wait

- For older classes Synchronized blocks can be used to achieve the same results

- Often threads unconditionally block other threads from asynchronous access to certain methods - hampers performance

- To improve Performance - use wait(), notify(), notifyAll() methods

- wait() - Tells calling thread to go to sleep till notified

- notify() - Wakes up thread that called wait() on same object
- notifyAll() - Wakes up all threads that called wait() on same obj.
- Producer - Consumer algorithm is a technique for Generating requests and Processing the pending requests
- Producer produces requests, Consumer consumes generated requests
- Both work as independent threads
- Working :
    - Consumer must wait while Producer is producing
    - Once Producer has produced it would send signal to Consumer
    - Producer must wait while Consumer is consuming
    - Once Consumer has consumed it would send signal to Producer
- Thread priorities are used to schedule thread execution
- Higher priority threads get more CPU time and may preempt lower priority threads
- Standard Priorities :
    - MIN_PRIORITY, MAX_PRIORITY, NORM_PRIORITY
    - These are constants with values 1, 10, 5
- Functions to set and get priorities :
    - final void setPriority (int level)
    - final int getPriority()

Let Us JAVA 7th Edition

Generics

CHAPTER 18

Generalizations are good. Especially when the Compiler handles the specializations...

Contents

- Generic Functions
- Multiple Argument Types
- Generic Classes
- Bounded Generics
- Exercises
- KanNotes

Generics are a mechanism that make it possible to use one function or class to handle many different data types. By using generics, we can design a single function/class that operates on data of many types, instead of having to create a separate function/class for each type. In this chapter we would first look at using generics with functions and then move on to using generics with classes.

Generic Functions

Suppose you wish to print contents of an integer array. To achieve this, we can write a function as shown below:

```
void printIntArr ( int [ ] arr )
{
    for ( int i : arr )
        System.out.println ( i ) ;
}
```

Here the function **printIntArr( )** is defined to receive an **int** array and then print all its elements through a **for** loop. What if we wish to print a **float** array—we would be required to write a completely new function **printFloatArr( )**. Similarly, to print a **char** array we would be required to write **printCharArr( )**—a separate version of the same function.

You would agree that this is a suitable case for overloaded functions, as all these functions have different names but essentially carry out the same activity—printing elements of an array passed to them. This way, at least the names of all these functions can be the same. These overloaded functions are given below:

```
// printArr for ints
void printArr ( int [ ] arr )
{
    for ( int i : arr )
        System.out.println ( i ) ;
}
// printArr for floats
void printArr ( float [ ] arr )
{
    for ( float i : arr )
        System.out.println ( i ) ;
}
```

```
// printArr for chars
void printArr ( char [ ] arr )
{
    for ( char i : arr )
        System.out.println ( i ) ;
}

// etc...
```

Have we gained anything by writing these overloaded functions? Not much, because we still have to write a separate definition for each type. This results in three disadvantages:

(a) Rewriting the same function body over and over for different types is time consuming.

(b) The program consumes more disk space.

(c) If we decide to modify one such function, we need to remember to make the modification in other overloaded functions.

Will it not be nice if we could write such a function just once, and make it work for many different data types. This is exactly what function generics do for us.

The following program shows how to write the **printArr( )** function as a generic function, so that it will work with any standard type. We have invoked this function from **main( )** for different data types.

```
// Defining and using generic function
package genericfunctionproject ;
public class GenericFunctionProject
{
    public static <T> void printArray ( T[ ] arr )
    {
        for ( T i : arr )
            System.out.printf ( "%s ", i ) ;

        System.out.println( ) ;
    }
    public static void main ( String args[ ] )
    {
        Integer[ ] intarr = { 10, -2, 37, 42, 15 } ;
        Float[ ] floatarr = { 3.14f, 6.28f, -1.5f, -3.44f, 7.234f } ;
        Character[ ] chararr = { 'Q', 'U', 'E', 'S', 'T' } ;
```

```
        printArray ( intarr ) ;
        printArray ( floatarr ) ;
        printArray ( chararr ) ;
    }
}
```

Here's the output of the program:

```
10 -2 37 42 15
3.14 6.28 -1.5 -3.44 7.234
Q U E S T
```

As you can see, the **printArr( )** function now works with different data types that we use as arguments.

Isn't this code reuse? Yes, but of a different type. Inheritance provides a way to reuse object code. Generics provide a way to reuse the source code. Generics can significantly reduce source code size and increase code flexibility.

Let us now understand what grants the generic function the flexibility to work with different data types. Here is the definition of the **printArr( )** function...

```
public static <T> void printArray( T[ ] arr )
{
    for ( T i : arr )
        System.out.printf ( "%s ", i ) ;

    System.out.println( ) ;
}
```

In this generic function a data type has been represented by a name (**T** in our case) that can stand for any type. There's nothing special about the name **T**. We can use any other name like **type**, **mytype**, etc. Throughout the definition of the function, wherever a specific data type would ordinarily be written, we substitute it with type **T**.

Notice that while calling **printArr( )** function, we have passed to it an array of **Integers**, **Floats** and **Characters** and not an array of **ints**, **floats** and **chars**. This is because a generic function can work only with reference types and not with primitives like **int**, **float**, **double**, **char**, etc.

To help you fix your ideas about generics, here is another program that uses a generic function. This one obtains the minimum of two quantities using a generic **minimum( )** function.

```
// More complex generic function
package minusinggenericsproject ;
public class MinUsingGenericsProject
{
    public static <T extends Comparable <T> > T minimum ( T a, T b )
    {
        if ( a.compareTo ( b ) < 0 )
            return a ;
        else
            return b ;
    }
    public static void main ( String[ ] args )
    {
        Float a = 3.14f, b = -6.28f, c ;
        c = minimum ( a, b ) ;
        System.out.println ( c ) ;

        Character ch = 'A', dh = 'Z', eh ;
        eh = minimum ( ch, dh ) ;
        System.out.println ( eh ) ;

        Double d = 1.1, e = 1.11, f ;
        f = minimum ( d, e ) ;
        System.out.println ( f ) ;
    }
}
```

Given below is the output that the program produces on execution.

```
-6.28
A
1.1
```

Note how we have defined the generic **minimum( )** function.

```
public static < T extends Comparable <T> > T minimum ( T a, T b )
{
    ...
```

```
}
```

The above definition means that this function would work with all those types which implement the **Comparable** interface. In our case the classes **Integer**, **Float**, and **Character** implement this interface, so we can use the **minimum( )** function with these types.

Note that this function cannot compare two **Integer** or two **Float** objects using relational operators like >, <, etc. Hence to actually carry out the comparison we have used the **compareTo( )** function of **Integer** / **Float** / **Character** class.

We can extend the same comparison logic and write a program that sorts **Integer**s, **Float**s, **Character**s using a generic sorting function. Here it is...

```
// Sorting using generics
package genericsortingproject ;
public class GenericSortingProject
{
	public static void main ( String[ ] args )
	{
		Float num[ ] = { 5.4f, 3.23f, 2.15f, 1.09f, 34.66f } ;
		Integer arr[ ] = { -12, 23, 14, 0, 245, 78 , 66, -9 } ;
		int i ;

		sort ( num, 5 ) ;
		for ( i = 0 ; i <= 4 ; i++ )
			System.out.print ( num[ i ] + " " ) ;
		System.out.println( ) ;
		sort ( arr, 8 ) ;
		for ( i = 0 ; i <= 7 ; i++ )
			System.out.print ( arr[ i ] + " " ) ;
	}
	public static <T extends Comparable <T> > void sort ( T[ ] n, int size )
	{
		int i, j ;
		T t ;

		for ( i = 0 ; i <= size - 2 ; i++ )
		{
			for ( j = i + 1 ; j <= size - 1 ; j++ )
			{
```

```
                if ( n[ i ].compareTo ( n[ j ] ) > 0 )
                {
                    t = n[ i ] ;
                    n[ i ] = n[ j ] ;
                    n[ j ] = t ;
                }
            }
        }
    }
}
```

The output of the program is given below:

```
1.09 2.15 3.23 5.4 34.66
-12 -9 0 14 23 66 78 245
```

We do not intend to explain the actual working of the sorting logic. This topic has been dealt with thoroughly in all the standard books on Data Structures. What you need to concentrate on here is how to write generic functions that can work for a variety of data types.

Multiple Argument Types

In all the programs that we have seen so far in this chapter, the generic functions worked only with one type. But we can very well write a generic function that takes different types of arguments during a call. The following code shows such a generic function.

```
// Generics with multiple types
package mulitpletypesgenericfunctionproject ;
public class MulitpleTypesGenericFunctionProject
{
    public static void main ( String[ ] args )
    {
        Integer i = 10 ;
        Float j = 3.14f ;
        Character ch = 'A' ;
        printTypes ( i, j, ch ) ;
    }
    public static <T, S, Z> void printTypes ( T a, S b, Z c )
    {
        System.out.println ( "a = " + a ) ;
        System.out.println ( "b = " + b ) ;
```

```
        System.out.println ( "c = " + c ) ;
    }
}
```

The **printTypes( )** function can receive three different types of arguments represented by **T**, **S** and **Z**. It simply prints all the arguments that it receives. Would the function work if we pass to it arguments of same types? Yes, it will. So, the following call would be perfectly valid.

```
Integer i = 10, m = 20, n = 30 ;
printTypes ( i, m, n ) ;
```

Generic Classes

The concept of generics can be extended even to classes. Generic classes are often used for data storage. In fact, Java provides a library of container classes that implement data structures like stack, queue, linked lists, binary tree, hash map, etc. These implementations are based on generic classes.

Let us try implementing a Stack class as a generic class. This class should be able to maintain a stack of **Integer**s, **Float**s, **Character**s etc. Here is a program with this generic stack class in action.

```
// Generic stack class
package genericstackproject ;
public class GenericStackProject
{
    public static void main ( String[ ] args )
    {
        Stack <Integer> s1 ;
        s1 = new Stack <Integer> ( 10 ) ;

        if ( ! s1.isFull( ) )
            s1.push ( 10 ) ;
        if ( ! s1.isFull( ) )
            s1.push ( 20 ) ;
        if ( ! s1.isFull( ) )
            s1.push ( 30 ) ;

        int data1 ;
        if ( ! s1.isEmpty( ) )
        {
```

```
            data1 = s1.pop( ) ;
            System.out.println ( data1 ) ;
        }
        if ( ! s1.isEmpty( ) )
        {
            data1 = s1.pop( ) ;
            System.out.println ( data1 ) ;
        }

        Stack <Float> s2 ;
        s2 = new Stack <Float> ( 10 ) ;

        if ( ! s2.isFull( ) )
            s2.push ( 10.5f ) ;
        if ( ! s2.isFull( ) )
            s2.push ( 20.5f ) ;
        if ( ! s2.isFull( ) )
            s2.push ( 18.5f ) ;

        float data2 ;

        if ( ! s2.isEmpty( ) )
        {
            data2 = s2.pop( ) ;
            System.out.println  ( data2 ) ;
        }
        if ( ! s2.isEmpty( ) )
        {
            data2 = s2.pop( ) ;
            System.out.println  ( data2 ) ;
        }

        Stack <Complex> s3 ;
        s3 = new Stack <Complex> ( 10 ) ;

        Complex c1 = new Complex ( 1.1f, 2.2f ) ;
        Complex c2 = new Complex ( 3.3f, 4.4f ) ;
        Complex c3 = new Complex ( 5.5f, 6.6f ) ;

        if ( ! s3.isFull( ) )
            s3.push ( c1 ) ;
```

```
        if ( ! s3.isFull( ) )
            s3.push ( c2 ) ;
        if ( ! s3.isFull( ) )
            s3.push ( c3 ) ;

        Complex c ;
        if ( ! s3.isEmpty( ) )
        {
            c = s3.pop( ) ;
            c.printData( ) ;
        }
        if ( ! s3.isEmpty( ) )
        {
            c = s3.pop( ) ;
            c.printData( ) ;
        }
    }
}
class  Stack <T>
{
    private T arr[ ] ;
    private int  top ;
    private int size ;
    Stack ( int sz )
    {
        size = sz ;
        top = -1 ;
        arr = ( T[  ] ) new Object[ sz ] ;
    }
    boolean isFull( )
    {
        if ( top == size )
            return true ;
        else
            return false ;
    }
    void push ( T  data )
    {
            top++ ;
            arr [ top ] = data ;
    }
```

```
    boolean isEmpty( )
    {
        if ( top == -1 )
            return true ;
        else
            return false ;
    }
    T pop( )
    {
        T val ;
        val = arr [ top ] ;
        top-- ;
        return val ;
    }
}
class Complex
{
    float r, i ;

    public Complex ( float rr, float ii )
    {
        r = rr ;
        i = ii ;
    }
    public void printData( )
    {
        System.out.println ( "Real = " + r + " Imag = " + i ) ;
    }
}
```

We have created three stacks here—**s1**, **s2** and **s3** and pushed three objects on each one. Then we popped up the values from the three stacks and displayed them on the screen. **s1** and **s2** maintain stacks of ready-made classes **Integer** and **Float**. We have also declared a class called **Complex** and then pushed/ popped **Complex** objects to/from stack **s3**. Here's the output of the program...

```
30
20
18.5
20.5
Real = 5.5 Imag = 6.6
```

Real = 3.3 Imag = 4.4

You can observe that the order in which the elements are popped from the stack is exactly reverse of the order in which they were pushed on the stack.

The way to build a generic class is like the one used for building a generic function. The **<T>** signals that the class is going to be a generic class. This is precisely how we have defined the **Stack** class. Its skeleton is shown below.

```
class Stack <T>
{
    // code that uses the type T
}
```

It the **Stack** class, the type **T** is used at every place in the class where there is a reference to the type of the array **arr**. There are four such places—the definition of **arr**, the constructor, the argument type of the **push( )** function, and the return type of the **pop( )** function. Do take a look at these four functions in our program.

To create objects of this generic class we have used statements like,

```
Stack <Integer> s1 ;
s1 = new Stack <Integer> ( 10 ) ;
```

While creating object **s1** we are passing 10 to the constructor of generic stack class. The value 10 indicates the size of the array that is going to hold the values pushed into the stack. In the constructor we have created this array through the statement

```
arr = ( T[ ] ) new Object[ sz ] ;
```

Here, firstly an array of **Object**s is created, and the address of this array is typecasted into an address of array of type **T**.

In the constructor, to indicate emptiness of stack, we have initiated **top** to a value -1. This variable is going to act as an index into the array in which the values pushed into the stack are going to be stored. We have also preserved the value of array size in the variable **size**. Later, in functions **isEmpty( )** and **isFull( )** we have used these values to check whether stack is empty or full.

Note that it is also possible to inherit a new class from a generic class.

Bounded Generics

Let us now define and use a generic class called **Statistics**. This class obtains an average of **Integer**s or **Float**s. This should be simple. However, the twist here is, we should not be allowed to find average of types for whom average does not make any sense, strings for example. This means that the **Statistics** class should not work for strings. Such classes are known as Bounded Generics. It is very simple to accomplish this. While defining the **Statistics** class we should define it as:

```
class Statistics <T extends Number>
```

This ensures that **Statistics** class can work only with those types that are derived from **Number**. Incidentally, **Integer** and **Float** both are derived from **Number** class, so **Statistics** can work with objects of these classes. Here is the full-fledged program.

```
// Bounded generics
package statsdemoproject ;
public class StatsDemoProject
{
    public static void main ( String[ ] args )
    {
        Integer iarr[ ] = { 1, 2, 3, 4, 5 } ;
        Statistics <Integer> iobj ;
        double avg1 ;

        iobj = new Statistics <Integer> ( iarr ) ;
        avg1 = iobj.getAverage( ) ;
        System.out.println ( "avg1 = " + avg1 ) ;

        Float farr[ ] = { 1.1f, 2.1f, 1.0f } ;
        Statistics <Float> fobj ;
        double avg2 ;

        fobj = new Statistics <Float> ( farr ) ;
        avg2 = fobj.getAverage( ) ;
        System.out.println ( "avg2 = " + avg2 ) ;
    }
}
class Statistics <T extends Number>
{
```

```
    private T arr[ ] ;

    Statistics ( T[ ] obj )
    {
        arr = obj ;
    }
    public double getAverage( )
    {
        double sum = 0.0 ;

        for ( int i = 0 ; i < arr.length ; i++ )
            sum = sum + arr[ i ].doubleValue( ) ;

        return ( sum / arr.length ) ;
    }
}
```

The program is straight-forward, and we think you can understand it easily. The **doubleValue( )** method returns the value of the specified number as a **double**.

Exercises

[A] State whether the following statements are True or False:

(a) Java supports generic classes but not generic functions.

(b) We can inherit a new class from a generic class.

(c) Using generic functions saves memory.

(d) Generic functions cannot work for primitives like **int**, **float**, **char**, etc.

(e) A generic function can receive multiple argument types.

(f) Bounded generics can work only with the objects of a specified class.

(g) Generics are extensively used in Java collection classes.

(h) Generic function arguments can take default values.

(i) Generic classes describe the functionality without being bound to any type.

[B] Answer the following:

(a) Write a program that will implement a linked list through a generic class.

(b) Write a program that has a generic class that can sort dates and strings apart from integers and floats.

[C] Pick up the correct alternative for each of the following questions:

(a) If **printArray( )** is a generic function capable of printing any numeric array then which of the following is the CORRECT way to call it?

(1) int[ ] arr = { 10, 20, 30, 40, 50 } ;
printArray (arr) ;
(2) float[ ] arr = { 1.1, 1.2, 1.3, 1.4, 1.5 } ;
printArray (arr) ;
(3) Integer[ ] arr = { 10, 20, 30, 40, 50 } ;
printArray (arr) ;
(4) char[ ] arr = { 'A', 'B', 'C', 'D', 'E' } ;
printArray (arr) ;

(b) A generic function can work with
(1) byte
(2) char
(3) float
(4) Float

(c) Which of the following statements is CORRECT about the **fun( )** function given below:

```
public static < T > void fun ( T[ ] arr )
{
    for ( T i : arr )
        System.out.println ( i ) ;
}
```

(1) It is a generic function.
(2) It is receiving an array of any reference type
(3) It is printing all elements of the array that it is receiving
(4) (1), (2) and (3)

(d) Which of the following statements is CORRECT about the code snippet given below:

```
public static < T > T minimum ( T a, T b )
{
    if ( a.compareTo ( b ) < 0 )
        return a ;
    else
        return b ;
}
```

(1) It returns the smaller of the 2 arguments that it receives
(2) It works only with those types that are derived from Number class
(3) It works only with those types which implement a **Comparable** interface
(4) It can work with any type of primitive

KanNotes

- Generics promote source-code level reuse, whereas Inheritance promotes byte-code level reuse
- It is possible to create generic functions as well as generic classes
- Once the generic function / class is ready we can use them with any reference type
- Primitives are often called value types, whereas classes are called reference types
- Syntax of defining and calling a generic function :

```
// call to generic function
Integer[ ] intarr = { 10, -2, 37, 42, 15 } ;
printArray ( intarr ) ;

// generic function definition
public static <T> void printArray ( T[ ] arr )
```

```
{
    ..
}
```

- Generic function that can work with types that implements a Comparable interface

```
public static <T extends Comparable <T> > T min ( T a, T b )
{
    ...
}
```

- Generic function that can receive multiple types

```
public static <T, S, Z> void printTypes ( T a, S b, Z c )
{
    System.out.println ( "a = " + a + " b = " + b + " c = " + c ) ;
}
```

- Syntax for using and defining a generic class :

```
// using generic class
stack <Integer> s1 ;
s1 = new stack <Integer> ( 10 );
s1.push ( 10 ) ;

// defining generic class
class stack <T>
{
    ..
}
```

- Bounded generic class restricts its usage only by those reference types which are derived from the specified type
- For example, the following class would work only for those types that are derived from the Java API Number class :

```
class Statistics <T extends Number>
{
    ..
}
```

Chapter 19

Java Collections

There are many standard ways of storing and accessing data. Let Java Collections handle that, so that you can concentrate on building something bigger using them...

Contents

- What is Collections Framework?
- Array of Names and Numbers
- Maintaining a Stack
- Maintaining a Queue
- Maintaining a Linked List
- Maintaining a Set
- Maintaining a Tree
- Maintaining a HashMap
- Using the Algorithms
- Exercises
- KanNotes

As Java became a popular choice amongst programmers to implement solutions, a need was felt to have a standard way to handle the data in the program. So, a set of classes and interfaces were made available in Java API to handle the data in memory. These classes came to be known as Java Collections Framework. Let us now understand its details.

What is Collections Framework?

Suppose in a program we wish to store, retrieve, and manipulate numbers and strings. An easy and intuitive way to handle this situation would be to create arrays of numbers and strings. However, this approach has the following limitations:

(a) We may not want fixed-size arrays. We may want arrays to grow dynamically as we keep adding new elements to it. This requirement cannot be met by normal arrays, at least not without an effort of allocating space for bigger-sized array, copying existing elements into this space, etc.

(b) There may be a need to maintain data in different ways like array (where order of insertion is important) or Key-Value maps (where order of insertion is unimportant).

(c) There may be a need to access data in different ways—from beginning to end, or last-in-first-out order (as in a stack), or first-in-first-out order (as in a queue).

To handle all these scenarios a library called Java Collections Framework was introduced. It is based on Generics. It contains Collection classes, Interfaces and Algorithms (set of static functions). Some of the highlighting features of this collection framework are:

(a) Since the collections framework is based on generics it lets you handle virtually any type of data.

(b) The collections framework provides a set of very efficient classes to carry out most in-memory data management functionality.

(c) It contains readymade classes for most Data Structures like stack, queue, linked list, binary tree, hash map, etc.

(d) There is a lot of consistency in usage of the collection classes. For example, the same **add( )** function is available for adding new data to different collections. So, no matter how a stack or a linked list organizes the data internally, the call that the programmer must make to add a new element to them remains same.

(e) Rather than doing the entire implementation from scratch, it is easily possible to extend the collections framework using the usual inheritance rules, to suit our specific needs.

Figure 19.1 shows the classes and interfaces (selected few) available in the collections framework. Each transparent box represents an interface, whereas each filled box represents a class. The classes and interfaces of the collections framework are defined in **java.util** package.

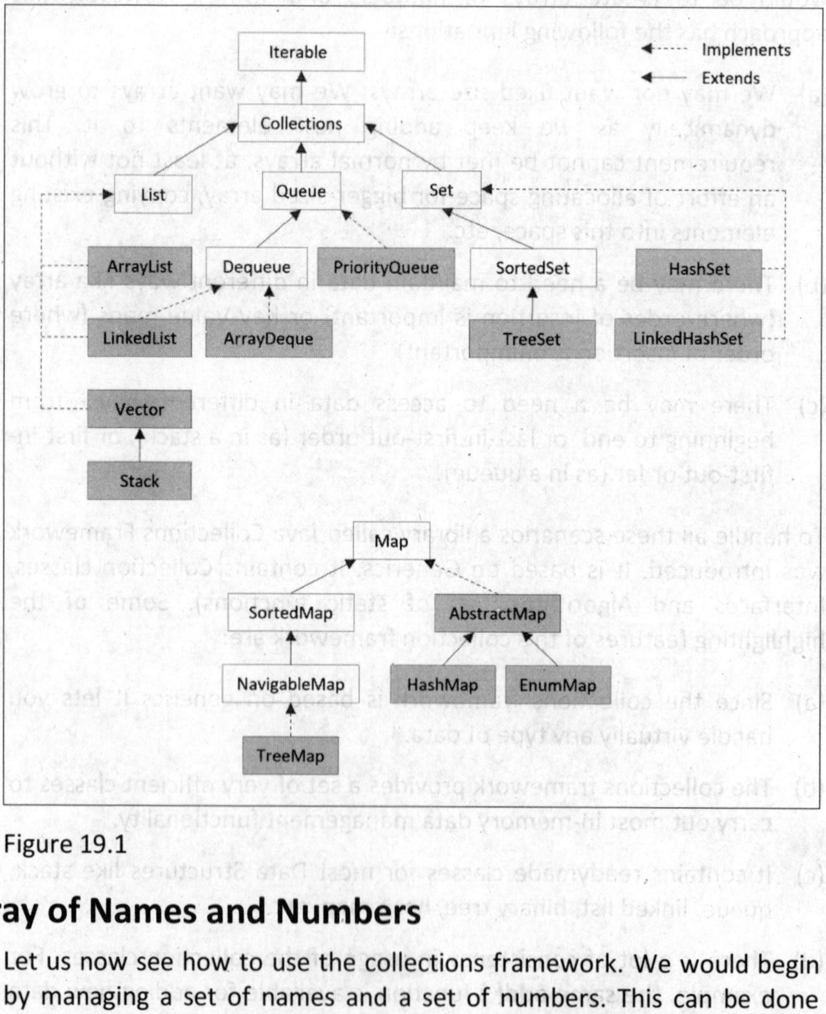

Figure 19.1

Array of Names and Numbers

Let us now see how to use the collections framework. We would begin by managing a set of names and a set of numbers. This can be done using the **ArrayList** collection class. Given below is a program that shows how this can be done.

```
// Using an ArrayList
package arraylistproject ;
import java.util.* ;
public class ArrayListProject
{
    public static void main ( String[ ] args )
    {
        ArrayList <String> alnames ;

        alnames = new ArrayList <> ( ) ;
        alnames.add ( "Shashank" ) ;
        alnames.add ( "Prasanna" ) ;
        alnames.add ( "Nimesh" ) ;
        alnames.add ( "Karun" ) ;
        alnames.add ( "Rajgopal" ) ;

        System.out.println ( "contents of al: " + alnames ) ;
        alnames.add ( 2, "Aditya" ) ;
        alnames.remove ( 3 ) ;
        alnames.remove ( "Karun" ) ;
        System.out.println ( "contents of al: " + alnames ) ;

        if ( alnames.contains ( "Aditya" ) )
            System.out.println ( "Aditya is present in the array list" ) ;

        ArrayList <Integer> alnums ;
        alnums = new ArrayList <>( ) ;
        alnums.add ( 10 ) ;
        alnums.add ( 20 ) ;
        alnums.add ( 30 ) ;
        alnums.add ( 40 ) ;

        int sum = 0 ;
        for ( int i = 0 ; i < alnums.size( ) ; i++ )
            sum = sum + alnums.get ( i ) ;

        System.out.println ( "sum = " + sum ) ;

        Integer arr[ ] = new Integer [ alnums.size( ) ] ;
```

```
        arr = alnums.toArray ( arr ) ;

        sum = 0 ;
        for ( int n : arr )
            sum += n ;

        System.out.println ( "sum = " + sum ) ;
    }
}
```

Here is the output of the program...

```
contents of alnames: [Shashank, Prasanna, Nimesh, Karun, Rajgopal]
contents of alnames: [Shashank, Prasanna, Aditya, Rajgopal]
Aditya is present in the array list
sum = 100
sum = 100
```

The program begins by creating an **ArrayList** object for storing strings and then adding a few names to it using **add( )** function. If we wish, we can also pass the initial size of the array list by passing the size to the constructor while creating the **ArrayList** object. After creating the object, we have added a new name at a specific position (using the overloaded **add( )** function) and removed name from a specific position (using the **remove( )** function). Thus addition, insertion and deletion operations are straight-forward.

There is a very simple way to print the entire **ArrayList** contents using **println( )**. Note that the **ArrayList** maintains the list in a dynamic fashion. Nowhere have we specified its size. It keeps growing as we keep adding new elements. The **contains( )** function helps us figure out whether a specific element is present in the array list or not.

What is important for you to notice is that the usage of **ArrayList** class does not change at all when it comes to maintaining an array of numbers instead of names.

We have obtained the sum of all integers by retrieving each integer using the **get( )** function. Note that **get( )** returns an **Integer**, not an **int**. The **size( )** function yields the current size of the array list.

The array maintained by array list can be converted into the normal Java array using the **toArray( )** function. This array can then be traversed using the special **for** loop as shown in the program.

Maintaining a Stack

A Stack is a data structure in which the addition of a new element or deletion of an existing element always takes place at the same end. This end is often known as **top** of stack. This situation can be compared to a stack of plates in a cafeteria where every new plate added to the stack is added at the **top**. Similarly, every plate taken off the stack is also from the **top** of the stack. Thus, stack is a last-in-first-out (LIFO) list. When an item is added to a stack, the operation is called **push**, and when an item is removed from the stack the operation is called **pop**.

Given below is a program that maintains a stack of city names using the collection class called **Stack**. Note that before calling the **pop( )** function we need to ascertain whether the stack has any element left in it. This is done by calling the **isEmpty( )** function.

```
// Maintaining a stack
package stackdemoproject ;
import java.util.* ;
public class StackDemoProject
{
    public static void main ( String args[ ] )
    {
        Stack < String > s ;
        s = new Stack <> ( ) ;
        s.push ( "Delhi" ) ;
        s.push ( "Nagpur" ) ;
        s.push ( "Indore" ) ;
        s.push ( "Raipur" ) ;
        s.push ( "Mysore" ) ;
        s.push ( "Mumbai" ) ;

        String str ;
        if ( ! s.isEmpty( ) )
        {
            str = s.pop( ) ;
            System.out.println ( str ) ;
        }
        if ( ! s.isEmpty( ) )
        {
            str = s.pop( ) ;
            System.out.println ( str ) ;
```

```
        }
    }
}
```

Maintaining a Queue

Queue is a linear data structure that permits insertion of new element at one end and deletion of an element at the other end. The end at which the deletion of an element takes place is called **front**, and the end at which insertion of a new element takes place is called **rear**.

The first element that gets added into the queue is the first one to get removed from the list. Hence, queue is also referred to as first-in-first-out (FIFO) list. Figure 19.3 gives a pictorial representation of a queue.

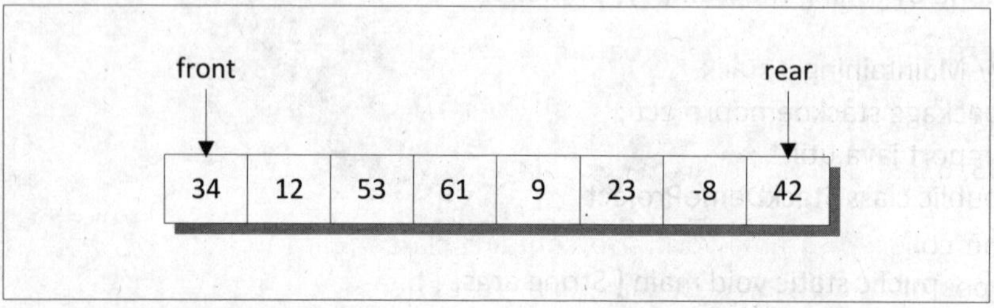

Figure 19.3

In Figure 19.3, 34 is the first element and 42 is the last element added to the queue. Similarly, 34 will be the first element to get removed and 42 will be the last element to get removed from the queue.

The queue data structure is widely used in job scheduling, print spooling, maintaining message queues in event-driven architectures, handling requests in web applications, manage incoming calls in call centers, etc.

The program given below uses the collection class **LinkedList** to maintain a queue of numbers. Note that the LinkedList collection class implements the **List** as well as the **Queue** interface.

```
// Maintaining a queue
package queuedemoproject ;
import java.util.* ;
public class QueueDemoProject
{
    public static void main ( String[ ] args )
```

```
    {
        Queue <Integer> q ;
        q = new LinkedList <Integer> ( ) ;
        q.add ( 34 ) ;
        q.add ( 12 ) ;
        q.add ( 53 ) ;
        q.add ( 61 ) ;
        q.add ( 9 ) ;
        System.out.println ( q ) ;
        q.remove( ) ;
        q.remove( ) ;
        System.out.println ( q ) ;
    }
}
```

Here is the output of the program...

```
[34, 12, 53, 61, 9]
[53, 61, 9]
```

The collection framework also contains classes that implement special types of queues. For example, the **ArrayDeque** class uses a resizable array and allows us to add or remove an element from both ends of the queue. The **PriorityQueue** class can be used when the elements must be processed based on priority.

Maintaining a Linked List

Linked list is a very common data structure often used to store similar data in memory. While the elements of an array occupy contiguous memory locations, those of a linked list are not constrained to be stored in adjacent locations. The individual elements are stored "somewhere" in memory, rather like a family dispersed, but still bound together. The order of the elements is maintained by explicit links between them. For instance, the marks obtained by different students can be stored in a linked list as shown in Figure 19.2.

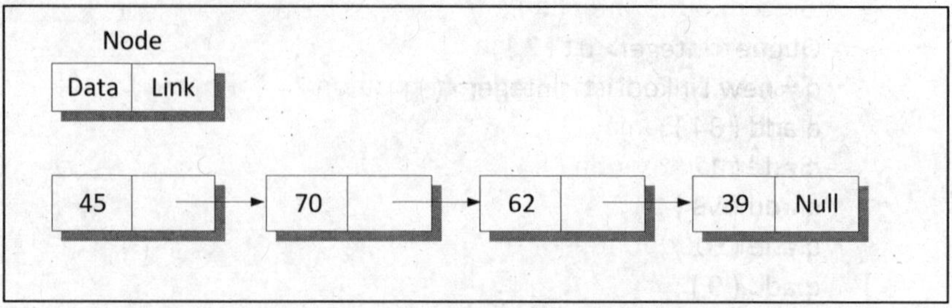

Figure 19.2

Observe that the linked list is a collection of elements called nodes, each of which stores two items of information—an element of the list and a link. A link is a reference or an address that indicates explicitly the location of the node containing the successor of the list element. In Figure 19.2, the arrows represent the links. The **data** part of each node consists of the marks obtained by a student, and the **link** part is a pointer to the next node. The **NULL** in the last node indicates that it is the last node in the list.

Instead of marks, we can maintain a linked list of names. If we want, we can maintain both in each node. The program given below uses the collection class **LinkedList** to maintain a linked list of names of students. Most of the operations in the program are self-explanatory. Go through the program carefully, step at a time.

```
// Maintaining a linked list
package linkedlistdemoproject ;
import java.util.* ;
public class LinkedListDemoProject
{
    public static void main ( String[ ] args )
    {
        LinkedList <String> ll ;
        ll = new LinkedList <> ( ) ;
        ll.add ( "Subhash" ) ;
        ll.add ( "Rahul" ) ;
        ll.add ( "Joe" ) ;
        ll.add ( "Vineeta" ) ;
        for ( String s : ll )
            System.out.println ( s ) ;

        ll.set ( 2, "Neha" ) ;
```

```
            System.out.println ( ll ) ;
            String name = ll.get ( 2 ) ;
            System.out.println ( "String at position 2 = " + name ) ;
            ll.add ( 3, "Sanjay" ) ;
            System.out.println ( ll ) ;
            ll.remove ( 1 ) ;
            System.out.println ( ll ) ;
      }
}
```

Here is the output of the program...

```
Subhash
Rahul
Joe
Vineeta
[Subhash, Rahul, Neha, Vineeta]
String at position 2 = Neha
[Subhash, Rahul, Neha, Sanjay, Vineeta]
[Subhash, Neha, Sanjay, Vineeta]
```

Maintaining a Set

Set data structure is an unordered collection of objects in which duplicate values cannot be stored. To create and maintain this data structure, collections framework provides a **Set** interface which is implemented by classes **HashSet**, **TreeSet**, and **LinkedHashSet**. Each of these implementations have unique characteristics.

If we need a fast set with no specific ordering requirements, we should use **HashSet**. If we need elements sorted in a specific order, we should use **TreeSet**. Lastly, if we want to maintain the order of insertion and still have good performance, we should use **LinkedHashSet**. The choice between these classes depends on the specific use case and the requirements of the application.

Given below is a program that maintains a set of numbers using the collection class **HashSet**.

```
// Maintaining a set
packafe setdemoproject ;
import java.util.* ;
public class SetDemoProject
{
```

```
public static void main ( String[ ] args )
{
    HashSet<Integer> numSet = new HashSet<>( ) ;
    numSet.add ( 5 ) ;
    numSet.add ( 10 ) ;
    numSet.add ( 15 ) ;
    numSet.add ( 20 ) ;
    numSet.add ( 25 ) ;

    System.out.println ( numSet ) ;

    // Adding a duplicate element (it will not be added)
    numSet.add ( 10 ) ;
    System.out.println ( numSet ) ;

    numSet.remove(15);
    System.out.println ( numSet ) ;

    int ele = 20 ;
    if ( numSet.contains ( ele ) )
        System.out.println ( ele + " is present in the HashSet" ) ;
    else
        System.out.println ( ele + " is not present in the HashSet" ) ;
  }
}
```

Here is the output of the program...

```
[20, 5, 25, 10, 15]
[20, 5, 25, 10, 15]
[20, 5, 25, 10]
20 is present in the HashSet
```

Maintaining a Tree

The data structures such as linked lists, stacks and queues are linear data structures. As against this, trees are non-linear data structures. In a linked list each node has a link which points to another node. In a tree structure, however, each node may point to several other nodes (which may then point to several other nodes, etc.). Tree data structure is used for a wide variety of applications. For example, we can use it to represent a person and all his or her descendants as shown in Figure 19.4.

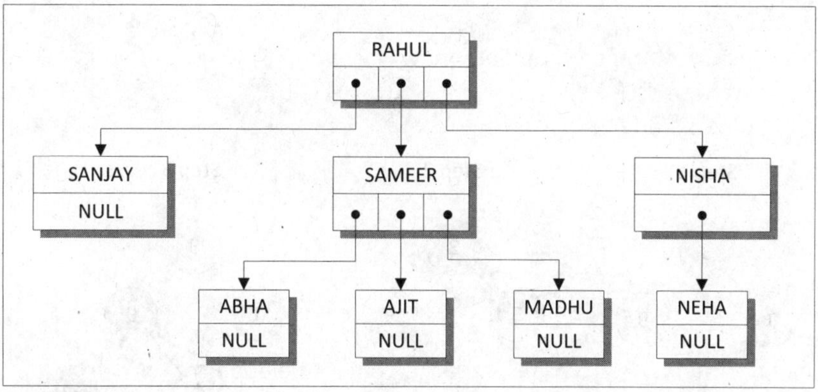

Figure 19.4

Notice that each tree node contains a name for data and one or more pointers to the other tree nodes.

Although the nodes in a general tree may contain any number of pointers to the other tree nodes, many data structures have at the most two pointers to the other tree nodes. This type of tree is called a **Binary Tree**.

Many algorithms that use binary trees proceed in two phases. The first phase builds a binary tree, and the second traverses the tree. A simple logic to build a binary tree is to compare the element to be inserted with the element in the root node and then take the left branch if the element is smaller than the element in the node, and a right branch if it is greater or equal to the element in the node. Thus, if the input list is

3, 9, 1, 4, 7, 11

Then using this insertion method, the binary tree shown in Figure 19.5 would be produced.

Such a binary tree has the property that all the elements in the left sub-tree of any node **n** are less than the contents of **n**. And all the elements in the right sub-tree of **n** are greater than or equal to the contents of **n**. A binary tree that has these properties is called a **Binary Search Tree (BST)**.

If a binary search tree is traversed in in-order, i.e., in the order left child, root, and right child and the contents of each node are printed as each node is visited, the numbers are printed in ascending order.

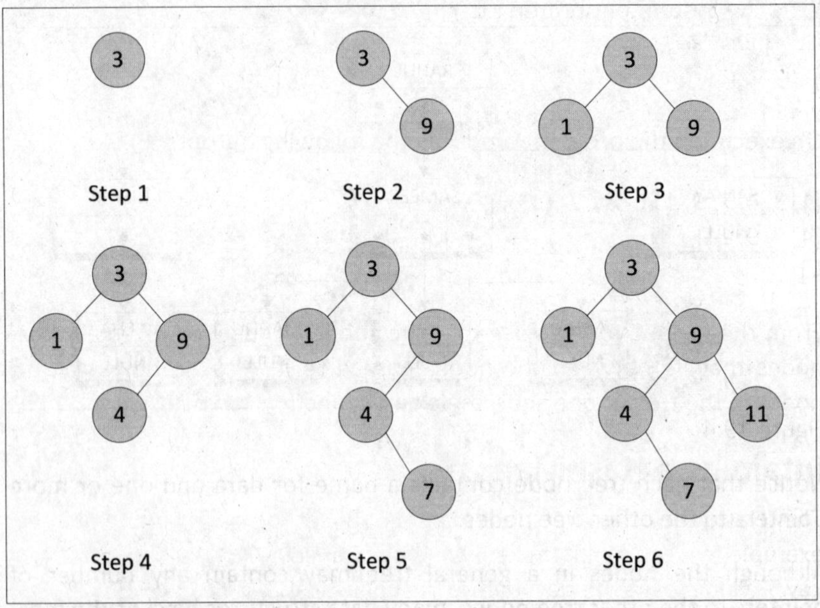

Figure 19.5

There isn't a class specifically designed for a Binary Search Tree (BST). However, we can use the **TreeSet** class to achieve a similar effect. This is demonstrated in the program given below.

```
// Maintaining a tree
package treesetdemoproject ;
import java.util.* ;
public class TreeSetDemoProject
{
    public static void main ( String args[ ] )
    {
        TreeSet <Integer> ts ;
        ts = new TreeSet <> ( ) ;
        ts.add ( 3 ) ;
        ts.add ( 9 ) ;
        ts.add ( 1 ) ;
        ts.add ( 4 ) ;
        ts.add ( 7 ) ;
        ts.add ( 11 ) ;

        System.out.println ( ts ) ;
        System.out.println ( ts.subSet ( 4, 11 ) ) ;
        ts.clear( ) ;
```

```
        System.out.println ( ts ) ;
    }
}
```

On execution the program produces the following output:

```
[1, 3, 4, 7, 9, 11]
[4, 7, 9, 11]
[ ]
```

From the output you can see that the **subSet( )** function gives all those nodes that lie between the nodes passed to it. Also, to delete all the nodes in the tree at one shot, the **clear( )** function can be used.

Maintaining a HashMap

The **HashMap** class lets us maintain a set of key-value pairs. For example, we can maintain key-value pairs of cell numbers and names, or key - value pairs of day names in English and Hindi. A map cannot contain duplicate keys. The key - value pairs may not be stored in the same order as the order of insertion. We can get the order in which they are being maintained by printing out the hash map. We can also retrieve or update the values using the key. This is shown in the following program.

```
// Maintaining a hash map
package hashmapdemoproject ;
import java.util.* ;
public class HashMapDemoProject
{
    public static void main ( String args[ ] )
    {
        HashMap < String, String> hm ;
        hm = new HashMap < > ( ) ;
        hm.put ( "Sun", "Ravi" ) ;
        hm.put ( "Mon", "Som" ) ;
        hm.put ( "Tue", "Mangal" ) ;
        hm.put ( "Wed", "Budh" ) ;
        hm.put ( "Thu", "Guru" ) ;
        hm.put ( "Fri", "Shukra" ) ;
        hm.put ( "Sat", "Shani" ) ;

        System.out.println ( hm ) ;    // prints entire hash map
```

```
        // print one entry at a time
        for ( Map.Entry<String, String> e : hm.entrySet( ) )
            System.out.println ( e.getKey( ) + ":" + e.getValue( ) ) ;
        String str ;
        str = hm.get ( "Wed" ) ;
        System.out.println ( "Wed in hindi is " + str ) ;
    }
}
```

The output of the program is shown below. Note that the **get( )** function can be used to obtain the value stored against the key passed to it. The **entrySet( )** method creates a set out of the elements in a map.

```
{Thu=Guru, Tue=Mangal, Wed=Budh, Sat=Shani, Fri=Shukra, Sun=Ravi,
Mon=Som}
Thu:Guru
Tue:Mangal
Wed:Budh
Sat:Shani
Fri:Shukra
Sun:Ravi
Mon:Som
Wed in hindi is Budh
```

If we wish to store multiple values against each key, then these values must be wrapped in an object. For example, against a cell number as a key we can store an object containing the name, address, and photograph.

The classes **TreeMap**, **HashMap**, and **EnumMap** all implement the **Map** interface. We should **HashMap** when order is not important, and you need efficient basic operations. We should use **TreeMap** when we need elements sorted by keys. Lastly, we should use **EnumMap** when we wish to work with **enum** keys.

Using the Algorithms

There are many operations that we wish to perform on collections. These include searching, sorting, finding minimum value, finding maximum value, etc. In terminology of collections framework these are called algorithms and are available for use in the form of **static** methods of the **Collections** class. A smaller version of the same is also available in the **Arrays** class. The program given below shows how to use these algorithms from the **Arrays** class.

```
// Using algorithms
package arraysdemoproject ;
import java.util.* ;
public class ArraysDemoProject
{
    public static void main ( String[ ] args )
    {
        int arr[ ] = new int[ 5 ] ;
        Random r = new Random( ) ;

        for ( int i = 0 ; i < arr.length ; i++ )
        {
            arr[ i ] = r.nextInt ( 25 ) ;
            System.out.println ( arr[ i ] ) ;
        }
        Arrays.sort ( arr ) ;
        System.out.println ( "After sorting: " ) ;
        for ( int i = 0 ; i < arr.length ; i++ )
            System.out.println ( arr[ i ] ) ;

        Arrays.fill ( arr, 2, 4, -3 ) ;
        System.out.println ( "After filling: " ) ;
        for ( int i = 0 ; i < arr.length ; i++ )
            System.out.println ( arr[ i ] ) ;

        int pos ;
        pos = Arrays.binarySearch ( arr, -3 ) ;
        System.out.println ( "pos = " + pos ) ;
    }
}
```

Here is the output of the program.

```
15
13
13
2
18
After sorting:
```

2
13
13
15
18
After filling:
2
13
-3
-3
18
pos = 2

The program generates random numbers using **nextInt( )** function of **Random** class and then populates the array **arr** with these randomly generated integers. Next, it calls the **sort( )** function to sort these numbers.

The call to **fill( )** function fills the array with -3 starting from 2nd position up to and excluding the 4th position. Then the program uses the **binarySearch( )** function to search for the position of first occurrence of -3 in the array.

We hope now you have got a fair idea of how to use the Java collections framework. You can explore the other collection classes, interfaces, and algorithms of the framework on your own.

Exercises

[A] State whether the following statements are True or False:

(a) Java collections framework provides common algorithms through **static** functions of **Collections** class.

(b) The Java collection framework is based on Generics.

(c) Key - value pairs can be maintained using **ArrayList** class.

(d) In a hashmap the order of insertion and order of access are the same.

(e) **ArrayList** class can grow and shrink an array dynamically.

(f) Elements of a linked list are stored in adjacent memory locations.

(g) Stack is a FIFO list.

(h) All binary trees are maintained by **TreeSet** class as binary search trees.

(i) It is possible to maintain elements of **ArrayList** in sorted order.

[B] Answer the following questions:

(a) Write a program that will implement a linked list where each node consists of name, age, and salary of a person.

(b) Write a program that maintains a tree of city names in sorted order.

(c) Write a program that maintains a hash map of 10 cell numbers as keys and the name of the person and his email address as values.

[B] Pick up the correct alternative for each of the following questions:

(a) Which of the following is the CORRECT import statement for using classes in Java collection framework?
(1) import java.io.*
(2) import java.util.*
(3) import java.*
(4) import java.collections.*

(b) Java collections maintain data in the form of
(1) int
(2) float
(3) double
(4) Any reference type

(c) Consider the following code snippet:

```
ArrayList < int > num = new ArrayList < > ( ) ;
num.add ( 10 ) ;
num.add ( 20 ) ;
```

What change should be made to make the above code work?

(1) Replace **ArrayList** with **Vector**
(2) Replace **ArrayList** with **LinkedList**

(3) Replace **int** with **Integer**
(4) The code will work perfectly

(d) Consider the following code snippet:

```
ArrayList < Integer > num = new ArrayList < Integer > ( ) ;
num.add ( 10 ) ;
num.add ( 20 ) ;
num.add ( 30 ) ;
num.add ( 40 ) ;
Integer arr [ ] = new Integer[ num.size( ) ] ;
// add statement here
for ( int n: arr )
    System.out.println ( n ) ;
```

Which statement will you add for the code to work?

(1) arr = num.toArray (arr) ;
(2) arr = num ;
(3) arr = num.convert (arr) ;
(4) arr = convert (arr) ;

(e) Which of the following is NOT an interface in the Java Collection framework?
(1) TreeSet
(2) Set
(3) SortedSet
(4) NavigableSet

KanNotes

- To store, retrieve and manipulate multiple numbers / strings arrays can be used
- Arrays suffer from 2 limitations :
  - They have no mechanism to maintain data in different ways like Key -Value maps, Dictionary, etc.
  - Arrays have no means to access data in FIFO, LIFO, Sorted order, etc.

- Instead of arrays we should use ready-made library called Java Collection Framework
- Advantages of using Java Collection f/w
  - Very efficient, time tested, written by experts
  - Readymade classes for most data structures, so we can concentrate on program rather than building data structures
  - It is possible to extend the collection classes to suit our needs
- Collection framework contains :
  - Collection classes - ArrayList, LinkedList, TreeSet, PriorityQueue, HashMap, etc.
  - Interfaces - Collection, List, Set, SortedSet, NavigableSet, Queue, DeQueue, etc
  - Algorithms – fill( ), max( ), min( ), reverse( ), shuffle( ), binarySearch(), sort(), etc.
- Algorithms are static methods of Arrays class
- All collection classes are implemented as Generics, hence can work only with reference types
- Vector class and ArrayList class both can maintain arrays that grow dynamically
- Vector is synchronized class, so slow. ArrayList is not synchronized, so fast
- For a Vector class :
  - capacity indicates how many elements can be stored in the vector
  - size indicates number of elements present in it
  - grow size indicates by how much would the capacity increase, when we store an element once the capacity is full
- Vector / ArrayList should be used if we are to store and process their elements sequentially
- LinkList should be used if frequent insertions / deletions of elements is required

- Rule for inserting elements in a Binary Search Tree (BST)- Greater to Right, Smaller to Left of Root
- The sequence of visiting nodes in BST in Inorder traversal – Left, Root, Right
- When elements are accessed using Inorder Traversal, they get accessed in ascending order
- The order in which we insert entries into a HashMap and the order in which they are stored may be different

Lambdas and Functional Programming

Let Us JAVA 7th Edition

CHAPTER 20

Lambdas and Functional programming are modern features that Java has to offer. Learn them or you will soon perish...

Contents

- Functional Interface
- Lambda Expression
- Creating and Using Lambda
- Assigning Lambda to Variable
- Generic Functional Interface
- Using Lambda in Multithreading
- Using Lambda with Collections
- Functional Programming
- Stream API
- Map, Filter, Reduce
- Mutable and Immutable Lists
- Standard Functional Interfaces
- default and static Methods of Standard Functional Interfaces
- Lazy and Eager Operations
- More Programs
- KanNotes
- Exercises

Lambdas and Functional Programming unlock the power of modern programming paradigms. In this chapter we will explore the principles of functional programming, a programming style that treats computation as the evaluation of mathematical functions. We will also experience the elegance and efficiency that lambdas (anonymous functions) bring to Java, enabling us to write more expressive and concise code. Let us begin this journey by understanding what a functional interface is.

Functional Interface

An interface that contains only one abstract method is called a functional interface. A functional interface can contain any number of **default** or **static** methods. Here is an example of a functional interface.

```
@FunctionalInterface
public interface MyInterface
{
    void method1( ) ;        // method signature
    default void method2( )
    {
        // default implementation for method2
    }
    static void method3( )
    {
        // implementation for method3
    }
}
```

Note that using **@FunctionalInterface** notation is not mandatory for the interface to be treated as a functional interface. But it is a good idea to use it, because if we use it and then by mistake add one more method signature, the compiler will report an error. Since a functional interface contains a single abstract method, it is also called a SAM.

Interfaces like **Runnable**, **Callable**, **Comparator**, etc. in Java library are functional interfaces. The **Runnable** and **Callable** interfaces are used in multithreading applications, whereas the **Comparator** interface is used for sorting a collection of objects or arrays. In addition to them, functional interfaces like **Predicate**, **Consumer**, **Function**, **Supplier**, **UnaryOperator**, **BinaryOperator**, **BiFunction**, etc. have been provided in **java.util.function**.

Lambda Expression

Lambda expression (often simply called lambda) provides a clear and concise way to implement single abstract method present in a functional interface using an expression. A Lambda expression can be assigned to a variable or passed to a function.

A lambda expression doesn't have a name and can take one of the following forms:

```
( ) -> expression
( ) -> statement ;
( ) -> { statements ; }
( parameters ) -> expression
( parameters ) -> statements ;
( parameters ) -> { statements ; }
```

Parameters are like method parameters, but without explicit types. If there is only one parameter, we can omit parentheses. If there are no parameters, we still need empty parentheses. The arrow (->) separates parameters from the body of the lambda expression. The expression or statements represent the body of the lambda expression. For a single expression, we can omit the braces. Here are a few examples of lambdas.

```
( ) -> "Hi!"                          // receives nothing, returns "Hi"
( x ) -> x * x * x                    // receives x, returns x cube
( a, b, c ) -> ( a + b + c ) / 3      // receives a, b, c, returns average
( s ) -> System.out.println ( s )     // receives s, returns nothing
(x, y ) -> {                          // receives x, y, returns ( x + y ) * 2
        int sum = x + y ;
        return sum * 2 ;
    }
```

Creating and Using Lambda

We know that a class that implements a functional interface must define the method declared in the interface. An abstract method **print( )** in an **ISample** interface can be implemented in **MySample** class and called from **doPrinting( )** method as shown below.

```
// Creating and using lambda
@FunctionalInterface
interface ISample
```

```
{
    public void print( ) ;
}
class MySample implements ISample
{
    public void print( )
    {
        System.out.println ( "Hello" ) ;
    }
}
public class Main
{
    public static void main ( String[ ] args )
    {
        MySample s = new MySample( ) ;
        doPrinting ( s ) ;
    }
    public static void doPrinting ( ISample ms )
    {
        ms.print( ) ;
    }
}
```

In **main( )** we have created an object of **MySample** class and passed it to **doPrinting( )** method which collected it in **ISample ms**. Then using **ms** we have called the **print( )** method. The only thing that we can do with **ms** is call the implementation of **print( )** method (**print( )** being the only method in the functional interface **ISample**). But to do this we had to do a whole bunch of things. We had to declare a **Sample** class that implements the **ISample** interface. Then we had to implement the **print( )** method in it. Then we had to create a **Sample** object and pass it to the **doPrinting( )** method.

This is where lambdas come in. To achieve the same functionality lambda allows us to pass the implementation of **print( )** method as an **ISample** parameter. If we do so, the call to **doPrinting( )** would look like this:

```
doPrinting ( public void print( )
{
    System.out.println ( "Hello" ) ;
}) ;
```

However, we need to make some adjustments to this code to adhere to lambda syntax. So we will have to pass the implementation of **print( )** as follows:

```
doPrinting ( ( ) -> System.out.println ( "Hello" ) ) ;
```

Thus, instead of passing an object that contains the implementation of **print( )** method, we are passing the implementation (code) of **print( )** function to the **doPrinting( )** method. Since a function represents behavior, it is often said that lambda facilitates passing behavior to a method.

Assigning Lambda to Variable

Continuing with the program of the previous section, we can assign the behavior to a variable and pass that variable to **doPrinting( )** as shown below:

```
ISample lambdams = ( ) -> System.out.println ( "Hello" ) ;
doPrinting ( lambdams ) ;
```

Thus, lambdas permit us to turn method implementations into objects and save them in variables and pass them to other methods.

If we alter the **print( )** method to receive a prefix and suffix string and print them along with "Hello", we must alter the code as shown below.

```
// Assigning lambda to a variable
@FunctionalInterface
interface ISample
{
    public void print ( String prefix, String suffix ) ;
}
public class Main
{
    public static void main ( String[ ] args )
    {
        ISample lms = ( p, s ) -> System.out.println ( p + "Hello" + s ) ;
        doPrinting ( lms ) ;
    }
    public static void doPrinting ( ISample ms )
    {
        ms.print ( "**", "!!" ) ;
```

```
    }
}
```

If instead of printing the string, the **print( )** method wishes to return the string, then the interface and lambda should be altered as follows:

```
@FunctionalInterface
interface ISample
{
    public String print ( String prefix, String suffix ) ;
}
// other code
ISample lms = ( p, s ) -> p + "Hello" + s ;
```

Here the expression **p + "Hello" + s** becomes the return string, without using the **return** statement. If we have multiple statements in a lambda then we must explicitly use the **return** statement as shown below.

```
ISample lms = ( p, s ) -> {
    // other statements
    return p + "Hello" + s ;
} ;
```

Generic Functional Interface

A functional interface may contain a SAM that receives and returns a generic type as shown below:

```
interface ISample <T, R>
{
    R apply ( T t ) ;
}
```

The **apply( )** method takes an argument of type **T** and returns a result of type **R**. It represents the operation to be applied to the input value during functional programming. Let us now write a program that uses this generic functional interface.

```
// Defining and using generic functional interface
interface IFunc <T, R>
{
    R apply ( T t ) ;
}
```

```
public class Main
{
    public static void main ( String[ ] args )
    {
        // use the generic functional interface to concatenate strings
        IFunc <String, String> concatenator = s -> s + "!!!" ;
        String result = process ( "Hello", concatenator ) ;
        System.out.println ( "Result: " + result ) ;

        // use the generic functional interface to square numbers
        IFunc <Integer, Integer> squareFunction = n -> n * n ;
        int squaredResult = process ( 5, squareFunction ) ;
        System.out.println ( "Squared Result: " + squaredResult ) ;
    }
    private static <T, R> R process ( T input, IFunc <T, R> processor )
    {
        return processor.apply ( input ) ;
    }
}
```

Here the behavior (i.e. either **concatenator** or **squareFunction**) is passed to the **process( )** method as an argument. When the **apply( )** method is called within the **process( )** method, the appropriate implementation associated with the passed functional interface gets invoked. This aligns with the concept of functional programming, where behaviors can be treated as first-class citizens and passed around as arguments to methods.

Using Lambda in Multithreading

We know that the popular way to launch a thread is by implementing the functional interface **Runnable**. This interface contains a SAM **run( )**. The following program launches a thread and then prints its name 10 times in the **run( )** method.

```
// Normal multithreading program
public class  Main
{
    public static void main ( String args[ ] )
    {
        Runnable  x = new Ex( ) ;
        Thread  t  = new  Thread ( x, "One" ) ;
```

```
        t.start( ) ;
        for ( int  i = 0 ; i < 10 ; i ++ )
            System.out.println ( "Main thread" ) ;
    }
}
class Ex implements Runnable
{
    public void run( )
    {
        for ( int i = 0 ; i < 10 ; i++ )
            System.out.println ( Thread.currentThread( ).getName( ) ) ;
    }
}
```

Now let us achieve the same effect by using a lambda for the **run( )** method.

```
// Multithreading using lambda
public class Main
{
    public static void main ( String[ ] args )
    {
        Runnable x = ( ) -> {
            for ( int i = 0 ; i < 10 ; i++ )
                System.out.println ( Thread.currentThread( ).
                                                getName( ) ) ;
        } ;
        Thread t = new Thread ( x, "One" ) ;
        t.start( ) ;
        for ( int i = 0 ; i < 10 ; i++ )
            System.out.println ( "Main thread" ) ;
    }
}
```

Consider the statement that uses the lambda. It represents the **run( )** method of the **Runnable** interface. It prints the name of the current thread ten times. When a new **Thread** object is created, the **Runnable** instance **x** is passed to it along with the name of the thread. When the **start( )** method is called on the **Thread** instance **t**, it initiates the execution of the **run( )** method in a new thread. As a result, the code inside the lambda expression will be executed concurrently with the main thread. You will appreciate that by using the lambda expression the code becomes very concise.

Using Lambda with Collections

Lambda expressions are often used in conjunction with Java Stream API and collections. An example of using lambda with **ArrayList forEach** method is given below.

```
import java.util.* ;
public class Main
{
    public static void main ( String[ ] args )
    {
        ArrayList <String> names = new ArrayList <> ( ) ;
        names.add ( "Shashank" ) ;
        names.add ( "Prasanna" ) ;
        names.add ( "Nimesh" ) ;
        names.forEach ( n -> System.out.println ( "Hi " + n ) ) ;
    }
}
```

Let us see one more example of the use of lambda with collections. Here we will maintain an **ArrayList** of **Person** objects, with each object containing the name and age of a person. Then we will use a lambda expression to sort the **ArrayList** first time using name of person and next time using age of person. Here is the code that achieves this.

```
// Using lambda with collections
import java.util.* ;
class Person
{
    private String name ;
    private int age ;
    public Person ( String n, int a )
    {
        name = n ;
        age = a ;
    }
    public String getName( )
    {
        return name ;
    }
```

```
    public int getAge( )
    {
        return age ;
    }
}
public class Main
{
    public static void main ( String[ ] args )
    {
        ArrayList <Person> people = new ArrayList < > ( ) ;
        people.add ( new Person ( "Ajay", 25 ) ) ;
        people.add ( new Person ( "Vijay", 31 ) ) ;
        people.add ( new Person ( "Sanjay", 22 ) ) ;
        people.add ( new Person ( "Tanmay", 26 ) ) ;
        people.add ( new Person ( "Anuj", 30 ) ) ;
        people.add( new Person ( "Aditya", 22 ) ) ;

        System.out.println ( "Sorted by name:" ) ;
        Collections.sort ( people, ( p1, p2 ) ->
                    p1.getName( ).compareTo ( p2.getName( ) ) ) ;
        people.forEach ( n -> System.out.println ( n.getName( ) + " : "
                    + n.getAge( ) ) ) ;
        System.out.println ( "\nSorted by age:" ) ;
        Collections.sort ( people, ( p1, p2 ) -> Integer.compare (
                    p1.getAge( ), p2.getAge( ) ) ) ;
        people.forEach ( n -> System.out.println ( n.getName( ) + " : "
                    + n.getAge( ) ) ) ;
    }
}
```

Through the lambda expressions we are providing the implementation of the **compareTo( )** method of the **Comparable** functional interface.

Functional Programming

Programming paradigm/model is a style of building the structure and elements of computer programs. Java was initially designed as an object-oriented programming (OOP) language. It encouraged developers to organize code around objects, promoting principles like encapsulation, inheritance, and polymorphism. Furthermore, it employed structured programming concepts, allowing developers to organize methods and code into modular structures such as classes and methods, enhancing code readability and maintainability.

In a significant evolution, Java introduced functional programming features with the release of Java 8. The introduction of lambda expressions and the Stream API enabled developers to embrace functional programming principles. The Stream API facilitates functional-style operations on sequences of elements, bringing powerful and declarative approaches to Java programming. Thus, today Java programs can incorporate multiple programming paradigms—OOP, structured programming, and functional programming.

Let us now compare the older imperative style code (used in structured programming) with the new declarative style used in functional programming. Suppose the task at hand is to convert a list of strings to its uppercase equivalent and print it. The following program demonstrates how this can be done using the declarative style that we are familiar with.

```
// imperative programming style
import java.util.* ;
public class Main
{
    public static void main ( String[ ] args )
    {
        List <String> lcNames, ucNames ;
        lcNames = Arrays.asList ( "rahul", "siva", "sundar", "abhijeet" ) ;
        ucNames = toUpperCase ( lcNames ) ;
        System.out.println ( ucNames ) ;
    }
    public static List <String> toUpperCase ( List <String> lcn )
    {
        List <String> ucn = new ArrayList < > ( ) ;
        for ( String n : lcn )
            ucn.add ( n.toUpperCase( ) ) ;
        return ucn ;
    }
}
```

Here we have passed the list of lowercase names to the method **toUpperCase( )**. This method iterates through the list, converting each name into its uppercase equivalent. I am sure you will find this code familiar. Let us now do the same job using declarative (functional) programming.

```
// declarative programming style
import java.util.* ;
import java.util.stream.Collectors ;
public class Main
{
    public static void main ( String[ ] args )
    {
        List <String> lcNames, ucNames ;
        lcNames = Arrays.asList ( "rahul", "siva", "sundar", "abhijeet" ) ;
        ucNames = lcNames
                    .stream( )
                    .map ( name -> name.toUpperCase( ) )
                    .collect ( Collectors.toList( ) ) ;
        System.out.println ( ucNames ) ;
    }
}
```

This program achieves the conversion job through clean and concise code. It uses the Stream API methods **stream( )**, **map( )** and **collect( )** along with a lambda expression **name -> name.toUpperCase( )** to get the job done. We will discuss **stream( )**, **map( )** and **collect( )** functions later in this chapter.

From these two programs we can note one important point. In imperative programming emphasis is not only on "what to do" (convert a list to uppercase), but also on "how to do it" (how to do the uppercase conversion). Contrasted with this, in declarative programming, emphasis is on "what to do". In short, declarative programming lets us express the intent of its business logic rather than the mechanics of how it's achieved. This helps us write easier-to-read code that is reliable, easy to maintain and less error-prone.

With the rise of powerful multicore CPUs and efficient JVMs, the focus today is more on writing clean, maintainable code that uses libraries, rather than on code that's efficiently using every CPU clock cycle and every byte of memory.

Stream API

Along with the language enhancements introduced in Java 8, an important addition was made in the form of Stream API. A Java stream provides access to a sequence of elements, and we can perform various operations on them without modifying the original data source. The stream API provides a powerful and expressive way to process collections of data in a functional and declarative manner. It consists of two main types of methods:

(a) Termination methods - These methods are responsible for producing a result or a side effect. Examples of termination methods include **forEach( )**, **count( )**, **collect( )**, **reduce( )**, and **anyMatch( )**. These operations signal the end of the stream processing and trigger the execution of the stream pipeline.

(b) Transformation methods - These methods transform the elements of the stream and create a new stream as a result. Examples of transformation methods include **map( )**, **filter( )**, **flatMap( )**, **distinct( )**, and **sorted( )**. These methods modify or filter the data in the stream without producing the final result until a termination method is invoked.

Together, these two types of methods enable developers to perform complex data manipulations with concise and readable code, promoting a more functional and modular approach to stream processing in Java.

The commonly used methods of Stream API are discussed below.

(a) **stream( )** : It converts a collection or another data source into a sequence of elements that supports various functional-style operations such as filtering, mapping, and collecting results.

(b) **flatMap( )** : It transforms each element of the stream into a new stream and then flattens these streams into a single stream. It is useful for scenarios like converting a stream of lists into a stream of their elements.

(c) **distinct( )** : It filters out duplicate elements from a stream, ensuring that only unique elements are retained, providing a clean and distinct set of values.

(d) **sorted( )** : It orders the elements of a stream based on their natural order or a provided comparator, allowing us to obtain a sorted stream of elements.

(e) **forEach( )** : It performs an action for each element in the stream, providing a concise way to iterate over and perform operations on each element.

(f) **count( )** : It returns the number of elements in a stream, providing a quick way to obtain the size of the stream.

(g) **min( )** : It returns the minimum element of a stream based on the natural order or a provided comparator. It is useful for finding the smallest element in the stream.

(h) **max( )** : It returns the maximum element of a stream based on the natural order or a provided comparator. It is useful for finding the largest element in the stream.

(i) **anyMatch( )** : It checks if any element of the stream satisfies a given predicate (discussed later), returning true if at least one element matches the condition. It is useful for determining if any element meets a specific criteria in the stream.

(j) **collect( )** : It performs a terminal operation that transforms the elements of a stream into a different form, usually a collection such as a List, Set, or Map.

(k) **map( )** : Applies a function to a stream of values, producing another stream of new values. For example:

- Finding square roots of all numbers in the list and returning a list of these roots.
- Converting all characters in the list to uppercase and returning the uppercase characters' list.

(l) **filter( )** : Applies a function to a stream of values, and retains only those values in the stream for which the function returns true. For example:

- Checking whether each element in a list is an alphabet and returning a list of alphabets.

- Checking whether each element in a list is odd and returning a list of odd numbers.

(m) **reduce( )** : It combines values in a single result by applying a rolling computation to sequential pairs of values. For example:

- Obtaining product of a list of integers and returning the product.
- Concatenating all strings in a list and returning the final string.

Map, Filter, Reduce

Usually, the map, filter, reduce operations would need a **for** loop and/or **if** statement to control the flow while iterating over a collection. Instead, if we use the functions **map( )**, **filter( )**, **reduce( )** we do not need a **for** loop or **if** statement to control the flow. This lets us focus on the actual computation rather than on the details of loops, branches, and control flow.

Given below is a program that demonstrates how to use these methods of Stream API.

```
// Using map( ), filter, reduce( )
import java.util.* ;
import java.util.stream.Collectors ;
public class Main
{
    public static void main ( String[ ] args )
    {
        List <String> names ;
        names = Arrays.asList ( "rahul", "siva", "john", "abhijeet" ) ;

        // print name and length of each name
        List <String> greetNames = names
                    .stream( )
                    .map ( n -> n + " : " + n.length( ) )
                    .collect ( Collectors.toList( ) ) ;
        System.out.println ( greetNames ) ;

        // filter names whose length is more than 4
        List <String> filteredNames = names
                    .stream( )
                    .filter ( n -> n.length( ) > 4 )
                    .collect ( Collectors.toList( ) ) ;
```

```
        System.out.println ( filteredNames ) ;

        // find the total length of all names
        int totalLength = names.stream( )
                .map ( n -> n.length( ) )
                .reduce ( 0, ( x, y ) -> x + y ) ; // 0 is the initial value
        System.out.println ( "Total Length of Names: " + totalLength ) ;
    }
}
```

Here is the output of the program...

```
[rahul:5, siva:4, john:4, abhijeet:8]
[rahul, abhijeet]
Total Length of Names: 21
```

Here is one more program that will help you fix your ideas about these popular stream API functions.

```
import java.util.* ;
import java.util.stream.Collectors;
public class Main
{
    public static void main ( String[ ] args )
    {
        List <Integer> lst1 ;
        lst1 = Arrays.asList ( 5, 10, 18, 27, 25 ) ;

        // obtain a list of squares of all numbers
        List <Integer> lst2 = lst1
                .stream( )
                .map ( n -> n * n )
                .collect ( Collectors.toList( ) ) ;
        System.out.println ( lst2 ) ;

        // filter those numbers which are multiples of 5
        List <Integer> lst3 = lst1
                .stream( )
                .filter ( n -> n % 5 == 0 )
                .collect ( Collectors.toList( ) ) ;
        System.out.println ( lst3 ) ;

        // obtain product of all numbers in the list
```

```
        int product = lst1
                    .stream( )
                    .reduce (1, ( x, y ) -> x * y ) ;
        System.out.println ( "Product = " + product ) ;
    }
}
```

Here is the output of the program...

```
[25, 100, 324, 729, 625]
[5, 10, 25]
Product = 607500
```

Mutable and Immutable Lists

A mutable list can be modified after its creation, allowing for the addition, removal, or modification of elements. In contrast, an immutable list, once created, cannot be changed.

While both approaches have their advantages and use cases, they cater to different scenarios. A mutable list provides flexibility for dynamic scenarios where the collection of elements needs to change during the program's execution. Immutable lists are beneficial when you want to guarantee the integrity of the data and prevent unintended modifications.

The following code-snippet shows how mutable and immutable lists can be created.

```
List <Integer> mutableList = new ArrayList < > ( ) ;
mutableList.add ( 10 ) ;
mutableList.add ( 20 ) ;
mutableList.add ( 30 ) ;
mutableList.add ( 40 ) ;          // can add
mutableList.set ( 1, 55 ) ;       // can modify
mutableList.remove ( 40 ) ;       // can delete

List <Integer> immutableList = List.of ( 10, 20, 30, 40 ) ;
immutableList.add ( 50 ) ;        // exception, cannot add
mutableList.set ( 1, 55 ) ;       // exception, cannot modify
immutableList.remove ( 40 ) ; // exception, cannot delete
```

Apart from the two methods shown above, there exists one more way to create a list. Using it we can create a fixed-size list. We can change the values of individual elements of this list, but we cannot add or remove elements, or change the size of the list. This is demonstrated below.

```
List <Integer> lst = Arrays.asList ( 10, 20, 30, 40 ) ;
lst.add ( 50 ) ;              // exception, cannot add
lst.set ( 1, 55 ) ;           // can modify
lst.remove ( 40 ) ;           // exception, cannot delete
```

Standard Functional Interfaces

Standard functional interfaces provided in package **java.util.function** package are widely used with streams and lambdas while processing collections. To begin with let us concentrate on the following three:

```
public interface Function <T, R>
{
    R apply ( T t ) ;      // receives a type T, returns a type R
}
public interface Predicate <T>
{
    boolean test ( T t ) ;     // receives T, performs test, returns boolean
}
public interface BinaryOperator <T>
{
    T apply ( T t1, T t2 ) ;    // receives 2 args, does opn, returns result
}
```

The prototypes of **map( )**, **filter( )** and **reduce( )** functions suggest that they take **Function**, **Predicate** and **BinaryOperator** as their arguments. So, instead of using lambdas in these functions, we can assign them to **Function**, **Predicate** and **BinaryOperator** type variables and pass these variables to **map( )**, **filter( )** and **reduce( )**. This is shown in the following program.

```
// Using standard functional interfaces
import java.util.* ;
import java.util.function.* ;
import java.util.stream.Collectors ;
public class Main
{
    public static void main ( String[ ] args )
    {
        List <Integer> lst1 = Arrays.asList ( 5, 10, 18, 27, 25 ) ;
```

```
        // use Function to square a number
        Function <Integer, Integer> squareFunction = n -> n * n ;
        List<Integer> lst2 = lst1
                .stream( )
                .map ( squareFunction )
                .collect ( Collectors.toList( ) ) ;
        System.out.println ( lst2 ) ;

        // use Predicate to check if a number is a multiple of 5
        Predicate <Integer> multipleOfFivePredicate = n -> n % 5 == 0 ;
        List<Integer> lst3 = lst1
                .stream( )
                .filter ( multipleOfFivePredicate )
                .collect ( Collectors.toList( ) ) ;
        System.out.println ( lst3 ) ;

        // use BinaryOperator for multiplication
        BinaryOperator<Integer> multBinaryOperator = ( x, y ) -> x * y ;
        int product = lst1
                .stream( )
                .reduce ( 1, multBinaryOperator ) ;
        System.out.println ( "Product = " + product ) ;
    }
}
```

What did we achieve in this program? Well, by defining functional interfaces and providing their explicit implementations, our code is now more readable and reusable. Also, by giving meaningful names to these functional interfaces, the intention of the code becomes clearer. This approach aligns with the principles of functional programming and enhances the maintainability of the code.

There are three more standard functional interfaces of interest. These are given below.

```
public interface UnaryOperator<T> extends Function <T, T>
{
    // Inherits the apply method from Function
}
public interface Supplier<T>
{
```

```
    T get( ) ;
}
public interface Consumer<T>
{
    void accept ( T t ) ;
}
```

Of these, **UnaryOperator** is a specialized version of the **Function** interface where the input and output types are the same. It represents an operation on a single operand, making it useful for cases where a value needs to be transformed in-place.

The Supplier functional interface represents a supplier of results and takes no arguments. It is often used for providing values on demand.

The Consumer functional interface represents an operation that takes a single argument and returns no result. It is typically used for side-effect operations, like printing elements or updating external state. In streams, it is often employed in the **forEach( )** operation.

The following program shows very simple usage of these interfaces.

```
import java.util.function.Consumer ;
import java.util.function.Supplier ;
import java.util.function.UnaryOperator ;
public class Main
{
    public static void main ( String[ ] args )
    {
        // use Supplier to generate a value
        Supplier <String> stringSupplier = ( ) -> "Hello, World!" ;
        String suppliedString = stringSupplier.get ( ) ;
        System.out.println ( "Supplied String: " + suppliedString ) ;

        // use Consumer to print a message
        Consumer <String> stringConsumer = message ->
            System.out.println ( "Consumed Message: " + message ) ;
        stringConsumer.accept ( "This is a message to consume" ) ;

        // use UnaryOperator to transform a number
        UnaryOperator <Integer> squareOperator = n -> n * n ;
        int originalNum = 5 ;
        int squaredNum = squareOperator.apply ( originalNum ) ;
```

```
        System.out.println ( "Original Number: " + originalNum ) ;
        System.out.println ( "Squared Number: " + squaredNum ) ;
    }
}
```

Supplier allows us to encapsulate the logic for generating values in a way that it can be easily parameterized and passed around in a clean and functional manner. Similarly, **Consumer** encapsulates the logic for using the generated values. Thus, value generation gets decoupled from the usage of values. The caller doesn't need to know how the values are generated; it only needs to know how to retrieve them.

default and *static* Methods of Standard Functional Interfaces

To enhance the utility of standard functional interfaces, static and default methods are provided in some of these interfaces. For example, apart from the abstract method **test( )**, the **Predicate** functional interface contains default methods **and( )**, **or( )**, **negate( )** and **static** methods **not( )** and **isEqual( )**.

Of these, **and( )**, **or( )** and **negate( )** work like the usual and, or and not operators. What can be achieved using the default **negate( )** method can also be achieved using the static **not( )** method. The **isEqual( )** method is used to compare objects. The following program shows how to use these methods.

```
// Using default and static methods of standard functional interfaces
import java.util.ArrayList ;
import java.util.List ;
import java.util.function.Predicate ;
class Student
{
    private String name ;
    private int age ;
    private double salary ;

    public Student ( String name, int age, double salary )
    {
        this.name = name ;
        this.age = age ;
        this.salary = salary ;
```

```
    }
    public String getName( )
    {
        return name ;
    }
    public int getAge( )
    {
        return age ;
    }
    public double getSalary( )
    {
        return salary ;
    }
    @Override
    public String toString( )
    {
        return "{ " + name + " " + age + " " + salary + " }" ;
    }
}
public class Main
{
    public static void main ( String[ ] args )
    {
        List <Student> stdList = new ArrayList <>( ) ;
        stdList.add ( new Student ( "Ajay", 25, 50000.0 ) ) ;
        stdList.add ( new Student ( "Vijay", 30, 60000.0 ) ) ;
        stdList.add ( new Student ( "Charlie", 22, 45000.0 ) ) ;
        stdList.add ( new Student ( "Meena", 23, 43000.0 ) ) ;
        stdList.add ( new Student ( "Neha", 27, 41000.0 ) ) ;

        Predicate <Student> agePred ;
        agePred = student -> student.getAge( ) > 22 ;

        Predicate <Student> salaryPred ;
        salaryPred = student -> student.getSalary( ) > 48000.0 ;

        Predicate <Student> namePred ;
        namePred = student -> student.getName( ).equals ( "Charlie" ) ;

        // using default methods
        List <Student> lst1 = stdList
```

```
                    .stream( )
                    .filter ( agePred.and ( salaryPred ) )
                    .toList( ) ;
        System.out.println ( lst1 ) ;

        List <Student> lst2 = stdList
                    .stream( )
                    .filter ( salaryPred.or ( namePred ) )
                    .toList( ) ;
        System.out.println ( lst2 ) ;

        List <Student> lst3 = stdList
                    .stream( )
                    .filter ( namePred.negate( ) )
                    .toList( ) ;
        System.out.println ( lst3 ) ;

        // using static methods
        List <Student> lst4 = stdList
                    .stream( )
                    .filter ( Predicate.not ( namePred ) )
                    .toList( ) ;
        System.out.println ( lst4 ) ;

        Student st = stdList.get ( 0 ) ;
        List <Student> lst5 = stdList
                    .stream( )
                    .filter ( Predicate.isEqual ( st ) )
                    .toList( ) ;
        System.out.println ( lst5 ) ;
    }
}
```

Here is the output of the program...

```
[{ Ajay 25 50000.0 }, { Vijay 30 60000.0 }]
[{ Ajay 25 50000.0 }, { Vijay 30 60000.0 }, { Charlie 22 45000.0 }]
[{ Ajay 25 50000.0 }, { Vijay 30 60000.0 }, { Meena 23 43000.0 }, { Neha
27 41000.0 }]
[{ Ajay 25 50000.0 }, { Vijay 30 60000.0 }, { Meena 23 43000.0 }, { Neha
27 41000.0 }]
[{ Ajay 25 50000.0 }]
```

You can note that in this program instead of using the **collect(Collectors.toList( ))** method to create the list, we have used to **toList( )** method.

On similar lines you can explore the default and static methods of other standard functional interfaces.

Lazy and Eager Operations

Lazy and eager evaluation refers to different approaches in processing elements of a collection. Lazy evaluation means that operations on the elements of a stream are deferred until an actual result is needed. In other words, the processing of elements is postponed until a terminal operation is invoked. This deferred execution allows for more efficient use of resources, especially when working with large datasets, as only the necessary elements are processed. Lazy evaluation is a key feature of the Stream API, promoting optimization and avoiding unnecessary computations. Here is an example of lazy evaluation:

```
List <Integer> numbers = Arrays.asList ( 1, 2, 3, 4, 5 ) ;
Stream <Integer> squaredNumbers = numbers.
                                  stream( ).
                                  map ( n -> n * n ) ;
List <Integer> result = squaredNumbers.collect ( Collectors.toList( ) ) ;
```

Here the mapping operation is only performed when the terminal operation (collect) is invoked.

On the other hand, eager evaluation involves the immediate execution of operations on the elements of a stream. Eager evaluation performs computations eagerly as soon as they are encountered in the stream pipeline, regardless of whether the final result is needed. While this approach may be simpler to understand, it might lead to suboptimal performance for large datasets, as it processes all elements even if the result requires only a subset. Let us now see an example of eager evaluation.

```
List <Integer> numbers = Arrays.asList ( 1, 2, 3, 4, 5 ) ;
List <Integer> squaredNumbers = numbers
                          .stream( )
                          .map ( n -> n * n )
                          .collect ( Collectors.toList( ) ) ;
```

Here the entire stream pipeline, including the mapping operation, is executed immediately when the collect operation is encountered.

Striking the right balance between lazy and eager evaluation is crucial for achieving efficient and effective stream processing.

More Programs

The more you use the stream API, the more comfortable you get with it. With that in view, given below are a few programs that are self-explanatory. Feel free to play around with them to improve your familiarity with stream API.

Program 1: Get a new list by eliminating the duplicates from a list.

```
import java.util.* ;
public class Main
{
    public static void main ( String[ ] args )
    {
        List <Integer> numList = Arrays.asList ( 23, 42, 23, 67, 92, 67 ) ;
        List <Integer> uniqueList = numList
                                    .stream( )
                                    .distinct( )
                                    .toList( ) ;
        System.out.println ( uniqueList ) ;
    }
}
```

Program 2: Partition the elements in a list into two lists.

```
import java.util.* ;
import java.util.stream.Collectors ;
public class Main
{
    public static void main ( String[ ] args )
    {
        List <Integer> numList = Arrays.asList ( 23, 42, 23, 67, 92, 67 ) ;

        Map <Boolean, List <Integer>> m ;
        m = numList
            .stream( )
            .collect ( Collectors.partitioningBy (
            e -> numList.indexOf ( e ) != numList.lastIndexOf ( e ) ) ) ;
```

```
        List <Integer> duplicates = m.get ( true ) ;
        List <Integer> unique = m.get ( false ) ;
        System.out.println ( "Duplicate Elements: " + duplicates ) ;
        System.out.println ( "Unique Elements: " + unique ) ;
    }
}
```

Program 3: Count elements in a list and determine the maximum and minimum element in it.

```
import java.util.* ;
import java.util.stream.* ;
public class Main
{
    public static void main ( String[ ] args )
    {
        List <Integer> numList = Arrays.asList ( 23, 42, 23, 67, 92, 67 ) ;
        long num = numList
                        .stream( )
                        .count( ) ;
        System.out.println ( "Number of elements in list = " + num ) ;
        Integer min = numList
                        .stream( )
                        .min ( ( a, b ) -> a.compareTo ( b ) ).orElse ( null ) ;
        Integer max = numList
                        .stream( )
                        .max ( ( a, b ) -> a.compareTo ( b ) ).orElse ( null );
        if ( min != null && max != null )
        {
            System.out.println ( "Minimum Value: " + min ) ;
            System.out.println ( "Maximum Value: " + max ) ;
        }
        else
            System.out.println ( "List is empty" ) ;
    }
}
```

Program 4: Sort elements in ascending and descending order.

```
import java.util.* ;
public class Main
{
```

```
    public static void main ( String[ ] args )
    {
        List <Integer> numList = Arrays.asList ( 23, 42, 23, 67, 92, 67 ) ;
        List <Integer> asc = numList
                                .stream( )
                                .sorted ( Comparator.naturalOrder( ) )
                                .toList( ) ;
        List <Integer> dsc = numList
                                .stream( )
                                .sorted ( Comparator.reverseOrder( ) )
                                .toList( ) ;
        System.out.println ( "Ascending Order: " + asc ) ;
        System.out.println ( "Descending Order: " + dsc ) ;
    }
}
```

Program 5: Get the n th highest number from a list.

```
import java.util.* ;
public class Main
{
    public static void main ( String[ ] args )
    {
        List <Integer> numList = Arrays.asList ( 23, 42, 23, 67, 92, 67 ) ;
        int n = 2 ; // change this to the desired nth value

        // remove duplicates and sort in descending order
        List <Integer> distinctSorted = numList.stream( )
                .distinct( )
                .sorted ( Comparator.reverseOrder( ) )
                .toList( ) ;

        if ( n > 0 && n <= distinctSorted.size( ) )
        {
            int nthHighest = distinctSorted.get ( n - 1 ) ;
            System.out.println ( n + "th highest = " + nthHighest ) ;
        }
        else
            System.out.println ( "Invalid value of n" ) ;
    }
}
```

The Method Reference Operator ::

Lambda expressions help us create on-the-fly anonymous functions. But sometimes, they just call an existing method we already have. In such cases we can remove lambda expressions and simply refer to the existing method by name using the method reference operator ::.

There are four types of method references possible:

(a) Reference to a static method
(b) Reference to an instance method of a particular object
(c) Reference to an instance method of an arbitrary object of a particular type
(d) Reference to a constructor

The following program illustrates the first 3 of these cases.

```
// Using method reference operator
import java.util.function.BiFunction ;
public class Main
{
    public static <T extends Number> T calc ( T a, T b,
                                        BiFunction<T, T, T> opn )
    {
        return opn.apply ( a, b ) ;
    }
    public static int add ( int a, int b )
    {
        return a + b ;
    }
    public int subtract ( int a, int b )
    {
        return a - b ;
    }
    public static void main ( String[ ] args )
    {
        Main m = new Main( ) ;

        // using lambda expressions
        System.out.println ( calc ( 5, 3, ( x, y ) -> add ( x, y ) ) ) ;
        System.out.println ( calc ( 4, 1, ( x, y ) -> m.subtract ( x, y ) ) ) ;
        System.out.println ( calc ( 1.1, 3.1, ( x, y )->Double.max (x, y))) ;
```

```
        // using reference to a static method
        System.out.println ( calc ( 5, 3, Main :: add ) ) ;

        // using reference to instance method of a particular object m
        System.out.println ( calc ( 4, 1, m :: subtract ) ) ;

        // using reference to an instance method of an arbitrary object
        // of type Double
        System.out.println ( calc ( 1.1, 3.1, Double :: max ) ) ;
    }
}
```

Here is the output of the program...

```
8
3
3.1
8
3
3.1
```

Here the **calc( )** method accepts two values of a generic numerical type **T extends Number** and a **BiFunction** that defines the operation to be performed on those values. The **BiFunction** functional interface represents a function that receives two input values of type **T** and returns the result of type **T**. Not that in other situations Bifunction can receive types **T** and **U** and return a type **R**.

The first three calls to **calc( )** use a lambda expression to perform addition, subtraction and max operations. The lambda expressions can be replaced by specific calls to **add( )**, **subtract( )** and **max( )** using :: operator. The call to **add( )** method represents reference to static method. The call to **subtract( )** represents reference to instance method of a specific object **m**. Finally, the call to **max( )** represents reference to instance method of an arbitrary object of type **Double**.

Here is one more example of using method reference instead of lambda expression.

```
import java.util.* ;
public class Main
{
    public static void main ( String[ ] args )
```

```
    {
        List <String> n1, n2 ;
        n1 = Arrays.asList ( "Apple", "banana", "cherry", "apricot" ) ;
        n1.sort ( ( String s1, String s2 )->s1.compareToIgnoreCase( s2));
        System.out.println ( n1 ) ;
        n2 = Arrays.asList ( "Apple", "banana", "cherry", "apricot" ) ;
        n2.sort ( String :: compareToIgnoreCase ) ;
        System.out.println ( n2 ) ;
    }
}
```

The **sort( )** method of the **List** class expects a **Comparator** object as an argument. A **Comparator** is an **interface** that defines a single method called **compare( )**. This **compare( )** method takes two objects as arguments and returns an integer value based on the comparison.

So, the lambda expression is essentially implementing the **compare( )** method of the **Comparator** interface. It compares two strings (**s1** and **s2**) using the **compareToIgnoreCase( )** method, which performs a case-insensitive comparison. The result of this comparison (negative, zero, or positive) is returned by the lambda expression.

Since the lambda expression is calling a specific method **compareToIgonreCase( )** of **String** class, we may as well call it explicitly using the method reference operator as in

```
n2.sort ( String :: compareToIgnoreCase ) ;
```

Here we are using the :: operator to refer to instance method of an arbitrary object of a particular type (**String**).

And now an important question—how do we choose between a lambda expression and a method reference? Well, if the logic you need is complex or requires additional code within the lambda body, a lambda expression might be more suitable. If the logic is already implemented in a well-named method, a method reference can improve code readability and conciseness.

Exercises

[A] State whether the following statements are True or False:

(a) A functional interface can contain multiple abstract method signatures.

(b) A functional interface can contain only one static and one default method.

(c) lambda function cannot be used with **reduce( )** function.

(d) lambda, **map( )**, **filter( )**, **reduce( )** can be combined in one single expression.

(e) Though functions can be assigned to variables, they cannot be called using these variables.

(f) Functions can be passed as arguments to function and returned from function.

(g) Lambda functions are always nameless.

[B] Answer the following questions:

(a) Define a **Person** class containing data **name**, **age**, and **salary** and methods **compareByAge( )** and **compareByName( )**. In **main( )** create a list of **Person** objects and then sort them by name and by age.

(b) Write lambda expressions performing for the following operations:

Receive an argument and return its cube.
Receive 3 arguments and return their average.
Receive a string and return the uppercase version of the string.

(c) Write a program to create a list of 10 random integers. Use the **map( )** function with lambda expressions to perform following operations:

Print a list of radians of all values in the list.
Print a list of factorial of all values in the list.
Print a list of squares of all values in the list.

(d) Write a program to create a list of names and numbers. Filter the list using lambda expression to create a new list containing only numbers.

(e) Suppose there are two lists, one containing numbers from 1 to 6, and other containing numbers from 6 to 1. Write a program to obtain a list that contains elements obtained by adding corresponding elements of the two lists.

(f) The following data shows names, ages, and marks of students in a class:

Anil, 21, 80
Sohail, 20, 90
Sunil, 20, 91
Shobha, 18, 93

Write a program to sort this data based on multiple keys in the order name, age, and marks.

(g) Suppose a dictionary contains key-value pairs, where each key is an alphabet, and each value is a number. Write a program that obtains the maximum and minimum values from the dictionary.

[C] Using lambda, **map( )**, **filter( )** and **reduce( )** or a combination thereof to perform the following tasks:

(a) Suppose a dictionary contains type of pet (cat, dog, etc.), name of pet and age of pet. Write a program that obtains the sum of all dog's ages.

(b) Consider the following list:

lst = [1.25, 3.22, 4.68, 10.95, 32.55, 12.54]

The numbers in the list represent radii of circles. Write a program to obtain a list of areas of these circles.

(c) Consider the following lists:

nums = [10, 20, 30, 40, 50, 60, 70, 80]
strs = ['A', 'B', 'C', 'D', 'E', 'F', 'G', 'H']

Write a program to obtain a list of lists, where each list contains a number from one list and a string from another, in the same order in which they appear in the original lists.

(d) Suppose a dictionary contains names of students and marks obtained by them in an examination. Write a program to obtain a list of students who obtained more than 40 marks in the examination.

(e) Consider the following list:

lst = ['Malayalam', 'Drawing', 'madamlamadam', '1234321']

Write a program to print those strings which are palindromes.

(f) A dictionary contains the following information about 5 employees:

First name
Last name
Age
Grade (Skilled, Semi-skilled, Highly-skilled)

Write a program to obtain a list of employees (first name + last name) who are Highly-skilled.

KanNotes

- A functional interface can contain only 1 abstract method and one or more default and static methods
- A lambda expression is an anonymous function that implements the single abstract method of a functional interface
- A lambda expression can be assigned to a variable
- A functional interface can use generics
- A lambda expression is popularly used in multithreading and in processing collections
- Stream API brings functional programming aspects to Java programming
- Stream API contains many terminal methods and transformation methods
- Java API provides several standard functional interfaces
- Lazy evaluation defers operations on stream elements until an actual result is needed
- Eager evaluation performs immediate operations on the elements of a stream

User Interfaces

Let Us JAVA 7th Edition

CHAPTER 21

Text is gone! Graphics is the way forward. Learn how to build Graphical User Interfaces in Java...

In today's GUI-centric world it is expected that Java programs would let a user interact with it using GUI elements like text boxes, list boxes, combo boxes, push button, radio buttons, check boxes, scroll bars, etc. To facilitate this interaction Java provides three libraries—Active Window toolkit (AWT), Swing and JavaFX. Of these, AWT is the older library. In fact, Swing internally uses AWT.

However, the popularity of Java desktop applications has waned in favor of their web and mobile counterparts. While Java offers robust features and functionalities, users today prefer the flexibility and accessibility of web apps and the convenience of mobile apps. This shift requires developers to be familiar with technologies like React or Angular for web development, as opposed to the desktop-specific libraries like AWT, Swing, or JavaFX. While Java desktop applications haven't entirely disappeared, their development space has certainly shrunk in the face of these evolving trends.

Hence, we have decided to make this chapter available only in downloadable form. So those who are interested in it can download it from:

https://tinyurl.com/yzjyxpz5

Its contents are as follows:

Contents

- A Simple Swing Application
- Event Handling
- One More GUI Application
- Adapter Classes
- What Next?
- Exercises
- KanNotes

Chapter 22

JDBC

The world is full of data. You are in a commanding position if you know how to deal with it in a professional manner...

J Contents

- Data Organization
- Common Database Operations
- Database Operations through Java
- JDBC Architecture
- JDBC Driver Types
- MySQL Database Installation
- Common JDBC API Components
- Putting it to Work
- Exercises
- KanNotes

Data is the King! In today's digital world an enormous amount of data is being generated and exchanged. All this data finally gets stored in a database. As a Java programmer one must know how to handle this data programmatically. To help us do this Java provides an API called JDBC. It stands for Java Database Connectivity. This API lets us write Java programs that can interact with a wide range of databases. How this can be done is discussed in this chapter.

Data Organization

Modern way of organizing data is storing it in a Relational Database Management System or RDBMS. Different vendors provide this RDBMS software. These include Oracle, Microsoft, IBM, etc. There are several open-source implementations available as well, the most popular amongst which is MySQL. All these RDBMSs are accessible through the JDBC API.

Each of these RDBMS organizes the data in the form of different tables. One database may contain multiple tables. Each table contains data organized in the form of records (rows). Each record may contain multiple fields (columns).

For example, a company may have a database containing Employees table containing records about employees working in an organization. Each record may contain fields like Name, Age, Salary, etc.

Likewise, a university database may consist of tables for students, professors, courses, examinations, payments, etc. It is also possible to establish relationships between tables. For example, if a student pays fees, then the record of fees paid can be linked to his record in the student table. This would be a one-to-one relationship. If the same student pays fees multiple times, then it would become a one-to-many relationship.

Common Database Operations

There is a set of typical operations that one needs to carry out on a database of any kind. These are as follows:

(a) Create Table - Create a table by specifying its name and the fields that it would contain along with the type of each field.

(b) Modify Table - Modify the specifications of different fields or add / delete certain fields.

(c) Drop Table - Delete the table from the database including all the records present in it.

To carry out these operations a simple language has been created. It is called SQL, standing for Structured Query Language. This language provides simple English like statements to perform database operations. SQL is supported by almost every RDBMS and it allows you to work with a database independently of the underlying RDBMS.

Given below are some sample SQL statements for carrying out database operations. The comments before each SQL statement would help you understand the operation being performed by the SQL statement.

```
// Create a table called Persons containing two fields EmpID of the type
// int and Name of the type variable length string of 255 characters
CREATE TABLE Persons ( EmpID int, Name varchar ( 255 ) )

// Modify Persons table by adding a field DateOfBirth of the type date
ALTER TABLE Persons ADD DateOfBirth date

// Modify the Persons table by deleting the column DateOfBirth
ALTER TABLE Persons DROP COLUMN DateOfBirth

// Delete the Customers table
DROP TABLE Customers
```

SQL also provides statements that let you work with the records of each table. Common operations on a table include **C**reate new record(s), **R**ead existing record(s), **U**pdate existing record(s), **D**elete existing record(s). In short these are known as CRUD operations. The SQL statements that carry out these operations are often known as SQL queries. Given below are some sample SQL statements for carrying out CRUD operations.

```
// Insert a new record in Persons table, with values 101 and Sunil in the
// EmpID and Name respectively
INSERT INTO Persons ( EmpID, Name) VALUES ( 1001, 'Sunil' )

// Read all records from Employees table
SELECT * FROM Employees

// Modify record whose Employee ID is 1001 by changing its Name field
// to hold a value Satish
```

UPDATE Persons SET Name = 'Satish' WHERE EmpID = 1001

// Delete that record from the Persons table whose Employee ID is 1244
DELETE FROM Persons WHERE EmpID = 1244

Database Operations through Java

The operations mentioned in the previous section were performed using SQL. Let us now see how these operations can be carried out through Java. Creation, Modification and Deletion of a table are infrequent operations. By this what I mean is Customers or Students table is not going to get created, altered, or deleted every other day. In fact, once you have set up all the fields in a table to your satisfaction, you would rarely change it. More common operations would be the CRUD operations.

Hence usually the operation of creation of tables is done manually using the tools that come with each RDBMS. For example, in this chapter we propose to use MySQL RDBMS and perform these operations using the MySQL WorkBench that comes with MySQL.

The CRUD operations can be performed using the JDBC objects called **Connection**, **Statement** and **ResultSet**. The purpose of each of these objects is mentioned below.

(a) Connection – To establish connection with database
(b) Statement – To execute SQL statements
(c) Resultset – To process results of a SQL query

Before we can use these objects in our Java program, we need to understand the JDBC architecture and install a RDBMS. Our choice of database would be MySQL, primarily because it is free of charge and quite popular amongst the open-source community. The JDBC architecture and MySQL installation are discussed in the following sections.

JDBC Architecture

To help programmers communicate with the database, vendors provide vendor-specific JDBC driver software. For example, Oracle provides a JDBC driver to help programmers communicate with databases maintained by it. Likewise, Microsoft provides a JDBC driver to help programmers communicate with databases maintained by MS SQL.

Java programmers must have a standard and uniform way to communicate with any third-party JDBC driver. To facilitate this, an interface called **Driver** is declared in the **java.sql** package. The third-party database vendors implement this interface in their driver.

To manage different JDBC drivers there is a component called Driver Manager. For example, through a Java program when we attempt to connect to a database, the Driver Manager would load the suitable JDBC driver. Thus, JDBC Manager ensures correct driver usage to access each database.

Once the driver is loaded, we have to use the different classes present in JDBC API to interact with the database.

The various layers of JDBC Architectures are shown in Figure 22.1.

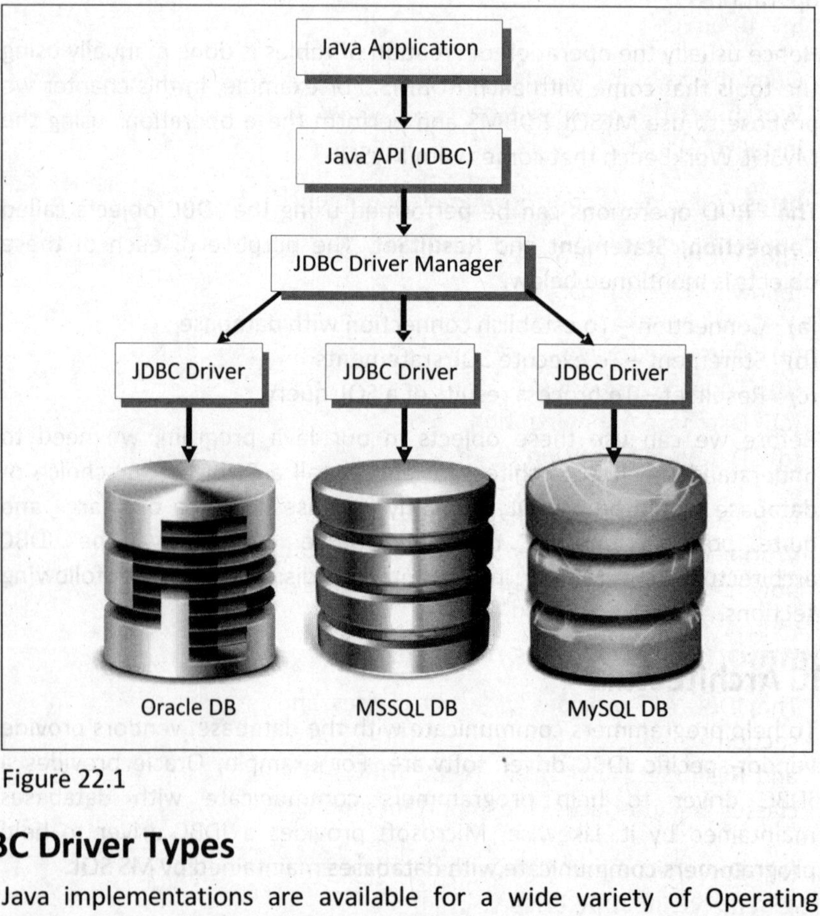

Figure 22.1

JDBC Driver Types

Java implementations are available for a wide variety of Operating Systems and hardware. These platforms themselves have evolved over the years. There are different JDBC driver implementations for these different platforms. All these drivers are classified into 4 categories—Type 1 driver, Type 2 driver, Type 3 driver, and Type 4 driver. Most legacy applications would use Type 1, 2, or 3 driver, whereas to connect with modern databases Type 4 driver is used. For programs in this book Type 4 driver would have to be installed.

MySQL Database Installation

We wish to install MySQL on a Windows machine. To do this we need to first download the MySQL Installer. This is available for download at https://dev.mysql.com/downloads/windows. Once downloaded, execute this MySQL Installer. When presented with options to install components, choose MySQL database and JDBC driver. At the time of writing this book the JDBC driver was available in mysql-connector-java-5.1.40-bin.jar.

Once the MySQL database and driver stand installed, download MySQL Workbench for your version of Windows from URL given below and install it.

https://dev.mysql.com/downloads/workbench/

The Workbench provides an integrated tool for carrying out the following operations:

(a) Database Design
(b) Trying SQL queries
(c) Database Administration
(d) Database Migration

In a later part of the chapter, we would see how to use the MySQL Workbench to create a database and its tables(s). We would also see how to use the JDBC driver to work with the database programmatically.

Common JDBC API Components

The JDBC API provides different classes and interfaces. In a previous section we had seen the purpose three classes—**Connection, Statement** and **ResultSet**. Apart from them, JDBC API also provides several other classes and interfaces. The important amongst them are as follows:

(a) **DriverManager**: This class provides services for loading and managing JDBC drivers.

(b) **Driver**: This is an interface. Each JDBC driver implements this interface. It handles the communications with the database server. In a Java program we rarely interact with **Driver** directly. Instead, we use **DriverManager** objects, which in turn manages the **Driver** objects.

(c) **SQLException**: This class handles any errors that occur in a database application.

Putting it to Work

We have now understood the data organization, SQL statements for database operations, JDBC architecture and JDBC API components. We have also seen how to install MySQL and MySQL Workbench. So, it is now time to write a Java program that accomplishes the following:

(a) Create a Schema called "study". Insert a table in it called "Accounts" and add three fields to it—ID, Name and Balance.

(b) Add 4 records to the table using MySQL Workbench containing following data:

ID	Name	Balance
1011	Neha	4000.50
1023	Sunil	5000.00
1021	Rohit	6000.75
1044	Rahul	5600.55

(c) Create a record with field values 1001, Joe, 5000.00.

(d) Retrieve and print all existing records.

(e) Update record – Change Sunil to Sanjay.

(f) Delete record whose ID is 1044.

Out of these, steps (a) and (b) are to be performed using MySQL workbench, whereas the rest are to be performed through the Java program.

So let us now create a schema, add table to it and then add 4 records to it. Carry out the following steps to achieve this:

(a) Start MySQL workbench by double-clicking its icon. Create a new schema (database) by selecting from the menu File | New Model.

By default, a schema by the name **mydb** would get created. It would be shown under the "Physical Schemas" tab.

(b) Double click on **mydb** schema. A dialog would popup. Through this dialog change the **Name** of this schema to "study".

(c) From the "study" tab double click the "Add Table" icon. Given the table name as "Accounts".

(d) Click on the Columns tab at the bottom of the page and create three columns with following properties.

Column Name	Datatype	Primary Key
ID	INT	Yes
Name	VARCHAR(255)	No
Balance	FLOAT	No

(e) Click on "Inserts" tab at the bottom of the screen. The columns ID, Name and Balance would be shown. Add 4 records with values mentioned in the problem statement above.

Now finally we have reached a stage where we can write a Java program to carry out steps (c), (d), (e) and (f) given in the problem statement. Here is the program...

```
package myjdbccrudproject ;
import java.sql.* ;
public class MyJdbcCRUDProject
{
    static final String jdbcDriver = "com.mysql.jdbc.Driver" ;
    static final String dbURL = "jdbc:mysql://localhost/study" ;

    public static void main ( String[ ] args ) throws Exception
    {
        Connection conn = null ;
        Statement stmt = null ;
        ResultSet rs = null ;

        try
        {
            Class.forName ( jdbcDriver ) ;
            conn = DriverManager.getConnection ( dbURL,
                                        "root", "admin" ) ;
```

```
                stmt = conn.createStatement( ) ;

                String sql ;
                sql = "INSERT INTO Accounts VALUES ( 1001, 'Joe',
                    5000.0 )" ;
                stmt.executeUpdate ( sql ) ;

                sql = "UPDATE Accounts SET NAME = 'Sanjay'
                            WHERE ID = 1023" ;
                stmt.executeUpdate ( sql ) ;

                sql = "DELETE FROM Accounts WHERE ID = 1044" ;
                stmt.executeUpdate ( sql ) ;

                sql = "SELECT * FROM  Accounts" ;
                rs = stmt.executeQuery ( sql ) ;

                int id ;
                String name ;
                float balance ;
                while ( rs.next( ) )
                {
                    id = rs.getInt ( "ID" ) ;
                    name = rs.getString ( "Name" ) ;
                    balance = rs.getFloat ("Balance") ;

                    System.out.println ( id + " " + name + " " + balance ) ;
                }
                rs.close( ) ;
                stmt.close( ) ;
            }
            finally
            {
                if ( conn != null)
                    conn.close( ) ;
            }
        }
    }
```

Let us now to try to understand the program. The project name given was **MyJdbcCrud**, hence the classes in this program would belong to the package **myjdbccrud**, as indicated in the package statement at the beginning of the program.

The **import** statement ensures that the classes declared in **java.sql** package for database access are available to the program.

Now we need to open a communication channel with the database. For this we need to load and register the JDBC driver. This registration needs to be done only once in the program. We have done this registration through the call

```
Class.forName ( jdbcDriver ) ;
```

where **jdbcDriver** is a string that has been initialized to "com.mysql.jdbc.Driver". This call dynamically loads the driver's class file into memory, which automatically registers it. Naturally if we use a different RDBMS than MySQL then the driver's name and hence the string would change as given below.

ORACLE RDBMS - oracle.jdbc.driver.OracleDriver
DB2 RDBMS - COM.ibm.db2.jdbc.net.DB2Driver

Now we need to open a connection with the database. This is done using the statement

```
conn = DriverManager.getConnection ( dbURL, "root", "admin" ) ;
```

The **getConnection( )** method needs three parameters—the database URL which indicates the name and location of the database, login name and password to access the database. We have initialized the **dbURL** to "jdbc:mysql://localhost/study".

Here **localhost** refers to the local machine and **study** refers to the database name. If the database is present on a different machine, then **localhost** should be replaced by IP address or name of the machine where the database is hosted.

Once again for Oracle and DB2 the **dbURL** string would be different. For these databases the following strings should be used:

Oracle RDBMS - jdbc:oracle:thin:@hostname:port Number:databaseName
DB2 RDBMS - jdbc:db2:hostname:port Number/databaseName

While creating the database we have given the login name as "root" and password as "admin". Hence same have been used in the call to **getConnection( )**. This call creates a **Connection** object and returns it, which we promptly collect in **conn**.

Once the connection with the database is established, we have performed the CRUD operations. For this we have to create a **Statement** object by calling **createStatement( )** on the connection object. Next, we have to create the query string and pass it to **executeUpdate( )** method of **Statement** object to execute the query. This sequence of operations is shown below.

```
stmt = conn.createStatement( ) ;
String sql ;
sql = "INSERT INTO Accounts VALUES ( 1001, 'Joe', 5000.0 )";
stmt.executeUpdate ( sql ) ;
```

Create, update and delete operations are similar in the sense that to perform all of them the **executeUpdate( )** method has to be called. The Read operation is a bit different. For it we need to call the **executeQuery( )** method on the **Statement** object. When we do this, the query is fired on the database and all the records that qualify the query are returned in the form of a **ResultSet** object. For example, when we fire the query "SELECT * from Accounts" all the records in the **Accounts** table would qualify this query and hence would be returned together in a **ResultSet** object.

We can iterate through all the records in the **ResultSet** object through a **while** loop. Each time through the loop we can extract the individual field values in the record by calling the **ResultSet** methods as shown below.

```
id = getInt ( "ID" ) ;
name = rs.getString ( "Name" ) ;
balance = rs.getFloat ( "Balance" ) ;
```

We have extracted the values and displayed them on the screen. Once all the records have been iterated, **rs.next( )** returns a false, whereupon the loop is terminated.

That brings us to the final stage of the program where we need to do the cleanup operations. We do this by calling the **close( )** methods on **Statement**, **ResultSet** and **Connection** objects.

One small thing needs to be done before you can execute the program. We need to add the JDBC library. Carry out the following steps to do this:

(a) Right click on "Libraries" node of the "MyJDBCCrud" project in the project window.

(b) From the menu that pops up select "Add JAR/Folder".

(c) Navigate to the suitable directory where you have downloaded the "mysql-connector-java-5.1.40-bin" file.

(d) Click Open followed by OK.

Once the library has been added we can now build and execute the program.

Exercises

[A] State whether the following statements are True or False:

(a) A database can contain multiple tables.

(b) MySQL is an open-source RDBMS.

(c) Modern databases use T3 type of JDBC driver.

(d) Advantage of JDBC is that the same driver can be used to connect multiple RDBMSs.

(e) A call to **class.forName( )** loads and registers the JDBC driver.

(f) Records from a table can be deleted using call to **executeQuery( )** method of **Statement** object.

(g) To read a set of records from a table we must use the **executeUpdate( )** method of the **Statement** object.

(h) **Driver** class's method should be called from your program to obtain a **Connection** object to interact with the database.

(i) Different **dbURL** connection strings should be used to connect to different RDBMSs.

(j) A set of records is returned while reading a database table into a **RecordSet** object.

[B] Answer the following questions:

(a) Write a program which lets you carry out the CRUD operations through a GUI shown below. Use the same database and table discussed in the section "Putting it to Work".

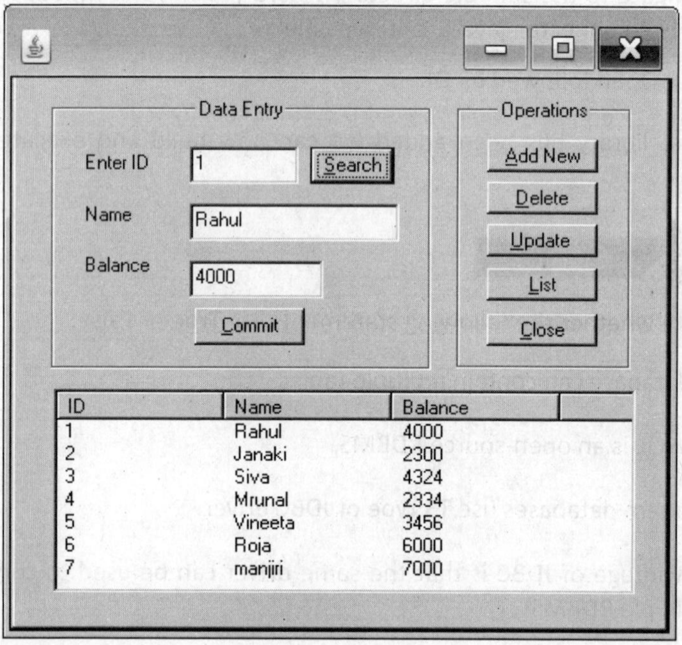

Note that all the records added to the table should get displayed in the list box. Before carrying out Delete or Update operations the record should be searched using the ID. A new record should be added or the existing record should be modified on clicking the Commit button.

[C] Pick up the correct alternative for each of the following questions:

(a) What do CRUD operations stand for?

(1) CREATE, READ, UPDATE, DELETE
(2) CREATE, REMOVE, UPDATE, DROP
(3) CLEANUP, REMOVE, UPGRADE, DROP
(4) CLEANUP, RECTIFY, UPGRADE, DELETE

(b) Consider the following code snippet:

```
Connection conn ;
conn = DriverManager.getConnection ( dbURL, "root", "admin" ) ;
```

Which of the following is the CORRECT way to create a **Statement** object?

(1) Statement stmt = conn.createStatement( ) ;
(2) Statement stmt = createStatementObject( ) ;
(3) Statement stmt = new StatementObject( ) ;
(4) Statement stmt = conn.createStatementObject( ) ;

(c) Which statement should be added to following code snippet to insert a new record in **Accounts** table?

```
Statement stmt ;
Stmt = conn.createStatement( ) ;
String sql = "INSERT INTO Accounts VALUES ( 1001, "Joe", 5000.0 )" ;
// add statement here
```

(1) stmt.executeQuery (sql) ;
(2) stmt.executeStatement (sql) ;
(3) stmt.executeUpdate (sql) ;
(4) stmt.executeInsert (sql) ;

(d) Which of the following is the CORRECT way to make available **Statement**, **Connection** and **ResultSet** objects?
(1) import Statement, Connection, ResultSet
(2) import Statement, Connection, ResultSet from SQL
(3) import java.sql.*
(4) Import sql.*

KanNotes

- Terminology :
  - Field - Individual item of information
  - Record - Collection of fields
  - Table - Collection of records
  - Database - Collection of tables
- Different vendors provide RDBMS. Ex. : Oracle, MS SQL, MySQL

- All DB use SQL to carry out operations on a database or tables
- SQL statements are often called Queries and are English like statements
- All RDBMS are accessible through Java API - JDBC. To these API functions SQL queries must be passed
- Common database operations - Create / Modify / Drop Table
- Examples of database operations :
    - CREATE TABLE Persons (ID int, Name varchar (255))
    - ALTER TABLE Persons ADD DateOfBirth date
    - ALTER TABLE Persons DROP COLUMN DateOfBirth
    - DROP TABLE Customers
- These database operations are usually done using Tools that come with each DB. Ex. : MySQL WorkBench that comes with MySQL
- Common operations on Table – CRUD (Create, Read, Update, Delete)
- Examples of operations on a table :
    - INSERT INTO Persons (ID, Name) VALUES (1001, 'Sunil')
    - SELECT * FROM Employees
    - UPDATE Persons SET Name = 'Satish' WHERE EmpID = 1001
    - DELETE FROM Persons WHERE EmpID = 1244
- These operations are done programmatically using JDBC objects
- Common JDBC objects used are :
    - Connection object – establishes connection with database
    - Statement object – executes SQL statements
    - Resultset object – processes results of a query
- Add library "mysql-connector-java-5.1.40-bin" before using JDBC objects
- Software Installations required - MySQL Installer and Workbench

Let Us JAVA 7th Edition

CHAPTER 23 Network and Internet Programming

The ability to do multiple things simultaneously is a great asset in life. So also in programming...

All successful people are usually well connected. Computing has taken this connectedness to the next logical step. 'Every device and person would ultimately get connected to every other device and person'—that is where Network Programming is headed. Hence learning network programming has become very important.

However, in modern Java web development, raw network programming has largely been replaced by higher-level frameworks like Spring Web and Jersey. They allow developers to focus on application logic rather than managing the intricacies of network protocols. These tools offer features like automatic request and response handling, object serialization/deserialization for data exchange, support for common web communication patterns (like RESTful APIs), etc.. This not only reduces development time but also improves code maintainability and promotes consistency across web applications.

Hence, we have decided to make this chapter available only in downloadable form. So those who are interested in it can download it from:

https://tinyurl.com/yzjyxpz5

Its contents are as follows:

Contents

- Networking Concepts
- Networking Model
- Protocols
- Packets
- IP Addresses
- Sockets
- Port Numbers
- What's The Time Now
- Communicating with Whois Server
- Give Me the Home Page
- Two-Way Communication
- Multiuser Chat Application
- File Transfer Using UDP
- Exercises

Miscellany

Let Us JAVA 7th Edition

CHAPTER 24

Features that are useful, but a bit separated from mainstream Java...

Contents

- CLASSPATH Variable
- *strictfp* Modifier
- Bitwise Operators
- Annotations
- Packages
  - Creating and Using a Package
- Split Packages
- Different Packages, Same Type
- Nested Packages
- Package FAQs
- Packages and Access Mechanism
- KanNotes
- Exercises

The topics discussed in this chapter were either too large or far too removed from the mainstream Java programming for inclusion in the earlier chapters. These topics provide certain useful programming features and could prove to be of immense help in certain programming strategies. These include CLASSPATH variable, *strictfp* modifier, packages, and bitwise operators. Let us understand them one by one.

CLASSPATH Variable

Our Java program may use types stored in other .class files. CLASSPATH is a mechanism that helps Java runtime environment locate the other .class files. It is an environment variable, and it contains a list of directories that contain third-party and user-defined types.

CLASSPATH variable is different than the PATH environment variable. PATH is used by Operating System to locate executable files, whereas CLASSPATH is used to locate the .class files. The default value of CLASSPATH is '.'. This means by default the search for .class files is carried out only in current directory or its sub-directories.

In Windows the CLASSPATH variable can be set permanently through Control Panel or at command prompt. Given below is an example of setting it at command prompt.

```
set CLASSPATH=%CLASSPATH%;.;C:\ProgramFiles\Java\mylib
```

Here %CLASSPATH% gives the existing value of CLASSPATH variable. We have two directories in the list, '.' and 'C:\ProgramFiles\Java\mylib' separated by a semicolon (;). The .class files would be first searched in the current directory. If not found they would be searched in mylib directory.

If we wish to set the CLASSPATH value temporarily, we can do so as shown in the following example:

```
java -classpath .;c:\ProgramFiles\Java\mylib sample.jar
```

If executed under Linux remember to replace \ and ; with / and : respectively.

strictfp Modifier

Floating-point calculations are platform dependent. So, the same floating-point operation may give different results when the same class file is executed on different platforms. This happens because floating point precision may vary from one platform to another. It can be mitigated using the **strictfp** keyword.

As the name suggests, the **strictfp** modifier stands for strict floating-point operations. It ensures that we get the same result on every platform while performing float operations. **strictfp** can be applied to a class, a method, or an interface, but not to abstract method, variable or on constructor. A sample usage of **strictfp** is shown below.

```
strictfp class StrictMath
{
    public double calculateArea ( double radius )
    {
        double pi = 3.14159;
        return pi * Math.pow ( radius, 2 ) ;
    }
}
```

Bitwise Operators

Bitwise operators permit us to work with individual bits of a byte. There are many bitwise operators available in Java. These include:

~ - complement operator
<< - left shift
>> - right shift
>>> - unsigned right shift
& - and
| - or
^ - xor

The usage of these bitwise operators is shown in the following code snippet:

```
int ch, dh, eh, fh, a, b, c ;
ch = 32 ;
dh = ~ch            // toggles 0s to1s and 1s to 0s
eh = ch << 3        // << shifts bits in ch 3 positions to left
fh = ch >> 2        // >> shifts bits in ch 2 positions to right
a = 45 & 32         // and bits of 45 and 32
b = 45 | 32         // or bits of 45 and 32
c = 45 ^ 32         // xor bits of 45 and 32
```

Note that except ~ all other bitwise operators are binary operators. Remember the following tips while using bitwise operators:

(a) Any bit value ANDed with 0 is 0.
(b) Any bit value ORed with 1 is 1.
(c) 1 XORed with 1 is 0.
(d) << - As bits are shifted from left, zeros are pushed from right.
(e) >> - As bits are shifted from right, left-most bit is copied from left.
(f) >>> - As bits are shifted from right, zeros are pushed from left.

The purpose of each bitwise operator is given below:

~ - Convert 0 to 1 and 1 to 0
<< - Shift out desired number of bits from left
>>, >>> - Shift out desired number of bits from right
& - Check whether a bit is on / off. Put off a particular bit
| - Put on a particular bit
^ - Toggle a bit

There are a few more bitwise operators known as bitwise compound assignment operators. These include operators like <<=, >>=, &=, |= and ^=. They offer a shortcut as shown in the following statements:

```
a <<= 5  // is same as a = a << 5
b &= 2   // is same as b = b & 2
```

Annotations

Annotations provide data about program elements either to compiler or to Java runtime. Annotations can be applied to declaration of classes, data members, member functions and other program elements. Annotations begin with a symbol '@' to indicate that what follows is an annotation. There are some standard annotations defined in Java API. These include **@Deprecated**, **@Override**, **@SuppressWarnings**, **@Retention**, **@Documented**, **@Target**, **@Inherited**, etc.

Java also lets us create our own annotations. Given below is a code snippet that shows how to define and use annotations.

```
// annotation declaration
@interface ClassOwnership
{
    String name( ) ;
    int version( ) ;
```

```
    String date( ) ;
}

// annotation usage
@ClassOwnership ( name = "Saket", version = 7, date = "15/02/23" )
class Circle extends Shape
{
    @Override
    void draw( )
    {
    }
}
```

Here **@Override** is a pre-defined annotation that is being used to indicate that the **draw( )** method declared in the base class **Shape** is being overridden in the derived class **Circle**. This annotation does not have any elements and is often known as a marker annotation. Unlike this, **ClassOwnership** is a user-defined annotation. We have first declared this annotation using the **interface** keyword. This annotation includes elements **name**, **version**, and **date**. Once declared, we have used this annotation while declaring the **Circle** class by specifying the actual values for these elements.

Here are some tips about annotations:

(a) If the annotation has no elements, then ( ) can be dropped as in **@Override**.

(b) It is possible to apply multiple annotations to a program element as shown below:

```
@Testing
@ClassOwnership ( name = "Saket", version = 7, date = "15/02/23" )
class Circle extends Shape
{
    // some code
}
```

(c) While declaring an annotation it is possible to assign default values to its elements as shown below:

```
@interface BackupSchedule
```

```
{
    int hour( ) default 12 ;
    int minute( ) default 30 ;
    int second( ) default 0 ;
}
```

Packages

A reasonably big Java software would contain many classes, interfaces, enumerations, and annotations. Java helps you organize them properly by storing related classes, interfaces, enumerations, and annotations in a logical container called Package. This organization is helpful in three ways:

(a) Packages make it easy to locate and use types (i.e., classes, interfaces, enumerations, and annotations).

(b) Two different packages may contain types with the same names. So, if a library package contains a type called **class Student** and we also define a type called **class Student**, so long as they belong to two different packages, we can use both. Thus, packages help avoid naming conflict.

(c) Through packages we can control which type within it can be accessed from outside the package.

To enforce a good design practice Java follows certain rules about packages and directory structure. These are as follows:

(a) A new folder is created for every new package. Moreover, package name and folder name are always the same.

(b) A .java file can contain only one public type. Its name is same as the name of the .java file.

Creating and Using a Package

Let us now see how to create our own package and use it. Here are the specifications of the package.

Package name: **sample**
Filename: Sample.java
Class name: **Sample** containing a method **show( )**
And now the actual program...

```
// Package Declaration – Sample.java
package sample ;
public class Sample
{
    public void show( )
    {
        System.out.println ( "Bye" ) ;
    }
}
```

We wish to call **show( )** from **main( )** present in a class **Client** present in file Client.java. Here is the program to do this...

```
// Package Usage – Client.java
package client ;
import sample.Sample ;
public class Client
{
    public static void main ( String args[ ] )
    {
        Sample a = new Sample( ) ;
        a.show( ) ;
    }
}
```

Given below are the steps to be followed to create these packages in NetBeans.

(a) Create a new project by name Client. This will create a file called Client.java containing a package **client**, which contains a public class, **Client**.

(b) Add a new package called **sample**. For this right-click Source Packages. A menu will pop up. From this menu select New | Java Package – sample. This action will create a package **sample**.

(c) Once the **sample** package is created, right-click **sample** package. A menu would pop up. From this menu select New | Java class – **Sample**. This action will create a public class **Sample** in a file Sample.java in the package **sample**.

(d) Define **show( )** method in the **Sample** class.

Let us now examine the directory structure. The source code would get created in the following files:

~\Client\src\client\Client.java
~\Client\src\sample\Sample.java

On compilation the bytecode gets stored in the following files:

~\Client\build\classes\client\Client.class
~\Client\build\classes\sample\Sample.class

As you can appreciate the directory structure reflects the package structure. As a result, it becomes easy to locate a type.

Note that if we do not import the **Sample** class from sample package using an **import** statement, we can still use the **Sample** class. This can be done by using a fully qualified name as shown below:

```
sample.Sample  a = new sample.Sample( ) ;
```

Split Packages

It is possible to split a package across multiple files. This means a package can contain multiple public types stored in different files. This suits software development teams as different developers can develop different types and store them in different files. All these types can belong to the same package. The following program demonstrates split packages.

```
// File: Sample1.java
package sample ;
public class Sample1
{
    public void show( )
    {
        System.out.println ( "Bye" ) ;
    }
}

// File: Sample2.java
package  sample ;
public class Sample2
```

```
{
    public void display( )
    {
        System.out.println ( "Hi" ) ;
    }
}
```

Let us now look at code that uses these split packages.

```
// File: Client.java
package client ;
import sample.Sample1 ;
import sample.Sample2 ;
class Client
{
    public static void main ( String args[ ] )
    {
        Sample1 s1 = new Sample1( ) ;
        s1.show( ) ;
        Sample2 s2 = new Sample2( ) ;
        s2.display( ) ;
    }
}
```

Given below are the steps to be followed to create these packages in NetBeans.

(a) Create a new project by name Client. This will create a file called Client.java containing a package **client**, which contains a public class, **Client**.

(b) Add a new package called **sample**. For this right-click Source Packages. A menu will pop up. From this menu select New | Java Package – sample. This action will create a package **sample**.

(e) Once the **sample** package is created, right-click **sample** package. A menu would pop up. From this menu select New | Java class – **Sample1**. This action will create a public class **Sample1** in a file Sample1.java in the package **sample**.

(c) Define **show( )** method in the **Sample1** class.

(d) Again right-click **sample** package. A menu would pop up. From this menu select New | Java class – **Sample2**. This action will create a public class **Sample2** in a file Sample2.java in the package **sample**.

(e) Define **display( )** method in the **Sample2** class.

The source code would get created in the following files:

~\Client\src\client\Client.java
~\Client\src\sample\Sample1.java
~\Client\src\sample\Sample2.java

On compilation the bytecode gets stored in the following files:

~\Client\build\classes\client\Client.class
~\Client\build\classes\sample\Sample1.class
~\Client\build\classes\sample\Sample2.class

Different Packages, Same Type

It is possible that different packages contain types that have the same names. For example, two packages sample1 and sample2 may contain two different classes by the same name Sample. This is shown in the following code.

```
// File: Sample.java, Package: sample1
package sample1 ;
public class Sample
{
    public void show( )
    {
        System.out.println ( "Bye" ) ;
    }
}

// File: Sample.java, Package: sample2
package sample2 ;
public class Sample
{
    public void display( )
    {
        System.out.println ( "Bye" ) ;
```

```
    }
}
```

Let us now look at client code that uses these Sample class from two different packages.

```
// File: Client.java, Package: client
package client ;
import sample1.Sample ;
import sample2.Sample ;
class Client
{
    public static void main ( String args[ ] )
    {
        sample1.Sample s1 = new sample1.Sample( ) ;
        s1.show( ) ;
        sample2.Sample s2 = new sample2.Sample( ) ;
        s2.display( ) ;
    }
}
```

The source code would get created in the following files:

```
~\Client\src\client\Client.java
~\Client\src\sample1\Sample.java
~\Client\src\sample2\Sample.java
```

On compilation the bytecode gets stored in following files:

```
~\Client\build\classes\client\Client.class
~\Client\build\classes\sample1\Sample.class
~\Client\build\classes\sample1\Sample.class
```

Note that while creating objects of **Sample** class from two different packages, we should use the fully qualified name to help understand which **Sample** class we are planning to use for object creation, as shown below:

```
sample1.Sample s1 = new sample1.Sample( ) ;
sample2.Sample s2 = new sample2.Sample( ) ;
```

Nested Packages

It is also possible to create nested packages. This is especially helpful while creating big libraries containing numerous types. For example, the classes in Java library are organized in many nested packages like **java.io**, **java.awt**, **java.lang**, etc. Note that all packages in Java API begin with **java** or **javax**. Let us now create nested packages for user-defined classes.

```
// File: Sample.java, Package: sample
package sample ;
public class Sample
{
    public void show( )
    {
        System.out.println ( "Bye" ) ;
    }
}

// File: Trial.java, Package: sample.trial
package sample.trial ;
public class Trial
{
    public void display( )
    {
        System.out.println ( "Hi" ) ;
    }
}
```

Let us now look at client code that uses the **Sample** class present in **sample** package and the **Trial** class present in the nested package **sample.trial**.

```
package client ;
import sample.Sample ;
import sample.trial.Trial ;
class Client
{
    public static void main ( String args[ ] )
    {
        Sample s = new Sample( ) ;
        s.show( ) ;
```

```
        Trial e = new Trial( ) ;
        e.display( ) ;
    }
}
```

The source code would be created in the following files:

~\Client\src\client\Client.java
~\Client\src\sample\Sample.java
~\Client\src\sample\trial\Trial.java

On compilation the bytecode gets stored in the following files:

~\Client\build\classes\client\Client.class
~\Client\build\classes\sample\Sample.class
~\Client\build\classes\sample\trial\Trial.class

Package FAQs

Often there are questions in programmers' mind about packages and import statements. We have compiled below these FAQs.

(a) What if package name is absent in a .java file?

All types in the file belong to a package called default package. This practice should however be discouraged.

(b) Should package name be in small case?

It is a good idea and is used by many Java development environments including NetBeans. This helps avoid name conflict with class/interface names.

(c) How do I ensure uniqueness in package names?

Use reversed Internet domain names like com.ykanetkar.sample, com.ykanetkar.trial, etc. Since domain names are unique, their reversed forms are also unique.

(d) Which packages are imported by default?

default package, java.lang

(e) Which packages would get imported through the statement:

import graphics.A*

None. It does not import all packages that begin with letter A. It would result in compilation error.

(f) Can the following set of statements be replaced by import java.awt.*?

```
import java.awt.shape.*
import java.awt.color.*
```

No. * can be used to signify all types in a package, and not all packages nested in a package.

(g) What do the following import statements mean?

```
import example.ex1.* ;
import example.ex2.ex3.* ;
```

Here the first statement means import all public types from directory C:\~\example\ex1. Second statement means import all public types from directory C:\.....\example\ex2\ex3.

Packages and Access Mechanism

We are already familiar with access specifiers **private, protected,** and **public**. If we do not use any of them then the data member or member function is treated to have a **default** access specifier. For example, **num** and **fun( )** in the following code are considered to have **default** access specifier.

```
package p1 ;
class Myclass
{
    int num = 40 ;
    void fun( )
    {
    }
}
```

There are following possibilities when we attempt to access **num** and **fun( )**:

(a) They are accessed from the same class
(b) They are accessed from the same package's class
(c) They are accessed from a different package's class
(d) They are accessed from the same package's sub-class

(e) They are accessed from a different package's sub-class

Keep the following guidelines in mind while deciding whether they would accessible or not.

(a) private members are accessible within the class.
(b) default members are accessible within the package.
(c) protected members are accessible within package and in sub-classes.
(d) public members are accessible anywhere.
(e) Within a package behavior of default, protected and public are same.
(f) Default members are not accessible across package boundary.
(g) Protected members can be accessed outside the package only through child class object.

These guidelines have been captured in Figure 24.1.

	Package pkg1			Package pkg2	
Access Specifier (in class A)	class A	class B	class D extends A	class C	class E extends A
public	Yes	Yes	Yes	Yes	Yes
protected	Yes	Yes	Yes	No	Yes
default	Yes	Yes	Yes	No	No
private	Yes	No	No	No	No

Figure 24.1

Exercises

[A] State whether the following statements are True or False:

(a) *strictfp* modifier should be used on variables to ensure accurate floating-point operations.

(b) On using *strictfp* modifier we get the same answers on Windows and Linux machines.

(c) CLASSPATH is an environment variable.

(d) CLASSPATH indicates the path for library and user-defined classes.

(e) CLASSPATH contains a list of paths separated by semicolon.

(f) Elements of a user-defined annotation can take default values.

(g) The access to data members and member functions is controlled only through keywords **private**, **protected**, and **public**.

(h) A package can contain only one public type.

(i) A package can be split across files.

(j) A package can be nested within another package.

[B] Answer the following questions:

(a) What would be the values of different variables after performing the operations given below.

```
short i = 32, j = 65, k, l, m, n, o, p ;
k = i | 35 ;   l = ~k ;   m = i & j ;
n = j ^ 32 ;   o = j << 2 ;   p = i >> 5 ;
```

(b) Rewrite the following expressions using bitwise compound assignment operators:

```
a = a | 3        a = a & 0x48        b = b ^ 0x22        c = c << 2
```

(c) Consider an integer in which the rightmost bit is numbered as 0. Write a function **checkbits (x, p, n)** which returns true if all "n" bits starting from position "p" are turned on, false otherwise. For example, **checkbits (x, 4, 3)** will return true if bits 4, 3 and 2 are 1 in number **x**.

(d) Write a program to scan an 8-bit number into a variable and check whether its 3rd, 6th and 7th bit is on.

(e) Write a program to receive a 16-bit integer and then exchange the contents of its 2 bytes using bitwise operators.

(f) Write a program to receive an 8-bit number into a variable and then exchange its higher 4 bits with lower 4 bits.

(g) Write a program to receive an 8-bit number into a variable and then set its odd bits to 1.

(h) Write a program to receive an 8-bit number into a variable and then check if its 3rd and 5th bit are on. If these bits are found to be on, then put them off.

(i) Write a program to receive an 8-bit number into a variable and then check if its 3rd and 5th bit are off. If these bits are found to be off, then put them on.

KanNotes

- CLASSPATH is an environment variable that contains a list of directories separated by ; (: in Linux)
- JRE searches directories in CLASSPATH to locate .class files that contain third-party and user-defined types.
- When the same class file containing floating-point operations is executed on different platforms it may give different results.
- When strictfp is applied to a class, a method or an interface it ensures that we get same result of floating-point operations on different platforms
- Packages are logical containers that may contain related classes, interfaces, enumerations and annotations
- A package may be split across files
- Two different packages may contain types with same names
- Through packages we can control which type within it can be accessed from within and outside the package

- A new folder is created for every new package with the same name as name of the package

- A .java file can contain only one public type. Its name is same as the name of the .java file

- Bitwise Operations :

  Set a bit to a value 0/1 → Write operation
  Check whether bit is 1 (on) or 0 (off) → Read operation

- Bitwise operators available in Java are ~, <<, >>, >>>, &, |, ^, <<=, >>=, &=, |=, ^=.

The Next Level

Let Us Java 7th Edition

CHAPTER 25

There are many Java programmers and then there are 'good' Java programmers. Board the train which will help you make the transition from a Java programmer to a 'good' Java programmer...

Contents

- Place of Declaration of Local Variables
- Proper *for* Loop
- *BigDecimal* instead of *float, double*
- Unnecessary Use of Boxed Primitives
- Enums over Strings
- Short Method Parameter List
- Fail-fast Approach
- Data Validation
- Refer Objects by their Interfaces
- Optional Type
- Established Object Creation Patterns
  - Static Factory
  - Singleton
  - Builder
  - Dependency injection

In the previous 24 chapters we have tried to explain different features of Java language and Java library. The more thoroughly you know them, the stronger programming foundation you will have. Once you are done with them, read this chapter which contains topics that would take a good Java programmer to the next level.

Place of Declaration of Local Variables

Java lets us declare variables where it is first used, rather than at the beginning of a method. If we declare a variable at the beginning of a method, by the time the variable is used, the reader might not remember the variable's type or initial value.

Proper *for* Loop

Do not use the following form of **for** loop to iterate through a collection or array if the sole intention is to print the element or do something else with it.

```
int[ ] marks = { 55, 65, 75, 56, 78, 78, 90 } ;
for ( int i = 0 ; i <= marks.length - 1 ; i++ )
    System.out.println ( marks[ i ] ) ;

List <String> names ;
names = Arrays.asList ( "rahul", "siva", "sundar", "abhijeet" ) ;
for ( int i = 0 ; i < names.size( ) ; i++ )
    System.out.println ( names.get ( i ) ) ;
```

Instead, prefer this uncluttered form:

```
for ( String n : names )
    System.out.println ( n ) ;

for ( int m : marks )
    System.out.println ( m ) ;
```

However, we will have to fall back on the conventional **for** loop in two situations:

(a) if we wish to manipulate the array/collection elements as shown below:

```
int[ ] num = { 55, 65, 75, 56, 78, 78, 90 } ;
```

```
for ( int i = 0 ; i <= num.length - 1 ; i++ )
        num[ i ] = num[ i ] * 2 ,
```

(b) If we wish to traverse multiple arrays/collections simultaneously as shown below:

```
int[ ] num1 = { 55, 65, 75, 56, 78, 78, 90 } ;
int[ ] num2 = { 55, 65, 75, 56, 78, 78, 90 } ;
for ( int i = 0 ; i <= num1.length - 1 ; i++ )
        System.out.println ( num1[ i ] + " " num2[ i ] ) ;
```

BigDecimal instead of *float, double*

Do not use the **float** or **double** in financial or scientific calculations as using them may result in loss of precision. Instead, we should use **BigDecimal**, as shown in the following example:

```
float a = 0.3f, b = 0.2f ;
System.out.println ( a - b ) ;                // prints 0.10000001

double c = 1.03, d = 0.42 ;
System.out.println ( c - d ) ;                // prints 0.6100000000000001

BigDecimal i = new BigDecimal ( "0.3" ) ;
BigDecimal j = new BigDecimal ( "0.2" ) ;
System.out.println ( i.subtract ( j ) ) ;     // prints 0.1

BigDecimal x = new BigDecimal ( "1.03" ) ;
BigDecimal y = new BigDecimal ( "0.42" ) ;
System.out.println ( x.subtract ( y ) ) ;     // prints 0.61
```

The disadvantage of **BigDecimal** is that it's slower. Also using a **BigDecimal** is a bit non-intuitive as we have to use methods like **add( )**, **subtract( )**, **multiply( )** and **divide( )** with them instead of **+**, **-**, *****, and **/**.

Unnecessary Use of Boxed Primitives

If we are to create a list of integers or floats, we cannot use the primitives **int** and **float**. Instead, we should use the boxed primitives **Integer** and **Float**.

```
List <int> lst1 ;          // error
List <float> lst2 ;        // error
List <Integer> lst3 ;      // works
```

```
List <Float> lst4 ;        // works
```

As we know, we cannot put primitives in collections, we must put boxed primitives. However, do not use boxed primitives unnecessarily. They may cause errors, as shown in the following code snippet.

```
Integer i = new Integer ( 34 ) ;
Integer j = new Integer ( 34 ) ;
if ( i == j )
    System.out.println ( "Match" ) ;
```

Here **i** and **j** contain reference to two distinct **Integer** objects having same value. When we compare, the references get compared, not the values. Since references refer to two distinct objects, they can never be equal. Also, boxed primitives work slower than primitives, hence do not overuse them.

Enums over Strings

Let's consider an example where we need to represent the days of the week in a program. We can use an enum to define a type-safe representation of the days of the week:

```
public enum Day
{
    MON, TUE, WED, THUR, FRI, SAT, SUN
}
```

With this enum, we ensure that only valid days of the week can be used throughout the program. For example, if we have a method that takes a day of the week as an argument, we can use the **Day** enum instead of a string:

```
public class Schedule
{
    public void setMeeting ( Day d )
    {
        // Logic to schedule a meeting on the specified day
    }
}
```

By using the **Day** enum, we gain type safety because the compiler ensures that only valid day values are passed to the **setMeeting( )** method. If we try to pass a string instead of an enum constant:

```
Schedule sch = new Schedule( ) ;
sche.setMeeting ( "Mon" ) ; // Compile-time error: incompatible types
```

The compiler will produce an error because "Mon" is not of type **Day**, thus preventing potential runtime errors caused by using incorrect or misspelled string literals.

In summary, using enums provides type safety by restricting the valid values that can be used, leading to more reliable and maintainable code. The same type safety cannot be ensured if we use a string in place of an enum.

Short Method Parameter List

While defining a method do not create parameter lists with more than 4 parameters. If you do, it will be difficult to remember and without constant reference to its documentation. The parameter list can be shortened in the following ways:

(a) Break the method into multiple methods, each of which requires only a sub-set of the parameters. For example, consider the **processOrder( )** method shown below that receives 6 parameters:

```
// method with a long parameter list
public void processOrder ( String custName, String[ ] items, double
pricePerItem, int discountPercentage, String shippingAddress,
String paymentMethod )
{
    // process the order
}
```

This method can be broken into the following methods:

```
public Order createOrder ( String customerName, String[ ] items,
                                    double pricePerItem)
{
}
public Order applyDiscount ( Order order, int discountPercentage )
{
    // apply discount, store it in order
    return order ;
}
public void processPayment ( Order order, String paymentMethod )
{
```

```
        // payment processing logic
    }
    public void shipOrder ( Order order, String shippingAddress )
    {
        // order shipping logic
    }
```

This example demonstrates that breaking down functionality into multiple methods improves code modularity, readability, and maintainability. Each method has clear responsibility and shorter parameter lists, making the code easier to understand and modify.

(b) Create a helper class to hold groups of parameters. For example, consider the **applyFilter( )** method shown below that receives 6 parameters:

```
class ImageEditor
{
    public void applyFilter ( String imagePath, String filterType,
        double brightness, double contrast, double saturation)
    {
        // image editing logic based on provided parameters
    }
}
```

The parameter list of **applyFilter( )** can be shortened by creating a helper class as shown below.

```
// Helper class to group image adjustments
class ImageAdjustments
{
    private final double brightness, contrast, saturation ;
    public ImageAdjustments (double b, double c, double s )
    {
        brightness = b ;
        contrast = c ;
        saturation = s ;
    }
    // Getters for adjustments
    public double getBrightness( )
    {
        return brightness ;
```

```
        }
        public double getContrast( )
        {
            return contrast ;
        }
        public double getSaturation( )
        {
            return saturation ;
        }
}
class ImageEditor
{
        public void applyFilter ( String imagePath, String filterType,
                                ImageAdjustments adjustments )
        {
            // image editing logic
        }
}
public class Main
{
        public static void main ( String[ ] args )
        {
            String imagePath = "image.jpg";
            String filterType = "Sepia";
            double brightness = 1.1, contrast = 1.2, saturation = 0.8 ;
            ImageAdjustments adj = new ImageAdjustments (
                                        brightness, contrast, saturation ) ;
            ImageEditor editor = new ImageEditor( ) ;
            editor.applyFilter ( imagePath, filterType, adj ) ;
        }
}
```

This approach improves code readability and maintainability by grouping related parameters into a dedicated class. It also reduces the number of individual parameters passed to the method, making it clearer and less error prone.

Fail-fast Approach

Many methods and constructors impose restrictions on the values accepted by their parameters, such as requiring non-negative values or non-null object references. In such cases we should check parameter values at the beginning of the method body. This principle of detecting errors as soon as possible after they occur is called fail-fast approach. This is illustrated in the following program.

```
public class AgeValidator
{
    public static boolean isAdult ( int age )
    {
        if ( age < 0 )
            throw new IllegalArgumentException ("Age is negative " ) ;
        return age >= 18 ;
    }
    public static void main ( String[ ] args )
    {
        int userAge = -5;
        try
        {
            if ( isAdult ( userAge ) )
                System.out.println ( "You are an adult" ) ;
            else
                System.out.println ( "You are not an adult" ) ;
        }
        catch ( IllegalArgumentException e)
            System.out.println ( "Error: " + e.getMessage( ) ) ;
    }
}
```

Failing to perform such checks early in the method can lead to various undesirable outcomes.

Data Validation

Data validation is a crucial step before constructing objects. It ensures the integrity of our program by guaranteeing that only valid data is used to create objects. Imagine building a house with faulty materials - the whole structure could be compromised. Similarly, constructing objects with invalid data can lead to unexpected behavior, errors, and ultimately, a malfunctioning program. Data validation not only improves the robustness of our code but also simplifies debugging by pinpointing potential problems early on.

We can validate the data by using techniques like using the method **Objects.requireNonNull( )** for null checks or custom logic for specific formats and ranges. This is shown in the following program.

```
import java.util.Objects ;
class User
{
    private String name ;
    private int age ;
    public User ( String n, int a )
    {
        name = Objects.requireNonNull ( n, "Name cannot be null" ) ;
        if ( age < 0 )
            throw new IllegalArgumentException ( "Age is negative" ) ;
        age = a ;
    }
    public String getName( )
    {
        return name ;
    }
    public int getAge( )
    {
        return age ;
    }
}
public class Main
{
    public static void main ( String[ ] args )
    {
        try
        {
            User user1 = new User ( "Rahul Verma", 30 ) ;
            System.out.println ( "User: " + user1.getName( ) ) ;
            System.out.println ( "Age: " + user1.getAge( ) ) ;
            User user2 = new User ( null, 25 ) ;
        }
        catch ( NullPointerException e )
        {
            System.out.println ( "Error: " + e.getMessage( ) ) ;
        }
        catch ( IllegalArgumentException e )
        {
```

```
                System.out.println ( "Error: " + e.getMessage( ) ) ;
            }
        }
}
```

While creating **user2**, since we are passing **null** for name, a **NullPointerException** would be thrown by **requireNonNull( )** method. When this exception is caught in **main( )**, the message "Name cannot be null" is extracted by **e.getMessage( )**. Thus, data validation acts as a quality control checkpoint, ensuring only well-formed objects are created, laying a solid foundation for a reliable and predictable program.

This technique for checking for null can also be used in any other method, apart from the constructor.

Refer Objects by their Interfaces

While passing an object to a method or returning an object from it, you should use interface (if it exists) rather than class to refer to an object. This will make the program more flexible.

Let us understand this with the help of an example. Suppose we wish to maintain inventory of items using a hash map and a tree map. We wish to print inventory items using a method **printContents( )**. We can either write two versions of this method, one that receives a **HashMap** and another that receives a **TreeMap**. However, since both **HashMap** and **TreeMap** implement the **Map** interface, we can define **printContents( )** method to receive a **Map** instead of a **HashMap** or a **Treemap** or any other custom map. This will make the **printContents( )** method more flexible. Also, this approach makes the method testable. The implementation of this idea is given below.

```
import java.util.* ;
public class Main
{
    public static void printContents ( Map <String, Integer> inventory )
    {
        if ( inventory.isEmpty( ) )
        {
            System.out.println ( "Inventory is empty." ) ;
            return ;
        }
        System.out.println ( "Inventory:" ) ;
```

```
        for ( Map.Entry<String, Integer> entry : inventory.entrySet( ) )
        {
            String item = entry.getKey( ) ;
            int quantity = entry.getValue( ) ;
            System.out.println ( " - " + item + ": " + quantity ) ;
        }
    }
    public static void main ( String[ ] args )
    {
        // create a HashMap
        HashMap <String, Integer> hm = new HashMap< >( ) ;
        hm.put ( "Shirt", 10 ) ;
        hm.put ( "Pants", 5 ) ;
        hm.put ( "Hat", 2 ) ;

        // create a TreeMap
        TreeMap <String, Integer> tm = new TreeMap< >( ) ;
        tm.put ( "Shirt", 10 ) ;
        tm.put ( "Pants", 5 ) ;
        tm.put ( "Hat", 2 ) ;

        System.out.println ( "Printing HashMap:" ) ;
        printContents ( hm ) ;

        System.out.println ( "\nPrinting TreeMap:" ) ;
        printContents ( tm ) ;
    }
}
```

Let us now see how the same flexibility can be ascertained while returning an object from a method. Suppose there are two methods **getOrderedFruits( )** and **getDiverseFruits( )**. One method creates a **LinkedHahSet** object and the other creates a **HashSet** object. Both methods return the objects by referring to it as a **Set**, an interface that is implemented by **LinkedHashSet** and **HashSet**. This ensures that the methods adhere to the contract of returning a **Set** while still maintaining the specific behavior of **LinkedHashSet** (preserving order and uniqueness) and **HashSet** (not preserving order but preserving uniqueness). Also, we can now use only one **Set** reference to refer to both the objects. The following program puts this concept into action.

```
import java.util.* ;
```

```
public class Main
{
    public static Set<String> getOrderedFruits( )
    {
        LinkedHashSet<String> fruits = new LinkedHashSet< >( ) ;
        fruits.add ( "Apple" ) ;
        fruits.add ( "Banana" ) ;
        fruits.add ( "Orange" ) ;
        fruits.add ( "Mango" ) ;
        fruits.add ( "Apple" ) ; // duplicate will be ignored
        return fruits ;
    }
    public static Set<String> getDiverseFruits( )
    {
        HashSet<String> fruits = new HashSet< >( ) ;
        fruits.add ( "Apple" ) ;
        fruits.add ( "Banana" ) ;
        fruits.add ( "Orange" ) ;
        fruits.add ( "Mango" ) ;
        fruits.add ( "Apple" ) ; // duplicate will be ignored
        return fruits ;
    }
    public static void main ( String[ ] args )
    {
        Set<String> fruitSet ;

        fruitSet = getOrderedFruits( ) ;
        System.out.println ( "Collected LinkedHashSet Fruits:" ) ;
        for ( String fruit : fruitSet )
            System.out.println ( fruit ) ;

        fruitSet = getDiverseFruits( ) ;
        System.out.println ( "Collected HashSet Fruits:" ) ;
        for ( String fruit : fruitSet )
            System.out.println ( fruit ) ;
    }
}
```

Here is the output of the program...

```
Collected LinkedHashSet Fruits:
Banana
```

```
Apple
Orange
Mango
Collected HashSet Fruits:
Apple
Mango
Orange
Banana
```

Optional Type

Consider the following code:

```
import java.util.* ;
class Person
{
    private String name ;
    private int age ;

    public Person ( String n, int a )
    {
        name = n ;
        age = a ;
    }
    public String getName( )
    {
        return name ;
    }
    public int getAge( )
    {
        return age ;
    }
}
class DataProcessor
{
    private ArrayList<Person> people ;

    DataProcessor( )
    {
        people = new ArrayList < > ( ) ;
        people.add ( new Person ( "Ajay", 25 ) ) ;
        people.add ( new Person ( "Vijay", 31 ) ) ;
```

```
        people.add ( new Person ( "Sanjay", 22 ) ) ;
        people.add ( new Person ( "Tanmay", 26 ) ) ;
        people.add ( new Person ( "Anuj", 30 ) ) ;
        people.add ( new Person ( "Aditya", 22 ) ) ;
    }
    public Person getPersonByName ( String n )
    {
        for ( Person p : people )
        {
            if ( p.getName( ).equals ( n ) )
                return p ;
        }
        return null ;
    }
}
public class Main
{
    public static void main ( String[ ] args )
    {
        DataProcessor dp = new DataProcessor( ) ;
        Person p ;

        p = dp.getPersonByName ( "Aditya" ) ;
        System.out.println ( p.getAge( ) ) ;

        p = dp.getPersonByName ( "Rahul" ) ;
        System.out.println ( p.getAge( ) ) ;
    }
}
```

Here the **Person** class is very simple and needs no explanation. The **DataProcessor** class has a method **getPersonByName( )** that receives a name. Ideally this method should search for this name in a database, retrieve the other data against the name, construct a **Person** object from this data and return the **Person** object. If the search is unsuccessful, the method should return null. For the sake of simplicity, we have avoided the database and maintained an **ArrayList** of **Person** objects. So, search is carried out in **ArrayList** rather than the database.

The **main( )** method is fraught with danger. It believes that the name being searched will indeed be present in the **ArrayList**, which is not the case with the name "Rahul". So in this case **p** will be set to null, and when we call **p.getAge( )** it will result in a **NullPointerException**. This is a very common phenomenon and can be mitigated by checking for null as follows:

```
p = dp.getPersonByName ( "Rahul" ) ;
if ( p == null )
    System.out.println ( "Rahul does not exist" ) ;
else
    System.out.println ( p.getAge( ) ) ;

p = dp.getPersonByName ( "Aditya" ) ;
if ( p == null )
    System.out.println ( "Aditya does not exist" ) ;
else
    System.out.println ( p.getAge( ) ) ;
```

However, this solution has an obvious disadvantage. Every time a method returns an object, we must remember to perform the null check. If we forget to do that, disaster is not far away. Moreover, the code becomes clumsy if it involves several such null checks.

So, something needs to be done in the method definition that reminds the user of a possibility that the method may return a null and force him to address that possibility without using the clumsy null checks. The solution comes in the form of a new generic class introduced in **java.util** called **Optional**. If a method is returning an **Optional** type, it means it is advertising that there is a possibility that the method may return a null. Once known, the user of the method can account for the possibility by replacing the null checks with suitable methods of **Optional** class. This is shown in the following program.

```
class Person
{
    private String name ;
    private int age ;

    public Person ( String n, int a )
    {
        name = n ;
        age = a ;
    }
```

```
    public String getName( )
    {
        return name ;
    }
    public int getAge( )
    {
        return age ;
    }
}
class DataProcessor
{
    private ArrayList<Person> people ;

    DataProcessor( )
    {
        people = new ArrayList< > ( ) ;
        people.add ( new Person ( "Ajay", 25 ) ) ;
        people.add ( new Person ( "Vijay", 31 ) ) ;
        people.add ( new Person ( "Sanjay", 22 ) ) ;
        people.add ( new Person ( "Tanmay", 26 ) ) ;
        people.add ( new Person ( "Anuj", 30 ) ) ;
        people.add ( new Person ( "Aditya", 22 ) ) ;
    }
    public Optional<Person> getPersonByName ( String n )
    {
        for ( Person p : people )
        {
            if ( p.getName( ).equals ( n ) )
                return Optional.of ( p ) ;
        }
        return Optional.empty( ) ;
    }
}
public class Main
{
    public static void main ( String[ ] args )
    {
        DataProcessor dp = new DataProcessor( ) ;
        Optional<Person> op ;
        Person p ;
        op = dp.getPersonByName ( "Rahul" ) ;
```

```
            p = op.orElse ( new Person ( "Unknown", 0 ) ) ;
            System.out.println ( p.getName( ) + " " + p.getAge( ) ) ;
            op = dp.getPersonByName ( "Aditya" ) ;
            p = op.orElse ( new Person ( "Unknown", 0 ) ) ;
            System.out.println ( p.getName( ) + " " + p.getAge( ) ) ;
    }
}
```

Note that the return type of **getPersonByName( )** is **Optional<Person>**. If the name is found in the **ArrayList**, the **Person** object is wrapped in **Optional** type by the **static** method **of( ).** If it is not found then null is wrapped in **Optional** type by the **static** method **empty( ).**

On the client side, the null checks are replaced by the statements:

```
Optional<Person> op ;
Person p ;
op = dp.getPersonByName ( "Rahul" ) ;
p = op.orElse ( new Person ( "Unknown", 0 ) ) ;
```

The **orElse( )** method sets **p** with a **Person** if it is present in **op**. If **op** contains null, **p** is set up with an object which has 'Unknown' name and '0' age.

Established Object Creation Patterns

We know that a class usually exposes a public constructor(s) as the way for external code (clients) to create instances (objects) of that class. However, classes can provide other ways to create object(s) from it. We will discuss here 4 of these common ways. These are discussed below.

Static Factory

Often there are situations where we are required to create a class for others to use. In such situations we want objects created from our class to be immutable. This means that once the object is created its fields should not change.

To achieve this, we can make the constructor of our class **private** and provide a **public static** method (called factory method) to create objects. When we call this method, it in turn invokes the **private** constructor for each object. The following program shows how to define and call the factory method.

```
class Example
{
    private Example( )
    {
    }
    // factory method
    public static Example getInstance( )
    {
        Example ex = new Example( ) ;
        return ex ;
    }
}
public class Main
{
    public static void main ( String[ ] args )
    {
        Example ex1 = Example.getInstance( ) ;
        Example ex2 = Example.getInstance( ) ;
    }
}
```

The advantage of the static factory method is that, based on its input parameter, it can return different objects. For example, if **Dog** and **Cat** classes are derived from an **Animal** class, then the static factory method in **Animal** class can return either a **Dog** object or a **Cat** object depending on the input parameter passed to it. This is shown in the following program.

```
package com.Book;
import java.util.Objects ;
enum AnimalType { cat, dog }
class Animal
{
    private final String name ;
    protected Animal ( String n )
    {
        name = n ;
    }
    public static Animal createAnimal ( AnimalType at, String name )
    {
        Objects.requireNonNull ( at, "AnimalType cannot be null" ) ;
        if ( at == AnimalType.dog )
```

```
            return Dog.getInstance ( name ) ; // return subtype ( Dog )
        return Cat.getInstance ( name ) ; // return subtype  ( Cat )
    }
}
class Dog extends Animal
{
    private Dog ( String name )
    {
        super ( name ) ;
    }
    static Dog getInstance ( String name )
    {
        return new Dog ( name ) ;
    }
}
class Cat extends Animal
{
    private Cat ( String name )
    {
        super ( name ) ;
    }
    static Cat getInstance ( String name )
    {
        return new Cat ( name ) ;
    }
}
public class Main
{
    public static void main ( String[ ] args )
    {
        Animal a1 = Animal.createAnimal ( AnimalType.dog, "Tobby" ) ;
        Animal a2 = Animal.createAnimal ( AnimalType.cat, "Kitty" ) ;
        Animal a3 = Animal.createAnimal ( null, "Bosco" ) ;
    }
}
```

Note a few important things about the program:

(a) **Animal** class's field **name** has been marked **final**. This will ensure that once initialized it cannot be modified, ensuring immutability.

(b) **Animal** class's constructor has been marked **protected**. This is necessary to make it available in the inheritance chain, when we call **super( )**.

(c) While creating **a3**, since the first parameter passed to **createAnimal( )** is null, the **requireNonNull( )** method will throw a **NullPointerException**.

One disadvantage of a static factory method is that, unlike a constructor, it is not easy to identify it from its name. Commonly used names for static factory method is **getInstance( )**, **createInstance( )**, **newInstance( )**, **of( )**, **valueOf( )**, **from( )**, etc.

Singleton

Sometimes a system has some component that is unique. For example, there is only one Vice Chancellor in a University system. In such a case we should be able to create a **ViceChancellor** class from which only one object can be created. Such a class is called a singleton class. There are two ways to create it. These are shown in the following programs.

```
// Approach 1
class Example
{
    // private constructor
    private Example( )
    {
    }
    public static final Example INSTANCE = new Example( ) ;
    // other methods of the class
}
public class Main
{
    public static void main ( String[ ] args )
    {
        Example ex1 = Example.INSTANCE ;
        Example ex2 = Example.INSTANCE ;
        if ( ex1 == ex2 )
            System.out.println ( "Both refer to one object" ) ;
    }
}
```

Note that here the constructor is private, so it cannot be called from outside the class. It gets called only once when **public static final** variable **INSTANCE** is initialized, and an **Example** object gets created. The expression **Example.INSTANCE** always gives reference to the same object since **INSTANCE** field is **final**.

If we wish, we can keep the **INSTANCE** field **private** and then access it through a **static getInstance( )** method (factory method). This is shown in the following program.

```
// Approach 2
class Example
{
    // private constructor
    private Example( )
    {
    }
    private static final Example INSTANCE = new Example( ) ;
    public static Example getInstance( )
    {
        return INSTANCE ;
    }
    // other methods of the class
}
public class Main
{
    public static void main ( String[ ] args )
    {
        Example ex1 = Example.getInstance( ) ;
        Example ex2 = Example.getInstance( ) ;
        if ( ex1 == ex2 )
            System.out.println ( "Both refer to one object" ) ;
    }
}
```

Builder

Often an object has a long list of fields. In principle we can create such objects using either a public constructor or a static factory pattern. However, both these methods share the following disadvantages:

(a) The parameter list will be too long.

(b) A long sequence of parameters, especially if the types of adjacent parameters are same can cause bugs. If by mistake we interchange the order of two adjacent parameters of same type, the compiler won't report an error, but the object would be set up wrongly, which may result in a runtime error later.

Also, some fields out of the long list of fields in an object might be absolutely necessary for the creation of an object, whereas some others may not be strictly necessary. For example, a **Book** class may have following required and optional fields:

Required fields: title, ISBN, author

Optional fields: publication year, edition, number of pages, rating, genre, publisher, synopsis, awards received

To deal with this problem we may think of providing multiple overloaded constructors or multiple static factory methods with different combinations of parameters. However, this is a clumsy approach.

A better approach is to construct such objects using a Builder pattern. It helps us address all three issues—immutability, long parameter list and optional/required fields. Let us now see how to implement this pattern.

In the **Book** class define the following:

(a) All the required and optional fields. Mark them as **final**, to ensure the immutability of objects created from **Book** class.

(b) Getter methods for all the fields.

(c) A **public static Builder** class nested inside the **Book** class.

(d) A **private** constructor that receives a **Builder** object and sets up values of all fields of **Builder** object into corresponding fields of **Book** object.

(e) A **public static** method **getBuilder( )** that returns a **Builder** object.

In the **Builder** class define the following:

(a) Setter methods (or builder methods) for every field. Each setter method should return the **Builder** object itself, allowing for method chaining (calling multiple setter methods in a row).

(b) An empty private constructor

(c) A **build( )** method that invokes the **private** constructor of **Book** class to construct the object.

The following program puts the Builder pattern into action.

```
package com.Book;

import java.util.Objects ;
import java.util.Optional ;

class Book
{
    private final String title, ISBN, author ;
    private final int yearOfPublication, edition, numberOfPages, rating ;
    private final String genre, publisher, synopsis, awardsReceived ;

    private Book ( Builder b )
    {
        title = b.title ;
        ISBN = b.isbn ;
        author = b.author ;
        yearOfPublication = b.yearOfPublication ;
        edition = b.edition ;
        numberOfPages = b.numberOfPages ;
        rating = b.rating ;
        genre = b.genre ;
        publisher = b.publisher ;
        synopsis = b.synopsis ;
        awardsReceived = b.awardsReceived ;
    }
    public String getTitle( )
    {
        return title ;
    }
    public Optional<String> getPublisher( )
    {
```

```
        return Optional.ofNullable ( publisher ) ;
    }
    public int getNumberOfPages( )
    {
        return ( numberOfPages ) ;
    }
    // add other getter methods like getIsbn( ), getAuthor( ), etc.
    public static Builder getBuilder( )
    {
        return new Builder( ) ;
    }
    public static class Builder
    {
        // required parameters
        private String title, isbn, author ;
        // optional parameters
        private int yearOfPublication, edition ;
        private int numberOfPages, rating ;
        private String genre, publisher, synopsis, awardsReceived ;
        private Builder( )
        {
        }
        public Builder setTitle ( String val )
        {
            title = val;
            return this;
        }
        public Builder setIsbn ( String val )
        {
            isbn = val ;
            return this ;

        }
        public Builder setAuthor ( String val )
        {
            author = val ;
            return this ;
        }
        public Builder setGenre ( String val )
        {
            genre = val ;
```

```
        return this ;
    }
    public Builder setPublisher ( String val )
    {
        publisher = val ;
        return this ;
    }
    public Builder setSynopsis ( String val )
    {
        synopsis = val ;
        return this ;
    }
    public Builder setAwardsReceived ( String val )
    {
        awardsReceived = val ;
        return this ;
    }
    public Builder setYearOfPublication ( int val )
    {
        yearOfPublication = val ;
        return this ;
    }
    public Builder setEdition ( int val )
    {
        edition = val ;
        return this ;
    }
    public Builder setNumberOfPages ( int val )
    {
        numberOfPages = val ;
        return this ;
    }
    public Builder setRating ( int val )
    {
        rating = val ;
        return this ;
    }
    public Book build( )
    {
        Objects.requireNonNull ( title, "Title cannot be null" ) ;
        Objects.requireNonNull ( isbn, "ISBN cannot be null" ) ;
```

```
            Objects.requireNonNull ( author, "Author can't be null" ) ;
            return new Book ( this ) ;
        }
    }
}
public class Main
{
    public static void main ( String[ ] args )
    {
        Book b = Book.getBuilder( )
                    .setTitle ( "LUJ" )
                    .setIsbn ( "0306805900" )
                    .setAuthor ( "YK AK" )
                    .setYearOfPublication ( 2020 )
                    .setEdition ( 7 )
                    .setNumberOfPages ( 550 )
                    .setRating ( 4 )
                    .setGenre ( "IT" )
                    .setPublisher ( "BPB" )
                    .setSynopsis ( "Simple Java programming book" )
                    .setAwardsReceived ( "3" )
                    .build( ) ;
        System.out.println ( "Book title = " + b.getTitle( ) ) ;
    }
}
```

Note the following important tips as you try to understand this program:

(a) In **main( )** the call **Book.getBuilder( )** returns a **Builder** object. Using this object the various setter methods of **Builder** class are called in a chain.

(b) In the chain of calls if we do not call a setter method for the required fields, the program will throw a null pointer exception. So, this will force the caller to call the setter methods for the required fields to be able to construct an object.

(c) Since a **Book** object has many optional fields, we can identify those which we want to set up and make a call for those setter methods. We can drop the remaining setter calls from the chain of calls.

(d) In the chain, the last call is to the **build( )** method of **Builder** class. Here the data for required parameters is validated before calling **Book**'s **private** constructor.

(e) Since every consumer of **Book** class is not going to set up every optional field, optional field data is not validated.

(f) The getter method for required fields will always have a valid value in them, so that value will be returned.

(g) An optional field may or may not have been set up. Hence the getter method for optional fields (like **getPublisher( )**) will return an **Optional** type if it is returning an object (like **String**).

(h) For getter method for an **int** field (like **getNumberOfPages( )**) use of **Optional** is not necessary, since it will either return a 0 or a set non-zero value.

Go through the program thoroughly, and reassure yourself that immutability, long parameter list and optional/required fields have been addressed properly by the program.

The Builder pattern offers several advantages for creating complex objects. These are listed below.

(a) By separating the object construction into a separate nested class the code becomes easier to read and understand. The Builder class encapsulates the construction steps, making the main class cleaner and less cluttered.

(b) The Builder pattern elegantly handles optional parameters. You can specify only the required parameters or set additional information using the builder's setter methods. This promotes flexibility and avoids long constructors with many arguments.

(c) The Builder pattern can be used to create immutable objects. Since the Builder manages the construction process, the final object's state cannot be modified after creation. This leads to safer and more predictable code behavior.

(d) When creating objects with many dependencies or nested objects, the Builder pattern can simplify the process. It allows for step-by-step construction, making it easier to manage complex object hierarchies that involve inheritance.

(e) The Builder pattern can aid in unit testing. We can create mock objects with specific configurations by controlling the builder's behavior, making it easier to isolate and test different aspects of our code.

Overall, the Builder pattern can be a valuable tool for designing well-structured and maintainable programs, especially when dealing with complex object creation scenarios.

Dependency injection

Consider a scenario where we need to process data through a **DataProcessor** class as per different processing strategies like filtering, sorting, etc. Instead of **DataProcessor** creating **FilteringStrategy** or **SortingStrategy** object, we can inject one of these objects as a dependency while creating a **DataProcessor** object. This pattern of injecting an object (**FilteringStrategy** or **SortingStrategy**, or any other strategy) as a dependency for creating a **DataProcessor** object is called Dependency Injection.

By injecting the strategy, the **DataProcessor** doesn't need to know the specifics of filtering or sorting logic. It simply delegates the processing task to the injected strategy. This allows us to easily switch between filtering and sorting or even introduce new processing strategies in the future without modifying the core **DataProcessor** logic. Thus, Dependency Injection promotes flexible and loosely coupled code design. The following program implements this dependency injection pattern.

```
import java.util.* ;
interface DataProcessorStrategy
{
    List<Integer> processData ( List<Integer> data ) ;
}
class DataProcessor
{
    private final DataProcessorStrategy strategy ;

    public DataProcessor ( DataProcessorStrategy strat )
    {
```

```
        strategy = strat ;
    }
    public List<Integer> processData ( List<Integer> data )
    {
        return strategy.processData ( data ) ;
    }
}
class FilteringStrategy implements DataProcessorStrategy
{
    @Override
    public List<Integer> processData ( List<Integer> data )
    {
        List<Integer> filteredData = new ArrayList< >( ) ;
        for ( int number : data )
        {
            if ( number % 2 == 0 )
                filteredData.add ( number ) ;
        }
        return filteredData ;
    }
}
class SortingStrategy implements DataProcessorStrategy
{
    @Override
    public List<Integer> processData ( List<Integer> data )
    {
        Collections.sort ( data ) ; // sort data in ascending order
        return data ;
    }
}
public class Main
{
    public static void main ( String[ ] args )
    {
        List <Integer> data = new ArrayList< >( ) ;
        data.add ( 1 ) ;
        data.add ( 5 ) ;
        data.add ( 3 ) ;
        data.add ( 4 ) ;
        data.add ( 2 ) ;
```

```
        DataProcessorStrategy dpstrat ;
        DataProcessor processor ;
        List <Integer> processedData ;

        dpstrat = new FilteringStrategy( ) ; // filter even numbers
        processor = new DataProcessor ( dpstrat) ; // dep. injection
        processedData = processor.processData ( data ) ;
        System.out.println ( "Original data: " + data ) ;
        System.out.println ( "Processed data: " + processedData ) ;

        dpstrat = new SortingStrategy( ) ; // Sort data
        processor = new DataProcessor ( dpstrat) ; // dep. injection
        processedData = processor.processData ( data ) ;
        System.out.println ( "Original data: " + data ) ;
        System.out.println ( "Processed data: " + processedData ) ;
    }
}
```

Here is the output of the program...

```
Original data: [1, 5, 3, 4, 2]
Filtered data: [4, 2]
Original data: [1, 2, 3, 4, 5]
Sorted data: [1, 2, 3, 4, 5]
```

This program demonstrates how we can easily switch between different processing strategies (filtering or sorting) by injecting the desired strategy into the **DataProcessor**. This allows us to process data in different ways without modifying the core processing flow in **DataProcessor**. The **DataProcessor** class remains reusable with different data manipulation needs. This exemplifies the flexibility provided by Dependency Injection.

Note that in real-world scenarios, data structures and processing logic would be more complex based on your specific needs.

With that we come to the end of this chapter. We would await suggestions from you at **kanetkar@kicit.com** about what more you want us to include in this chapter in future editions.

OTHER TITLES OF INTEREST

The **Ultimate Power Query Cookbook** for **Power BI** & **Excel**
ISBN: 9789355517395

200+ Excel Formulas & **Functions**
ISBN: 9789355513786

Excel 2022 Pro 100+ PivotTables, Charts & Reports
ISBN: 9789355512475

Mastering Advanced Excel with **ChatGPT**
ISBN: 9789355518651

Excel for **Finance** & **Accounting**
ISBN: 9789355517999

Advanced Analytics with **Excel 2019**
ISBN: 9789389845808

Excel 2019 All-In-One
ISBN: 9789388511582

Microsoft Excel Professional 2021 Guide
ISBN: 9789355510457

Management Science using **Excel**
ISBN: 9789355518811

EXCEL FUNCTIONS & **FORMULAS**
ISBN: 9788183331821

Mastering SEQUENCE
ISBN: 9789355518545

Excel BI & **Dashboards in 7 Days**
ISBN: 9789355519467

Power BI for Jobseekers
ISBN: 9789355518149

Self-Service Analytics with **Power BI**
ISBN: 9789355518200

Power BI Data Modeling
ISBN: 9789389328837

Mastering Power BI
ISBN: 9789391030728

Periodic Tests

Let Us JAVA 7th Edition

CHAPTER 26

You should never take a test when you are not prepared. You should never give up an opportunity to get tested when you are fully prepared and confident. This chapter would help you check your strengths and weaknesses, once you are prepared and confident...

Periodic Test I
(Based on Chapters 1 to 6)

Time: 90 Minutes **Maximum Marks: 40**

[A] Fill in the blanks: [5 Marks, 1 Mark each]

(1) Java interpreter converts Java source code into ______.

(2) _____ type of values cannot be checked using **switch-case**.

(3) In the expression **condition1 & condition2**, **condition2** would get executed only if **condition1** is ______.

(4) The size of an **int** data type is ______ bytes.

(5) Exponentiation operation can be performed using _____ function.

[B] State True or False: [5 Marks, 1 Mark each]

(1) **$salary** is a correct variable name in Java.

(2) A java program compiled for one JVM must be recompiled to make it work on a different JVM.

(3) If we are to run a Java program on a machine, it is enough if JRE is installed on it.

(4) Once a variable is declared as final its value cannot be changed.

(5) Consecutive cases with no statements between them enable the cases to execute a common set of statements.

[C] What would be the output of the following code snippets: [5 Marks, 1/2 Mark each]

(1) What would be the output of the following code snippet?

```
int a = 25543 ;
System.out.format ( "%10d\n", a ) ;
System.out.format ( "%+10d\n", a ) ;
System.out.format ( "%,10d\n", a ) ;
System.out.format ( "%,+10d\n", a ) ;
```

(2) Why is a function in a class marked public? Why is a class in a package marked public?

(3) What is JVM? What is a package?

(4) Write Java statements to sum odd integers between 1 and 99, using a **for** statement.

(5) What would be the output of the following code snippet?

```
int i = 1, j = 2, k = 3 ;
System.out.println ( j == 5 ) ;
System.out.println ( i <= k ) ;
System.out.println ( ! ( i <= j ) ) ;
System.out.println ( !i ) ;
```

(6) How would you ensure that a float result (2.5) gets stored in variable **a** in the following code snippet?

```
float a ;
int b = 5, c = 2 ;
a = b / c ;
```

(7) What would be the output of the following code snippet if value of **choice** is 1?

```
switch ( choice )
{
    case 1 :
    case 2 :
        System.out.println ( "Right choice" ) ;
}
```

(8) Would the following program run? If yes, what would be the output and if no, what would be the error? Assume that the value of **choice** is 3?

```
switch ( choice )
{
    case 1 - 5 :
        System.out.println ( "Right choice" ) ;
    default :
        System.out.println ( "Wrong choice" ) ;
}
```

(9) Point out the error, if any, in the following code snippet:

```
int i = 5, j = 10 ;
boolean flag ;
```

```
flag = ( i == 20 && j != 10 ) ? true : false ;
System.out.println ( flag ) ;
```

(10) Point out the error, if any, in the following code snippet:

```
boolean ret = 1, flag = 0 ;
System.out.println ( ret ) ;
System.out.println ( flag ) ;
```

[D] Match the following: [5 Marks, 1/2 Mark each]

(a) size of byte	(1) literal
(b) continue	(2) abandon loop
(c) break	(3) short-circuiting expression
(d) cond1 | cond2	(4) 1 bit
(e) size of short	(5) identifier
(f) constant	(6) 1 byte
(g) cond1 || cond2	(7) next iteration
(h) size of boolean	(8) 4 bytes
(i) size of int	(9) no short-circuiting expression
(j) variable	(10) 2 bytes

[E] Attempt the following: [20 Marks, 10 Marks each]

(1) According to a survey a popular social networking site hit one billion users in Jan 2019. If its user base grows at a rate of 8% per month, write a program to show how many months it will take for the site to grow its user base to 1.5 billion users? Print user base figures at the beginning and end of each month.

(2) Write a program that receives a 4-digit number as input and prints an equivalent encrypted number. The encryption should be done as follows:

Replace each digit with (digit + 7) mod 10
Interchange first digit with third digit
Interchange second digit with fourth digit

Also write the decryption logic to obtain the original number from the encrypted number.

Periodic Test II
(Based on Chapters 7 to 8)

Time: 90 Minutes **Maximum Marks: 40**

[A] Fill in the blanks: [5 Marks, 1 Mark each]

(1) _______ package should be imported to be able to use trigonometric functions.

(2) While defining a function that receives variable number of arguments _____ symbol is used to collect the values passed to the function in an array.

(3) During a function call the actual and formal arguments must match in ______, ______, and ______.

(4) A function should be marked with _____ keyword to indicate that it is not going to return any value.

(5) A function that calls itself is known as a _______ function.

[B] State True or False: [5 Marks, 1 Mark each]

(1) A fresh set of local variables gets created every time a function is called normally or recursively.

(2) A function can return only one value at a time.

(3) A function cannot be defined inside another function.

(4) Any function can be made a recursive function.

(5) It is possible to define a function that receives different number of arguments in different function calls.

[C] Answer the following: [10 Marks, 2 Marks each]

(1) Is this a correct statement? If not, why not?

```
return ( a, b, c ) ;
```

(2) What would happen on execution of the following statement? What value would it return to the calling function?

```
return ( a, b, c ) ;
```

(3) Write a code snippet that demonstrates that actual arguments passed to a function can be a constant, variable or expression, whereas the formal arguments must always be variables.

(4) Write a code snippet that calls a function **cal( )** and passes to it an angle in degrees. The function **cal( )** should return sum of sin and cos of the angle passed to it.

(5) A recursive call should always be subjected to an **if**. Why? Explain with an example.

[D] Attempt the following: [20 Marks, 10 Marks each]

(1) Define a function that receives 4, 5 or 6 integers and returns sum of the integers that it receives.

(2) Write a recursive function which prints the prime factors of the number that it receives when called from **main( )**.

Periodic Test III
(Based on Chapters 9 to 12)

Time: 90 Minutes **Maximum Marks: 40**

[A] Fill in the blanks: [5 Marks, 1 Mark each]

(1) In Java an array is implemented as an ______.

(2) An array is created in _____ memory and a reference to it is created in ______ memory.

(3) _______ method of a class gets called when garbage collector is about to collect an object.

(4) _____ is used by methods of a class to identify an object it is working on.

(5) Static functions in a class can access only ______ data.

[B] State True or False: [5 Marks, 1 Mark each]

(1) A string object cannot be mutated.

(2) Two strings represented by objects **s1** and **s2** can be compared using the statement **if (s1 == s2)**.

(3) In a 2D array all rows must have the same number of elements.

(4) Objects are passed to a function by reference.

(5) A class permits us to build user-defined data types.

[C] Answer the following: [10 Marks, 2 Marks each]

(1) Write a code snippet to print the name and ordinal value for each element of the following enum.

enum maritalstatus { single, married, divorced } ;

(2) Illustrate with a code snippet the difference between a **String** and **StringBuilder** class.

(3) What is the purpose of **static** block? When does it get invoked?

(4) Which of the following statements are true about an object?

- Each object's variables can have different values.
- An object can contain many methods using which we can access or manipulate its state.
- Objects can be created either on heap or on stack.
- An object behaves like a blueprint or template.

(5) What is the limitation of an array of pointers to strings? How can it be overcome?

[D] Attempt the following: [20 Marks, 10 Marks each]

(1) Create an array of strings containing names of 10 cities. Write a program that sorts the cities in reverse alphabetical order and prints this reversed list.

(2) Declare a class **Circle** containing private variables **radius**, **area,** and **circumference**. Provide a constructor to set up a value in **radius**. Create an array of 10 **Circle** objects, each with different radius. Define a method **calc( )** in the **Circle** class that calculates and prints **area** and **circumference** for a given **Circle** object. Call this method for each object in the array.

Periodic Test IV
(Based on Chapters 13 to 15)

Time: 90 Minutes **Maximum Marks: 40**

[A] Fill in the blanks: [5 Marks, 1 Mark each]

(1) The class at the top of exception class hierarchy is _______.

(2) In Java all function calls are resolved using the _________ mechanism.

(3) In an Inheritance chain Base class is also known _______ as and Derived class is also known as _______.

(4) In overloaded functions their arguments must differ in _______, _______, or _______ .

(5) _______ keyword should be used to prevent derivation of a new class from an existing class.

[B] State True or False: [5 Marks, 1 Mark each]

(1) Protected members are inaccessible in the inheritance chain.

(2) Protected members are accessible to classes in the same package.

(3) Inheritance makes use of "Has A" relationship.

(4) Inheritance, Containership and Generics are all code reuse mechanisms.

(5) Function overloading is an example of Polymorphism.

[C] Answer the following: [10 Marks, 2 Marks each]

(1) Which exception is likely to occur in the following code snippet?

```
int a, b, c ;
// receive b and c from keyboard
a = b / c ;
```

(2) What is the difference between checked and unchecked exceptions?

(3) What do you mean by exception propagation?

(4) If no exceptions are thrown in a try block, where does control proceed to when the try block completes execution?

(5) What happens if several **catch** blocks match the type of thrown object?

[D] Attempt the following: [20 Marks, 10 Marks each]

(1) Create a **Document** class. From it inherit a **Magazine** class and a **Book** class. Objects of each class should contain a **print( )** method. Create 5 objects each of **Magazine** and **Book** class. Store these objects in an array of references of **Document** class. Call **print( )** method using the array elements ensuring that appropriate class's **print( )** function gets called.

(2) Create the following class hierarchy:

Vehicle - base class
Car, Truck - derived classes, derived from Vehicle

Declare an interface **Storable** containing methods **serialize( )** and **deserialize( )**. Implement this interface in the derived classes. Call these functions from **main( )**.

Periodic Test V
(Based on Chapters 16 to 21)

Time: 90 Minutes **Maximum Marks: 40**

[A] Fill in the blanks: [5 Marks, 1 Mark each]

(1) The Java collection class that can be used for maintaining key-value pairs is _______.

(2) Common algorithms like searching, sorting, etc. can be applied on collection using functions present in ________ class.

(3) A thread can be created in a Java program by extending the _______ class or implementing the _______ interface.

(4) If two methods running in two different threads wish to access the same resource, then to ensure at a time only one thread accesses the resource the methods should be marked as _______.

(5) All Swing classes are defined in _______ package.

[B] State True or False: [5 Marks, 1 Mark each]

(1) Generic functions cannot work for primitives like int, float, char, etc.

(2) A generic function can receive multiple argument types.

(3) Bounded generics can work only with the objects of a specified class.

(4) Protected members are inaccessible in the inheritance chain.

(5) In Swing API there is one adapter class for each listener.

[C] Answer the following: [10 Marks, 2 Marks each]

(1) What are Sources, Events, Listeners, Adapters in context of GUI applications?

(2) Suppose you have connected to a database containing a table called Employees. Each record in this table contains Employee ID, Name, Age and Salary. Write a code snippet that would read and print all records present in this table.

(3) What does each function call in the following code snippet achieve?

```
static final String jdbcDriver = "com.mysql.jdbc.Driver" ;
static final String dbURL = "jdbc:mysql://localhost/study" ;
Connection conn = null ;
Statement stmt = null ;
String sql = sql = "INSERT INTO Accounts VALUES ( 1001, 'Joe' )" ;

Class.forName ( jdbcDriver ) ;
conn = DriverManager.getConnection ( dbURL, "root", "admin" ) ;
stmt = conn.createStatement( ) ;
stmt.executeUpdate ( sql ) ;
```

(4) What are CRUD operations?

(5) What are bounded generics? When are they used?

[D] Attempt the following: [20 Marks, 10 Marks each]

(1) Write a program that maintains a hash map of 10 Employee Ids as keys and name of the person, his email address, and his date of birth as values.

(2) Producer - Consumer algorithm is a popularly used algorithm in Computer Science. It is a technique for generating requests (by producer) and processing the generated requests (by consumer). Write a program to implement this algorithm to meet the following specifications:

- The Producer produces factorial value of numbers in sequence 0, 1, 2, ...
- Consumer consumes the produced factorial values by printing them
- Both Producer and Consumer work as independent threads
- Consumer must wait while Producer is producing
- Once the Producer has produced it would send a signal to Consumer
- Producer must wait while Consumer is consuming
- Once Consumer has consumed it should send a signal to Producer

I
Index

Search it, the easy way...

!

!, 69
!=, 61
%=, 85
&&, 64
&, 68
*=, 85
--, 85
++, 85
+=, 85
-=, 85
/=, 85
<, 61
<=, 61
==,61
>, 61
>=, 61
? :, 71
|, 68
||, 64
@override, 459
2-D array, 194
2-D jagged arrays, 197

A

Algorithms, 381. 394
ArrayList class, 382, 383
Arrays class, 395
abs( ), 45
abstract classes, 252
abstract functions, 252, 256
actual arguments, 117, 119
annotations, 459
append( ), 215
args, 24, 26
  command-line, 41
arithmetic instruction, 44
  type conversion, 46
array, 185, 186
array
  2-D arrays, 194
  accessing elements, 188
  bounds checking, 188
  declaration, 185
  initialization, 187
  jagged array, 197
  multi-dimensional, 194
  of objects, 193
  of strings, 215
  passing 2-D array, 196
  passing array reference, 189
  passing to function, 189
  resizing of arrays, 199
  returning an array, 190
  two dimensional, 194
associativity of operators, 50

B

BigDecimal, 478
Binary Search Tree, 390
Binary Tree, 390
BufferredInputStream, 312
BufferredOutputStream, 312
BufferredReader, 313
BufferredWriter, 313
binarySearch( ), 395
bitwise operators, 458
boolean data type, 37
bounds checking, 188
boxed primitives, 478
break, 89
byte, 35
bytecode, 7, 8, 10

C

C++, 9
CLASSPATH, 457

CRUD operations, 439
Collection Classes, 381
Complex class, 165
Containership, 151
Control Instructions, 53
calling function, 114, 118
canRead( ), 308, 312
canWrite( ), 308
case, 103, 104
catch block, 277, 278, 282
char data type, 37
character constant, 21
class, 157, 158
 ArrayList, 382
 Collections, 382
 Complex, 165
 HashMap, 393
 LinkedHashSet, 389
 LinkedList, 387
 Stack, 385
 StringBuilder, 215
 SQLException, 444
 TreeSet, 389
 constructors, 160, 162
 inner, 174
 terminology, 165
close( ), 314, 316, 318
command line arguments, 41
comment, 25
compareTo( ), 211, 213, 216
compareToIgnoreCase( ), 213
compilation, 28
compiler, 4, 8, 10, 11, 28
compound assignment operators, 84
concat( ), 211, 213
contains( ), 214
conditional operators, 71
console, 317
console output, 51
console output functions, 50, 51
 readLine( ) function, 40, 41
constant variables, 51
constants, 21
constructors, 160, 162
constructors,
 in inheritance, 237
continue, 91
control instructions, 53
 decision, 61
 case, 101
 loops, 81
copyValueOf( ), 211, 213
cos( ), 46
createStatement( ), 446, 448

D

DELETE, 441
DataInputSrteam, 312
DataOutputSrteam, 312
Data organization, 439
declaration
 place of local variables, 477
DriverManager class, 443
data type, 19, 35
 boolean, 37
 byte, 35
 char, 37
 enum, 218, 222
 integer, 35
 long, 35
 user-defined, 32
 real, 36
 short, 35
data validation, 483
decision control instructions, 61
default, 101
default method, 268
default method ambiguities, 268
delete( ), 215
directory operations, 305
do, 88
double, 36
do-while, 88
drive operations, 305

E

else, 61
else if clause, 65
enum, 218
  over strings, 479
enumerations, 218
  use of, 219
exceptions
  user-defined, 290
exception handling, 280
execution, 28
  executeUpdate( ), 446, 448
  executeQuery( ), 446, 448
exists( ), 306, 316, 320
explicit conversion, 48
exponential form, 37

F

Float, 39
File, 305, 306, 307
FileInputStream, 312, 318
File Operations, 305
FileOutputStream, 311, 313, 315
FilterOutputStream, 312, 314
FileReader, 313, 316
FileWriter, 313, 314
fail-fast approach, 482
false, 37
file decryption, 322
file encryption, 322
filter, 416
final, 50, 240
finalize method, 164, 165
finally block, 289, 290
float, 36
for, 85
  loop, 85, 86, 87
  multiple initializations, 88
  nesting, 87
  partial, 86
  proper, 477
formal arguments, 117, 119
format( ), 51
format specifiers, 52
function overloading, 129
functional interface, 403
  generic functional, 407
  standard, 419
functional Programming, 411
functions, 111
functions
  called function, 112
  calling function, 112, 116
  passing values between, 116
  function overloading, 129
  readLine( ) function, 50
  println( ) function, 51

G

garbage collector, 163, 164
generic classes, 369
generic functions, 363
generics, 361
  bounded, 374
getAbsolutePath( ), 306
getCanonicalPath( ), 214, 215
getConnection( ), 445, 447
getFloat( ), 448, 450
getInt( ), 448, 450
getName( ), 307
getParent( ), 306
getString( ), 446, 448

H

HashMap, 393
hierarchy, 48

I

I/O System
  Expectations, 305
IDE, 11
INSERT, 441
Input/Output, 305
InputStreamReader, 306, 313
Integer, 35, 39
Integrated Development
  Environment, 11
practical uses of
Interfaces - different
  implementations, 264
Interfaces - focused view, 261
Interfaces - unrelated inheritance,
  266
identifier, 21
if-else statement, 61
immutable lists, 418
incremental development, 241
indexOf( ), 212, 213
inheritance, 231
  constructors, 237
  uses, 234
insert( ), 215
instruction types, 41
instructions, 41
instructions
  arithmetic instruction, 41, 43
  control instruction, 41, 53
  exception handling, 41
  type declaration instruction, 41
int, 35
integer, 35
integer constant, 35
interface,
  practical uses, 260
interfaces
  refer objects by their 485
inter-thread communication, 354
isDirectory( ), 308
isEmpty( ), 214

J

J2SE, 14
JDBC, 439, 441
  Architecture, 441
  adding library, 449
  driver, 442
  driver manager, 442
  driver type, 442
James Gosling, 5
Java, 5, 6
  bytcode, 7, 8, 10
  data types, 19, 35
  instructions, 42
  keywords, 23
  library, 14
  streams, 310
JDK, 10, 11
JIT compiler, 10
JRE, 10, 11
JVM, 7, 8, 9
jagged array, 197, 198
java.sql package, 442, 447
joining and splitting strings, 214

K

keywords, 23

L

Linked List, 387
LinkedList class, 387, 388
Linux, 7, 8
lambda, 403
  assigning, 406
  creating, 404
  expression, 404
  use in multithreading, 408
  use with collections, 410

lastIndexOf( ), 213, 214
lazy and eager operations, 425
literal, 21, 37
log( ), 46
log10( ), 46
logical operators, 64, 68
long, 35
loops, 81
loops
  do-while loop, 88
  for, 85
  tips, 83
  while, 81

M

Math, 46
Multitasking, 337
Multithreading, 338
MySQL, 447
  Workbench, 441
  installation, 443
main( ), 24, 25, 26
map, 416
method
  default, 268
  default, of std fun interfaces, 422
  parameter list, 480
  static method, 268
  static, of std fun interfaces, 422
multiple exceptions, 287
mutable lists, 418

N

NetBeans, 11, 28
nested if-elses, 65
nesting of loops, 87
new, 157, 162

O

OOP, 141
OutputStreamWriter, 318, 319
object, 146, 160
  Connection, 441, 443, 445
  ResultSet, 441, 443, 445
  Statement, 443, 444, 445
object destruction, 163
object-oriented programming, 144
  classes, 147
  containership, 149
  inheritance, 147
  objects, 146
  polymorphism, 149
  reusability, 150
operators,
  associativity, 49
  bitwise, 458
  compound assignment operators, 84, 98
  conditional operators, 71
  hierarchy, 70
  logical operators, 64
  method reference, 429
  relational operators, 62
optional type, 488
overloading functions, 129

P

PrintWriter, 313
package, 24, 25, 461
  java.sql, 442
parseInt( ), 40, 51
parseFloat( ), 40
passing
  2-D array, 196
  array elements, 189
  array reference, 189
  parameters, 116

values, 116
pattern
builder, 496
dependency injection, 503
singleton, 495
static factory, 492
polymorphism, 249
pow( ), 46
primitives, 19
println( ), 24, 27, 51
protected, 239, 253
public, 159
private, 159

R

RDBMS, 439, 440
Reader, 313
Record I/O, 317
readLine( ) function, 40
real, 36
Recursion, 132
reduce, 416
reference type, 19
relational operators, 62
replace( ), 215
resizing of arrays, 199
return, 118
returning 1-D array, 190
reusability, 149
rules,
for constructing constants, 21
for constructing variables, 22

S

SELECT, 440, 446
Set, 389
SQLException class, 444
Solaris, 4
Stack class, 385
Stream API, 414
strictfp, 457
StringBuilder class, 215
schema, 444, 445
security, 8
short, 35
sin( ), 46
sort( ), 395, 396
split( ), 215
splitting strings, 214
sqrt( ), 45
standard exception, 291
standard functional interfaces
default method 422
static method, 422
static data, 170
static functions, 170
streams, 310
stream classes, 312
user-defined streams, 319
string Functions
charAt( ), 211, 212, 213
compareTo( ), 211, 213
concat( ), 211, 213
contains( ), 214
copyValueOf( ), 211, 213
format( ), 214
indexOf( ), 212, 213
isEmpty( ), 214
lastIndexOf( ), 212, 213
length( ), 213
replace( ), 213
substring( ), 212, 213
toUpperCase( ), 213, 214
strings,
array of, 215
reading, 315
sorting, 217
splitting, 214
structured programming, 142, 143
super, 236, 237, 238
switch, 103, 105, 107

T

Tree, 390
  Binary, 391
TreeSet class, 392
table,
  Alter, 440
  Create, 440
  Drop, 440
tan( ), 46
this reference, 169
thread
  launching, 340
  launching multiple threads, 343
  priorities, 354
  synchronization, 351
three dimensional array, 194
throw, 295
try, 296
toString( ), 314, 327
toUpperCase( ), 320
traditional programming model, 6
true, 37
two dimensional array, 194
typecasting, 49
type conversion, 46
type declaration instruction, 43

U

UPDATE, 441, 446
user-defined exceptions, 290
user-defined streams, 319

V

value type, 19
variable names,
  rules for constructing, 22
variables, 20, 22, 23
void, 24, 26, 27

W

Windows, 6, 7, 8, 11
Writer, 313, 314, 315
while, 81, 83
write( ), 315, 318
writeInt( ), 314, 315

OTHER TITLES FOR INTEREST

Prompt-Driven Development Handbook
ISBN: 9789365892932

Practical Generative AI on AWS
ISBN: 9789365894653

AI Success Beyond Perfect Data
ISBN: 9789365899313

Modern Data Architecture in AI
ISBN: 9789365899771

Practical Approach to Agentic AI
ISBN: 9789365891898

Generative AI Ethics, Privacy, and Security
ISBN: 9789365899566

Data Engineering for AI
ISBN: 9789365893403

Hands-on AI Networking
ISBN: 9789365898460

Build Your Own AI Assistant
ISBN: 9789365893526

Generative AI for Healthcare
ISBN: 9789365897821

Building Applications with AI Agents
ISBN: 9789365894790

AI in the Classroom
ISBN: 9789365891492

Generative AI for Everyone
ISBN: 9789365897388

Learn AI with Python - 2nd Edition
ISBN: 9789365895001

Infrastructure for AI Network Design and Architecture
ISBN: 9789365899085

Strategic AI Leadership Through Data
ISBN: 9789365895759

OTHER TITLES OF INTEREST

.NET MAUI Projects
ISBN: 9789365899924

Web Development with HTML, CSS, and JavaScript
ISBN: 9789365896909

Get Set Go
ISBN: 9789365898866

Flutter Solutions for Web Development
ISBN: 9789365898248

Domain-driven Design with Java
ISBN: 9789365894462

DevOps for Java Developers
ISBN: 9789365896015

Decoding JavaScript Design Patterns
ISBN: 9789365894899

Comprehensive Java Programming
ISBN: 9789365890112

Penetration Testing with Java
ISBN: 9789365899351

Java Real World Projects
ISBN: 9789365898972

Exploring Scientific Computing with Java
ISBN: 9789365897593

Microservices Design Patterns with Java
ISBN: 9789355517005

Mastering DevOps and Site Reliability Engineering
ISBN: 9789365890228

CompTIA CySA+ CS0-003 Exam Guide
ISBN: 9789365899900

Prompt-Driven Development Handbook
ISBN: 9789365892932

Cybersecurity and Ethics
ISBN: 9789365893151